INDIANS, SETTLERS, & SLAVES IN A FRONTIER EXCHANGE ECONOMY

THIS BOOK WAS THE WINNER OF

THE JAMESTOWN MANUSCRIPT PRIZE

FOR 1990

INDIANS,

THE LOWER MISSISSIPPI VALLEY

SETTLERS,

BEFORE 1783

& SLAVES

BY DANIEL H. USNER, JR.

IN A

PUBLISHED FOR THE OMOHUNDRO INSTITUTE OF EARLY

FRONTIER

AMERICAN HISTORY AND CULTURE, WILLIAMSBURG, VIRGINIA

EXCHANGE

BY THE UNIVERSITY OF NORTH CAROLINA PRESS

ECONOMY

CHAPEL HILL AND LONDON

The Omohundro Institute of Early American History and Culture is sponsored jointly by the College of William and Mary and the Colonial Williamsburg Foundation.

Manufactured in the United States of America

04   03   02   01   00
7   6   5   4   3

Epigraph from William Faulkner, "The Old People," in Go Down, Moses, published by Random House, copyright by William Faulkner 1940, 1941, 1942; copyright renewed 1968, 1969, 1970 by Estelle Faulkner and Jill Faulkner Summers.

The paper in this book meets the guidelines for permanence and durability of the Committee on Production Guidelines for Book Longevity of the Council on Library Resources.

Library of Congress Cataloging-in-Publication Data

Usner, Daniel H.

Indians, settlers, and slaves in a frontier exchange economy : the Lower Mississippi Valley before 1783 / Daniel H. Usner, Jr.

p.   cm.

Includes bibliographical references and index.

ISBN 0-8078-2014-8 (cloth : alk. paper).

— ISBN 0-8078-4358-X (pbk. : alk. paper)

1. Mississippi River Valley—History—To 1803.   2. Mississippi River Valley—Commerce—History—18th century.

I. Institute of Early American History and Culture (Williamsburg, Va.)   II. Title.

F352.U86   1992

977—dc20   91-26689

CIP

This volume received indirect support from an unrestricted book publication grant awarded to the Institute by the L. J. Skaggs and Mary C. Skaggs Foundation of Oakland, California.

To my parents,

Joyce Durel Usner

and

Daniel Henry Usner, Sr.

ACKNOWLEDGMENTS

I owe gratitude to a number of institutions and individuals for helping me find my way through the Lower Mississippi Valley both in the eighteenth century and in my own lifetime. The Newberry Library's Center for the History of the American Indian (now the D'Arcy McNickle Center for the History of the American Indian) provided financial support and intellectual nurture at the first stage of writing this work. Former Director Francis Jennings and former Associate Director William R. Swagerty took good care of me when I was a predoctoral fellow there in 1979–1980 and have continued to take an interest in my work ever since. The Return Jonathan Meigs research fund at Cornell University has covered many travel and other expenses that went into the making of this work. A grant from the American Council of Learned Societies helped me put finishing touches on the project in 1987–1988.

The staffs at many libraries and archives provided me with generous assistance. They patiently cooperated with the scattered inquiries of a social historian always hungry for more bits and pieces of descriptive information. Over many hot and humid summers in the Deep South, I enjoyed hospitable working conditions in air-conditioned comfort at the Earl K. Long Library of the University of New Orleans; the Historic New Orleans Collection; the Howard-Tilton Memorial Library of Tulane University, New Orleans; the Louisiana Division of the New Orleans Public Library; the Louisiana Historical Collection of the Louisiana State Museum, New Orleans; the Louisiana State University Library, Baton Rouge; the Loyola University of New Orleans Library; and the Mississippi Department of Archives and History, Jackson. In more northern climes, I have benefited from the John M. Olin Library of Cornell University; the Newberry Library, Chicago; the North Carolina Division of Archives and History, Raleigh; and the William R. Perkins Library of Duke University.

The Institute of Early American History and Culture is well known for its influential dedication to excellence in colonial scholarship. My respect for the Institute's reputation, mixed with a desire to entice its gaze westward beyond the English colonies, motivated me to send them my manuscript on French and Spanish Louisiana. Since the Institute accepted this project for publication in the winter of 1985–1986, several Editors and Visiting Editors of Publications have touched it. Two in particular left decisive marks on its progress. Before leaving his post for a teaching position at Florida State University, Philip Morgan urged me to rewrite and reorganize in ways that significantly improved my argument. Fredrika Teute, who is now the Institute's Editor of Publications, provided strong encouragement and good advice necessary to bring the revision to a close. Managing Editor Gil Kelly copy-edited the manuscript with an extraordinary blend of painstaking and witty attention. I want also to thank Michael McGiffert, editor of the Institute's *William and Mary Quarterly,* for demanding refinement of my essay, "The Frontier Exchange Economy of the Lower Mississippi Valley in the Eighteenth Century."

On my road to becoming a historian, three individuals made a difference at crucial intersections. As a teacher at De La Salle High School in New Orleans, Brother Peter Barnes instilled in me an irrepressible passion for history. With great fervor and humor he demonstrated to his students how important and satisfying it is to ask difficult questions of the past. At The Johns Hopkins University, William Freehling further cultivated my interest in history, paying considerable attention to the research and writing skills of his undergraduate students. Inspired by Bill to pursue nineteenth-century political history of the South, I went to Duke University for graduate study. There I had the great fortune of working with Peter Wood, whose scholarship and character were influential enough to detour me into eighteenth-century social history. His masterful study of slavery in colonial South Carolina and his innovative course on colonial history opened my eyes to the importance of early American history, especially for understanding this nation's complex cultural and geographical origins. I also owe thanks to Peter for being such a passionate scholar, conscientious teacher, and generous colleague.

Two different groups of colleagues indirectly influenced this book.

Although still relatively small in number, historians of French colonial Louisiana are a highly productive group of scholars. Mathé Allain, Carl Brasseaux, and Glenn Conrad of the University of Southwestern Louisiana's Center for Louisiana Studies deserve special recognition for their service in collecting, publishing, and interpreting documents from early Louisiana. A close reader of my notes will detect how important their work is in laying groundwork and constructing landmarks for what we hope will be a growing number of students interested in French Louisiana. Through their own works and their personal responses, Patricia Galloway of the Mississippi Department of Archives and History and Michael Foret of the University of Wisconsin at Stevens Point have also been helpful.

Cornell University's Department of History, the other group of colleagues, provided this beginner a decade ago with an environment too good to be true. The integral ties between teaching, scholarship, and service are genuinely respected here at Cornell's history department. I have benefited from the patience as well as example of all members of my department, but owe a special word of thanks to Mary Beth Norton and Tom Holloway for their steadfast faith and interest in my work. Steve Kaplan graced an early version of my chapter on food exchange with a keen critical reading that resulted in the publication of "Food Marketing and Interethnic Exchange in the Eighteenth-Century Lower Mississippi Valley" in *Food and Foodways*.

In dedicating this book to my mother and father, I express my loving gratitude for everything they have done over the years. Their undaunting devotion to family and generosity toward all people make them my greatest teachers. Rhonda Seals Usner has contributed much to this book from its very beginnings. To list the multitude of ways that she helped, from translating Spanish documents to exhorting me to finish, would only trivialize the spirit of partnership that guides all aspects of our relationship. Rhonda's own interest in Louisiana culture and history made researching and writing a joint adventure. Our sons Jacob and Jordan joined this journey along the way and introduced us to another enriching mixture of work and play. Their tolerance of their father's frenzied work habits earns them special thanks.

CONTENTS

ILLUSTRATIONS AND TABLES

PLATES

MAPS

TABLES

ABBREVIATIONS

AC, C13A   Archives des Colonies, Paris, Series C13A. These 54 volumes of Louisiana General Correspondence are docu-
ments received by the Ministry of Marine from officials in
Louisiana. The collection is available on microfilm in several repositories in Louisiana and Mississippi, the principal one used by the author being Loyola University of
New Orleans.

AGI, PC   Archivo General de Indias, Seville, Papeles Procedentes de
Cuba. A complete microfilm collection of the more than
500 *legajos* (bundles of documents) of correspondence, reports, censuses, and so forth regarding Louisiana is not
yet available in the United States. Transcripts are scattered
in various archives of the United States. Among those
used by the author are the Edward E. Ayer Collection,
Newberry Library, Chicago; Louisiana Historical Collection, New Orleans; and North Carolina Division of Archives and History, Raleigh.

AHQ   *Alabama Historical Quarterly.*

AR   *Alabama Review.*

EPR   English Provincial Records, 1763–1783. Ten volumes of
transcripts from the Colonial Office Records, British Public Record Office, in the Mississippi Department of Archives and History, Jackson.

JMH   *Journal of Mississippi History.*

LH   *Louisiana History.*

LHQ   *Louisiana Historical Quarterly.*

MPAED   *Mississippi Provincial Archives: English Dominion,* 1 vol. to date, ed. Dunbar Rowland (Nashville, Tenn., 1911–). Official English correspondence from the transcripts of Colonial Office Papers in the Mississippi Department of Archives and History, Jackson.

MPAFD   *Mississippi Provincial Archives: French Dominion,* I–III, ed. Dunbar Rowland and Albert Godfrey Sanders (Jackson, Miss., 1929–1932); IV–V, ed. Rowland and Sanders, rev. and ed. Patricia Kay Galloway (Baton Rouge, La., 1984). Translations of transcripts in the Mississippi Department of Archives and History, Jackson, mostly from the C13A Series of the Archives des Colonies.

RSCLHQ   "Records of the Superior Council," published intermittently in the *Louisiana Historical Quarterly,* I–XXII (1918–1939), serves as a calendar of the manuscript Records of the Superior Council in the Louisiana Historical Collection, New Orleans. A massive organization, microfilming, and cataloging of these judicial papers is presently underway and will supersede the summaries and translated excerpts in *LHQ.* All manuscripts in this collection examined by the author but not included in the *RSCLHQ* are cited by title and date of document.

SJRLHQ   "Spanish Judicial Records," *Louisiana Historical Quarterly,* VI–XXV (1923–1942). The same information about the *RSCLHQ* applies to this collection.

SMV   *Spain in the Mississippi Valley, 1765–1794,* ed. and trans. Lawrence Kinnaird, 3 parts, vols. II–IV of American Historical Association, *Annual Report for the Year 1945* (Washington, D.C., 1946–1949[?]), cited by part no. Translations of materials from the Spanish Archives in the Bancroft Library, University of California, Berkeley.

SPR   Spanish Provincial Records, 1763–1783. Ten volumes of transcripts from the Archivo General de Indias in the Mississippi Department of Archives and History, Jackson.

INDIANS, SETTLERS, & SLAVES IN A FRONTIER EXCHANGE ECONOMY

And as he talked about those old times and those dead and vanished men of another race from either that the boy knew, gradually to the boy those old times would cease to be old times and would become a part of the boy's present, not only as if they had happened yesterday but as if they were still happening, the men who walked through them actually walking in breath and air and casting an actual shadow on the earth they had not quitted. And more: as if some of them had not happened yet but would occur tomorrow, until at last it would seem to the boy that he himself had not come into existence yet, that none of his race nor the other subject race which his people had brought with them into the land had come here yet; that although it had been his grandfather's and then his father's and uncle's and was now his cousin's and someday would be his own land which he and Sam hunted over, their hold upon it actually was as trivial and without reality as the now faded and archaic script in the chancery book in Jefferson which allocated it to them and that it was he, the boy, who was the guest here and Sam Fathers' voice the mouthpiece of the host.

—William Faulkner, "The Old People,"
Go Down, Moses

INTRODUCTION

This book began in a study of early slavery in colonial Louisiana. Already steeped in the scholarship on society and politics in the antebellum South, I suddenly encountered a surprising world—where African slaves joined Indians in wars against colonial armies, Indian leaders pleaded pardons for deserting European soldiers, and German settlers hunted and farmed in a French province. As I followed these and other seemingly anomalous leads, the wider social relations among Indians, settlers, and slaves led me far beyond the institutional parameters of slavery. Not only was slavery itself very different in the eighteenth century from in the nineteenth century, but its formation within a sparsely settled French colony surrounded by numerous and populous American Indian societies had a significance that later events and perceptions would only obscure. In attempting to understand how peoples of different cultures influenced each other in early Louisiana, the Lower Mississippi Valley assumed meaning for me as an actual region within which distinct patterns of concord and conflict came to the fore.

In wandering through the sources, it did not take long to discover many signs of the profound change that eventually overcame earlier peoples and patterns in this region. The evolution of the stranger, older world into the more familiar antebellum Deep South, in fact, magnetized me. But my desire to explain the dramatic transformation during the late eighteenth and early nineteenth centuries was seriously hindered by the all too vague and misapprehending notions that readers would bring to the region's earlier period. I resolved this dilemma by bringing what had once been intended as a backdrop to its much-deserved front-stage position. Deeper examination into the formative years of the region, before 1783, shaped the ordinary patterns of cross-cultural interaction and the less perceptible forms of economic change into the principal subject of this work. In one sense, it is now a long prelude to what will be a separate study of the transformative period.

Personal resolution of this historiographical problem, however, did not rescue me from the question ringing throughout my efforts to reconstruct relations that existed among inhabitants of the Lower Mississippi Valley before 1783: Why has this region of North America interested relatively few professional historians? My own hesitancy as an aspiring historian to leave the more solid ground of other places and periods for the more uncertain terrain of the colonial Gulf South is a striking illustration of this neglect, since I am myself a native of New Orleans, who spent summer after summer swimming and fishing with my family off the Mississippi Gulf Coast. The answer to the question lies in a twofold syndrome by which this particular region was both overshadowed chronologically and trivialized geographically. Inherent in the orthodox historiography of the American South, as C. Vann Woodward has reminded us, is the predominance of an Old South by which other eras are measured.[1] Changes and continuities that went into the making (and perhaps unmaking) of the southern section of the United States have been long obfuscated by an obsession with that passing phase of its history known as the antebellum period. Only in the last few decades—a century after the Civil War—have historians begun to rescue older and newer Souths from a false sense of time, in which class and race relations seem frozen in images of docile slaves, deferential yeomen, and gentrified planters. Students of the colonial period, in particular, are disclosing how drastically different life was for the generations of settlers and slaves who inhabited southern North America, along with American Indians, before it became swept into the vortex of antebellum racism and sectionalism.[2]

---

1. C. Vann Woodward, *Thinking Back: The Perils of Writing History* (Baton Rouge, La., 1986), 62–69.

2. Important studies in this rescue of the colonial South from the Old South grip include Peter H. Wood, *Black Majority: Negroes in Colonial South Carolina from 1670 through the Stono Rebellion* (New York, 1974); Edmund S. Morgan, *American Slavery, American Freedom: The Ordeal of Colonial Virginia* (New York, 1975); Robert D. Mitchell, *Commercialism and Frontier: Perspectives on the Early Shenandoah Valley* (Charlottesville, Va., 1977); Rhys Isaac, *The Transformation of Virginia, 1740–1790*

The geographical trivialization of the Gulf South in colonial American historiography has certainly not helped us overcome this chronological obscurity of older Souths. The Lower Mississippi Valley has been borderland territory for historians as it once was for the English colonies of the Atlantic Coast, and its people have been largely ignored or casually dismissed as mere bit-players in the drama of American development— colorful, no doubt, but peripheral and unimportant. Before falling under the sovereignty of the United States, lands along the Mississippi River appear to be an amorphous area sojourned by French woodsmen and Indian warriors while waiting to be occupied by Anglo-American settlers and their African-American slaves. A determinatively eastern point of view toward regions beyond the Atlantic seaboard is echoed in phrases like Ulrich Bonnell Phillips's "redskins and Latins" and more recently in Bernard Bailyn's references to "exotic," "strange," and "bizarre" people living in the southeastern hinterland.[3] The trans-Appalachian South, in a

---

(Chapel Hill, N.C., 1982); Allan Kulikoff, *Tobacco and Slaves: The Development of Southern Cultures in the Chesapeake, 1680–1800* (Chapel Hill, N.C., 1986); James H. Merrell, *The Indians' New World: Catawbas and Their Neighbors from European Contact through the Era of Removal* (Chapel Hill, N.C., 1989); Rachel N. Klein, *Unification of a Slave State: The Rise of the Planter Class in the South Carolina Backcountry, 1760–1808* (Chapel Hill, N.C., 1990); Joyce E. Chaplin, "An Anxious Pursuit: Innovation in Commercial Agriculture in South Carolina, Georgia, and British East Florida, 1730–1815" (Ph.D. diss., Johns Hopkins University, 1986). The most neglected century of all in southern history, the 16th century, is finally receiving close attention, best represented by such works as Paul E. Hoffman, *A New Andalucia and a Way to the Orient: The American Southeast during the Sixteenth Century* (Baton Rouge, La., 1990); and Charles Hudson, *The Juan Pardo Expeditions: Exploration of the Carolinas and Tennessee, 1566–1568* (Washington, D.C., 1990).

3. "Redskins and Latins" is the title of a chapter in Ulrich Bonnell Phillips's *Life and Labor in the Old South* (Boston, 1929). Carl Bridenbaugh, in *Myths and Realities: Societies of the Colonial South* (Baton Rouge, La., 1952), viii, told an audience in, of all places, Baton Rouge for Louisiana State University's Walter Lynwood Fleming Lectures in Southern History about three "Old Souths" that preceded the more familiar Old South of antebellum America—without once mentioning colonial Louisiana. Granted, his listeners and readers understood that Bridenbaugh meant only to focus on the English colonies that became part of the original United States, but a powerful subliminal message was imparted when he noted in passing the "redskins and Latins" who walled in the English colony of South Carolina. For Bernard Bailyn's recent characterization of the southern frontier, see *The Peopling of British North America: An Introduction* (New York, 1986), 112–131. His case is elaborated in *Voyagers to the West: A Passage in the Peopling of America on the Eve of the Revolution* (New York, 1986).

word, has been only dimly realized by historians as a place with a history of its own and a people whose tale is worth telling in its own right.

Not that the vast region known in colonial times as Louisiana has been wholly neglected by noted historians. The likes of Francis Parkman, Justin Winsor, and Frederick Jackson Turner eloquently depicted it as an arena of international contests for empire. Historians based in the Mississippi Valley, beginning with Charles Gayarré in the 1850s, have vigorously studied French and Spanish Louisiana. But the focus on geopolitical affairs has long obscured the ordinary people who actually shaped society and economy within the region yet remain overshadowed by a few great men acting upon the grand stage of diplomacy. A growing cadre of scholars is now excavating details about government, immigration, slavery, and Indian affairs in the colony—with increasing emphasis on social and economic life. But what are conveniently classified as French colonial and Spanish borderlands histories still go slightly noticed by students of British North America and generalists in American history.[4]

Relegation of Louisiana and other non-English colonies to the margins of American history is partly due to a tendency among so-called Borderlands historians themselves to compare their subjects with standards set in English colonial history. The most devoted historians of Louisiana are quick to point out that the colony in the Mississippi Valley lagged behind, or failed in comparison with, the English colonies along the Atlantic seaboard. Louisiana indeed suffered from a low priority in the mercantile designs of both France and Spain. Immigration and population growth proceeded slowly, exportation of staple products to Europe fluctuated, and subsistence agriculture predominated over production of cash crops.[5]

4. The skewed emphasis in Louisiana colonial historiography, since Parkman and Gayarré, on explorers and other "great men" is noted in Carl A. Brasseaux, "French Louisiana," in Light Townsend Cummins and Glen Jeansonne, eds., *A Guide to the History of Louisiana* (Westport, Conn., 1982), 4; and Patricia K. Galloway, ed., *La Salle and His Legacy: Frenchmen and Indians in the Lower Mississippi Valley* (Jackson, Miss., 1982), xii–xiii.

For historiographical assessments of Louisiana colonial scholarship, see Brasseaux, "French Louisiana," and Light Townsend Cummins, "Spanish Louisiana," in *Guide to the History of Louisiana*, 3–25. The most comprehensive bibliographical guide is Glenn R. Conrad and Carl A. Brasseaux, *A Selected Bibliography of Scholarly Literature on Colonial Louisiana and New France* (Lafayette, La., 1982).

5. Reflecting the dominant tone in the scholarship, Joe Gray Taylor's chapters on the 18th century in his *Louisiana: A Bicentennial History* (New York, 1976) are entitled

But Louisiana's sparse colonial population and tentative transatlantic commerce can actually be used to the historian's advantage, allowing one to turn more attentively to social and economic relations that have been neglected in all colonial regions of North America.[6]

Colonial history has focused for a long time on the external linkages of colonies with their home countries, to the neglect of internal relationships forged by inhabitants. This neglect has been especially true among students of economic change who measure development according to the success of mercantile or colonial policies. In their analyses, production of commodities exported to the European Atlantic market overshadows economic activities oriented toward local or regional markets. More historians are now turning to social and economic interaction inside colonial regions, animated by an interest in how and when a commercial economy encroached upon a subsistence economy.[7] A greater understanding of the role played by people living in and around the colonies is consequently in the making. Whether looking at labor systems or regional markets, the outcome of colonization depended as much upon the influence of colonial and native inhabitants as upon the policies designed by official and commercial interests. The struggle between metropolitan plans and local purposes is, in fact, coming to dominate newer scholarship.[8]

"Colonial Louisiana: Study in Failure" and "A Holding Action: Louisiana as a Spanish Colony." The marginal position of Louisiana in the Atlantic economy is cogently explained in Donald J. Lemieux, "The Mississippi Valley, New France, and French Colonial Policy," *Southern Studies,* XVII (1978), 39–56.

6. The inhibiting effect of Borderlands scholars' emphasis on geopolitics and of their comparisons with Anglo-American regions upon integration into general United States history is convincingly demonstrated in Gerald E. Poyo and Gilberto M. Hinojosa, "Spanish Texas and Borderlands Historiography in Transition: Implications for United States History," *Journal of American History,* LXXV (1988–1989), 393–416.

7. For discussions of colonial economic historiography, see Jacob M. Price, "The Transatlantic Economy," Richard B. Sheridan, "The Domestic Economy," and James T. Lemon, "Spatial Order: Households in Local Communities and Regions," in Jack P. Greene and J. R. Pole, eds., *Colonial British America: Essays in the New History of the Early Modern Era* (Baltimore, 1984), 18–122; and John J. McCusker and Russell R. Menard, *The Economy of British America, 1607–1789* (Chapel Hill, N.C., 1985), 17–34.

8. John Robert McNeill, *Atlantic Empires of France and Spain: Louisbourg and Havana, 1700–1763* (Chapel Hill, N.C., 1985); Steve J. Stern, "Feudalism, Capitalism, and the World-System in the Perspective of Latin America and the Caribbean," *American Historical Review,* XCIII (1988), 829–872.

Here I examine the evolution and composition of a regional economy that connected Indian villagers across the Lower Mississippi Valley with European settlers and African slaves along the Gulf Coast and lower banks of the Mississippi. The term "frontier exchange" is meant to capture the form and content of economic interaction between these groups. For too long, "frontier" has connoted an interracial boundary, across which advanced societies penetrated primitive ones. But frontiers were more regional in scope, networks of cross-cultural interaction through which native and colonial groups circulated goods and services.[9] Small-scale production, face-to-face marketing, and prosaic features of livelihood in general must be taken more seriously by colonial historians in order to grasp how peoples of different cultures related to and influenced each other in daily life. I am less concerned with measuring the "impact" of a "colonial culture" upon a "native culture" than many readers might prefer, but rather assign myself the task of examining the economic context in which different peoples continuously interacted with each other. Without using any spatial models or formulas, I examine how Indians, settlers, and slaves produced and distributed goods at a regional level.[10]

In order to underscore this regional context of exchange, the Lower Mississippi Valley is here defined as a colonial region shaped by forms of

9. A redefinition of frontier from a linear to a regional perspective can be traced in Robin F. Wells, "Frontier Systems as a Sociocultural Type," *Papers in Anthropology,* XIV (1973), 6–15; D. W. Meinig, "The Continuous Shaping of America: A Prospectus for Geographers and Historians," *AHR,* LXXXIII (1978), 1186–1217; Robert F. Berkhofer, Jr., "The North American Frontier as Process and Context," in Howard Lamar and Leonard Thompson, eds., *The Frontier in History: North America and Southern Africa Compared* (New Haven, Conn., 1981), 43–75; Kenneth E. Lewis, *The American Frontier: An Archaeological Study of Settlement Pattern and Process* (Orlando, Fla., 1984); and Francis Jennings, *The Ambiguous Iroquois Empire: The Covenant Chain Confederation of Indian Tribes with English Colonies from Its Beginnings to the Lancaster Treaty of 1744* (New York, 1984), esp. 58–83.

10. I am indebted to anthropological works that focus on local and regional marketing, most notably Carol A. Smith, ed., *Regional Analysis,* 2 vols. (New York, 1976); Stuart Plattner, ed., *Markets and Marketing: Proceedings of the 1984 Meeting of the Society for Economic Anthropology* (Washington, D.C., 1985); Richard Hodges, *Primitive and Peasant Markets* (New York, 1988). For two ambitious studies that encompass all groups of participants in a regional analysis, see D. W. Meinig, *The Shaping of America: A Geographical Perspective on Five Hundred Years of History,* I, *Atlantic America, 1492–1800* (New Haven, Conn., 1986); and Thomas D. Hall, *Social Change in the Southwest, 1350–1880* (Lawrence, Kans., 1989).

production and means of exchange practiced commonly and regularly among its diverse inhabitants. Within this region, people produced and exchanged basic resources without much division of labor. Colonial officials and merchants tried to administer commerce with only limited success, and Indians, settlers, and slaves went on trading small quantities of goods directly and openly with each other. Upper Louisiana, or the area called Illinois country, is not examined here, because economic connections between the Upper Mississippi Valley and lower Louisiana were more impersonal and less predictable before the last quarter of the eighteenth century. The inhabitants of the Illinois settlements—numbering 768 French settlers, 445 black slaves, and 147 Indian slaves at midcentury—belonged to Louisiana politically but were more closely integrated economically into the Great Lakes region. The standard image of Louisiana as a vast territory spread along a thousand miles of the meandering Mississippi and sparsely occupied by Frenchmen and their Indian allies not only exaggerates the boundlessness of life in the valley but distracts attention from the substantial intraregional connections that differentiated lower Louisiana from upper Louisiana.[11] In 1762–1763 the Lower Mississippi Valley was partitioned into the Spanish province of Louisiana and the English province of West Florida. The latter colony, therefore, must be included in any study of the region's economy. The persistence of frontier exchange across the political boundary can too easily be overlooked when Louisiana and West Florida are treated separately.

Regional analysis of frontier exchange can also illuminate the diverse and dynamic participation of Indians, settlers, and slaves in a way that may prove useful to historians of other colonial regions. For colonies examined more thoroughly than are Louisiana and West Florida, racial categories dictate selection and organization of data by historians. African-Americans and American Indians are finally receiving scholarly attention commensurate with their presence and influence in colonial America, and the old tendency to read nineteenth-century race relations and racism back into earlier periods is being corrected. Nonetheless, analyses of colonial society and economy still tend to compartmentalize

11. W. J. Eccles, *France in America* (New York, 1972), 167; and John G. Clark, *New Orleans, 1718–1812: An Economic History* (Baton Rouge, La., 1970), 30. For the best modern inquiry into the Illinois country, see Carl J. Ekberg, *Colonial Ste. Genevieve: An Adventure on the Mississippi Frontier* (Gerald, Mo., 1985); and Winstanley Briggs, "Le Pays des Illinois," *William and Mary Quarterly,* 3d Ser., XLVIII (1990), 30–56.

ethnic and cultural groups by socioeconomic status and geographical location. During the 1980s Indians and Africans at last shared the forestage of colonial scholarship with Europeans, but mostly under separate (even if equally bright) spotlights.[12] But by tracing linkages between seemingly disparate sites within a region—Indian villages, colonial plantations, winter hunting camps, military outposts, and port towns—I hope to highlight the fluidity that characterized social and economic relations between all groups of people.

"Frontier exchange" describes intercultural relations that evolved within a geographical area in a way that emphasizes the initiatives taken by the various participants. Indians, settlers, and slaves had separate stakes in how the colonial region evolved. But in pursuit of their respective goals, they found plenty of common ground upon which to adapt. Part I of this study traces chronologically the formation of a colonial region in the Lower Mississippi Valley, focusing upon decisions and conditions that facilitated frontier exchange. Its four chapters are general sketches of change, none by any means comprehensive; it is hoped they will evoke deeper and more critical investigation into what is suggested. Part II probes the structure of the frontier exchange economy by dividing economic activities and relations into four spheres of interaction. These four chapters are more anatomical than chronological, dissecting the regional economy into its component patterns of production and exchange. Change in this socioeconomic structure occurred in slow shifts and slight cracks, which foreshadowed the subsequent era of drastic transformation.

In the responses of Indians, settlers, and slaves to changing demographic and economic conditions between 1763 and 1783, we observe "frontier exchange" beginning to evolve from a network of interaction into a strategy of survival. Toward the end of the eighteenth century,

12. For reviews of colonial historiography on Indians and blacks, see James Axtell, "The Ethnohistory of Early America: A Review Essay," *WMQ*, 3d Ser., XXXV (1978), 110–144; Peter H. Wood, "'I Did the Best I Could for My Day': The Study of Early Black History during the Second Reconstruction, 1960 to 1976," *WMQ*, 3d Ser., XXXV (1978), 185–225; T. H. Breen, "Creative Adaptations: Peoples and Cultures," in Greene and Pole, eds., *Colonial British America*, 195–232. For an assessment of colonial scholarship that directly confronts the compartmentalization and isolation of Indian studies, see James H. Merrell, "Some Thoughts on Colonial Historians and American Indians," *WMQ*, 3d Ser., XLVI (1989), 94–119.

Indians, settlers, and slaves had to struggle harder to preserve means of production and exchange that had routinely provided them flexibility and autonomy. Stronger government intervention and commercial infiltration into social and economic relations resulted from aggressive immigration policies of both Spain and Great Britain, expansion of plantation agriculture, and monopolization of Indian trade. Tougher laws controlling interaction among Indians, settlers, and slaves heightened ethnic tensions and accelerated the buildup of interracial barriers. The plantation economy began to replace the frontier exchange economy as the main framework of cross-cultural relations. Frontier exchange activities, however, never totally disappeared from the landscape of the Lower Mississippi Valley: the farming, herding, hunting, and trading practices devised over the eighteenth century persevered in the interstices of the expanding plantation society. Indeed, customary means of production and exchange would prove to be strong roots for popular livelihood and everyday resistance well into the nineteenth century.

THE EVOLUTION OF A

COLONIAL REGION, 1699–1783

1

TRADE AND SETTLEMENT IN THE

FORMATION OF A COLONIAL REGION

In late February 1699, a small group of sailors, soldiers, and a few artisans toiled on the sandy beach of Biloxi Bay beneath the tall pines on its eastern shore. As these men cut timber, constructed a fort, and hunted for food, Indian men, women, and children took time from their routine fishing and hunting along the Gulf of Mexico shore to observe from a cautious distance these newcomers whose skin seemed as white as the beach sand. Awkward moments of contact led to more relaxed attempts at communication, and by spring Indian groups from the Gulf Coast and the Mississippi River were establishing formal relations with the French post at Biloxi. The ceremonial entrance into Fort Maurepas of chiefs from nearby villages—Pascagoulas, Biloxis, Moctobis, and Capinas—was perhaps the grandest of several occasions in which the calumet, a long, hollow cane decorated with feathers and attached to a stone pipe, was offered to Pierre Le Moyne d'Iberville, commandant of this French occupation. Iberville, who would have preferred not to smoke, "did indeed draw some puffs" from the pipe and then had his face rubbed with white powder. This feast of the calumet lasted three days, during which the Indians sang and danced to the music of their drum and gourd rattles. On the third day they carried Iberville to a clearing in front of the fort, sat all the Frenchmen on deerskins around a stake, and one by one struck the post with their "wooden head-breakers" and boasted "noble deeds they had done in war." From the royal storehouse Iberville distributed among the Indian celebrants "knives, glass beads, vermilion,

13

guns, lead, powder, mirrors, combs, kettles, cloaks, hats, shirts, *braguets,* leggings, rings, and other such trinkets."[1]

This and other ceremonial exchanges marked the beginnings of a new colonial region in North America, although to the founders of Louisiana they probably paled beside the ambitious economic plans and political schemes that had renewed European interest in the Lower Mississippi Valley two decades earlier. Iberville's assignment to "select a good site that can be defended with a few men, and block entry to the river by other nations" resulted from a flurry of ventures toward the lower Mississippi River by competitive European interests.[2] Following the expedition of Father Jacques Marquette and Louis Jolliet through Illinois country and down the Mississippi to the Arkansas River, René Robert Cavelier, sieur de La Salle, began to expand his Great Lakes Indian commerce, based at his seigneurial grant of Fort Frontenac, into the Mississippi Valley. In the spring of 1682, he led a party of thirty-three Frenchmen and thirty-one Indian men, women, and children to the mouth of the Mississippi and extended offers of alliance, through skillful use of Indian diplomatic protocol, to Quapaw, Taensa, and Natchez villages along the river. Upon completing Fort St. Louis on the Illinois River the following year, La Salle granted concessions to settlers that included rights to trade with Indians down the Mississippi. These efforts to expand French commerce did not occur without some stiff competition. Seneca and other Iroquois Indians were trying to strengthen their own trade position vis-à-vis western tribes, and English traders sought direct avenues to Indian villages west of their colonies. La Salle's role in this commercial drive into the Lower Mississippi Valley ended with his assassination in 1687, after three years of struggling to save a colony that he established on the Texas coast. But his vision of developing fur commerce in the valley, particularly in bison robes, and of usurping Spanish colonial mines to the southwest continued to fuel the interests of royal officials, missionaries, and merchants.[3]

1. Richebourg Gaillard McWilliams, ed. and trans., *Fleur de Lys and Calumet: Being the Pénicaut Narrative of French Adventure in Louisiana* (Baton Rouge, La., 1953), 5–7 (hereafter cited as *Pénicaut Narrative*).

2. Richebourg Gaillard McWilliams, ed. and trans., *Iberville's Gulf Journals* (University, Ala., 1981), 4 (hereafter cited as *Iberville's Gulf Journals*).

3. For modern perspectives on French exploration in the Lower Mississippi Valley during the late 17th century, see Carl O. Sauer, *Seventeenth Century North America* (Berkeley, Calif., 1980), 137–192; Patricia K. Galloway, ed., *La Salle and His Legacy:*

French activity in the Lower Mississippi Valley remained minimal into the 1690s because of a convergence of factors. Canadian officials had to restrict Indian trade in a glutted beaver skin market, and France had military priorities on the European continent. Henri de Tonti and other associates of the deceased La Salle, nevertheless, sustained trade with central valley Indians from posts on the Illinois and Arkansas rivers. Meanwhile, Spanish expeditions into Texas, in search of La Salle's short-lived settlement near Matagorda Bay, led to the temporary formation of two missions between the Trinity and Neches rivers. And in 1698 Spain stationed a permanent garrison at Pensacola Bay. The most aggressive challenge to French claims to the lower Mississippi originated farther eastward in Carolina, where the English had established a colony in 1670. With assistance from Indian allies and from at least one known French expatriate, a voyageur named Jean Couture, English traders entered the Lower Mississippi Valley in pursuit of deerskins and Indian slaves. The apparent success of Carolina agents and the threat of direct English occupation of the Mississippi River under Daniel Coxe finally quickened the French Ministry of Marine to embark, on September 24, 1698, two royal frigates and two freighters to the Gulf Coast of Louisiana under the Canadian naval officer Iberville.[4]

Through the voyages of La Salle, Tonti, and Iberville, American Indians in the Lower Mississippi Valley came face to face with agents of France's mercantile economy. Based in Atlantic ports like La Rochelle and Bordeaux, French merchants and their allies in the court of Louis XIV at Versailles were propelling the movement of products and money over long distances. The sailors, soldiers, voyageurs, and missionaries from both Canada and France now approaching Louisiana did not necessarily represent the social mainstream of late seventeenth-century France, which like most of Europe was still a country of agricultural, inward-directed com-

Frenchmen and Indians in the Lower Mississippi Valley (Jackson, Miss., 1982); Monique Pelletier, "From New France to Louisiana: Politics and Geography," in Steven G. Reinhardt, ed., *The Sun King: Louis XIV and the New World* (New Orleans, 1984), 85–95; Peter H. Wood, "La Salle: Discovery of a Lost Explorer," *American Historical Review*, LXXXIX (1984), 294–323; Robert S. Weddle, ed., *La Salle, the Mississippi, and the Gulf: Three Primary Documents* (College Station, Tex., 1987).

4. Verner W. Crane, *The Southern Frontier, 1670–1732* (Durham, N.C., 1928); William Edward Dunn, *Spanish and French Rivalry in the Gulf Region of the United States, 1678–1702: The Beginnings of Texas and Pensacola* (Austin, Tex., 1917).

munities. But they performed roles abroad that did represent the intentions, however incongruent they were at times, of king, church, and company. As it made its appearance on the Gulf Coast, French mercantilist policy was designed to extract furs, minerals, or crops from remote lands for the benefit of the nation's commercial economy. The first step in this scheme was to enlist the inhabitants of these lands in order to secure territorial claims and military service against other European powers.[5]

I

French relations with Indians in the Lower Mississippi Valley began in the shadow of pressures originating with the earlier establishment of Atlantic Coast colonies. Needing a powerful ally against British expansionism, Indian nations quickly turned to Iberville's nascent colony for assistance. By the end of the seventeenth century, English traders from Charleston had reached the Mississippi River by way of Creek and Chickasaw travel routes. In search of deerskins and Indian slaves, they offered guns and ammunition to Creek, Chickasaw, and Natchez warriors who agreed to deliver captives taken from other tribes. As bands of Indians equipped with firearms attacked villages on both sides of the Mississippi, hundreds of Indians were killed and captured under a new type of warfare.[6] Thousands more died of smallpox and other foreign viruses. The spread of European diseases among the region's native inhabitants actually dated back to the coastal reconnaissance and interior expeditions that were carried out by Spanish explorers during the sixteenth century. The populous and centralized chiefdoms encountered by Hernando de Soto in 1540 had collapsed into smaller societies largely in consequence of virulent epidemics.[7] Since Native Americans lacked immunity to viruses that

5. Charles Woolsey Cole, *French Mercantilism, 1683–1700* (New York, 1943); Pierre Goubert, *Louis XIV and Twenty Million Frenchmen,* trans. Anne Carter (New York, 1970); Philippe Jacquin, "The Colonial Policy of the Sun King," in Reinhardt, ed., *Sun King,* 73–83; Mathé Allain, *"Not Worth a Straw": French Colonial Policy and the Early Years of Louisiana* (Lafayette, La., 1988).

6. The extent and experience of Indian enslavement in the colonial South are best represented in J. Leitch Wright, Jr., *The Only Land They Knew: The Tragic Story of the American Indians in the Old South* (New York, 1981), 126–150.

7. George R. Milner, "Epidemic Disease in the Postcontact Southeast: A Reappraisal," *Midcontinental Journal of Archaeology,* V (1980), 39–56; Marvin T. Smith,

originated across the Atlantic Ocean, diseases like influenza, measles, cholera, typhus, dysentery, and yellow fever had been sweeping through vulnerable Indian populations for many years. The seventy thousand or so American Indians still inhabiting the Lower Mississippi Valley in 1700, therefore, were far fewer than the population in the sixteenth and seventeenth centuries.[8]

When the French built their first post on Biloxi Bay in the spring of 1699, Indian villages in the immediate vicinity were already wrenched by epidemics and slave raids reaching them from the Atlantic seaboard. The establishment of a Spanish fort at Pensacola Bay only a few months before Iberville's three ships arrived, and now the presence of Frenchmen, exposed these people to an even closer source of infection and conflict. Six groups of Indians, numbering approximately thirty-five hundred men, women, and children, lived within a few days' reach of the earliest French settlement. The Biloxis, Pascagoulas, Moctobis, and Capinas occupied separate villages on small bluffs overlooking the Pascagoula River, situated near enough to the coast to take advantage of its rich fishing resources but far enough to be protected from spring floods and autumn hurricanes. To the east of Biloxi Bay, clusters of Mobilian and Tohomé villages enjoyed similar positions along the Mobile River. Traveling up the Pascagoula River in April 1700 and up the Mobile two years later, Iberville noticed several deserted villages and found signs of epidemic sickness within the villages still occupied.[9]

In the midst of hazardous conditions all around, the need of Louisiana Indians for military protection conveniently complemented the need of French colonial personnel for subsistence. When chiefs of the Tohomés and Mobilians requested protection against Creek marauders in May 1701, Sauvolle de La Villantry "did not hesitate to send men there in the

Archaeology of Aboriginal Culture Change in the Interior Southeast: Depopulation during the Early Historic Period (Gainesville, Fla., 1987), 54–112; Ann F. Ramenofsky, *Vectors of Death: The Archaeology of European Contact* (Albuquerque, N.M., 1987), 42–71.

8. Henry F. Dobyns, *Native American Historical Demography: A Critical Bibliography* (Bloomington, Ind., 1976); Pauline A. Keehn, *The Effect of Epidemic Diseases on the Natives of North America: An Annotated Bibliography* (London, 1978); Russell Thornton, *American Indian Holocaust and Survival: A Population History since 1492* (Norman, Okla., 1987). For an overview of diseases transmitted across the oceans, see William H. McNeill, *Plagues and Peoples* (Garden City, N.Y., 1976), 199–234.

9. *Iberville's Gulf Journals,* 140–141, 169.

pressing necessity in which I found myself for lack of provisions." By sending a group of Canadians to these villages "with some beads, axes and other little things," the governor provided these Indians with the protection and support needed to continue cultivating their fields but also guaranteed a part of their harvest for the colony's sustenance. Early in 1702 Iberville moved the colonial headquarters from Biloxi to Mobile Bay in order to place his garrison in the vicinity of these productive Indian towns and also to be at the mouth of a river network that reached other tribal territories.[10]

French ambitions for wider alliance and commerce with Indians advanced significantly on March 26, 1702, when the Choctaws and Chickasaws from the piney hill country up the Tombigbee River met with the French at the new Mobile post. Seven Chickasaw and four Choctaw dignitaries quietly listened to the speech of Iberville being interpreted by his younger brother, Jean-Baptiste Le Moyne de Bienville. The Canadian-born naval officer harangued the Chickasaws for having "foolishly followed the advice of the English" and threatened to arm the Choctaws, Mobilians, and Tohomés against them if they did not drive all Englishmen away. Upon Iberville's request for a "family by family" count of men in their nations, the Indian delegates reported that eighteen Chickasaw villages included 588 cabins and thirty-eight Choctaw villages numbered 1,146 cabins (see Table 1). Told that three to four men lived in each cabin, the French estimated a population of two thousand warriors for the Chickasaws and five thousand warriors for the Choctaws.[11] Further discussion at the assembly revealed that in the course of ten years of warfare, stirred by slave dealers from Carolina who had already armed seven

10. *MPAFD*, II, 9–10. The first decade of French Louisiana is examined in extraordinarily rich detail in Jay Higginbotham, *Old Mobile: Fort Louis de la Louisiane, 1702–1711* (Mobile, Ala., 1977). Also see Marcel Giraud, *A History of French Louisiana*, I, *The Reign of Louis XIV, 1698–1715* (1953), trans. Joseph C. Lambert (Baton Rouge, La., 1974).

11. A copy of this village-by-village list of the number of households was later made by geographer Claude Delisle and has been found in the Archives Hydrographiques, Paris. Its publication in the *Louisiana Historical Quarterly* revealed that the actual totals from the census differed slightly from those specified in Iberville's Journal (see Table 1). It is possible that not all of the Choctaw villages were represented at this meeting, since most estimates of their number exceeded 50. On Apr. 29, 1700, the Pascagoulas told Iberville that more than 6,000 men lived in 50 different villages (*Iberville's Gulf Journals*, 141).

hundred Chickasaws with muskets, more than eighteen hundred Choctaws had been killed and another five hundred taken captive while the Chickasaws themselves lost "more than 800 men, slain on various war parties." The Chickasaw and Choctaw leaders agreed to live in peace with each other and with Iberville's colonists, "provided I would engage in trading with them, about which we came to an agreement over prices." Each tribe then received its gift of "200 pounds of powder, 200 pounds of bullets, 200 pounds of game-shot, 12 guns, 100 axes, 150 knives, some kettles, glass beads, gun flints, awls, and other hardware."[12]

Despite the Le Moyne brothers' diplomatic overtures, continuing inter-colonial hostility between Great Britain and France destabilized Indian tribal relations with each other and with the newborn colony of Louisiana. After arranging what turned out to be a short-lived peace between Choctaw and Chickasaw delegates at Mobile, the French counseled the Alibamons to discontinue their warfare against the Chickasaws, Mobilians, and Tohomés. Inhabiting several towns around the confluence of the Coosa and Tallapoosa rivers (near present-day Montgomery, Alabama), the Alibamons were one of three populous tribes in the Alabama River drainage system who eventually became known as the Upper Creeks. Altogether the Tallapoosas, Abehkas, and Alibamons numbered more than ten thousand people at the opening of the eighteenth century.[13] In the spring of 1703, a delegation of Alibamons offered to relieve Mobile's food shortage by trading their surplus corn for French merchandise. But on their upriver journey to trade for this grain, three Canadians were assassi-

12. *Iberville's Gulf Journals*, 171–174. The details of this treaty, particularly the role of Henri de Tonti in bringing the Choctaw and Chickasaw delegates to Mobile, are thoroughly recounted in Jay Higginbotham, "Henri de Tonti's Mission to the Chickasaw, 1702," *LH*, XIX (1978), 285–296. For an exemplary ethnohistorical analysis of Tonti's own account of his diplomatic mission through Choctaw and Chickasaw country, see Patricia Galloway, "Henri de Tonti du village des Chacta, 1702: The Beginning of the French Alliance," in Galloway, ed., *La Salle and His Legacy*, 146–175.

13. *MPAFD*, III, 536–537; Higginbotham, *Old Mobile*, 117–118. Thirty-six different Alibamon, Tallapoosa, and Abehka towns were named to Charles Lavasseur in 1700 by an Alibamon informant from the town of "Maugoulacho." The list is printed in Vernon J. Knight, Jr., and Sherée L. Adams, "A Voyage to the Mobile and Tomeh in 1700, with Notes on the Interior of Alabama," *Ethnohistory*, XXVIII (1981), 179–194, which is a translation and ethnographic analysis of the journal of Levasseur's expedition up the Mobile River.

TABLE 1. *Choctaw and Chickasaw Villages, 1702*

Chaqta Villages and Number of Huts

Ayanabe augoula	30	Iscananba Thousena Togrule	30
Bauctoucoula	40	Abiska	20
Coincha thoucoua logoule	33	Touacha	20
Ougilousa	30	Albamon	50
Boucfalaya	20	Itouichacou	30
Yty thipouta	30	Mogoulacha	10
Pouscouiche tacase	40	Yacho	20
Mogoulacha	50	Calouche	10
Yachou	40	Tabogoula	10
Cachetacha	40	Thata tascanan gouchy	40
Tohia sale	20	Touacha thoucoua togoule	30
Cafeta saya	20	Bita bogoula	60
Abiska Thocologoule	40	Tolistache	30
Bitabogoula	20	Ocouhinan	23
Suabonloula	10	Alibamon cheusare Lagoute	30
Thicacho oulasta	20	Onsacousba	30
Bouctoucoulo	40	Abisca	40
Ahipata bita Brugoula	60	Choutoua togoule	30
Boulistache	40	Busca	10
		Total number of huts	1,146

nated by a band of Alibamons allegedly influenced by Carolina provoca-
teurs. Two punitive expeditions led by Bienville had little effect upon the
Alibamons, who continued to raid French-allied villages as well as Indian
missions in Spanish Florida. In 1709, six hundred to seven hundred
Alibamon warriors attacked the Mobilian village, burning it down and
capturing nearly thirty women and children. A combined French, Mobilian, and Tohomé force quickly pursued these raiders, killing thirty-four
persons and taking five prisoners, who were then burned in their village as
retribution by the bereaved Mobilians.[14]

14. Jean-Baptiste Bernard de La Harpe, *The Historical Journal of the Establishment
of the French in Louisiana*, ed. Glen R. Conrad, trans. Joan Cain and Virginia Koenig
(Lafayette, La., 1971), 59–60, 64 (hereafter cited as La Harpe, *Journal*); *Pénicaut*

TABLE I. *Continued*

Chicacha Villages and Number of Huts

Apile faplimengo	10	Onthaba atchosa	50
Ayarraca	20	Thanbolo	40
Tolatchao	40	Sebafone	40
Tascaouilo	20	Thoucaliga	50
Chatata	30	Ayebisto, fortified village	30
Gouytola	20	Alaoute	60
Tanyachilca	50	Oucahata	40
Ayeheguiya	10	Oucthambolo	40
Thouquoa fola	30	Chinica	8
		Total number of huts	588

Source: A list, as recorded in meeting at Mobile, compiled by Claude Delisle, Archives Hydrographiques, Paris, published in George Kernion, trans., "Documents concerning the History of the Indians of the Eastern Region of Louisiana," *LHQ,* VIII (1925), 38–39.

Indians in the lowlands along the Mississippi River also suffered from intertribal and colonial warfare caused directly or indirectly by early European rivalry. In one documented instance, Carolina traders purchased from Natchez and Yazoo warriors a group of Chaouachas captured far down the Mississippi.[15] Among several different groups living below the mouth of the Red River, the Bayogoulas and Chitimachas probably suffered the worst series of hardships during the early years of French colonization. Occupying a natural levee on the west bank of the Mississippi, just above the mouth of Bayou Lafourche, the Bayogoulas' town enjoyed access to a wide range of seasonally diverse resources in the delta country: numerous species of fishes trapped in backwater lakes after spring floods receded, harvests of nuts and berries in scattered hammocks of hardwood forests, deer and bear hunted in the lowland forests, and

Narrative, 62–66; *MPAFD,* II, 23–24, III, 19–23, 136; Higginbotham, *Old Mobile,* 383–385; Alexander Moore, ed., *Nairne's Muskhogean Journals: The 1708 Expedition to the Mississippi River* (Jackson, Miss., 1988).

15. *Pénicaut Narrative,* 159.

small fields of corn planted on the narrow levees along the Mississippi and connecting bayous. But when Iberville first visited the Bayogoulas in March 1699, "smallpox, which they still had in the village, had killed one-fourth of the people." Surrounding the still sizable village, with an adult male population of some 250, stood platforms covered with the bodies of their dead.[16] Arriving at Bayogoula a year later to establish a short-lived mission, Father Paul Du Ru observed how the residents, people who had already suffered a great deal of sickness and death, seemed unwilling to hunt, fish, and plant, and interpreted what were obviously the physical and psychological effects of smallpox as "the dominant preference of these tribes for indolence."

The Bayogoulas did not hesitate, however, to entertain the Jesuit priest with many kinds of games and dances, impressing him with their efforts to preserve order and tradition in a village that Du Ru gathered was more than six hundred years old. Two temples of about equal size, made of thatch and covered with cane mats, stood at the ends of a huge plaza. One belonged to the Bayogoulas and the other to the Mongoulachas, a neighboring tribe recently accepted into the village. Du Ru compared their shape with the dome of the portal at the College du Plessis. Carved figures resembling roosters sat atop the steeples of these temples (see Plate 1 for a drawing of a similar temple). The French missionary "entered both of them and saw the lamp of eternal fire which is maintained because there is no other light when the door is closed. I saw there many rows of packages piled one on the other. These are the bones of the dead chiefs which are carefully wrapped in palm mats." Residential cabins in the village were large, "especially those of the chiefs, where nearly 300 persons can be assembled."[17]

The Bayogoulas were assimilating a number of refugees from other villages already destroyed by disease or warfare. This merging of remnant groups was not an uncommon or unreasonable response to such disruption, although it might have accelerated the spread of infection. The Mongoulachas mentioned by Du Ru were soon followed by Quinipissas

16. *Iberville's Gulf Journals,* 63. Problems in locating and estimating the size of delta tribes during these years are explored in Marco J. Giardino, "Documentary Evidence for the Location of Historic Indian Villages in the Mississippi Delta," in Dave D. Davis, ed., *Perspectives on Gulf Coast Prehistory* (Gainesville, Fla., 1984), 232–257.

17. Ruth Lapham Butler, trans., *Journal of Paul Du Ru (February 1 to May 8, 1700), Missionary Priest to Louisiana* (Chicago, 1934), 19–22, 52–53.

PLATE I. *Temple and Cabin of the Chief, Acolapissa, 1732.* By Alexandre de Batz. Pen and ink drawing. *Courtesy of Peabody Museum of Archaeology and Ethnology, Harvard University, Cambridge, Mass.*

who abandoned their own village in the vicinity of present-day New Orleans.[18] Then in the summer of 1706, the Taensa Indians were driven from their villages on Lake St. Joseph and sought refuge downriver with the Bayogoulas. These more numerous and aggressive newcomers, however, suddenly turned against their hosts, killing many Bayogoulas and capturing several Chitimacha villagers. Directing anger toward the French, a band of Chitimachas in late November assassinated Father Jean-François Buisson de Saint-Cosme as he was descending the Mississippi from Natchez. This action gave Louis Juchereau de Saint-Denis, a young lieutenant commanding Fort La Boulaye, the opportunity to escape the tedium of isolated garrison life in the delta. With a force of twenty fellow Canadians and about eighty warriors from villages around Lake Pontchartrain, Saint-Denis destroyed the nearest Chitimacha village on Bayou Lafourche and took a score of prisoners. These Chitimacha captives, most of them women and children, were sold to settlers for two hundred livres each. French and allied Indian warfare against this tribe continued for another decade, capturing many more Chitimachas and making them the core of Louisiana's earliest slave population.[19]

II

Like other North American colonies, Louisiana floundered during its earliest years. Under economic stress at home and overextended in other parts of the world, Louis XIV failed to support his latest colonial venture with adequate supplies and reinforcements. "The King seemed to be maintaining a small garrison there," Bienville recalled, "only to preserve for himself the possession of such a vast extent of country."[20]

18. Jay Higginbotham, ed. and trans., *The Journal of Sauvole: Historical Journal of the Establishment of the French in Louisiana by M. de Sauvole* (Mobile, Ala., 1969), 31; *Iberville's Gulf Journals*, 111.

19. *MPAFD*, III, 38–39, 115–116; La Harpe, *Journal*, 75; *Pénicaut Narrative*, 101–102; Higginbotham, *Old Mobile*, 93–94, 288–293.

20. *MPAFD*, III, 523. The factors behind Louisiana's early paucity of immigrants are examined closely in Mathé Allain, "French Emigration Policies: Louisiana, 1699–1715," and Carl A. Brasseaux, "The Image of Louisiana and the Failure of Voluntary Emigration, 1683–1731," in Alf Andrew Heggoy and James J. Cooke, eds., *Proceedings of the Fourth Meeting of the French Colonial Historical Society* (Washington,

Hunger and fever afflicted the small number of men stationed on the Gulf Coast, making them almost entirely dependent upon food provided by local Indian villagers. By 1708 the colonial population of Louisiana numbered only 122 soldiers and sailors, 80 Indian slaves, and 77 settlers, or habitants (24 men, 28 women, and 25 children). "Everybody," according to special commissioner Martin d'Artaguette, was asking for gunpowder "to trade with the Indians for the things we need."[21] The few colonists willing to consider developing this isolated outpost into a productive colony saw their only hope in acquiring African slaves "to clear the land." Bienville proposed that since the Indians being captured by Frenchmen and their allies deserted too easily, although "very good for cultivating the earth," settlers be allowed to "sell these slaves in the American islands in order to get negroes in exchange." Aware of the disorder and animosity incurred by the English slave trade in Indians from Carolina, the French minister of Marine prohibited this practice in 1710. Meanwhile, Bienville and a Monsieur Chateaugue managed to acquire at least six of Louisiana's first black slaves from the plunder captured by Iberville from the English island of Nevis during the War of Spanish Succession.[22]

Beginning principally as an avenue to food for settlers, trade with

D.C., 1979), 39–56. For a thorough analysis of the weak colonial policy within which Louisiana was founded, see Allain, *"Not Worth a Straw."*

21. *MPAFD*, II, 32–34; Carl A. Brasseaux, "La Délaissée: Louisiana during the Reign of Louis XIV, 1699–1715," in Reinhardt, ed., *Sun King,* 97–103.

22. *MPAFD*, II, 38–39, 115–116; Higginbotham, *Old Mobile,* 302, 541. These inauspicious beginnings of African-American slavery in Louisiana were the extension of two concurrent developments in the labor system under way in other French colonies in the Western Hemisphere. Enslavement of North American Indians diminished as their desertion, high mortality, and revenge warfare proved too disruptive—especially endangering the fur trade. Meanwhile, in the French Antilles, rebelliousness among white indentured servants was being muted during the late 17th century by the accelerated enslavement of West Africans, a process marked by the formulation of the Code Noir in 1685. See William B. Cohen, *The French Encounter with Africans: White Response to Blacks, 1530–1880* (Bloomington, Ind., 1980), 35–58. For the parallel process in English colonies, see Peter H. Wood, *Black Majority: Negroes in Colonial South Carolina from 1670 through the Stono Rebellion* (New York, 1974), 13–62; Edmund S. Morgan, *American Slavery, American Freedom: The Ordeal of Colonial Virginia* (New York, 1975), 295–337; Allan Kulikoff, *Tobacco and Slaves: The Development of Southern Cultures in the Chesapeake, 1680–1800* (Chapel Hill, N.C., 1986), 23–44.

Indians quickly became an important means of both military protection and commercial development in Louisiana. Access to trade goods and the protocol employed to distribute them, therefore, were critical issues in French-Indian relations. In 1711 Bienville, governing the colony since his brother Iberville had died of yellow fever at Havana five years earlier, declared that the Choctaws "are the key to this country" and that they must be provided with "cloth to clothe them and weapons to defend themselves." The Chickasaws, however, had already made it clear that "not being able to obtain from us their needs which have become indispensable to them they find themselves obliged to take them from the English." According to exchange customs that extended widely across North America, Indians in the Lower Mississippi Valley required that presents be distributed to them whenever any agreement or transaction was made. They traded among themselves, and now with Europeans, not only to acquire scarce products or ritual items but, as importantly, to demonstrate a willingness to maintain peaceful political relations.23 Gift-giving, smoking the calumet, and other hospitable acts served as symbolic expressions of sociable ties between host and guest parties. As one early French official keenly observed, Louisiana Indians would be conciliated only by "the presents that are given them, the justice that is done them and even more the food that one must not let them lack when they come on visits, together with caresses and evidences of friendship."24

23. *MPAFD*, III, 159–160. Goals and changes in the Le Moyne brothers' Indian policy are highlighted in Charles Edwards O'Neill, *Church and State in French Colonial Louisiana: Policy and Politics to 1732* (New Haven, Conn., 1966), 28–41, 50–77.

Concerning trade between tribal communities, Claude Lévi-Strauss stated: "There is a link, a continuity, between hostile relations and the provision of reciprocal prestations. Exchanges are peacefully resolved wars, and wars are the result of unsuccessful transactions" (*The Elementary Structures of Kinship* [1969], 67, quoted and further discussed in Marshal Sahlins, *Stone Age Economics* [Chicago, 1972], 301–303). The role of Indian exchange customs in the formation of another colonial region is most thoroughly explored in Neal Salisbury's *Manitou and Providence: Indians, Europeans, and the Making of New England, 1500–1643* (New York, 1982).

24. *MPAFD*, II, 128. In a contribution to the continuing discussion over the origins and diffusion of the calumet ceremony, Ian W. Brown argues that French explorers promoted its spread into southern regions of the Mississippi Valley because it "provided balance in a rapidly changing world" for all participants. "The Calumet Ceremony in the Southeast and Its Archaeological Manifestations," *American Antiquity*, LIV (1989), 311–331, quote at 311.

Through fixed prices and gift exchange, Indians hoped to make colonial commerce fit their political customs as well as their immediate needs. Presents distributed annually to each tribe served as a kind of tribute from the colony for occupying and using native land, as suggested in various speeches and negotiations, but more fundamentally displayed to the Indians the peaceful intentions of the colonial populace. An absence of trade goods and of gifts signaled potential disruption and often resulted in conflict between colonial and native groups. Although Bienville hoped "to put them on another basis" after 1706, Indians in Louisiana received more than six thousand livres worth of presents from Louis XIV during the hunting season of 1706–1707. Despite repeated complaints over cost from officials on both sides of the Atlantic Ocean, the Choctaws along with other Indian nations in the Lower Mississippi Valley received an increasing amount of gift merchandise throughout the century, reaching twenty thousand livres per year by 1732.[25]

When the company of Antoine Crozat took over Louisiana in 1712, the mercantile interests of company officials immediately clashed with frontier economic relationships that were being forged in the colony. Settlers and soldiers still depended heavily upon trade with Indian villagers for both subsistence and security. Many purchased food directly from Indians, and some acquired peltry from them that they then exchanged for imported grains and meats. Deer, bear, and even raccoon skins were essential export commodities. Early colonists used Indian-produced furs, along with planks sawed from coastal timber, to purchase products like sugar, wine, and wheat from the nearby Spanish garrison at Pensacola or from the French ships that occasionally arrived. In order to establish a monopoly over Louisiana commerce, Crozat prohibited trade with Pensacola and other Spanish colonial bases and marked up the prices of merchandise as much as 300 percent. The company also refused to buy deerskins at more than one livre apiece, but managed to sell them in France at nearly double this price. In pursuit of their own strategies of survival and gain, settlers resorted to now illegal trade practices, bartering independently with Indians and diverting products from company chan-

---

25. *MPAFD*, II, 23–24, III, 52, 575–576. Cornelius J. Jaenen, "The Role of Presents in French-Amerindian Trade," in Duncan Cameron, ed., *Explorations in Canadian Economic History: Essays in Honor of Irene M. Spry* (Ottawa, 1985), 231–250, argues convincingly that gifts signified mutual interdependency.

nels. The eight thousand livres worth of bear- and deerskins that did manage to fall into the hands of Crozat's Louisiana agent in 1713 resulted from innumerable social and economic exchanges occurring between colonial residents and native villagers beyond the company's control.[26]

With deerskins fast becoming the colony's major export commodity, an extensive network of trading posts developed over the next decade. Outposts established along interior waterways facilitated the movement of peltry to company warehouses on the coast but functioned more instantly as marketplaces for personal exchange, especially of food, between colonists and Indians. In 1714 the French built a storehouse on the east bank of the Mississippi at Natchez, located some 250 miles above the mouth of the river, in order to acquire deerskins from upcountry villages and to counteract English intrigue and commerce at a most propitious moment. Joining the Atlantic coastal Yamasees in a pan-tribal war against South Carolina, the Alibamons, Tallapoosas, and Abehkas ousted English traders from their villages. In 1715 these Upper Creek Indians began to carry their deerskins to Mobile and in 1717 allowed Bienville to build Fort Toulouse near the junction of the Coosa and Tallapoosa rivers.[27]

In 1716 Fort Rosalie was constructed among the Natchez Indians, a highly centralized and densely populous nation whose several villages occupied mixed pine and hardwood bluffs overlooking the east bank of the Mississippi. For some time, Canadian voyageurs and missionaries had been visiting the Natchez, whose gatherings around French camps looked to Father Du Ru "like one of our ports in France, or like a Dutch fair." Frequent contact with Europeans exposed the Natchez and neighboring tribes, particularly the Taensas and Tunicas, to a high rate of epidemics and wars. So the positioning of Fort Rosalie at this strategic location occurred under volatile circumstances.[28] In the fall of 1715, Natchez

26. *MPAFD,* II, 81–89, 129–132, III, 177–178; Giraud, *History of Louisiana,* trans. Lambert, I, 296. For an illustration of how the Crozat monopoly was bypassed by colonists, see Carl A. Brasseaux, "The Cadillac-Duclos Affair: Private Enterprise versus Mercantilism in Colonial Mobile," *AR,* XXVII (1984), 257–270.

27. *MPAFD,* III, 183, 187–188; La Harpe, *Journal,* 91–92. For a detailed discussion of this important southeastern Indian revolt against English colonialism, see Crane, *Southern Frontier,* 162–186.

28. Butler, trans., *Journal of Paul Du Ru,* 34–37. Like the Chitimachas downriver, the Natchez seemed to be adopting refugee groups into their villages while their own numbers were rapidly diminishing. John R. Swanton, *Indian Tribes of the Lower Mississippi Valley and Adjacent Coast of the Gulf of Mexico,* Bureau of American

leaders were insulted by Antoine de La Mothe Cadillac, the disreputable founder of Detroit and governor of Louisiana during most of the Crozat years, when on a downriver voyage he refused to stop and smoke their calumet. Interpreting this negligence as a sign of hostility, a Natchez war party assassinated four traders and pillaged ten thousand livres worth of merchandise from the Crozat company's local warehouse.[29] In the following spring Bienville led a small army of thirty-five men upriver to the Indian town of Tunica. There he negotiated with a group of Natchez leaders, took some of them hostage, and demanded the heads of all persons responsible for the deaths. The brother of the grand chief, called Petit Soleil by the French, returned with only three heads, pleading that he was unable to impose any more police power over his people. Bienville then had four of the hostages, including two apparent leaders of the revolt, tomahawked to death in a brash effort to assert his dubious strength. As many as a thousand Natchez warriors were available against the commandant's small army, but the execution worked. The Natchez agreed to settle the matter by building a new fortified post to be occupied by a French garrison and to facilitate trade relations. In 1719 Fort St. Pierre was established up the Yazoo River, extending Louisiana's trade sphere among the Ofogoulas, Chachiumas, and other northern neighbors of the Natchez.[30]

Ethnology Bulletin, no. 43 (Washington, D.C., 1911), is still the best place for any student of Natchez history to begin inquiry. The Lower Mississippi Survey conducted by the Peabody Museum, Harvard University, is examining systematically how material remains will enhance our understanding of colonial-Indian and Indian-Indian relations in the Natchez area. For an update on this project, see Ian W. Brown, "An Archaeological Study of Culture Contact and Change in the Natchez Bluffs Region," in Galloway, ed., *La Salle and His Legacy*, 176–193.

29. *MPAFD*, III, 193–194, 198. The events discussed here and Natchez-French relations throughout this period have been closely examined, from different perspectives, in Andrew C. Albrecht, "Indian-French Relations at Natchez," *American Anthropologist*, N.S., XLVIII (1946), 321–354; Patricia D. Woods, "The French and the Natchez Indians in Louisiana: 1700–1731," *LH*, XIX (1978), 413–435. Woods has also produced a general narrative of Louisiana Indian affairs in *French-Indian Relations on the Southern Frontier, 1699–1762* (Ann Arbor, Mich., 1980).

30. *MPAFD*, III, 213; La Harpe, *Journal*, 93–98; *Pénicaut Narrative*, 177–182, 215–216; Ian William Brown, "Early Eighteenth Century French-Indian Culture Contact in the Yazoo Bluffs Region of the Lower Mississippi Valley" (Ph.D. diss., Brown University, 1979), chap. 4. Fort St. Pierre was destroyed and abandoned during the Natchez Revolt of 1729–1730.

To promote trade alliances up the Red River, which flows into the Mississippi from the west, the French stationed a garrison among the Caddo Indians. Back in 1700 Bienville had visited the villages of Natchitoches, Doustionis, and Yatasis, where the people planted crops in fields scattered along the Red River and hunted deer and other wildlife in adjacent oak- and pine-forested hills. In addition to the four hundred or so men counted by Bienville in these towns, another five or six hundred warriors were estimated to be living farther upriver in the Kadohadacho division of the Caddo confederacy. The main French post was situated near the Natchitoches village in 1716, and a subsidiary trade station was established at an upriver Indian town called Upper Nasoni in 1719.[31] Only twenty miles southwest of Natchitoches, the Spanish—who had been gradually edging toward the Red River—constructed a military post at Los Adaes, among the Hasinai Indians, in 1721. Louis Juchereau de Saint-Denis, appointed commandant of French Natchitoches in 1719, had been trading with both Spaniards and Indians in the area for some time. He offered no objection to the Spanish presence, "because of the assistance that could be obtained from them in the future both in livestock and in money." In order to secure Louisiana's relationship with the Caddoes and their neighbors, the colonial council decided in 1719 to strengthen the garrison and to "give one hundred livres of presents to the Natchitoches nation, the same sum to the Dulchionis, sixty livres worth to the Adais, three hundred livres to the Cenis; to the Nasonis, Caddoes, Nanatsohos and Nacogdoches three hundred livres for all." The Hasinais soon came under the Spanish mission system being established across Texas and therefore remained outside French Louisiana's political and economic network, although some individual trading with Frenchmen and their Indian allies persisted throughout the eighteenth century.[32]

By the 1720s the contour of Louisiana's network of Indian trade al-

---

31. *MPAFD,* III, 515, 529–530; La Harpe, *Journal,* 130–142. A precise location of the Upper Nasoni post and the relative situation of other Caddo sites are identified in Mildred Mott Wedel, *La Harpe's 1719 Post on Red River and Nearby Caddo Settlements* (Austin, Tex., 1978).

32. *MPAFD,* III, 267–268, 314–315; Fray Isidro Felis de Espinosa, "Descriptions of the Tejas or Asinai Indians, 1691–1722," pt. 4, trans. Mattie Austin Hatcher, *Southwestern Historical Quarterly,* XXXI (1927–1928), 150–180; Herbert Eugene Bolton, *The Hasinais: Southern Caddoans as Seen by the Earliest Europeans,* ed. Russell M. Magnaghi (Norman, Okla., 1987).

liances was firmly established. Carolina traders resumed their commerce with the Chickasaws and some Upper Creek towns, but henceforth trade in the Lower Mississippi Valley flowed mainly from the Indian villages around the interior French posts to the Gulf Coast ports of Mobile and New Orleans. French control of the central valley was reinforced in 1721 when a small detachment of soldiers from the Yazoo River garrison joined a group of settlers at the lower Arkansas River, where the Quapaw Indians had allowed Henri de Tonti to situate his short-lived trade house back in 1686. Most of the peltry exported from Louisiana, numbering "fifty thousand deerskins every year" Bienville estimated in 1726, originated among tribes situated within a 350-mile radius of New Orleans. The outer limits, or periphery, of this network included the Upper Creeks to the northeast, the Quapaws due north, and the Caddoes to the northwest. The Choctaws and most of their neighbors in the region formed a relationship with French Louisiana similar to that existing between the Iroquois nations and the English colony of New York. Previous conflicts with one colony, Canada in the case of the Iroquois and Carolina in the case of the Choctaws, greatly influenced their decision to ally and trade with another European colony.[33]

III

The formation of this regional network of Indian trade occurred mainly while Louisiana remained a deprived and isolated satellite of the French empire. As of 1718 the colonial populace consisted of "no more than three hundred and fifty to four hundred people," most of them soldiers, officers, and other royal employees scattered among six administrative posts: Dauphin Island, Mobile, and Pascagoula on the Gulf Coast, Fort Toulouse at the forks of the Alabama River, Natchitoches on

33. Stanley Faye, "The Arkansas Post of Louisiana: French Domination," LHQ, XXVI (1943), 665–666; MPAFD, III, 538. For insights into the parallel intercolonial position of the Iroquois nations, see Thomas Elliot Norton, The Fur Trade in Colonial New York, 1686–1776 (Madison, Wis., 1974); Richard Aquila, The Iroquois Restoration: Iroquois Diplomacy on the Colonial Frontier, 1701–1754 (Detroit, Mich., 1983); Francis Jennings, The Ambiguous Iroquois Empire: The Covenant Chain Confederation of Indian Tribes with English Colonies from Its Beginnings to the Lancaster Treaty of 1774 (New York, 1984).

the Red River, and New Orleans just being constructed on the Mississippi.[34] A drastic change in the size and composition of Louisiana, however, was already under way. France ceded the colony to John Law's Company of the Indies in August 1717, after Crozat relinquished his title. Amid the surging commercial activity generated initially by Law's Company of the West and other assorted schemes, several financial and landed families in France invested in the colonization of the Mississippi Valley. Through the Company of the Indies, which unlike Law's bank and other projects survived the collapse of 1720 and his exile from France, investors hoped to receive a return from the colony in the form of tobacco, indigo, or some other agricultural staple.[35]

Between 1717 and 1721 the Company of the Indies transported in forty-three shipments seven thousand Europeans to the Gulf Coast, and eight vessels brought two thousand slaves from West Africa.[36] Among the European immigrants there were 977 soldiers and 122 officers. The company itself employed 302 workers and 43 clerks, warehouse keepers, and artisans. Only 119 immigrants, known as *concessionaires,* had been granted land concessions, while 2,462 laborers, or *engagés,* had contracted to serve them for an average term of three years. Illicit salt dealers, tobacco smugglers, army deserters, and other criminals taken from the streets and prisons of French cities constituted another 1,278 of the people

34. This estimate was made by a Company of the Indies director who reached Louisiana in August 1718 (Glenn R. Conrad, ed. and trans., *Immigration and War: Louisiana, 1718–1721: From the Memoir of Charles Le Gac* [Lafayette, La., 1970], 1). Also see Giraud, *History of French Louisiana,* trans. Lambert, I, 277–279.

35. Pierre Heinrich, *La Louisiane sous la Compagnie des Indes, 1717–1731* (Paris, 1908). For a convenient summary of the role of John Law's schemes in the European economy, see Glyndwr Williams, *The Expansion of Europe in the Eighteenth Century: Overseas Rivalry, Discovery, and Exploitation* (London, 1966), 53–55.

36. A compilation of the number and classification of European immigrants to Louisiana during this period was included in a Memoir on Louisiana, AC, C13A, VI, 329–331v, and published in Conrad, ed. and trans., *Memoir of Charles Le Gac,* 42. The passenger lists have been published in Glenn R. Conrad, comp. and trans., *The First Families of Louisiana,* 2 vols. (Baton Rouge, La., 1970), I, 1–140. Also see Mathé Allain, "L'immigration française en Louisiane, 1718–1721," *Revue d'histoire de l'Amérique française,* XXVIII (1975), 555–564. The number of African immigrants is derived from La Harpe's record of arrivals between June 6, 1719, and Oct. 15, 1721 (*Journal,* 113, 154, 167–173).

transported to Louisiana by the company.[37] In addition to this male population of 5,303 immigrants, 1,215 women and 502 children traveled aboard the ships. Although most of these people were natives of France, some 1,300 of them had been recruited from various parts of Germany.[38] The Negro slaves of diverse nationalities who reached Louisiana during the same period came from entrepôts at Goré, on the coast of the Senegal region, and Juida, farther south and east on the West African coast at the Bight of Benin. Most were people called Bambara, Malinke-speaking captives from the interior, but slaves exported from Senegambia also included such coastal ethnic groups as the Wolof and Sereer.[39]

Although at a lower rate than that experienced by Indians, death overcame many of these different migrants to Louisiana. "Numbers died of misery or disease," remarked Father Pierre de Charlevoix, "and the country was emptied as rapidly as it had filled." Of the seven thousand whites who entered the Lower Mississippi Valley from 1717 to 1721, at least half of them either perished or abandoned the colony before 1726. The ap-

37. James D. Hardy, Jr., "The Transportation of Convicts to Colonial Louisiana," *LH*, VII (1966), 207–220; Glenn R. Conrad, *"Emigration Forcée:* A French Attempt to Populate Louisiana, 1716–1720," in Heggoy and Cooke, eds., *Proceedings of the Fourth Meeting of the French Colonial Historical Society,* 57–66. For an analysis of the various factors that inhibited French migration to North America, see Peter N. Moogk, "Reluctant Exiles: Emigrants from France in Canada before 1760," *William and Mary Quarterly,* 3d Ser., XLVI (1989), 463–505.

38. Alice D. Forsyth and Earlene L. Zeringue, comps. and trans., *German "Pest Ships,"* 1720–1721 (New Orleans, 1969). For closer examination of this German migration to early Louisiana, see J. Hanno Deiler, *The Settlement of the German Coast of Louisiana and the Creoles of German Descent* (Philadelphia, 1909); Marcel Giraud, *Histoire de la Louisiane française,* IV, *La Louisiane après le système de law (1721–1723)* (Paris, 1974), 154–167; Reinhart Kondert, "Les Allemands en Louisiane de 1721 à 1732," *Revue d'histoire de l'Amérique française,* XXXIII (1979–1980), 51–65; and Kondert, "German Immigration to French Colonial Louisiana: A Reevaluation," in Heggoy and Cooke, eds., *Proceedings of the Fourth Meeting of the French Colonial Historical Society,* 70–81.

39. André Delcourt, *La France et les établissements français au Sénégal entre 1713 et 1763* (Ifan-Dakar, 1952); Philip D. Curtin, *The Atlantic Slave Trade: A Census* (Madison, Wis., 1969); Curtin, *Economic Change in Precolonial Africa: Senegambia in the Era of the Slave Trade* (Madison, Wis., 1975), 176–188. The long-neglected French slave trade is examined with thoroughness in Robert Louis Stein, *The French Slave Trade in the Eighteenth Century: An Old Regime Business* (Madison, Wis., 1979).

proximately seven thousand blacks transported to Louisiana on slave ships between 1718 and 1731 experienced a similar rate of diminution. Removed from their homelands where they had inherited or developed substantial immunities to the common maladies of the region, these new-comers found their health threatened by the deprivations of oceanic trans-portation and the unfamiliar viruses of a different disease environment. European immigrants to the Gulf Coast and other parts of the coastal South were particularly vulnerable to malarial fevers caused by infectious transmission from the anopheles mosquito. West Africans, like the resi-dents of Sicily and other traditionally malarious regions, had developed through genetic selection a sickle cell trait in some blood cells that pro-vided substantial hereditary immunity to malaria. But if Africans usually avoided the debilitating "fevers and ague" experienced by their white counterparts, other contagious and chronic illnesses had a fatal effect upon these enslaved colonial workers. Respiratory and intestinal viruses contracted from Europeans, in addition to sicknesses caused by the condi-tions of their enslavement and transportation, took a heavy toll upon the lives of African-Louisianians.[40]

The fate of two particular groups of colonists reaching Louisiana in August of 1718 dramatically reflects the general experience of immigra-tion at the time. Concessionaire Mathieu Brossard and Jean Baptiste Bernard de La Harpe, with ten and thirty-eight engagés respectively, had been directed by the company to settle on the Red River. After most of his people "died of fever" on their way to this destination from New Orleans, Brossard abandoned his project. But the ambitious La Harpe insisted on continuing up the Red River, where he hoped to establish himself among the Kadohadachos. Finally, according to a company director, La Harpe "was forced to abandon his people who were sick and dying of fever and exhaustion due to a lack of proper supplies." Of the nearly forty people

40. Pierre François Xavier de Charlevoix, *History and General Description of New France,* 6 vols., trans. John Gilmary Shea (New York, 1866–1872), VI, 69; John Duffy, ed., *The Rudolph Matas History of Medicine in Louisiana,* 2 vols. (Baton Rouge, La., 1958–1962), I, 8–28, 126–136; Philip D. Curtin, "Epidemiology and the Slave Trade," *Political Science Quarterly,* LXXXIII (1968), 190–216. The importance of health, particularly in regard to malaria, in the formation of slave colonies is incisively argued in Wood, *Black Majority,* 63–91. Also see the discussion of malaria and sickle cell in Todd L. Savitt, *Medicine and Slavery: The Diseases and Health Care of Blacks in Antebellum Virginia* (Urbana, Ill., 1978), 17–35.

accompanying him from Dauphin Island, this concessionaire left only seven or eight on the Red River and returned to the lower colony with ten others, whom he "handed over to some farmers in order that these *engagés* might fulfill the terms of their contracts."[41]

Most immigrants infected with malaria would have survived their illness had the colony been able to feed them properly. Although the Company of the Indies transported flour, cattle, and other supplies aboard its ships and even purchased large quantities of corn and meat from Indian villages, the continual flow of people from the vessels, through the coastal posts, and toward their concessions created a ubiquitous food shortage. The Scourion brothers' concession included eleven family members and sixty-six engagés, many of them skilled workers, and promised to become a successful settlement on the Yazoo River. But like other groups of passengers, these migrants "consumed great quantities of their supplies during the long journey from France to Dauphin Island." With only a fourth of the food needed for their journey inland, the Scourion party split into separate traveling groups. The concessionaires and a few of their associates managed to reach Natchez, but "the other half of the group traveled about sixty miles from Mobile and became stranded, causing its members to drift aimlessly." As reported by director Charles Le Gac, "the sum total of the whole enterprise was death for the greater part of this group."[42]

The forlorn immigrants stranded at the coastal posts of Dauphin Island, Mobile, and Biloxi lacked either the knowledge or the energy to gather fish and other available food sources, one group reduced instead to eating weevil-infested seed wheat in the winter of 1718–1719. The location of a principal settlement at Biloxi did not help matters, as Antoine Le Page Du Pratz denounced, "being nothing but a fine sand, as white and shining as snow, on which no kind of greens can be raised; besides . . . being extremely incommoded with rats, which swarm there in the sand, and at that time ate even the very stocks of the guns, the famine being there so very great, that more than five hundred people died of hunger." Fever and hunger along the Gulf Coast spiraled into a fatal cycle in which any available food went to people in makeshift hospitals and those who suffered malnutrition inevitably succumbed to sickness. A scarcity of

41. Conrad, ed. and trans., *Memoir of Charles Le Gac*, 4–5.
42. *Ibid.*, 7–8.

boats for transporting colonists and slaves to concessions along the Mississippi River kept too many people crowded at the ports for too long a time.[43] Jean François Benjamin Dumont, a lieutenant in charge of a shipment of exiled prisoners, vividly captured the Louisiana famine of 1719–1721:

> Although great care was taken in France to send abundantly provisions of every kind to the colony, yet all their care could not prevent want being felt there. It was so great that the commandant was obliged to send soldiers, workmen, and even officers, to the nearest Indians of the country, that of the Biloxis and Pascagoulas, who received them quite well, not indeed with bread, but with good hominy and sagamity, boiled with good store of meat or bear oil. As for the *concessionaires,* each remained at his place, living not over well, being brought down to beans and peas in no great quantity. To increase the dilemma, there arrived at this juncture a vessel loaded with negroes, who were distributed to such as could support them. At last, the famine was so severe that a great number died, some from eating herbs they did not know, and which, instead of prolonging life, produced death; others from eating oysters, which they went and gathered on the sea-shore. Most of those found dead by the heaps of shells were Germans. At last, in the height of this scourge, came the *Venus* loaded exclusively with provisions, and followed immediately by two other vessels. Then each one returned home, and the Indians were paid in goods for what they had given. At the same time the commandant raised at New Biloxi a third establishment, which being soon after completed he transported the whole colony to it, abandoning Old Biloxi, where his stay had been marked only by disastrous events [see Plate 2].[44]

43. *Ibid.,* 30, 34–35; Antoine Le Page Du Pratz, *The History of Louisiana,* ed. Joseph G. Tregle, Jr. (London, 1774; facs. rpt., Baton Rouge, La., 1975), 31–32. An incomplete list of those who died just at Fort Biloxi from Aug. 8, 1720, to Sept. 4, 1723, indicates that at least 172 persons perished at that post during a two-year period (Conrad, comp. and trans., *First Families of Louisiana,* II, 76–80).

44. Jean François Benjamin Dumont de Montigny, "Historical Memoirs of M. Dumont" (1753), in B. F. French, ed., *Historical Collections of Louisiana,* 5 vols. (New York, 1846–1853), V, 21. The *Venus* embarked from Lorient on Apr. 7, 1721, and reached Ship Island on July 15, 1721 (Conrad, comp. and trans., *First Families of Louisiana,* I, 135; La Harpe, *Journal,* 172).

In addition to the general food crisis encountered on the Gulf Coast, other specific factors contributed to a high rate of mortality among enslaved black immigrants. Whereas immigration of European settlers virtually halted after 1721, the Company of the Indies shipped additional cargoes of African slaves to Louisiana for another decade. Information regarding the fifteen known shipments of slaves between June 1719 and March 1729 indicates that about 20 percent of these Africans destined for Louisiana died in transit.[45] After months of imprisonment in such slave warehouses as Gorée near the mouth of the Senegal River, blacks were crowded into ships each carrying as many as 450 people. Unhealthy confinement, mistreatment, and malnutrition killed many passengers. Those who reached the pilot's station at the mouth of the Mississippi, known as Balize, still had to withstand several ailments. In 1727, for example, the *Prince de Conti* "arrived at the Balize on the twelfth of September *with 266 blacks,* rather fine, but a good part of these blacks were attacked on their arrival by two diseases, some by dysentery with a bloody flux and others by an inflammation on the eyes by which many have been left one-eyed and blind." The latter malady was probably trachoma, a contagious infection inside the eyelids and on the cornea easily contracted aboard unsanitary and crowded slave ships.[46]

Because of inadequate supplies of food, especially the lack of ascorbic acid found in citrus fruits, scurvy struck most slave ships during and after passage to Louisiana. The *Galatée* reached the mouth of the Mississippi on January 18, 1729, with only 260 of the 400 Africans who had boarded three months earlier at Gorée. "On account of the bad condition in which its crew and its negroes were," this ship had left 45 sick slaves, 9 sailors, and 1 officer at the port of La Caye on St. Domingue. Shortly after their arrival at Louisiana, 25–30 more Negroes died, "all of scurvy." Characterized by bleeding gums and loosening teeth, this disease accounted for a

45. A 20% rate of mortality is derived from available information about the numbers of slaves who boarded and disembarked six different ships (La Harpe, *Journal,* 167–173; MPAFD, II, 575–576, 620, 638). The mortality in transit of slaves transported by merchants of Nantes between 1715 and 1775 was 16.2%. During the actual period under discussion here, 1720–1731, an even higher mean rate of 18% prevailed (Curtin, *Atlantic Slave Trade,* 277).

46. MPAFD, II, 547. The literature on mortality rates of overseas migration in general is thoroughly cited in James C. Riley, "Mortality on Long-Distance Voyages in the Eighteenth Century," *Journal of Economic History,* XLI (1981), 651–656.

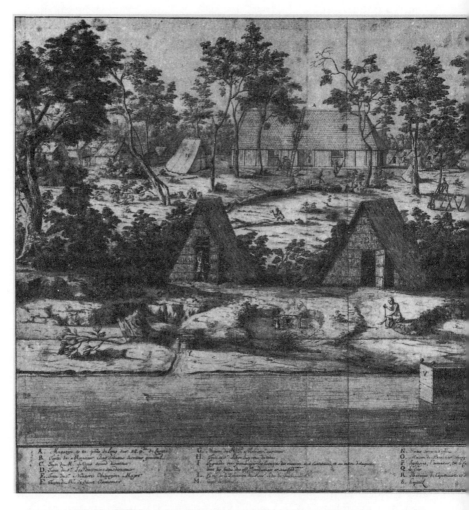

PLATE 2. *View of the Camp of the Concession of Monseigneur Law at New Biloxi, Coast of Louisiana, Drawn by Jean Baptiste Michel Le Bouteux, 10 December 1720. Pen, ink, and wash. Courtesy of Edward E. Ayer Collection, Newberry Library, Chicago*

large percentage of deaths among African immigrants. Of the 450 men, women, and children boarded on the *Venus* in 1729, 87 died during the voyage. En route from the mouth of the river to New Orleans, another 43 perished. Finally, 320 people reached the capital, but according to Governor Étienne Boucher de Périer and Commissioner Jacques de La Chaise, "they were so violently attacked by the scurvy that more than two-thirds of those who were sold at auction into the hands of the inhabitants have died." Principally concerned with the financial effects of this terrible mortality, the two officials reported on August 26, 1729, that settlers "outbid each other for the scurvied, consumptive and ulcerated and raise the price for them as high as one thousand livres. We saw some in this last auction as well as in the preceding ones die half a quarter of an hour after they had been awarded to them, and that in great numbers; others were not able to get them out of New Orleans; others remained with them only two days, and finally there are inhabitants who have taken as many as six or seven of them who have all died on their hands in less than a week."[47]

By the late 1720s Louisianians who endured ocean travel, disease, and hunger found themselves living in a stabilizing environment. They acquired greater immunity to infectious viruses and became acclimated to conditions in the Lower Mississippi Valley. Many colonists owed their survival to Indian villagers who provided food during the hard times. Settlers and slaves began to produce sufficient crops of grain and vegetables, and the quantity of hogs, cattle, and poultry slowly increased. Health hazards nonetheless persisted. Smallpox, dysentery, yellow fever, and typhus always threatened, especially young and elderly inhabitants. Overwork and mistreatment, although prohibited by the Code Noir, condemned slaves frequently to sickness and occasionally to death. Situated mostly below sea level and surrounded by mosquito-breeding waters, New Orleans was a promising site for commerce but potentially fatal to residents. A malignant fever "spread through the entire town" in the summer of 1723, attributed by La Chaise to "the stagnation of the water since it [the Mississippi River] did not retire until the beginning of July." Until the 1790s, however, the population of New Orleans remained small

---

47. *MPAFD*, II, 620, 659–660, 668–669. While the colonial bureaucracy worried over the financial implications of high mortality, the slaves themselves struggled to cure their illnesses. For a description of some remedies practiced by a "Negro physician" owned by the company, see Le Page Du Pratz, *History,* ed. Tregle, 378–380.

enough to avoid epidemic levels of contagious fever. Only then did yellow fever, and later cholera, become endemic in the Crescent City.[48]

IV

The nearly two thousand settlers and four thousand slaves inhabiting Louisiana by 1731 represented only about half of the number of people actually transported by the Company of the Indies. As distressing as this tragic rate of migrant mortality was in itself, company officials were equally concerned about the character of those who survived. Showing little eagerness to commit themselves to planting a commercial crop, colonial inhabitants constituted a weak population base for developing an agricultural export economy. As in other colonial regions, the Louisiana economy was evolving in a direction sharply divergent from the hopes and expectations of colonial planners and investors in France. During the 1720s the Company of the Indies promoted tobacco production through a series of measures: sending experienced tobacco workers to the colony, paying artificially high prices for the harvests, and even offering bounties to concession directors who chose to plant the crop.[49] But before the wave of immigration began, officials such as General Commissioner Marc-Antoine Hubert had detected a strong reluctance among settlers to till the soil, predicting in 1716 that they "will never be satisfied with this infallible resource, accustomed as they are to the trade with the Indians the easy profit from which supports them, giving them what they need day by day

48. *MPAFD*, II, 302; Duffy, *Rudolph Matas History of Medicine*, I, 191–219, 345–381; Albert E. Cowdrey, *This Land, This South: An Environmental History* (Lexington, Ky., 1983), 83–89, 103–107. The situation of Jamestown at the transition zone between salt and fresh water has been recently interpreted as a major cause of dysentery and typhus among early colonists in Virginia. See Carville V. Earle, "Environment, Disease, and Mortality in Early Virginia," in Thad W. Tate and David L. Ammerman, eds., *The Chesapeake in the Seventeenth Century: Essays on Anglo-American Society* (Chapel Hill, N.C., 1979), 96–125.

49. John Robert McNeill, *Atlantic Empires of France and Spain: Louisbourg and Havana, 1700–1763* (Chapel Hill, N.C., 1985). The official promotion and actual production of tobacco in French Louisiana are the subject of chaps. 12 and 13 in Jacob M. Price, *France and the Chesapeake: A History of the French Tobacco Monopoly, 1674–1791, and of Its Relationship to the British and American Tobacco Trades*, 2 vols. (Ann Arbor, Mich., 1973), I, 302–360.

the Indians who find their happiness in an idle and lazy life." Unable to control effectively the behavior of settlers and soldiers, much less of native villagers, promoters of Louisiana and of other colonial projects usually disparaged Indian life while reluctantly accepting patterns of trade and settlement very different from original schemes.[50]

Many Europeans arriving in Louisiana between 1717 and 1721 were unemployed and underemployed laborers or deported salt smugglers, prostitutes, and other illicit dealers who had moved freely across the countryside and in cities. *Rouleurs* (traveling workers) and *colpoteurs* (peddlers) carried small quantities of merchandise from place to place, in what one historian of eighteenth-century France has called a "makeshift subeconomy," and the practice of itinerant peddling proved useful and persistent in America. One official of the Company of the Indies observed that New Orleans by 1724 consisted of many "common people [*petites gens*] who were engaged in a commerce detrimental to the Colony and even to the interests of the Company." As soon as a ship landed at the levee, these "common people" petitioned the Superior Council for the orders needed to obtain merchandise from the company warehouse, quickly emptied it of all kinds of goods, and resold them at much higher prices. In March of 1725 the council restricted the distribution of these permits, declaring that the "number of little inhabitants who carry on no other business here than of trading" made it impossible to "find a servant or a workman to work in the fields that are in cultivation." One observer more sympathetic to those immigrants who did not want to work the land for someone else or could not begin their own farms described the importance of frontier exchange to them: "On their return from the Indians they disperse in the city their peltries or produce, which they bring in payment to those from whom they have borrowed in order to carry on their trade. This causes each one to share this commerce instead of it belonging exclusively to three or four persons who grow wealthy while the others die from hunger inside a settlement."[51]

50. *MPAFD,* II, 232. The implications of common settlers' recalcitrance toward the ideas and plans of their supposed superiors are insightfully examined in Nicholas Canny, "The Permissive Frontier: The Problem of Social Control in English Settlements in Ireland and Virginia, 1550–1650," in K. R. Andrews *et al.,* eds., *The Westward Enterprise: English Activities in Ireland, the Atlantic, and America, 1480–1650* (Detroit, 1979), 17–44.

51. Olwen H. Hufton, *The Poor of Eighteenth-Century France, 1750–1789* (Oxford, 1974), 120–121; Heloise H. Cruzat, trans., "Louisiana in 1724: Banet's Report

The importation of several thousand African slaves and the establishment of successful plantations during the 1720s helped reduce tensions between the *petits habitants* wanting to trade independently and the concessionaires demanding a tractable labor force. But few settlers could afford to purchase slaves, even on credit, from the company. Furthermore, the enslaved black workers themselves quickly adapted their own traditional economic practices to colonial life, turning to small-scale farming and frontier exchange to mitigate their bondage in America. Open interaction between Indians, settlers, and slaves—characteristic of most North American colonies during their early years—had already taken its course in other plantation societies, where governments turned exclusively to African-American slavery as a source of labor and took advantage of cultural differences to control social relations.[52] This process, however, did not unfold without intense conflict. Nor did it completely eliminate the strategies of exchange preferred by the people who struggled hardest to survive in a colonial region.

---

to the Company of the Indies, Dated Paris, December 20, 1724," *LHQ*, XII (1929), 125; *MPAFD*, II, 418–419; "Historical Memoirs of M. Dumont," in French, ed., *Historical Collections*, V, 27–28; Relation de la Louisiane [ca. 1735], 158–159 (anonymous MS), Edward E. Ayer Collection, Newberry Library, Chicago.

52. Daniel H. Usner, Jr., "From African Captivity to American Slavery: The Introduction of Black Laborers to Colonial Louisiana," *LH*, XX (1979), 25–48; T. H. Breen, "A Changing Labor Force and Race Relations in Virginia, 1660–1710," *Journal of Social History*, VII (1973–1974), 3–25; Wood, *Black Majority*, 218–238; Morgan, *American Slavery, American Freedom*. This tension between the trade interests of laborers and the agricultural interests of planters was first delineated for early Louisiana in James T. McGowan, "Planters without Slaves: Origins of a New World Labor System," *Southern Studies*, XVI (1977), 5–26, and his "Creation of a Slave Society: Louisiana Plantations in the Eighteenth Century" (Ph.D. diss., University of Rochester, 1976).

2

DIVERGENCE WITHIN COLONIAL

AND INDIAN SOCIETIES

Official plans to build a plantation system in Louisiana ran head-on against the interests of many people within colonial society as well as within neighboring Indian societies. With immigration of European settlers and African slaves slowing down by the mid-1720s, production of agricultural exports was naturally limited by the small size of Louisiana's colonial population. Altogether the nearly four thousand people inhabiting Louisiana settlements and outposts, combined with the approximately thirty-five thousand people still inhabiting the Indian villages around the year 1726, amounted to less than half the region's population of the 1680s.[1] Although relatively few, the free and enslaved inhabitants of Louisiana's formative colonial society interacted among

1. Daniel H. Usner, Jr., "Decline and Migration: A Population History of Indians in the Eighteenth-Century Lower Mississippi Valley." In this MS essay, my estimate of the Indian population for the mid-1730s includes 1,700 Biloxis, Pascagoulas, Moctobis, Capinas, Mobilians, and Tohomes along the Gulf Coast; 24,500 Choctaws, Chickasaws, and Upper Creeks; 3,000 Ouachas, Chaouachas, Mongoulachas, Bayogoulas, Chitimachas, Atakapas, Opelousas, Houmas, and Acolapissas in the Lower Mississippi Delta country; 4,400 Tunicas, Yazoos, Natchez, Taensas, and Quapaws in the central Mississippi Valley; and 1,500 Avoyelles, Natchitoches, Doustionis, Yatasis, and Kadohadachos along the Red River. My efforts to compile in a systematic way this population data were originally inspired by Peter H. Wood's population project on the entire Southeast. See Wood, "The Changing Population of the Colonial South: An Overview by Race and Region, 1685–1790," in Wood et al., eds., *Powhatan's Mantle: Indians in the Colonial Southeast* (Lincoln, Nebr., 1989), 35–103.

themselves and with native villagers in ways that made construction of a colony according to some mercantile blueprint all the more difficult. Settlers, servants, slaves, and soldiers moved along divergent paths in the evolution of a plantation economy. Contrary to retrospective impressions about race, not all Europeans had equal stakes in the enslavement of Africans or Indians. Most settlers could not afford to purchase slaves; some barely survived their own indentured servitude or military service. Not all slaves were African in origin, and some Africans managed to acquire freedom. And whether African or Indian, slaves fell into a wide range of roles in colonial society. If the budding foundations for plantation slavery were to be reinforced in Louisiana, policies designed to divide and rule an otherwise fluid populace would have to be implemented.

Comparable to the diverse composition of Louisiana colonial society, its Indian neighbors were not all alike either. An inclination to view Indians one-dimensionally as a single group of people has long obscured not only the cultural diversity among Indian societies but also the many different paths taken by Indians in their relations with colonists. Numerous Indians became subordinate members of colonial society as slaves. Bondage on plantations or in towns sharply distinguished these individuals from Indian people living freely in their own communities. Scattered among colonial settlements, the remnants of Indian nations reduced by disease or war formed another kind of relationship with Louisiana. By the 1720s there were nearly twenty different *petites nations,* as the French called these communities, situated around Mobile, New Orleans, and other centers of colonial population. Providing essential goods and services to the colony daily, these people tried to balance their political autonomy with their economic interdependency by staying on the margins of colonial society. In contrast with the close contact experienced by the smaller, coastal groups, Indian nations across the Louisiana hinterland communicated with the colony through more formal channels. Positioned between competing European colonies, tribes like the Choctaws and Chickasaws were treated diplomatically. They traded and fought principally as allies.

Tensions mounting in and around colonial society, as it evolved in Louisiana during the 1720s, exploded into open conflict by 1729. The Natchez Indians found themselves socializing with colonists on the most precarious of paths. Still living in populous villages at strategic locations, the Natchez developed strong trade ties with Louisiana. But the promotion of tobacco production around their villages, on some of the region's most promising soil, rapidly impinged on Natchez society. Their land became a more important resource to some colonial officials than their deerskins and foodstuffs. The Natchez decided to ward off what seemed to many an inexorable displacement and domination—by wiping out all French settlers in their territory. Indian war magnified insecurity inside colonial society, providing slaves with an opportunity to challenge their French masters. Although a slave revolt in New Orleans was aborted in the summer of 1730, the prospects of joint African and Indian resistance provoked official efforts to guard bridges between colonial society and its Indian neighbors more vigilantly.

I

The Louisiana census of 1726 divided the colonial population into four broad categories. *Habitants* were those 1,663 settlers, single persons and family members, who could move about and acquire land. By the mid-1720s any farmer or discharged soldier and servant was entitled to a few arpents (arpent = about .85 acre) of frontage on the Mississippi or some other river if he assumed responsibility for building a levee as well as for cultivating the land. *Engagés,* those laborers still serving out terms of indenture, were reduced to only 245 people by both a high rate of mortality and some movement into the habitant category. Military personnel stationed in Louisiana numbered 332 noncommissioned officers and soldiers. Soldiers employed by the Ministry of Marine were obliged to serve for a specified period of time, like the indentured servants, and therefore had less mobility than ordinary settlers. *Esclaves*—those men, women, and children held in bondage for life—numbered 159 Indians and 1,385 blacks. Of the total number of colonial inhabitants, 44 percent were habitants, 41 percent esclaves, 9 percent soldats, and 6 percent engagés (see Table 2). By 1732, largely because of additional shipments of slaves, the proportion of African-American inhabitants rose to about 60 percent. The proportion of soldiers fluctuated according to military conditions, while that of engagés declined to a negligible point.[2] In the almost

2. My compilation of Louisiana's 1726 population is summarized in Table 2. For the population in 1732, see *Census Tables,* 113, 123; and AC, C13A, XV, 105.

instant rise of African-American slaves over European servants as the colony's major labor force, Louisiana resembled the English colonies of South Carolina and Georgia. The process occurred more gradually in the Chesapeake Bay, because it had been settled earlier, before the flow of white indentured servants was altered by demographic changes in England. Until the 1780s blacks continued to constitute a majority within the Louisiana colonial population, making it similar to South Carolina and some Caribbean colonies.[3]

As in most colonies during their formative years, Louisiana experienced a high ratio of men to women in 1726. Since 1704, when a group of some two dozen women was first sent to the colony, officials had sought ways to acquire girls and young women needed, in the words of Commissioner d'Artaguette, to "draw in the backwoodsmen" from Indian villages and to "make that many more settlers." Most of the female participants in the 1718–1721 migration were the wives and daughters of concessionaires, farmers, workers, soldiers, and even convicts, but at least 150 "femmes" and "jeunes filles" came directly from poorhouses and prisons in France. The workers on board the *Loire* in 1720, bound for the St. Catherine concession at Natchez, included 26 single women with various occupations. Among these immigrants from the port of Lorient were Marie Delarue, a dressmaker, Françoise Chatrency, a laborer, and Perrine, a Negro cook.[4]

Male immigrants far outnumbered their female counterparts. By 1726,

3. The more delayed replacement of indentured servants by African slaves in the Chesapeake is the central subject of Edmund S. Morgan, *American Slavery, American Freedom: The Ordeal of Colonial Virginia* (New York, 1975). Also see Lorena S. Walsh, "'Till Death Us Do Part': Marriage and Family in Seventeenth-Century Maryland," and Lois Green Carr and Russell R. Menard, "Immigration and Opportunity: The Freedman in Early Colonial Maryland," in Thad W. Tate and David L. Ammerman, eds., *The Chesapeake in the Seventeenth Century: Essays on Anglo-American Society* (Chapel Hill, N.C., 1979), 126–152, 206–242. The process in South Carolina is examined in Peter H. Wood, *Black Majority: Negroes in Colonial South Carolina from 1670 through the Stono Rebellion* (New York, 1974). For a quantitatively systematic profile of indentured servant migration to English colonies, see David W. Galenson, *White Servitude in Colonial America: An Economic Analysis* (Cambridge, 1981). Indentured servitude and slavery in the French Caribbean are examined in Gabriel Debien, *Les engagés pour les Antilles (1634–1715)* (Paris, 1952), and his *Les esclaves aux Antilles Françaises, XVIIe–XVIIIe siècles* (Basse Terre, Guadeloupe, 1974).

4. MPAFD, II, 57, 73; Conrad, comp. and trans., *First Families of Louisiana*, I, 26–28, 30–31, 64–65, 117.

TABLE 2. *The Colonial Population in the Lower Mississippi Valley,*
1726

Location	Habitants Total (Men/Women/ Children)	Slaves Negro/ Indian	Others Engagés/ Soldiers	Total
Interior Settlements and Post				
Natchitoches	96 (48/22/26)	32/1	6/25	160
Arkansas	14 (11/3/0)	0/1	0/0	15
Black and Yazoo rivers	6 (4/2/0)	0/0	0/15	21
Natchez	105 (49/29/27)	65/9	45/35	259
Alibamons (Fort Toulouse)	2 (2/0/0)	0/0	0/15	17
Settlements along Mississippi River, below Red River (Descending Order)				
Village of Tunicas (east bank)	48 (17/14/17)	0/0	5/0	53
Pointe Coupée (west bank)	17 (6/3/8)	0/0	4/0	21
Bayogoula (west bank)	4 (2/2/0)	15/1	6/0	26
Village of Houmas (east bank)	10 (4/3/3)	2/3	5/0	20
Village of Acola-pissas (east bank)	25 (11/7/7)	0/0	1/0	26
German Village (west bank)	152 (47/50/55)	0/0	3/0	155
Cannes Bruslées (east bank)	23 (11/7/5)	52/4	6/0	85
Providence (east bank)	16 (7/4/5)	0/0	0/0	16

TABLE 2. *Continued*

Location	Habitants Total (Men/Women/ Children)	Slaves Negro/ Indian	Others Engagés/ Soldiers	Total
Chapitoulas (east bank)	21 (5/3/13)	385/11	21/0	438
Bienville's land (east bank)	28 (12/9/7)	13/2	13/0	56
New Orleans (east bank)	603 (265/170/168)	78/30	60/130	901
Settlements behind New Orleans	49 (15/11/23)	52/8	17/0	126
Below German Village (west bank)	86 (33/23/30)	210/4	20/0	320
Balize, at mouth of river	4 (4/0/0)	31/0	11/20	66
Gulf Coast Settlements				
Biloxy	8 (2/2/4)	13/0	0/7	28
Pascagoula	27 (12/6/9)	56/12	2/0	97
Mobile	261 (93/72/96)	144/50	7/85	547
Isle Dauphine and outlying settlements	10 (4/2/4)	11/3	1/0	25
Grand total	1,663 (688/454/521)	1,385/159	245/332	3,784

Sources: Charles R. Maduell, comp. and trans., *The Census Tables for the French Colony of Louisiana from 1699 through 1732* (Baltimore, 1972), 25–76; Glenn R. Conrad, comp. and trans., *The First Families of Louisiana*, 2 vols. (Baton Rouge, La., 1970), I, 277.

women composed 40 percent of the adult habitant population, indicating a ratio of 1.5 men to 1 woman; but when soldiers and engagés are included, the sex ratio among whites increases to 2.8:1, a more realistic representation of the overall scarcity of women in the colony. Figures on the sexual composition of transported Africans and the black population in 1726 are not available, but impressionistic and comparative information suggests that an unbalanced sex ratio existed among slaves as well and probably resembled that of the habitants. Beyond question is the fact that a relatively large white male population in early Louisiana, especially at Mobile, New Orleans, Natchez, and Natchitoches, made women of all nationalities and classes invaluable partners, sexually and otherwise, in colonial households. The Code Noir issued for Louisiana in 1724 prohibited sexual intercourse between slaves and settlers. But cohabitation across this legal barrier, like so many other acts forbidden by colonial laws, certainly did not end, since many Indian and black women lived with Frenchmen as mistresses or common law wives. On May 18, 1726, Father Raphaël, the Capuchin vicar general of Louisiana, complained of the violations of the Code Noir being committed by colonists, "for although the number of those who maintain young Indian women or negresses to satisfy their intemperance is considerably diminished, there still remain enough to scandalize the church and to require an effective remedy."[5]

The geographical distribution of colonial society also played an important part in shaping patterns of exchange and influence among Indians, settlers, and slaves (see Map 1). In 1726 only 500 people occupied the posts and surrounding settlements scattered across the interior of the Lower Mississippi Valley—Fort Toulouse, Natchez, Yazoo, Arkansas, and Natchitoches. This left nearly 90 percent of the colonial population concentrated in the Gulf Coast settlements of Mobile, Pascagoula, and Biloxi and in settlements along the lower Mississippi River between Tunica and Balize. The towns of Mobile and New Orleans included 38 percent of all colonial inhabitants (14 percent and 24 percent, respectively), a relatively large urban population for such a sparsely settled

5. *MPAFD,* II, 521. The origins and administration of the Code Noir are discussed in Mathé Allain, "Slave Policies in French Louisiana," and Carl A. Brasseaux, "The Administration of Slave Regulations in French Louisiana, 1724–1766," *LH,* XXI (1980), 127–158.

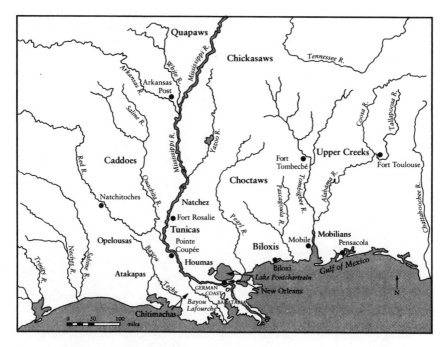

MAP 1. *The Lower Mississippi Valley in the 1730s*

colony.[6] Slaves were the most geographically concentrated group, with just over three-fourths of their number living along the Mississippi below the settlement of Cannes Bruslées. Already, the emergence of a small, slaveowning elite was beginning to concentrate African-Americans within that agricultural area, for 28 percent of the total black population of Louisiana (385 people in all) inhabited only five separate concessions at Chapitoulas (see Plate 3). One-fourth of the colony's 639 households owned slaves. Excluding the town populations in New Orleans and Mobile, slaves were present in 30 percent of all rural households. Most of the white farming colonists who lived in sexually balanced households and who owned no slaves in 1726 were German families settled about twenty-

6. These and other geographical features of the colonial society are explored in J. Zitomersky, "Urbanization in French Colonial Louisiana (1706–1766)," in *Annales de démographie historique, 1974: Études, comptes rendus, documents, bibliographie* (Paris, 1974), 263–278.

PLATE 3. *Special Map of the Mississippi River Ten Leagues above and below New Orleans.* Anonymous. Circa 1723. *Courtesy of Cartes Marines, Newberry Library, Chicago*

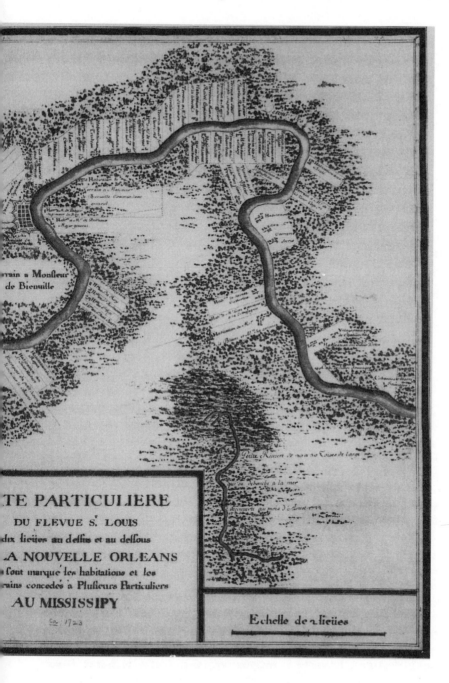

TE PARTICULIERE
DU FLEVUE S.T LOUIS
dix lieües au deſſus et au deſſous
LA NOUVELLE ORLEANS
s ſont marqué les habitations et les
rains concedés a Pluſieurs Particuliers
AU MISSISSIPY
ca. 1723

Echelle de 2 lieües

five miles above New Orleans and French families clustered around Natchez and Natchitoches.[7]

Most colonial inhabitants in the Lower Mississippi Valley were occupied by farming, herding, hunting-gathering-fishing, trading, military service and transportation, or by some combination of these dispersed economic activities (discussed in Part II, below). Like other early colonies and frontier regions, Louisiana in 1726 suffered a shortage of craftsmen, artisans, and professional occupations in general. Thirty-seven different occupations are identified within the New Orleans populace, but most of the individuals so listed in the census were day laborers (14), itinerant traders (12), indentured servants (11), sailors (11), and hunters and fishermen (7). Possessing skills in demand for shipping, construction, and repairs were 10 joiners, 9 carpenters, 4 coopers, 4 wagonmakers, 3 blacksmiths, 3 locksmiths, 2 turners, and 1 gunsmith. Other professionals included 7 tailors, 4 bakers, 4 physicians and surgeons, 3 Capuchin priests, 3 shoemakers, 2 surveyors, an engineer, a bookkeeper, a goldsmith, a wigmaker, a chandelier, a brewer, and a miller.[8]

As the principal employer of most skilled workers during the 1720s, the Company of the Indies tried to secure their services at minimal expense, in ways that profoundly influenced colonial society. As early as 1716 Gen-

7. Maduell, comp. and trans., *Census Tables,* 25–76. Politically, settlements and posts in Louisiana were organized into districts. Post commandants served as both military and civil officials in these districts, under the supervision of the Superior Council. The administrative and judicial center of provincial government in French Louisiana, the Superior Council consisted of the governor, commissioner, and attorney general, all selected by the crown, and of several councillors, some chosen from the resident planter-merchant class. This governing body enforced laws received from the Ministry of Marine and also enacted statutes and ordinances relating to local affairs. As the supreme court of the colony, the council heard all criminal and civil cases that either originated in the New Orleans area or could not be resolved by post commandants. Governance in French Louisiana is closely examined in Charles Edwards O'Neill, *Church and State in French Colonial Louisiana: Policy and Politics to 1732* (New Haven, Conn., 1966); James D. Hardy, Jr., "The Superior Council in Colonial Louisiana," in John Francis McDermott, ed., *Frenchmen and French Ways in the Mississippi Valley* (Urbana, Ill., 1969), 87–101; Donald Jile Lemieux, "The Office of Commissaire Ordonnateur in French Louisiana, 1731–1763: A Study in French Colonial Administration" (Ph.D. diss., Louisiana State University, 1972); Carl A. Brasseaux, *Denis-Nicolas Foucault and the New Orleans Rebellion of 1768* (Ruston, La., 1987).

8. Maduell, comp. and trans., *Census Tables,* 65–76.

eral Commissioner Hubert had recommended that Indian and Negro slaves could "be used very advantageously to learn the different trades of the workmen . . . in order that they may serve to replace them." "Since there is no blacksmith at all at Mobile and since individuals of this trade cost immense sums," the company in 1720 exchanged three African slaves for "Mr. de Bienville's negro named Laurent who is a good blacksmith." Efforts to regiment artisans receiving wages and rations from the company the way soldiers, sailors, and unskilled laborers were regimented proved very difficult. In order to keep workmen at Balize from returning to France, the Superior Council on November 8, 1724, raised the wages of Le Bas the carpenter by one hundred livres to six hundred livres per year and granted a daily wage of sixteen sous and eight deniers to a soldier who worked as blacksmith.[9] Over ensuing decades some soldiers brought skilled trades to Louisiana and joined other artisans in the colony after their military service. But to meet immediate needs and to cut costs in 1728, the colonial government was "placing negroes as apprentices with all the workmen who we think are good and honest men . . . although the workmen do not seek to perfect the negroes in their trades because they feel distinctly that that will harm them in the future." Within three months of this measure, they reduced the income of carpenters and blacksmiths to three hundred livres per year, and "those who appeared not to be satisfied were told that they only had to take their leave."[10]

Channeling slaves into skilled occupations undoubtedly heightened racial tensions, generating resentment among some European workers toward Africans' being used to lower their bargaining power. But many successful artisans themselves realized that ownership of skilled slaves greatly enhanced their businesses. The widespread participation of black Louisianians, at plantations and towns alike, in a multitude of occupations contributed to the flexibility and fluidity that in the long run characterized the region's frontier exchange economy. The census of New Orleans in 1732 indicates that 37 of the 252 Negroes then residing in the city belonged to skilled white craftsmen. Carpenters, joiners, and blacksmiths owned more Negro slaves than did other artisans, but blacks worked at a variety of specialties, ranging from hospital service to ironworking. Some

9. *MPAFD*, II, 230, III, 239, 282, 439–440, 442–443.
10. *Ibid.*, II, 599, 623–624, 654.

African craftsmen brought appropriate skills from Senegambia, where woodworkers, weavers, and blacksmiths belonged to distinct occupational castes. Whether African-Americans were learning new skills or applying familiar ones, their presence in workshops, kitchens, and stores facilitated intimate as well as occupational interaction with other Louisianians and provided an avenue for many slaves to purchase their freedom.[11]

II

American Indians mixed with colonial society in the Lower Mississippi Valley in a variety of ways that further made regulation and domination by governing authorities more difficult. An undetermined number of Indians entered or passed through Louisiana settlements as slaves. French and English colonies in North America allowed and periodically encouraged the enslavement of Indian people from enemy tribes or distant territories. Most captives were transported from one region to another, as in the case of Indians exported from Charleston to New England and Caribbean buyers during the early eighteenth century.[12] Many enslaved Indians, however, remained in their locales, to be joined by imported black and other Indian slaves. The 159 Indian slaves counted in the 1726 census of Louisiana came from several different tribes. "Panis" (a generic name) were Indians captured on the Great Plains, but most of the Indian slaves living in lower Louisiana's colonial households were

11. Maduell, comp. and trans., *Census Tables*, 123–141; *MPAFD*, II, 558–559; Marcus Christian, *Negro Ironworkers of Louisiana, 1718–1900* (Gretna, La., 1972). For the occupational caste system in Senegambia, see Philip D. Curtin, *Economic Change in Precolonial Africa: Senegambia in the Era of the Slave Trade* (Madison, Wis., 1975), 29–34.

12. Almon Wheeler Lauber, *Indian Slavery in Colonial Times within the Present Limits of the United States* (New York, 1913), is still the most comprehensive treatment of enslaved Indians in North America. For recent examination of particular regions, see Yasuhide Kawashima, "Indian Servitude in the Northeast," Peter H. Wood, "Indian Servitude in the Southeast," Albert H. Schroeder and Omer C. Stewart, "Indian Servitude in the Southwest," and Robert F. Heizer, "Indian Servitude in California," in William C. Sturtevant et al., eds., *Handbook of North American Indians*, IV, *History of Indian-White Relations* (Washington, D.C., 1988), 404–416.

captured from nearby tribes—like the Alibamons, Taensas, and Chiti-machas—against whom the French waged war before the 1720s.[13]

The dispersal of Indians among slaveowners in the towns and coun-tryside brought them into intimate contact with European and African Louisianians. The 30 Indian slaves listed in New Orleans for 1726 resided in various household arrangements. On Rue Royalle 2 Indian and 4 Negro slaves lived with carpenter Thomas Dezery, and 1 Indian slave lived in the household of a locksmith named Sulpice L'Évique with his wife and 3 children. Seven lived in another conjugal household on Rue St. Louis, that of François St. Amand, his wife, and his 2 children. On Rue Du Quay an Indian slave inhabited the house of Reboul, a hunter, perhaps as a female companion or a male assistant. At the settlement of Chapitoulas, just above New Orleans along the Mississippi, 11 Indian slaves lived on four separate plantations along with 11 European servants and 302 Negro slaves. At Bayou St. John and Gentilly, on the northeastern outskirts of the capital, 8 Indian slaves also worked beside white and black laborers on several different farms.[14]

Although the sex of slaves is not specified in the 1726 census, a sig-nificant percentage of Indians living in Louisiana households as slaves were women, raising controversy over intercultural sexual relationships. Whereas some marriages between Frenchmen and Indian women were blessed by priests at early Louisiana settlements, where few white women lived, most officials and clergymen condemned soldiers and settlers who cohabited with their female servants. Accusations of laxness toward this practice flew across factional lines in the colonial government. In a mem-oir written after his return to France in 1710, the former pastor of the colony's main settlement at Mobile had denounced many Louisianians for preferring, over legitimate marriage, "to maintain scandalous concubi-nages with young Indian women, driven by their proclivity for the ex-

13. Richebourg Gaillard McWilliams, ed. and trans., *Fleur de Lys and Calumet: Being the Pénicaut Narrative of French Adventure in Louisiana* (Baton Rouge, La., 1953), 101–102 (hereafter cited as *Pénicaut Narrative*); Antoine Le Page Du Pratz, *The History of Louisiana*, ed. Joseph G. Tregle, Jr. (London, 1774; facs. rpt., Baton Rouge, La., 1975), 20–21; Marcel Giraud, *A History of French Louisiana*, I, *The Reign of Louis XIV, 1698–1715* (1953), trans. Joseph C. Lambert (Baton Rouge, La., 1974), 177–180.

14. Maduell, comp. and trans., *Census Tables*, 50–76.

tremes of licentiousness. They have bought them under the pretext of keeping them as servants, but actually to seduce them, as they in fact have done."[15] The immigration of hundreds of European women to Louisiana after 1717 began moving the colonial population toward a more balanced sex ratio, which made intimacy with Indian women less threatening to the colony's order.

A more serious threat to the designs of colonial planners was the general recalcitrance of Indian slaves and the potential for collaboration between enslaved Indians and Africans. Given their knowledge of the terrain and familiarity with local tribes, runaway Indian slaves held the key to unlocking mass rebellion against slavery and colonial rule. As in other slave colonies situated amid Indian societies, Louisiana officials depended upon local Indians to catch runaway slaves. As soon as ships began depositing enslaved West Africans on the Gulf shore, Indian villagers were offered bounties of munitions and alcohol for capturing and returning runaways. Alarmed by robbery and arson being committed by numerous bands of runaways, or marrons, in 1726, Attorney General François Fleuriau, himself the owner of eight Negroes, urged the Superior Council to "take prompt and sweeping action against runaway slaves" by hiring "neighborhood Indians" to pursue them. But this expedient for dividing peoples who otherwise might have conspired against a common enemy, the white planter, was inhibited by the fact that some of Louisiana's runaway slaves were Indians.[16]

Incidents of black and Indian slaves' cooperating with each other occurred frequently enough to alarm officials into discouraging further enslavement of Louisiana Indians. Following reports that "marrons sauvages" had raided cattle and attacked the Negro public executioner, a maroon camp called Natanapallé was discovered in 1727. Sancousy, an Indian slave who lost his owner's ox, fled to this makeshift village, where he met about fifteen African and Indian fugitives. These escaped slaves possessed enough guns and ammunition to defend themselves against any

15. AC, C13A, III, 390. For analyses of this controversy, see Giraud, *History of French Louisiana*, trans. Lambert, I, 278–280; Charles Edwards O'Neill, *Church and State in French Colonial Louisiana: Policy and Politics to 1732* (New Haven, Conn., 1966), 86–92, 248–255; Carl A. Brasseaux, "The Moral Climate of French Colonial Louisiana, 1699–1763," *LH*, XXVII (1986), 27–41.

16. *RSCLHQ*, III, 414; Conrad, comp. and trans., *First Families*, II, 42; Le Page Du Pratz, *History*, ed. Tregle, 29.

pursuers. The arrest of other runaways who had apparently seen this community influenced Governor Étienne Boucher de Périer to request that the trade in Indian slaves be terminated. Not only did this traffic incite costly wars between tribes, but "these Indian slaves being mixed with our negroes may induce them to desert with them, as has already happened, as they may maintain relations with them which might be disastrous to the colony when there are more blacks."[17]

Bondage of Indians was not officially prohibited in Louisiana until Spanish acquisition, but a convergence of factors shared with other North American colonies did slow down the rate of Indian enslavement. The decimation of Indians by disease, the desire to secure stable trade relations with neighboring tribes, the availability of African slaves, and the ease with which Indian captives could abscond all contributed to a declining number of Indian slaves in the Lower Mississippi Valley after the 1720s. Conflicts with the Natchez and Chickasaw nations, as will be seen presently, produced hundreds of Indian slaves, but most were shipped away from the region to the Caribbean. Also influencing the process was the tendency in both custom and law to classify slaves automatically as Negro or mulatto. Liaisons between Indian and African-American slaves produced children who were ascribed with increasing regularity to Negro or mulatto identities. A portion of Indians was also assimilated into the free segment of colonial society, as the offspring of Indian slave women and freemen grew up as free people of color or as whites. By 1732 Louisiana contained fewer than one hundred Indian slaves amid a colonial population of nearly six thousand.[18]

17. *RSCLHQ*, I, 109, III, 414, 443–444; *MPAFD*, II, 573–574. Classic works on Indian-black relations in colonial North America include Kenneth W. Porter, "Relations between Negroes and Indians within the Present Limits of the United States," *Journal of Negro History*, XVII (1932), 287–369; and William S. Willis, "Divide and Rule: Red, White, and Black in the Southeast," *Jour. Negro Hist.*, XLVIII (1963), 157–176. Foremost in modern scholarship are Theda Perdue, *Slavery and the Evolution of Cherokee Society, 1540–1866* (Knoxville, Tenn., 1979), 36–49; and J. Leitch Wright, Jr., *The Only Land They Knew: The Tragic Story of the American Indians in the Old South* (New York, 1981).

18. Maduell, comp. and trans., *Census Tables*, 113, 123; C13A, XV, 105; Virginia R. Domínguez, *White by Definition: Social Classification in Creole Louisiana* (New Brunswick, N.J., 1986). The conjunction of demographic and legal changes in Indian slavery among English colonies is investigated in A. Leon Higginbotham, Jr., *In the Matter of Color: Race and the American Legal Process, the Colonial Period* (New York,

III

Another context of Indian relationships with Louisiana was that of several groups situated near colonial settlements and towns who interacted closely with colonists while maintaining a substantial degree of cultural and political autonomy. Indians occupying these small communities lived on the margins of colonial society, not inside it where Indian slaves did. Like the praying towns of New England, the missions of Canada, New Mexico, and Florida, and the settlement tribes of the Chesapeake and Carolinas, these petites nations in the Lower Mississippi Valley developed ties and tensions with colonial people that differed sharply from those of larger Indian nations situated in more distant or insulated locations.[19] Diseases and wars already having reduced their population and power relative to interior tribes, Indian nations along the Gulf Coast and lower Mississippi River staked their future on establishing forms of mutually supportive exchange with colonial settlements. Some groups achieved this relationship even by moving from their native sites to areas more heavily populated by settlers and slaves. By the mid-1720s ten Indian villages, inhabited altogether by some seventeen hundred people, were clustered around Mobile and Biloxi. The Grand Tohomé, Petit Tohomé, Mobilian, Pensacola, Pascagoula, and Biloxi communities were the known survivors indigenous to this area, joined by four groups of refugees from other areas. The Taensas had abandoned their location along the lower Mississippi River during the heavy conflict of the early colonial years. English raids against native towns in Spanish Florida drove Apalache, Tawasa, and Chahto refugees westward into French Louisiana, where by 1704 they had established three new villages on Mobile Bay.[20]

1978); Wright, *The Only Land They Knew*, 126–150, 248–278; Yasuhide Kawashima, *Puritan Justice and the Indian: White Man's Law in Massachusetts, 1630–1763* (Middletown, Conn., 1986).

19. While scholarship on these Indian communities and their relations with Atlantic coastal colonies has lagged behind that on the large interior tribes, several essays in Sturtevant *et al.*, eds., *Handbook of North American Indians*, XV, *Northeast* (Washington, D.C., 1978), esp. 177–189, 240–289, 466–480, focus on them. The most important contribution to this field, one that will serve as a model study for other scholars interested in similar Indian groups, is James H. Merrell, *The Indians' New World: Catawbas and Their Neighbors from European Contact through the Era of Removal* (Chapel Hill, N.C., 1989).

20. *Pénicaut Narrative*, 98, 102–103, 125, 161–162; MPAFD, III, 26–27, 136,

These villagers suffered more depopulation and relocation as time went on, but by the 1720s a pattern of close interaction with colonists was fixed. Indians from neighboring villages regularly provisioned Mobile and Biloxi with venison, corn, and other 'supplies. Women sold herbs, food-stuffs, and baskets, and men participated in such wage-earning occupations as rowing pirogues, carrying trade merchandise, and delivering messages between posts. These seasonal or occasional activities supplemented the villages' internal means of subsistence and allowed Indians flexibility in choosing how to benefit on the margins of colonial society.[21] Setting Gulf Coastal petites nations apart from all other Indian groups in the Lower Mississippi Valley was the adoption of Christianity by many of their members. Having been converted to Catholicism by Franciscan missionaries back in Florida, the Apalaches insisted that a priest live in their town. Through their influence, other Indians in the vicinity chose to be baptized into the church. In contrast with French Canada, missionary efforts among Indians in the Lower Mississippi Valley were otherwise negligible. A Capuchin priest was stationed at Apalache, but the Jesuits assumed responsibility for all other Indian missions in 1727. Their poorly supported efforts at Fort Toulouse, Arkansas, and the Choctaw village of Chickasawhay resulted in few conversions of Indian souls.[22]

Interspersed among settlements along the lower Mississippi River, an-

535–537; Albert S. Gatschet, *A Migration Legend of the Creek Indians* . . . (Philadelphia, 1884), 33–34, 109–112.

21. *MPAFD*, I, 167–178, IV, 161, V, 224–225; Le Page Du Pratz, *History of Louisiana*, ed. Tregle, 308–309; Marcel Giraud, *Histoire de la Louisiane française*, IV, *La Louisiane après le systeme de law (1721–1723)* (Paris, 1974), 421–422; Frank Norall, *Bourgmont, Explorer of the Missouri, 1698–1725* (Lincoln, Nebr., 1988), 99–103.

22. Claude L. Vogel, *The Capuchins in French Louisiana (1722–1766)* (New York, 1928), 60–64, 122; Jean Delanglez, *The French Jesuits in Lower Louisiana (1700–1763)* (Washington, D.C., 1935), 96, 420–490. For more modern scholarship on missionary work in colonial Louisiana, see Mary Veronica Miceli, "The Influence of the Roman Catholic Church on Slavery in Colonial Louisiana under French Domination, 1718–1763" (Ph.D. diss., Tulane University, 1979); and Miceli, "The Christianization of French Colonial Louisiana: A General View of Church and State in the Context of Eighteenth Century French Colonization and a Theory of Mission," *Southern Studies*, XXI (1982), 384–397. The role of religion in the formation of Indian mission communities in the Northeast is skillfully examined in James Axtell, *The Invasion Within: The Contest of Cultures in Colonial North America* (New York, 1985), 43–127, 218–286.

other three thousand or so Indian people lived in seven different petites nations. Before the 1720s this had been an extremely volatile area. Driven downriver by English and allied Indian raiders, Taensa and Tunica migrants triggered a chain reaction of conflicts and dislocations. The Taensas quickly migrated away from the Mississippi to Mobile Bay, after disrupting their Bayogoula hosts, and the Tunicas settled permanently at the village of the Houma Indians, who in turn fled downriver to resettle eventually several miles below Bayou Lafourche. Since 1706 the French had been waging war against the Chitimachas. But with the establishment of concessions along the Mississippi River under way by 1718, Chitimacha overtures of peace were finally accepted by Louisiana officials.[23] At the site where construction of New Orleans had just begun, Chitimacha delegates solemnly marched to the cadence of their own voices from the riverbank to Bienville's cabin. After they sat on the ground and poised their faces in their hands, the word-bearer rose to light the sacred pipe. He smoked and passed it on to the governor and then to everyone assembled. After presenting Bienville with the pipe and a gift of deerskins and other pelts, the elderly Chitimacha bemoaned the years of warfare with the French. Present at this ceremony and assisted by the translation of a Chitimacha woman whom he had recently purchased, Antoine Le Page Du Pratz recorded the word-bearer's speech. At the conclusion of his talk, the Indian orator eloquently expressed the hope of a people beleaguered by years of war and eager to live in peace:

> Formerly the sun was red, the roads filled with brambles and thorns, the clouds were black, the water was troubled and stained with blood, our women wept unceasingly, our children cried with fright, the game fled far from us, our houses were abandoned, and our fields uncultivated, we all have empty bellies and our bones are visible.
>
> Now the sun is warm and brilliant, the heaven is clear, there are no more clouds, the roads are clean and pleasant, the water is so clear that we can see ourselves within it, the game comes back, our women dance until they forget to eat, our children leap like young fawns, the heart of the entire nation laughs with joy, to see that we will walk

23. *MPAFD*, III, 527–529, 535–536; Jean-Baptiste Bernard de La Harpe, *The Historical Journal of the Establishment of the French in Louisiana*, ed. Glen R. Conrad, trans. Joan Cain and Virginia Koenig (Lafayette, La., 1971), 76 (hereafter cited as La Harpe, *Journal*); *Pénicaut Narrative*, 146, 216–219.

along the same road as you all, Frenchmen; the same sun will illuminate us; we will have but one word, our hearts will make but one, we
will eat together like brothers; will that not be good, what say you?[24]

By the time this treaty occurred, the villages of Chaouacha, Bayogoula,
Houma, Acolapissa, Chitimacha, and Tunica were all situated within a
hundred-mile radius of New Orleans and participated actively in the
evolving colonial economy. Like those along the Gulf Coast, these petites
nations provided goods and services that brought them into close contact
with colonial society. Despite the debilitating influences of disease and
alcohol that continued to threaten them, Indian communities along the
lower Mississippi persevered throughout the eighteenth century.[25] In
1722 the chief of Tunica looked like an entrepreneur to Father Pierre de
Charlevoix, who observed that this Indian had already acquired "fash-
ion" and "the art of laying up money" from the French in the course of
"supplying them with horses and poultry." At Acolapissa on the east bank
of the Mississippi, about thirty miles above New Orleans, Charlevoix was
welcomed with music played by a drummer "dressed in a long fantastical
parti coloured robe." Inquiring into the origin of this custom, he "was
informed that it was not very ancient; that a governor of Louisiana had
made a present of this drum to these Indians, who have always been our
faithfull allies; and that this sort of beadle's coat, was of their own
invention." Acolapissa hunters regularly supplied fresh meat to New
Orleans, and the Houmas raised abundant surpluses of corn for the city's
early grain market. The Houma village of some sixty cabins, according to
Bernard de La Harpe, "busies itself in raising hens and in the cultivation of
maize and beans." The one hundred men of the Acolapissas, Bienville
noted, "furnish us almost all the fresh meat that is consumed at New
Orleans without however their neglecting the cultivation of their lands
which produce a great deal of corn."[26]

24. Antoine Le Page Du Pratz, *Histoire de la Louisiane* . . . , 3 vols. (Paris, 1758), I,
106–114. The English translation of this speech is from John R. Swanton, *Indian
Tribes of the Lower Mississippi Valley and Adjacent Coast of the Gulf of Mexico*,
Bureau of American Ethnology Bulletin, no. 43 (Washington, D.C., 1911), 340–342.
    25. Daniel H. Usner, Jr., "American Indians in Colonial New Orleans," in Wood *et
al.*, eds., *Powhatan's Mantle*, 104–127.
    26. Pierre François Xavier de Charlevoix, *Journal of a Voyage to North America*,
2 vols. (London, 1761), II, 279–280, 285; La Harpe, *Journal*, 75–76; MPAFD, III,
527–529, 535. The rich archaeological and documentary data available for the Tunicas

For Indian nations situated farther from colonial settlements, relations with Louisiana during the 1720s were more formal. Interior trading posts operated as foci of exchange in the deerskin trade network. Trade among these larger tribes remained entangled in English-French rivalry. The Atakapas and Opelousas lived in the swamplands and savannahs west of Bayou Lafourche and just began contact with the French, who perceived them vaguely as nomadic and even cannibalistic people.[27] Tribes along the Red River, from the Avoyelles upriver to the Caddoes, strengthened their trade relations with Louisiana by producing a variety of furs and even herding livestock from Texas. Backcountry Indians did not escape the deleterious impact of epidemics, as witnessed firsthand by Father Charlevoix around the mouth of the Arkansas River. In December 1721 he found the Quapaw village of Ouyapes "in the greatest desolation." From a passing Frenchman infected with smallpox, the entire town was immobilized by the disease. All night in his tent, the priest "heard nothing but weeping, in which the men joined as well as the women, incessantly repeating the word *nihahani*." By 1727, according to one missionary, the Quapaws were reduced to "about twelve hundred souls," who congregated into three villages near the French post. Soldiers and travelers regularly purchased corn from the Quapaw village of Sotouris, some forty-one cabins and 330 inhabitants occupying a bluff just above the Arkansas River's spring flood level.[28]

---

are splendidly analyzed in Jeffrey P. Brain's two volumes: *Tunica Treasure,* Peabody Museum of Archaeology and Ethnology, Papers, LXXI (Cambridge, Mass., 1979); and *Tunica Archaeology,* Peabody Museum of Archaeology and Ethnology, Papers, LXXVIII (Cambridge, Mass., 1988).

27. *MPAFD,* III, 528–529. The Atakapas included in this study are only those who became principally involved in the Lower Mississippi Valley network of exchange, estimated by Bienville to number 200 warriors during the 1720s and referred to by anthropologists as the Atakapas Proper. Three other Atakapan-speaking groups—the Bidais, Akokisas, and Deadoses—lived west of the Sabine River and based their activities around Spanish missions and forts in Texas. Lawrence E. Aten, *Indians of the Upper Texas Coast* (New York, 1983); Elizabeth A. H. John, *Storms Brewed in Other Men's Worlds: The Confrontation of Indians, Spanish, and French in the Southwest, 1540–1795* (College Station, Tex., 1975), 349–350.

28. Le Page Du Pratz, *Histoire de la Louisiane,* I, 297–298; *MPAFD,* III, 529–530; La Harpe, *Journal,* 202; Charlevoix, *Journal of a Voyage,* II, 247–248; Reuben Gold Thwaites, ed., *The Jesuit Relations and Allied Documents: Travels and Explorations of the Jesuit Missionaries in New France, 1610–1791,* 73 vols. (Cleveland, Ohio, 1896–1901), LXVII, 319.

Across the interior hill country east of the Mississippi, the Choctaw and Chickasaw nations were deeply caught in a web of intercolonial competition for Indian trade. To neutralize the Chickasaws' now firm alliance with British South Carolina, Louisiana officials relied upon a policy of insurgence. At a council in Biloxi on February 8, 1721, they formalized a tariff of exchange rates for deerskins produced by Choctaws and announced formally their approval of warfare already in progress between the Choctaw and Chickasaw tribes. "In order to incite them to do well," the French promised Choctaw warriors "one gun, one pound of powder and two pounds of bullets" for each Chickasaw scalp and eighty livres of merchandise for each Chickasaw slave. As explained to the Superior Council by Governor Bienville, intertribal conflict not only discouraged a combination of these two populous nations against the French but compensated for the inability of the Company of the Indies to trade satisfactorily with both peoples. "If the Chickasaws became our allies and our friends, they would have to renounce all commerce with the English to trade with the French. It is impossible for us to do this because, in addition to the fact that we never have enough merchandise, the English furthermore trade for their peltries at a rate far higher than that at which the French receive them." With four hundred scalps and one hundred slaves in the hands of the French by 1723, the Chickasaws were becoming bitter and determined enemies of Louisiana. Consequently the colony grew increasingly dependent upon Bienville's bellicose deployment of Choctaw warriors.[29]

IV

Of all the different paths taken in Indian-colonial relations during the 1720s, that upon which the Natchez Indians found themselves was the most turbulent. In the Natchez country both internal divisions within colonial society and external tensions with Indian society came to a stormy impasse, leaving Louisiana with bitter lessons about the instability inherent in European commercial expansion. Natchez villages were not

29. MPAFD, III, 303, 343, 355–356, 375; Giraud, Histoire de la Louisiane française, IV, 420–421. Bienville's Chickasaw policy, more of which will be seen in the next chapter, is succinctly examined in Dawson A. Phelps, "The Chickasaw, the English, and the French: 1699–1744," Tennessee Historical Quarterly, XVI (1957), 117–133.

only populous communities capable of producing abundant foodstuffs and deerskins for Louisiana commerce, but they occupied one of the most attractive areas in the Lower Mississippi Valley for plantation agriculture. Unlike the banks of the lower Mississippi, fertile soil at Natchez was naturally protected from the river's annual inundation because of its location on a large bluff. The Company of the Indies granted land at this promising site to prospective producers of tobacco. By 1726 two large concessions—employing twenty-nine European engagés, fifty-six African slaves, and four Indian slaves—with about forty separate households of habitants were established near the Natchez villages (see Plate 4). This sudden increase in the colonial population around Fort Rosalie intensified the Natchez Indians' trade with settlers, slaves, and soldiers alike, leading planters and company officials to fear the effects of what Le Page Du Pratz called "our too familiar intercourse with them." Frequent episodes of personal exchange gave "occasion to vices," distracting colonists from the new tobacco fields. Indian elders also expressed regrets over the impact of this trade upon younger Natchez people, who were enticed by the convenience and pleasure of such foreign goods as muskets, cloth, and brandy.[30]

The spread of foreign diseases was still the most serious source of Natchez discontent during the early years of trade and settlement. Father Pierre de Charlevoix observed in 1721 that the great village of the Natchez, standing midway between the St. Catherine and White Earth plantations, was "at present reduced to a very few cabins." Except for the eternal fire burning inside, the grand temple lacked the ornaments and relics that had been widely publicized by earlier French visitors to this centrally located Indian chiefdom. The Jesuit priest speculated that "the neighborhood of the French made the Natchez fear that the bodies of their chiefs, and everything that was most precious in their temple, were in some danger if they did not convey them to another place." Contagious viruses introduced by Europeans and Africans, notably smallpox and influenza, were ravaging the Natchez people, and colonial settlement seemed to be closing in on their villages. From a population of more than thirty-five hundred before Louisiana began, the Natchez nation dropped to half that number and included only five villages by the mid-1720s.[31]

30. Le Page Du Pratz, *History of Louisiana*, ed. Tregle, 35, 106–107; Conrad, comp. and trans., *First Families of Louisiana*, II, 31–32.

31. Charlevoix, *Journal of a Voyage*, 140–149, 160–162, 170; Jean François Ben-

French-Natchez relations entered a new crisis in the autumn of 1722, when a quarrel over some corn owed to a Fort Rosalie sergeant led to the death of several Indian men inside the fort. To avenge this and other acts, which went unpunished by the French commandant, some Natchez groups decided to strike. Raids against the St. Catherine concession began on October 22 when warriors from the White Apple village, while "talking to the negroes who had stopped to eat," opened fire and killed a slave named Bougou. Within a week the Natchez killed eleven cattle, injured one black and one white laborer, and stole three horses, sixteen pigs, six quarts of flour, fifty quarts of corn, fifty quarts of potatoes, and forty quarts of beans.[32] Raids against the settlement continued sporadically for a year, until Bienville led an army of some six hundred soldiers and Indian allies into the Natchez country. Having already suffered innumerable attacks on their villages, the Natchez negotiated a peace with Bienville, who demanded "that they shall give up the heads of the men named Tchietchiomota, Capine, Ouyou, Nalcoa, Outchital, Yooua . . . [and] that they bring in dead or alive a negro who has taken refuge among them for a long time and makes them seditious speeches against the French nation and who has followed them on occasions against our Indian allies." Stung Serpent, war chief and brother of the Great Sun, managed to meet these conditions and restored peace between the Natchez and French people.[33]

But discontent over specific abuses and general influences of French colonization persisted among Natchez villagers. Warriors increasingly raided livestock on the concessions, hunting them like a new species of game and taunting their owners at the same time. Lieutenant Jean François Benjamin Dumont at Fort Rosalie observed that the Natchez considered it "brave and valiant" to mangle or kill horses, cows, and pigs,

---

jamin Dumont de Montigny, "Historical Memoirs of M. Dumont" (1753), in B. F. French, ed., *Historical Collections of Louisiana*, 5 vols. (New York, 1846–1853), V, 31–32; Le Page Du Pratz, *History of Louisiana*, ed. Tregle, 305–306; "Excerpt of a Letter Written by Mr. Faucond, Director General of the Colony at the Natchez, July 18th, 1721," *LHQ*, II (1919), 164–169.

- 32. *MPAFD*, III, 360; Dawson Phelps, ed. and trans., "Narrative of the Hostilities Committed by the Natchez against the Concession of St. Catherine, October 21, November 4, 1722," *JMH*, VII (1945), 3–10; "Journal of Diron d'Artaguiette," in Newton D. Mereness, ed., *Travels in the American Colonies* (New York, 1916), 33–41.

33. Le Page Du Pratz, *History of Louisiana*, ed. Tregle, 36–42; *MPAFD*, III, 385–387.

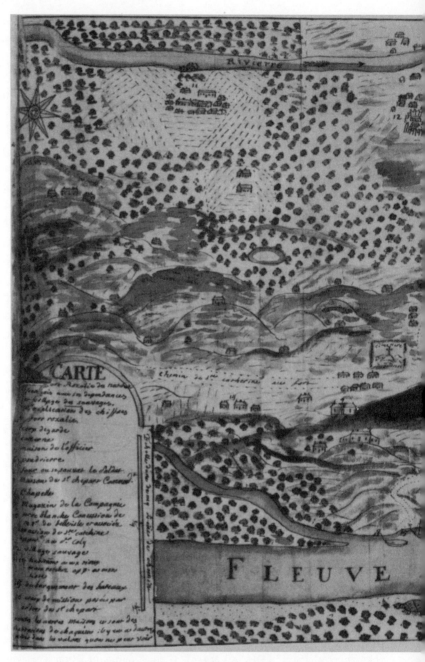

PLATE 4. *Drawing of Fort Rosalie of French Natchez with Its Dependencies and Indian Villages*. By Jean François Benjamin Dumont de Montigny. Circa 1729. *Courtesy of Edward E. Ayer Collection, Newberry Library, Chicago*

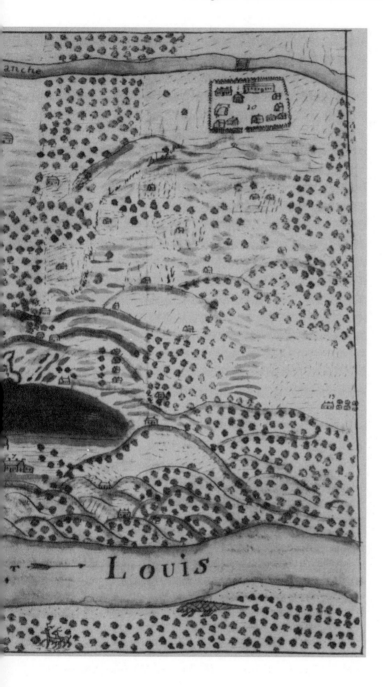

detecting in their harassment of colonial property a sporting test of Indian manhood. Irritated by repeated incidents of costly pillage, French officials imposed penal taxes on Natchez villages by demanding payments in produce for damages. Natchez leaders, especially the older generation, meanwhile resented not only the burdens imposed on the tribe's economy by colonial demands but, moreover, the toll being taken upon the people's cultural autonomy by European goods. Shortly before his death in 1725, Stung Serpent complained to Le Page Du Pratz how, before the French arrived, "Did we not live better than we do, seeing we deprive ourselves of a part of our corn, our game, and fish, to give a part to them?" Pointing to the men's reliance on guns and the women's recourse to blankets, the war chief reminded the Dutch-born colonist that earlier "we lived like men who can be satisfied with what they have; whereas at this day we are like slaves, who are not suffered to do as they please."[34]

A rapid succession of three French commandants at Fort Rosalie after 1723, reflecting political factionalism and transition in colonial leadership, only exacerbated French relations with the Natchez. When Captain de Merveilleux finally received the position, he briefly restored confidence among inhabitants and amity with Indian villagers. But in 1728 Étienne Boucher de Périer, who replaced Bienville as governor two years earlier, appointed Sieur De Chepart to the commandant post at Natchez. De Chepart, already known as a drunkard and a brash person, immediately "tyrannized the people and abused his power," as recalled by Lieutenant Dumont. When he removed a company of soldiers from the White Earth concession and thereby endangered its inhabitants, De Chepart was summoned before the Superior Council. The council found him guilty of "some acts of injustice," but Governor Périer pardoned De Chepart and restored him to his command.[35]

De Chepart actually returned to Natchez with some black slaves and ambitious plans to establish concessions there for both himself and Périer. In line with the tobacco designs of the Company of the Indies, De Chepart's immediate interests imminently clashed with the concerns of the Natchez Indians. The deaths of Stung Serpent in 1725 and of his brother,

34. "Journal of Diron d'Artaguiette," in Mereness, ed. *Travels*, 90–91; "Historical Memoirs of M. Dumont," in French, ed., *Historical Collections*, V, 59–61; Le Page Du Pratz, *History of Louisiana*, ed. Tregle, 44–45.

35. *MPAFD*, I, 128; "Historical Memoirs of M. Dumont," in French, ed., *Historical Collections*, V, 61–63.

the "great sun," in 1728 strengthened the influence of an anti-French leadership; the new grand chief was closely related to one of the White Apple chiefs whose skull went to the French in 1723. With intentions of building a plantation at the White Apple village, De Chepart insolently ordered its chief to relocate his people. Looking for time and discerning the commandant's greed, the village council asked that their people "be allowed to stay in their village till harvest, and till they had time to dry their corn, and shake out the grain; on condition each hut of the village should pay him in so many moons . . . a basket of corn and a fowl." De Chepart predictably accepted the proposition.[36]

The village chiefs and elders assembled again, this time to plan their revenge. The head chief, or Sun, urged them to choose "the best means of how to get rid of your bad neighbors without hazard." "Before the French came amongst us," exclaimed another elder, "we were men, content with what we had" and "we walked with boldness every road." "But now," he continued, "we go groping, afraid of meeting thorns, we walk like slaves, which we shall soon be, since the French already treat us as if we were such." Warning that for the least fault the French would tie young Natchez people "and whip them as they do their black slaves," the stirring orator asked, "Is not death preferable to slavery?" Within a week of deliberation, the council settled on a plot to "cut off the French to a man, in one day and one hour"—that fixed by the French commandant for the payment of their tribute. Several warriors were to "carry him the corn, as the beginning of their several payments, also carry with them their arms, as if going out to hunt: and that to every Frenchman in a French house, there shall be two or three Natchez; to ask to borrow arms and ammunition for a general hunting-match, on account of a great feast, and to promise to bring them meat; the report of the firing at the Commandant's, to be the signal to fall at once upon, and kill the French: that then we shall be able to prevent those who may come from the old French village [New Orleans], by the great water [Mississippi] ever to settle here."[37]

With all villages consenting to this plan, the Natchez began their elaborate preparations for war. In each town the war chiefs erected two poles painted red and ornamented with red feathers, arrows, and tomahawks. Warriors enlisted by smearing their faces with various colors and declar-

36. Le Page Du Pratz, *History of Louisiana,* ed. Tregle, 78–81.
37. *Ibid.,* 81–84.

ing their desire to die for their nation. They then drank kettles of "war medicine," an emetic made from boiled roots. The ceremony was "to swallow them with a single effort, and then to throw up immediately by the mouth, with efforts so violent that they can be heard at a great distance." After they danced before the sacred temple, sang their death songs, and boasted of their previous war feats, warriors marched from the village in single file.[38]

Perhaps because of the ceremonial nature of Natchez war preparation, rumors of attack spread among settlers during the autumn months of 1729. But De Chepart confidently disregarded all warnings and, as reported by Diron d'Artaguette, even "put in irons seven colonists who had asked to assemble to forestall the disaster with which they were menaced." One colonist wrote to Governor Périer requesting arms for his slaves, and the Natchez themselves recruited "several negroes, among others those of the White Earth at the head of whom were the two foremen who gave the other negroes to understand that they would be free with the Indians." On the morning of November 28, 1729, the Natchez implemented their plan with deliberate speed. They deceived De Chepart and his wards with generous quantities of tribute and friendly promises of meat and furs. A familiar pattern of frontier exchange now served as a subterfuge of the Indians' rebellious design. Within hours Natchez warriors killed 145 men, 36 women, and 56 children and captured nearly 300 Negro slaves in addition to some 50 white women and children.[39]

V

The anxiety among colonial officials and planters over intercultural collusion and their means of domination came to a violent head over the months of conflict that followed this Natchez attack. Hoping to allay the fear stirred in the New Orleans area by news of an Indian massacre and to generate antagonism between Africans and Indians,

---

38. *Ibid.*, 370–373; Thwaites, ed., *Jesuit Relations*, LXVIII, 143–147. For analysis of the use of emetics in southeastern Indian rituals, see Charles M. Hudson, ed., *Black Drink: A Native American Tea* (Athens, Ga., 1979).

39. *MPAFD*, I, 54, 58, 62–63, 76; "Historical Memoirs of M. Dumont," in French, ed., *Historical Collections*, V, 77; Patricia Dillon Woods, *French-Indian Relations on the Southern Frontier, 1699–1762* (Ann Arbor, Mich., 1980), 95–96.

Governor Périer dispatched a group of armed black slaves downriver from the capital on December 5, 1729, to destroy the Chaouachas, a neighboring village of only thirty warriors. This expedition, according to his report, "kept the other little nations up the river in a respectful attitude." Commending the slaves for their prompt and secret mission, the governor boasted, "If I had been willing to use our negro volunteers I should have destroyed all these little nations which are of no use to us, and which might on the contrary cause our negroes to revolt." He did not further employ these black soldiers "for fear of rendering [them] . . . too bold and of inclining them perhaps to revolt after the example of those who joined the Natchez." Defying customary practices more than once during his troublesome governorship, Périer was criticized for his genocidal assessment of local Indians, who, in fact, were very useful to colonial Louisiana.[40]

Encouraging enmity between racial groups without delivering to any one of them enough power to overthrow the colonial order was indeed like walking a tightrope. As feared by slaveowners, many of the Negro slaves taken from the upriver concessions during the November 28 attack did serve as allies, more than as hostages, of the Natchez rebels. On January 27, 1730, five hundred Choctaws under Sieur Jean-Paul Le Seur besieged the Natchez, killing about one hundred warriors and recovering most of the white women and children and about a hundred slaves. But as later discovered by Périer, "this defeat would have been complete if it had not been for the negroes who prevented the Choctaws from carrying off the powder and who by their resistance had given the Natchez time to enter the two forts." On February 8 the Choctaws were joined by two hundred troops from New Orleans, including fifteen blacks, and a protracted bombardment of the Natchez forts with cannons soon began. By February 25, the Natchez agreed to return the remaining hostages to the French, who promised to stop the siege. Within a few days the Natchez managed to slip by the French and cross the Mississippi. As the colonial army pursued the Natchez into the Ouachita River basin, the Choctaws returned to their villages with about thirty of the Negroes released from the fort.[41]

Wanting to guarantee themselves some kind of indemnity for their

---

40. *MPAFD*, I, 64–65, 71.
41. *Ibid.*, I, 68–69, 79–80; Thwaites, ed., *Jesuit Relations*, LXVIII, 189.

military services to the colony, the Choctaws realized the market value of slaves to colonial Louisianians. Eager to regain these slaves, Louisiana officials quickly sent Captain Joseph Christophe de Lusser to the Choctaw nation to negotiate for them. In the town square of Oskilakna on March 14, 1730, the "little chief" of this village berated the French for their failure to "pay for the death of their warriors" and criticized the performance of their cannons, which "had made much noise, but had had little effect." Finally, this chief disclosed a more general source of Choctaw discontent by stating that the French, who seemed to be everywhere, "stole the skins of the Indians by not giving a fair compensation in their goods." The Choctaws evidently hoped to reverse what seemed like a declining trade position by bargaining over the return of the Negroes now in their custody.[42]

The fate of all those African-Louisianians captured by the Choctaws during the Natchez War is indeterminate, but available evidence about some illuminates how distressing the status of slavery was for people caught between colonial and Indian societies. Eventually, at least twenty were purchased back into the colony, by either the government or individuals. Others reportedly fled to the Chickasaw villages or were sold to English traders. At Mobile in late October 1730, Choctaw spokesmen told Governor Périer that several Negroes whom they tried to return to Louisiana "killed themselves on the way." In the following spring three blacks being taken to Mobile by a chief known as Alibamon Mingo asked Ensign Regis Du Roullet to take them because, they told him, "the Indians make us carry some packages, which exhausts us, mistreat us much, and have taken from us our clothing." The French officer noticed that one "had a tomahawk wound on the head which went as far as the bone."[43]

During the summer of 1730, while the French were mobilizing several regiments upriver against the Natchez, African-American slaves in the New Orleans area plotted their own rebellion for June. Hints of a slave conspiracy did not take long to appear, as on the day when a black woman, after "receiving a violent blow from a French soldier for refusing

42. *MPAFD*, I, 105, IV, 56.

43. *RSCLHQ*, III, 76, IV, 97; *MPAFD*, I, 185–187, IV, 54, 60, 65–69. The changing contexts of Indian-black relations are explored with great discernment in James H. Merrell, "The Racial Education of the Catawba Indians," *Journal of Southern History*, L (1984), 363–384.

to obey him," shouted that "the French should not long insult negroes." The leaders and the plot quickly became known. Their plan, according to Lieutenant Dumont, "was for each first to kill his master at night . . . then being masters of all the keys, they would soon have guns, powder and lead, which would enable them to get rid of the troops on guard without difficulty." The official version of what might have happened, which Périer received as a warning from a Negro "domestic servant of the town," was that all Bambara-speaking slaves would begin to burn down the city "when everybody would be at mass" and then take over the colony. Several black men, including the overseer of the company plantation named Samba Bambara, were broken on the wheel, and one of the women conspirators was "hanged before their eyes."[44] Meanwhile, the French sent three Negroes accused of playing "the most active part" in the Natchez revolt to be burned by the Choctaws. This effective use of a divide-and-rule policy, as reported from New Orleans by Father Mathurin Le Petit on July 12, 1730, "has inspired all the Negroes with a new horror of the Savages, but which will have a beneficial effect in securing the safety of the Colony."[45]

Governor Périer, by now under heavy criticism in France, attempted to avert responsibility for the crisis of 1729–1730 by inflating events into a conspiracy among the Natchez, Chickasaws, and even some Choctaws. Trepidation over Indian and slave conspiracies and suspicion of English interference fueled this belief among many Louisiana colonists, but officials both in the colony and at home recognized Périer's ambitions for a plantation at Natchez and refuted his justification for negligence and repression. His military campaign against the Natchez over the winter of 1730–1731 did little toward reversing his disrepute, but the governor did manage to capture some five hundred prisoners, mostly women and children. In what proved to be the waning months of its dominion in Louisiana, the Company of the Indies shipped these Natchez captives as slaves to the Caribbean. The question pronounced by one of their elders at the war council—"Is not death preferable to slavery?"—must have echoed through their minds during this painful exodus from their homeland.[46]

44. Le Page Du Pratz, *History of Louisiana*, ed. Tregle, 77–79; "Historical Memoirs of M. Dumont," in French, ed., *Historical Collections*, V, 99–100; *MPAFD*, IV, 82, 104.

45. Thwaites, ed., *Jesuit Relations*, LXVIII, 198.

46. *MPAFD*, IV, 57–58, 79, 102–105.

VI

Like major Indian wars in other North American colonial regions—Powhatan's War in Virginia (1622), the Pequot War in New England (1637), the Pueblo Revolt in New Mexico (1680), and the Tuscarora and Yamasee wars in South Carolina (1711–1715)—the hostilities that swept across Louisiana marked a significant impasse. With mounting anxiety, colonial officials warned their superiors about the need for more colonists and troops to overcome the province's vulnerability to native demands. "The least little nation thinks itself our protector," Périer reported in August 1730, "whereas if we had forces to sustain ourselves by our own efforts the greatest nations would respect us and would very carefully seek an alliance with us, which would be as honorable as it would be useful for them." The obstinate governor's appeal for additional troops, however, had little chance of improving Louisiana's marginal status in France's empire.[47]

As a result of the Natchez War, a troubled Company of the Indies returned its monopoly over Louisiana to the French government. Louis XV reappointed Bienville, who had been away from the colony for seven years, as governor to replace the disreputable Périer. In the eyes of French officials, the commercial potential of Louisiana took a backseat to its geopolitical function. But the turbulence at the end of the 1720s left people actually living in the Lower Mississippi Valley with a more enduring legacy. Although Indian trade continued to be economically and politically important to Louisiana, some Indian trade partners could be sacrificed for the sake of other interests. When the Natchez resisted encroachment by Louisiana's most promising settlement, they became a nuisance to the colony. So their violence was met by a colonial retaliation amounting to near extermination. Initiatives taken by African slaves during these years also alerted colonial inhabitants to other costs incurred while building a plantation society. In order to continue exploiting the labor of a black majority in a colony surrounded by an even larger Indian populace, Louisiana officials and planters had to rely upon their own efforts. They improvised ways to impose a racially divided law and order upon peoples who crossed all kinds of boundaries whenever it suited their interests.

47. *Ibid.*, IV, 39–40.

3

THE INDIAN ALLIANCE NETWORK OF

A MARGINAL EUROPEAN COLONY

During the middle third of the eighteenth century, seemingly distant and disparate developments were changing the face of North
America. Most Indian tribes situated on the beachheads of successful
colonial landings had already been reduced by epidemics and wars to
enclave or refugee communities. The Natchez in Louisiana shared this
fate, for example, with the Pequots and Narragansetts of New England
and the Piscataways and Nanticokes of the Chesapeake. Many Indian
nations in the colonial hinterlands, in contrast, competed or negotiated
successfully for economic advantages and political power, especially as fur
trade networks expanded inland up the major rivers. The Choctaws firmly
held this position in the Lower Mississippi Valley, resembling the Iroquois
nations in New York and the Cherokees in Carolina. The security of
Louisiana depended heavily upon stable trade alliances, especially with
the Choctaws, whom the commandant of troops at New Orleans called
"the bulwark of the colony" in 1746. "None of those who have come to
the country," he explained, "fail to be aware of the impossibility of
keeping a country as vast as the one we occupy with the few troops and
settlers who are there and who would soon be obliged to depart from it if
the Choctaws refused us their assistance and decided to act against us."[1]

---

1. *MPAFD,* IV, 262. Economic and political change among interior Indian nations
and along major trade networks is becoming more comprehensible to us because of
such important regional studies as Arthur J. Ray, *Indians in the Fur Trade: Their Role*

Unlike other fur trade networks, however, French Louisiana was unable to expand significantly the volume of commerce with Indians across its hinterland, including with the powerful Choctaws. "The true means, my lord," advised the governor in 1744, "of making this colony, which is one of the finest in the world, flourish and of deriving from it all the advantages that one ought to expect from it is to procure peace and to bring about union among the Indian nations that serve as a barrier on this continent." In order to achieve this goal, "it would be necessary that an advance be made to this colony of about 100,000 livres in well-selected trade goods, in addition to the quantity of them that comes every year." But in quality as well as quantity of merchandise, Louisiana suffered a chronic shortage in its supply of imported goods available for the Indian trade; government and merchants in France continued to give lower priority to this colony than to other American possessions.[2]

To compensate for this disadvantage in competition with superior and more abundant English trade goods, the French relied upon political strategies to maintain a stable network of relations with Indian nations. War against the Chickasaws was necessary, even when they eagerly sought peace with Louisiana, because colonial governors "found it impossible to supply them with the things they need."[3] Unable to increase the volume of merchandise needed to entice Chickasaws away from the British, Louisiana officials chose annually to distribute a selection of gifts to the Choctaws, Chickasaws, and other Indian allies in order to prevent additional English inroads. This effectively coincided with the Indians' traditional synthesis of economic and political exchange, but the emergence of a faction discontented over both the Chickasaw strategy and the trade

---

as Trappers, Hunters, and Middlemen in the Lands Southwest of Hudson Bay, 1660–1870 (Toronto, 1974); Elizabeth A. H. John, Storms Brewed in Other Men's Worlds: The Confrontation of Indians, Spanish, and French in the Southwest, 1540–1795 (College Station, Tex., 1975); Francis Jennings, The Ambiguous Iroquois Empire: The Covenant Chain Confederation of Indian Tribes with English Colonies from Its Beginnings to the Lancaster Treaty of 1744 (New York, 1984); Gary Clayton Anderson, Kinsmen of Another Kind: Dakota-White Relations in the Upper Mississippi Valley, 1650–1862 (Lincoln, Nebr., 1984). The best overview of comparative processes in and around the English North American colonies is still Gary B. Nash, Red, White, and Black: The Peoples of Early America, 2d ed. (Englewood Cliffs, N.J., 1982).

2. MPAFD, IV, 221–222.

3. MPAFD, IV, 230.

limitations of the French wreaked temporary havoc in the Choctaw nation during the late 1740s. Except for this crisis, however, the political network of Indian trade with Louisiana remained intact before 1762. Retrenchment of relations within a nonexpanding trade region, in fact, helped to insulate the Lower Mississippi Valley from the international tremors of King George's War (1744–1748) and the Seven Years' War (1755–1762). The scarcity of merchandise in colonial warehouses enfeebled overtures, made by Louisiana governors during those conflicts, to the Cherokees and other tribes outside the region and, thereby, minimized intercolonial hostility to the familiarly chronic, but not destructive, ventures of Carolina and Georgia traders.[4]

Louisiana's marginal position in the French overseas empire also inhibited commercialization of economic relations within colonial society. A deepening commercial integration of other colonies into the Atlantic system, mainly as producers or shippers of agricultural exports, sharpened divisions between classes and races in North America during the mid-eighteenth century. Economic pressures for expanding the production of specialized commodities heightened barriers between African-American slaves and Euro-American colonists and circumscribed activities formerly pursued by blacks and Indians in and around colonies. With increasing vigor, colonial governments legislated and enforced laws that denied slaves much of the mobility previously gained through hunting, gardening, or petty trading. Blacks were increasingly confined to plantation production of export crops. Services once rendered freely by Indians became less tolerable as increasing numbers of settlers assumed their roles in local marketing or transportation. Indian communities surrounded by settlements and plantations suffered greater marginalization, becoming impoverished enclaves racially isolated from colonial society.[5]

4. Marc de Villiers Du Terrage, *The Last Years of French Louisiana* (1904), ed. Carl A. Brasseaux and Glenn R. Conrad, trans. Hosea Phillips (Lafayette, La., 1982), 82–92, 122–137.

5. Analysis of the restrictions on blacks is most pronounced in Peter H. Wood, *Black Majority: Negroes in Colonial South Carolina from 1670 through the Stono Rebellion* (New York, 1974), 218–238, 272–284; Allan Kulikoff, *Tobacco and Slaves: The Development of Southern Cultures in the Chesapeake, 1680–1800* (Chapel Hill, N.C., 1986), 381–420. On Indians, see William Cronon, *Changes in the Land: Indians, Colonists, and the Ecology of New England* (New York, 1983), 54–81; James H. Merrell, *The Indians' New World: Catawbas and Their Neighbors from European Contact through the Era of Removal* (Chapel Hill, N.C., 1989), 167–225.

Although it partly shared these general developments, French Louisiana lagged behind other colonies because of the mother country's relative indifference toward investment and settlement in the Lower Mississippi Valley. Except for the periodic movement of troops into and out of the region, large-scale migration of Europeans to Louisiana stopped after the 1720s. Between the censuses of 1726 and 1732, at least 1,688 more Africans entered the colony. But from then until the 1760s, not more than 400 additional slaves were shipped to the Lower Mississippi Valley. Numbering approximately 4,100 slaves, 3,300 settlers, and 600 soldiers in 1746, Louisiana did not approach the region's potential for commercial agriculture and overseas commerce.[6] Praising the soil and climate, although "the summer is to tell the truth, a little too warm and stormy," General Commissioner Honoré Michel de La Rouvillière called his financial charge in 1752 "the best land that there is in the world and the finest colony that the King could possess," and then warned:

> His Majesty will have reason in the future to repent not having profited by the considerable advantages that he was able to get from it. A small expenditure seasonably made would produce great benefits for the state. You know, my lord, that one must sow in order to reap, and the expense is not great in consideration of the result. It is a question only of sending here some intelligent settlers for the land and plenty of negroes, together with some credit for those to whom they are distributed. Competition has been awakened among the people for some time. The settlers, impressed by his Majesty's first bounties, have come out of their lethargy. They are all asking for

6. AC, C13A, XXVIII, 84–85; N. M. Miller Surrey, *The Commerce of Louisiana during the French Régime, 1699–1763* (New York, 1916), 236–245. Various failed schemes to import more slaves to Louisiana are discussed in Jacob M. Price, *France and the Chesapeake: A History of the French Tobacco Monopoly, 1674–1791, and of Its Relationship to the British and American Tobacco Trades,* 2 vols. (Ann Arbor, Mich., 1973), I, 339–360.

1746 population: AC, C13A, XXVI, 138–139, XXX, 256–257. Individuals and families occasionally migrated to Louisiana, but most new households sprang from already-settled families or from discharged soldiers who decided to settle in the colony. During the 1750s about 100 Alsacians migrated to Louisiana. See Glenn R. Conrad, "L'immigration alsacienne en Louisiane, 1753–1759," *Revue d'histoire de l'Amérique française,* XXVIII (1974–1975), 565–577.

negroes and really cannot succeed without that. Things are moving along very well. The colony is growing every day by itself. It is necessary, so to speak, only to spur it on.[7]

Under continuing neglect from France, the inhabitants of the Lower Mississippi Valley were left to their own designs. Colonial officials worked hard at preserving the Indian trade network that linked the interior posts (sweeping from east to west in an arc around the region) of Fort Toulouse, Fort Tombecbé, Arkansas, and Natchitoches to the Gulf Coast. Leaders of the interior Indian nations struggled to secure access to both alliance gifts and trade goods. Meanwhile, Louisiana settlers slowly and steadily increased cultivation of agricultural staples, mainly tobacco and indigo, enjoying at least some price supports that buffered them from the Atlantic economy's boom-bust cycles. Slaves also took initiatives in deciding what to produce and how to trade within the still flexible limits of a frontier exchange economy.

I

After the Natchez War Louisiana officials stepped up their policy of intimidation against the Chickasaws as an integral means of protecting the colony's borders. "The province of Louisiana will never be tranquil," Périer warned Minister of Marine Jean Frédéric Maurepas, "until the Chickasaws have been destroyed or until they have been obliged to go and settle outside the lands of the province." Inhabiting about ten fortified villages on the pine-forested ridges between the upper Yazoo and Tombigbee rivers, the Chickasaw nation maintained a lasting alliance with the English colonies to the east and, therefore, posed a chronic threat to French control over the Lower Mississippi Valley. Unable to meet the Chickasaws' trade demands, Louisiana employed Choctaw warriors against their villages and English caravans. This policy also served to divert Choctaw military power from the vulnerable French colony, keeping it aimed conveniently against another Indian nation. As one official of the Company of the Indies advised in 1730, total destruction of the Chickasaws was not desirable, since "the Choctaws, who will no longer

7. *MPAFD,* V, 115–116.

have this powerful nation to fear, might themselves become too powerful and be disposed to abuse it."[8]

During the decade after 1731, when the company returned Louisiana to the king, France expended an exceptional amount of resources trying to reduce the Chickasaw people and the Natchez refugees whom they welcomed to their villages. By the time Bienville returned to Louisiana as royal governor in early 1733, the Natchez Indians had already been reduced to only a few bands of refugees. Those who survived Périer's expedition of 1730–1731, which resulted in countless deaths and the exportation of five hundred Natchez slaves to the Caribbean, dispersed themselves into three major groups. One group of Natchez settled in the upcountry forest behind the Tunicas, whom they attacked by surprise in June 1731, killing at least twenty men and capturing some eight women. Another group occupied the west bank of the Mississippi. The largest, numbering about seventy-five warriors, formed a new village among the Chickasaws. Together, bands of Natchez and Chickasaw warriors waged a guerrilla resistance to French colonization, attacking the annual convoys between New Orleans and Illinois and marauding outposts along the Mississippi.[9]

Bienville mobilized Choctaw war parties against Chickasaw towns and attempted other means of reducing the threat of another large-scale Indian war. But orders from Minister of Marine Maurepas to destroy both the Chickasaws and Natchez forced him to assemble soldiers and supplies for a full-scale military campaign into Chickasaw country.[10] In early April 1736, an army of 460 whites and 140 blacks ascended the Mobile River in some sixty boats and encamped at "a place called Tombecbé" in Choctaw country, where an advance company of soldiers had already begun to build a fort. Around a partial palisade and makeshift cabins, the troops "immediately began to make earthen ovens and bake bread." On this large bluff situated near present-day Epes, Alabama (some sixty miles south-

8. *Ibid.*, IV, 47, 105.

9. *Ibid.*, I, 196–199, 234–235, III, 530–531, 622–625, IV, 73, 77–79, 102–103, 111–113.

10. *Ibid.*, I, 222, 236–237, 259–260; AC, C13A, XIX, 167v–169. For a detailed examination of Bienville's efforts during the early 1730s to pacify Indian insurgents, which carefully demonstrates his reluctance to wage a full-scale war against the Chickasaws, see Michael J. Foret, "War or Peace?: Louisiana, the Choctaws, and the Chickasaws, 1733–1735," *LH*, XXXI (1990), 273–292.

west of Tuscaloosa), Governor Bienville organized a separate company of Negro soldiers, arming 45 freemen and slaves and appointing a few free blacks as officers. He then met with Alibamon Mingo and other Choctaw chiefs to smoke the calumet of peace, to deliver the goods promised "for serving the French as auxiliaries," and to plan a strategy for the march against the Chickasaws. By May 24 a combined force of more than 1,200 colonial soldiers and Choctaw warriors camped near the Chickasaw town of Ackia. But when it began to march against the well-defended Chickasaw forts, Bienville's army fell under heavy fire from warriors hidden in the wooded hills surrounding the villages. This flank attack killed at least 100 men and forced the invading troops to withdraw. On returning to New Orleans, Bienville learned that the army of Frenchmen and Indians from Illinois that was supposed to join his troops had earlier suffered an identical ambush by the skilled woodland fighters of the Chickasaw nation.[11]

Although this expedition cost the French Ministry of Marine more than 120,000 livres, Bienville began almost immediately to plan a second campaign. Once again the colony deployed Choctaw war parties to raid Chickasaw cornfields and hunting camps, but now it also sent reconnaissance parties directly up the Mississippi River in order to find the best possible route to the Chickasaw villages. Heavy flooding in the spring of 1737 and widespread destruction of crops by worms in both native and colonial fields delayed preparations for war. Once the expedition did get under way, soldiers faced all kinds of sickness and long months of waiting. Slowly ascending the Mississippi from New Orleans during the autumn of 1738, crewmen on a convoy of six boats fell ill from drinking too much river water. They began to recover near the mouth of the Yazoo River, where some buffalo were hunted for their "good and succulent" meat. This detachment spent a month at the Quapaw villages on the lower Arkansas River, seeking Indian recruits, who did not come easily. "We

11. Jean François Benjamin Dumont de Montigny, "Historical Memoirs of M. Dumont" (1753), in B. F. French, ed., *Historical Collections of Louisiana*, 5 vols. (New York, 1846–1853), V, 105–107; MPAFD, I, 299–300, 307–310. For details surrounding construction of Fort Tombecbé, see Joe Wilkins, "Outpost of Empire: The Founding of Fort Tombecbé and de Bienville's Chickasaw Expedition of 1736," in Philip P. Boucher and Serge Courville, eds., *Proceedings of the Twelfth Meeting of the French Colonial Historical Society, Ste. Geneviève, May 1986* (Lanham, Md., 1988), 133–153.

listen to the words of our father," one village chief explained to the commandant, "but you know that we are not the masters of our warriors. We speak to them, but we cannot compel them to listen to us." A series of councils finally produced twenty-one Quapaw volunteers. Further reconnaissance of approaches to the Chickasaw towns was hampered by rains and floods, which also made winter quartering in the St. Francis basin very unpleasant. Construction of Fort Assumption (near present-day Memphis) began in January. A baking oven was speedily completed, and fresh bread eaten on the seventeenth; two boatloads of salted meat arrived several days later from the Arkansas.[12]

By mid-November 1739 an army of one thousand French soldiers, five hundred Indians, and more than three hundred African-Americans was assembled at Fort Assumption. Facing this large and heavily armed invading force, which included even warriors from Canadian and Great Lakes tribes, the Chickasaws immediately began negotiating for peace. After only a few skirmishes in February 1740, seven chiefs agreed to cease attacks on the Mississippi River and to return all Natchez refugees found among their people on condition that the Louisiana governor prevent Indian war parties of the upper valley from further raiding their villages. Bienville welcomed this offer, because, as he later admitted, his massive army could not have marched against the Chickasaws with enough speed to prevent them from slipping out of their forts and into the countryside.[13] Louisiana, already feeling the strain of military mobilization upon food supplies and manpower, was not prepared to withstand the protracted war that would have ensued. The generous mobilization of men and equipment of Louis XV for this campaign ended up costing three times the colony's regular annual budget. The movement of such a large number of

12. *MPAFD*, I, 351, 353, III, 693, 702–705; Jean Delanglez, ed. and trans., "The Journal of Pierre Vitry, S.J., 1738–1740," *Louisiana Studies*, III (1964), 247–309, esp. 259–266.

13. *MPAFD*, I, 447–461. The perseverance of the Chickasaws and the effectiveness of their guerrilla warfare against the invading army have been neglected as important factors in the outcome of Bienville's campaigns. Cf. Norman Ward Caldwell, *The French in the Mississippi Valley, 1740–1750* (Urbana, Ill., 1941), 83: "The lateness of the season, the ravages of disease among the troops, the great difficulties of the terrain, and the procrastination of Bienville, who was in command, doomed the expedition to failure." Actual shortcomings in planning and organizing the expedition are examined in Michael J. Foret, "The Failure of Administration: The Chickasaw Campaign of 1739–1740," *Revue de Louisiane/Louisiana Review*, XI (1982), 49–60.

people, many having recently arrived from abroad, was spreading disease across the Lower Mississippi Valley.[14]

Both Chickasaw expeditions, like the earlier war against the Natchez, illustrate that military service constituted an important sphere of intercultural exchange among Indians, settlers, and slaves in the Lower Mississippi Valley. Before and after these campaigns, petites nations along the lower Mississippi River—Ofogoulas, Tunicas, Houmas, and Bayogoulas—regularly provided scouts to help guard routes to the settlements and to guide militia patrols. When the Tunica village had been attacked by Natchez refugees, Diron d'Artaguette expressed fear that its demise would expose New Orleans and the colony's most lucrative plantations to enemy attack. In 1750 Governor Philippe de Rigault de Vaudreuil persuaded a group of Bayogoulas or Ouachas to settle opposite the German Coast for the sole purpose of guarding that settlement against attacks by rebellious Choctaws.[15] Local Indian villagers also continued to capture runaway slaves for bounty. A group of Indians on patrol for Bienville in the spring of 1738 caught a runaway black named La Fleur, who accused his owners of not providing him with enough food. In 1748 Jean Deslandes of the German Coast hired an Indian to accompany ten of his slaves on an attack against a camp of armed runaways. The Indian fired at the planter's command and seriously wounded one of the marrons.[16]

American Indians' participation in major campaigns was motivated by an obligation inherent in their alliance with Louisiana and by a self-interest in the strategic and material results of military action. The Choctaws' service in the Chickasaw War of 1736, for example, resulted in the construction of Fort Tombecbé, fulfilling a decade-long promise by the French to establish a post near their villages. Indians received valuable

---

14. AC, C13A, XXIV, 200–201, XXV, 212. See John Brice Harris, *From Old Mobile to Fort Assumption: A Story of the French Attempts to Colonize Louisiana, and Destroy the Chickasaw Indians* (Nashville, Tenn., 1959); and Patricia Dillon Woods, *French-Indian Relations on the Southern Frontier, 1699–1762* (Ann Arbor, Mich., 1980), for narrative details on the Chickasaw wars. Tactics and equipment employed by the French are examined in Joseph L. Peyser, "The Chickasaw Wars of 1736 and 1740: French Military Drawings and Plans Document the Struggle for the Lower Mississippi," *JMH*, XLIV (1982), 1–25.

15. *MPAFD*, IV, 37, 77, V, 40, 49; "Historical Memoirs of M. Dumont," in French, ed., *Historical Collections*, V, 96–97.

16. *RSCLHQ*, III, 414, V, 593–594, XIX, 1087–1088.

merchandise for various kinds of military assistance, including the taking of scalps. By encouraging presentation of enemy scalps for rewards, colonial officials in North America actually helped transform a practice traditionally used by Indian warriors to display their individual courage and to acquire power from the enemy into an economic incentive to kill as many enemies as possible. During the 1730s and 1740s Choctaw soldiers employed by the French to raid Chickasaw villages carried hundreds of scalps, mostly pieces of a smaller number of scalps, to Mobile. Separating scalps into pieces might have been a customary means of sharing military glory or supernatural power, but Louisiana administrators accepted them from the Choctaws, as explained to Maurepas by Diron d'Artaguette, "to induce them by this indirect compensation to destroy our enemies by stimulating them with competition."[17]

African Louisianians also took an active part in frontier military affairs, some in alliance with rebellious Indians, as seen during the Natchez War, and others in the service of the colonial government. In the Senegal River region of West Africa, whence most Louisiana slaves came during the 1720s, Bambara men earned a reputation for their military prowess. Many found themselves working for the French as enslaved soldiers. Beginning with the Natchez and Chickasaw wars, a group of freed Negroes became a permanent part of the Louisiana militia force. Some fifty "negres libres" constituted a separate company in 1740. A captain of this elite military group named Simon had distinguished himself, in the opinion of colonial officers, during the campaign of 1736. As described by one observer of the Chickasaw ambush of the invading army, Simon "started at a run on foot to the height on which the fort lay, and though the Indians sallied out, and balls were raining around him, he held on, and reaching a troop of horses at pasture, picked out a fine mare, sprang on her back, and rode back to the camp unscathed."[18] Such impressive action on the battle-

17. *MPAFD*, III, 702–705, IV, 138. For a discussion of the traditional role of scalping and related elements of Indian warfare in the region, see Charles Hudson, *The Southeastern Indians* (Knoxville, Tenn., 1976), 239–257. Two important interpretations of the intercultural dimension of warfare can be found in Cornelius J. Jaenen, *Friend and Foe: Aspects of French-Amerindian Cultural Contact in the Sixteenth and Seventeenth Centuries* (Ontario, 1976), 120–152; and James Axtell, *The European and the Indian: Essays in the Ethnohistory of Colonial North America* (New York, 1981), 16–35, 207–241.

18. "Historical Memoirs of M. Dumont," in French, ed., *Historical Collections*, V, 111. For the military role of slave-soldiers in the 18th-century Senegal Valley, see

field earned freedom for a number of Negroes during the French period, and the possibility of emancipation continued to draw some slaves into service. Most of those who participated in Indian and intercolonial campaigns, however, were given no choice but to assist troops as laborers and fighters. The three hundred or more Negro slaves employed in the 1739–1740 Chickasaw expedition as rowers, builders, and soldiers returned as slaves to their owners' indigo and tobacco plantations.[19]

II

As the military bulwark to Louisiana's security and its most populous trade partner, the Choctaw nation held the most powerful position in the Lower Mississippi Valley network of alliance. Chickasaw raids against French convoys and settlements resumed shortly after the 1740 war. Louisiana still lacked the volume of trade goods needed to replace English traders in Chickasaw villages. Bienville, therefore, continued to rely upon the Choctaws to carry out intimidating raids, which he hoped would debilitate the Chickasaws and drive out English trading parties. The Choctaws had their own reasons for cooperating with this French policy, particularly the need to avenge the deaths of fellow tribespeople. Year after year war parties of Choctaws (some fifteen hundred warriors reportedly out in September 1742) raided Chickasaw cornfields and English trade caravans—occasionally led by French officers and traders.[20]

Warfare against the Chickasaws soon took its toll on Choctaw society and strained the tribe's political order. Cultivation of crops was often neglected because of untimely military forays. Ammunition took precedence over cloth, tools, and other commodities available through trade with Louisiana. French insistence that hostility be perpetuated and English enticement with attractive trade goods fueled the rise of a peace faction within the Choctaw nation. The establishment of Georgia just

Philip D. Curtin, *Economic Change in Precolonial Africa: Senegambia in the Era of the Slave Trade* (Madison, Wis., 1975), 35, 115, 143.

19. Roland C. McConnell, *Negro Troops of Antebellum Louisiana: A History of the Battalion of Free Men of Color* (Baton Rouge, La., 1968), 3–14. The role of blacks in the frontier warfare of another North American colony is examined in Wood, *Black Majority*, 124–130.

20. *MPAFD*, I, 338, III, 716, 773–774, IV, 168–169, 172, 187–188, 199–203.

below South Carolina in 1733 had expanded English competition for Upper Creek and Choctaw trade. A party of Choctaws visited the Savannah River as early as the summer of 1734. Three years later six Englishmen brought fourteen horseloads of merchandise into two Choctaw towns. By 1738 the war chief of one of these villages, who had also led the 1734 delegation to Georgia, began to negotiate with the Chickasaws. Known by the name of his political position, Shulush Houma (or Red Shoes), this veteran of the Chickasaw wars told a French surveyor that "for too long a time the French have been causing the blood of the Indians to be shed."[21]

Red Shoes' peace overtures to the Chickasaws heightened political tension inside the Choctaw nation. The fluid dispersal of power characterizing the Choctaws' government might have allowed them to resolve this dispute. But Louisiana officials relentlessly demanded that loyalty come from the entire Indian nation. Into the 1740s the country of the Choctaws, numbering more than twelve thousand people, encompassed about fifty separate villages, which were divided into three geographical clusters. The Okla Hannali, People of the Sixtowns, lived in the southern district along the branches of the Chickasawhay River. In the western district the Okla Falaya, or Long People, villages clustered around the upper reaches of the Pearl River. The Okla Tannap, People of the Opposite Side, inhabited the eastern villages along Sugarnoochee River and other creeks winding eastward into the Tombigbee River.[22]

The colonial government had long been trying to identify and support a central chief with enough authority to direct the Choctaw alliance with Louisiana. But the dispersal of real authority among village leaders persisted and forced the French to distribute gifts widely in order to guarantee Choctaw loyalty. "All the villages are so many little republics in which each one does as he likes," reported Father Michel Baudouin. As the Jesuit

21. *Ibid.*, III, 711, IV, 139, 151–152. Relations of early Georgia with Indians in the interior are discussed in Phinizy Spalding, *Ogelthorpe in America* (Chicago, 1977), 76–97.

22. *MPAFD*, I, 21–54, 81–117, 136–154; Relation de la Louisiane [ca. 1735] (anonymous MS), Edward E. Ayer Collection, Newberry Library, Chicago. Pp. 118–165 of the latter manuscript, which includes valuable information on the political geography of the Choctaws, have been translated and published in John R. Swanton, "An Early Account of the Choctaw Indians," American Anthropological Association, *Memoirs*, V (1918), 53–72.

missionary who lived at the Choctaw village of Chickasawhay throughout the 1730s and most of the 1740s, Baudouin witnessed closely the divisive influences that French policy had on Choctaw political behavior. The "dignity of the Great Chief" was established for only about a quarter-century, "and in order to give credit to the one who was invested with it he was given a very considerable annual present." The Great Chief then had to share this present with "the principal chiefs of the different Choctaw villages" if he wanted them to follow his decisions. "But since the French have multiplied the presents," Baudouin noticed, "those who receive them directly from the French concern themselves very little about the Great Chief of their nation whose power they do not fear."[23]

By the 1740s a tribal chief, three district chiefs, war chiefs, dozens of village chiefs, and all their military and ceremonial assistants—more than one hundred men altogether—were attending annual meetings with colonial officials in Mobile as representatives of the Choctaw nation. Groups of emissaries usually traveled to Mobile either before the planting season or after harvest time in order to receive their presents, valued at more than fifty thousand livres by midcentury and often presented personally by the governor. Before entering the colonial town, they requested bread and brandy and received them in proportion to their numbers at the Mobilian Indian village, which served as a way station for Indians visiting Mobile.

23. *MPAFD*, I, 156, 194–195. Ethnographic data on Choctaw organization are compiled in John R. Swanton, *Source Material for the Social and Ceremonial Life of the Choctaw Indians*, Bureau of American Ethnology Bulletin, no. 103 (Washington, D.C., 1931), 55–102. Eighteenth-century Europeans commonly used the word *nation* to define political units observed among American Indians. *Tribe* is a modern anthropological concept applied to societies considered to be at a particular stage in political evolution, that is, somewhere between loosely connected bands of people and a centrally organized state. This static perspective misses an important historical dimension of tribalism, which the evidence here regarding the Choctaws suggests. The Choctaws identified and governed themselves as a separate society largely by kinship and language ties extending from village to village. Colonialism, however, created pressures that for the first time required a more centralized and stratified form of government to deal with European states. For a treatment of tribalism as a historical process rather than an evolutionary stage, see Morton H. Fried, *The Notion of Tribe* (Menlo Park, Calif., 1975). The forms of government that existed among American Indians before European contact varied considerably, from the autonomous towns of the Pueblos to the elaborate confederacy of the Iroquois.

On the following day they dressed in ceremonial clothes and accompanied an interpreter to the commandant. Each member of the band shook the commandant's hand, after which they smoked a pipe and made speeches. The Indians then withdrew to outlying woods while their guns were repaired and their gifts gathered. As soon as one band departed, another arrived. This process continued for three to six weeks and cost the commandant dearly, since he was obliged to share food and drink at his own table with the more distinguished members of each party.[24]

When ten or so Choctaw villages in the western district began openly to advocate peace with the Chickasaws and seek trade with the English, the Great Chief had the precarious responsibility of keeping them faithful to the French alliance. After a war party from the southern towns killed an esteemed Chickasaw leader in November 1738, a western Choctaw who happened to be in that chief's village during the raid sent several sympathetic warriors to "avenge this death." Fighting broke out among Choctaw villages. By the spring of 1739, however, order was restored when Choulkoulakta, war chief for the eastern district, organized a coalition of village war parties to raid the Chickasaws. Unfortunately, one of these parties mistakenly attacked some Abehkas, setting off a brief conflict with this Upper Creek tribe. Red Shoes, meanwhile, returned from a visit to the English displeased. He moved to oust the few English traders dealing in his village and then renewed his allegiance to French Louisiana by resuming hostilities against the Chickasaws. Bienville did not miss the opportunity, however, to "reproach him publicly" when Red Shoes and other chiefs met in Mobile during the winter of 1740–1741 to receive presents due them for two years.[25]

The internal consensus seemingly restored to the Choctaw nation in

24. *MPAFD*, IV, 215–216; Relation de la Louisiane, 121–125. For the most penetrating analysis of Choctaw-French diplomacy ever attempted, see Patricia K. Galloway, "The Barthelemy Murders: Bienville's Establishment of the *Lex Talionis* as a Principle of Indian Diplomacy," in E. P. Fitzgerald, ed., *Proceedings of the Eighth Annual Meeting of the French Colonial Historical Society* (Lanham, Md., 1985), 91–103; Galloway, "Talking with Indians: Interpreters and Diplomacy in French Louisiana," in Winthrop D. Jordan and Sheila L. Skemp, eds., *Race and Family in the Colonial South* (Jackson, Miss., 1987), 109–129; Galloway, " 'The Chief Who Is Your Father': Choctaw and French Views of the Diplomatic Relation," in Peter H. Wood *et al.*, eds., *Powhatan's Mantle: Indians in the Colonial Southeast* (Lincoln, Nebr., 1989), 254–278.

25. *MPAFD*, III, 722–731, 740; AC, C13A, XXV, 69.

1741 immediately lurched into another series of disruptive events. A smallpox epidemic "carried off many of their children" in the spring of 1742, on the heels of a year of costly fighting against the Chickasaws. Choctaw society was spinning in a traumatic pirouette of disease, warfare, and food shortage, as raids against Chickasaw villages and English caravans kept men from their fields and deadly microbes on the move.[26] In 1744 an acute shortage of trade merchandise caused some villages to welcome English traders and thus revived general agitation and division over the French alliance. Governor Philippe de Rigault de Vaudreuil, successor to Bienville, was intensifying pressure on the Choctaws to wage war against the Chickasaws, since a shortage of trade goods continued to plague Louisiana's Indian policy. Weary of fighting for the colony's security, Choctaw diplomats berated the French for not facing the Chickasaws themselves. Some Choctaws told Vaudreuil in October 1745 that the Chickasaws "are our enemies as well as theirs, and that for a number of years they have been bearing arms against a nation that has never done anything to them except to have been unfaithful to the French."[27]

To make matters worse, Louisiana received in the fall of 1745 a new general commissioner, Sebastien-François Ange Lenormant, assigned the task of cutting the colony's expenses. The *commissaire ordonnateur* immediately raised the price of merchandise sold by the crown to traders and soldiers from 50 percent to 100 percent above cost in France and ordered post commandants to cut back on the gifts distributed to Indian allies. The Choctaws stood to lose much by the higher cost of already scarce European merchandise; soldiers and traders exchanged imported goods for corn and deerskins with Indians around Fort Tombecbé. "We cannot carry on trade there on that basis," Governor Vaudreuil warned, "without running the risk of disgusting this nation with the French, and it would ask for nothing better than to have such pretexts in order to resort to the English." The scarcity and expense of imported trade goods was exacerbated by the outbreak of King George's War in Europe.[28]

26. *MPAFD*, III, 758–759, 765–767, 769. Other epidemics among the Choctaws over the mid-18th century are reported in AC, C13A, XIII, 173–178, XVIII, 153v–156; *MPAFD*, I, 183–184, IV, 58–60, 313. Choctaw spokesmen frequently requested the French to postpone or in some cases hurry military expeditions so that they could plant their crops. For examples, see *MPAFD*, I, 146; *SMV*, I, 419.

27. *MPAFD*, IV, 217, 230, 244.

28. *MPAFD*, IV, 246, 250–251.

III

The spark that ignited war inside the Choctaw nation occurred in August 1746. Three Frenchmen who were trading in the village
of Couechitto—a gentleman cadet named Verbois, a trader named Petit,
and a soldier named Replinque—were killed by Red Shoes' warriors, and
all other traders were driven from the western district.[29] Governor Vaudreuil responded by rushing Jadart de Beauchamp, major of the Mobile
garrison, into the southern district of the Choctaws to demand "three
heads, indiscriminately, for the three Frenchmen whom the rebel had
had assassinated." Leaders from villages throughout the nation met with
Beauchamp at Chickasawhay. Many chiefs and captains confirmed their
loyalty to the French and elaborated on their dependence upon the colony
for munitions and other merchandise. But these spokesmen unanimously
pleaded that they were unable to meet the governor's demand. On October 3 Alibamon Mingo from the eastern district, a chief unquestionably
loyal to the Louisiana government, argued that "he could not give us the
satisfaction . . . fearing to be attacked by the whole nation," and that "it
was necessary to wait for the chiefs of the western part, who are most
concerned with this affair." Speaking to the French officer six days later,
the western chiefs likewise conceded a lack of enough power to attack the
party under Red Shoes and urged the French to be patient. Despite caution
shown by Choctaw leaders over the risk of causing civil war by appeasing
the French, the conflagration began in June 1747. Encouraged by the
colony's offer of a bounty for the head of the rebel chief, a young Choctaw

---

29. *MPAFD*, IV, 299, 312–314. One of the most important conflicts in the colonial
South, the Choctaw War has gone largely unnoticed by historians until recently.
Charles W. Paape, "The Choctaw Revolt, a Chapter in the Intercolonial Rivalry in the
Old Southwest" (Ph.D. diss., University of Illinois, Urbana, 1946), remains the only
full-length study of the often contradictory details of the war. Two essays have mark-
edly advanced our understanding of this conflict: Richard White, "Red Shoes: Warrior
and Diplomat," in David G. Sweet and Gary B. Nash, eds., *Struggle and Survival in
Colonial America* (Berkeley, Calif., 1981), 49–68; and Patricia Galloway, "Choctaw
Factionalism and Civil War, 1746–1750," *JMH*, XLIV (1982), 289–327. Galloway
has further contributed through her splendid translation and annotation of documents
in vols. IV and V of the *Mississippi Provincial Archives: French Dominion*, which she
edited in 1984.

warrior assassinated Red Shoes while he was on an escort mission for an English trader.[30]

The ensuing revolt of western Choctaw villages spiraled violently into intratribal revenge warfare and quickly spread to the colonial populace. In addition to raids around Natchez and Mobile, Choctaw warriors attacked the German settlement above New Orleans in the spring of 1748, killing a settler and capturing his wife, daughter, and five slaves. By April a colonial force of about fifty soldiers and militiamen marched after the raiders. Across Lake Pontchartrain from New Orleans, this detachment mistook a peaceful Choctaw hunting camp for the rebels and opened fire in panic. Not until one soldier was killed and another two wounded did the two sides calm down. The head of the Choctaw party apologized for the incident, but argued that some runaway Negroes had actually fired the fatal shots. Groups of slave marrons were indeed camped in the area.[31]

Literally caught in the crossfire of slave resistance and Indian war, a young Louisiana-born Negro named François had recently fled into the woods behind the Boisclair plantation. His crossing of paths with Choctaw rebels offers a passing glimpse at the persistent network of marronage that many Louisiana slaves entered and left during the eighteenth century. François had been sold to a New Orleans merchant and did not want to leave family and friends. Running away, he survived in the forest by taking provisions from the slave cabins and milking his former owner's cows. In May 1748 he met five other runaway blacks, some of whom had come downriver from Pointe Coupée. Together they fed off cattle and poultry stolen from farms in the German Coast settlement. François soon joined up with a Chickasaw Indian named Joseph, a slave captured in one of the many raids against his people and now determined to return to them. Joseph, a Negro named Cezard, and an Indian woman had earlier rowed a pirogue into Lake Pontchartrain. At Bayou Tchefuncte these marrons were hailed by a band of about ten Choctaw rebels en route to raid the German Coast. Fearing the consequences of such an open attack against the French, Joseph separated himself from these warriors and was eventually captured along with François.[32]

30. MPAFD, IV, 269–297 (Alibamon Mingo's speech at 278), 311, 329; AC, C13A, XXXI, 98–101.

31. MPAFD, IV, 318–321.

32. RSCLHQ, XIX, 768–771.

When this war party of Choctaws returned from the German Coast to their villages of Couechitto and West Abeca, they were killed by pro-French members of their tribe. This was a typical incident in the vicious cycle of raids and counterraids committed between Choctaw factions over the next two years. The governor of Louisiana insisted throughout the war that all villages from which Choctaw raiders came must be destroyed. The bounty offered for enemy scalps was tripled. During the winter of 1748–1749, Vaudreuil received from the Choctaws at Mobile more than a hundred scalps and the heads of three men, allegedly chiefs responsible for starting the revolt. At the next annual meeting held in April 1750, he received another 130 scalps and the heads of three English traders and demanded that the two remaining pro-English towns of Caffetalaya and Cushtusha be destroyed.[33] Describing a battle fought the following August, two English packhorsemen reported that some pro-French warriors, "accompanied with eight French Men and two Negroes," surprised the pro-English group at the fort of Cushtusha, "which Engagement continued a Day and a half and the French Party being warmly received, retreated with the Loss of ten of their Men, and eight of ours, besides wounded on both Sides." Finally, the commandant of Fort Tombecbé led his garrison and about nine hundred loyal Choctaw warriors against both Caffetalaya and Cushtusha and forced the much-weakened rebels to surrender by November of 1750.[34]

The Choctaw War was a costly test of Louisiana's ability to preserve its Indian alliance network against great odds. Its marginality in the French empire made the Lower Mississippi Valley easy prey for aggressive English traders. Unable to import enough merchandise to trade equally with all Indian villages in the region, the Louisiana government resorted to a policy of generating splits not only between tribes but within tribes in order to counteract British infiltration. Situated on the Atlantic coast, the colonial governments of South Carolina and Georgia actively supported the extension of English commerce into as many villages within the French colonial sphere as possible. The limitations of Great Britain's geographical reach, however, became tragically apparent to the pro-English Choctaws

33. *MPAFD*, IV, 323, V, 15–25, 30, 40, 41–50, 136–137.

34. William L. McDowell, Jr., ed., *Documents Relating to Indian Affairs, May 21, 1750–August 7, 1754*, Colonial Records of South Carolina, 2d Ser. (Columbia, S.C., 1958), 40; *MPAFD*, V, 60–61; Paape, "Choctaw Revolt," 133–134.

when the depletion of ammunition from English traders forced them to defend their villages with bullets made from clay as well as with bows and arrows.[35] By the 1750s Louisiana managed to secure most of the Lower Mississippi Valley for its own limited trade. The Choctaw nation, Vaudreuil reported after spending more than two months with its representatives in Mobile, "is truly committed to remaining attached to us and to subscribing blindly to what we demand of it, provided, however, that we put it in the position of wanting nothing in regard to its needs." The English colonies, on the other hand, continued their commerce with the Chickasaws and made periodic inroads into some Upper Creek and Choctaw towns.[36]

Conflicts inside and between Indian nations have too often been interpreted as signs of cultural or political inferiority among Native Americans. But when examined closely in fuller context, such events as the Choctaw War disclose indomitable tribal independence in face of relentless European intervention. In Louisiana and other American colonies, officials patronized those chiefs most amenable to their interests, intensifying factionalism within Indian politics. Gift-giving, a native ceremonial institution designed to reaffirm alliances, became an instrument with which colonial governments bought services from Indian leaders. Loyal chiefs wore medallions engraved with the profiles of European rulers, which served as symbols of political allegiance between colony and village. Trade imposed a myriad of pressures upon Indian societies in North America. Villages, bands, and communities everywhere competed for highly prized European merchandise. Native groups vied for lucrative middleman positions between European traders and other Indians. Conflicts in the Lower Mississippi Valley during the mid-eighteenth century resulted largely from a struggle within and among Indian tribes over a relatively short supply of goods available in the regional trade network.

The Choctaw nation recovered from four years of civil war with re-

35. James Adair, *The History of the American Indians; Particularly Those Nations Adjoining to the Mississippi, East and West Florida, Georgia, South and North Carolina, and Virginia* . . . (London, 1775), 354. Adair, a trader to the Chickasaws between 1744 and 1768, was probably the most active Carolinian to encourage Red Shoes and other Choctaw leaders to replace French trade with English trade.

36. MPAFD, V, 111; Wilbur R. Jacobs, ed., *The Appalachian Indian Frontier: The Edmund Atkin Report and Plan of 1755* (Lincoln, Nebr., 1967), 43, 73.

markable political resilience. Under the leadership of Alibamon Mingo, the tribe resumed its regular commerce with the French and held on to its linchpin position in the Indian trade network of Louisiana. "As long as the Choctaws remain faithful to us," the official report on the 1750 peace treaty stated, "they will overawe the other nations." The Choctaws nevertheless continued to employ French-English competition to bargain for better terms. Meeting with Choctaw dignitaries in the summer of 1753, a new governor of Louisiana, Louis Billouart de Kerlérec, reproached "the facility with which they received the English traders." The Choctaw spokesmen, in turn, reminded him that the French "were the first to be in the wrong, since although we were the first Europeans whom they had known and who made them subject to the different needs that they can no longer now do without, we are no longer attentive, or at least not so much so as the English, to procuring for them in abundance everything that has become necessary for them for the trade."[37] Throughout the 1750s Choctaw villagers demanded more trade merchandise from Louisiana officials and produced more deerskins for exportation than did any other tribe in the region. Although many skins continued to reach English traders and the French always lagged behind in their gift obligation, the Choctaws maintained steady trade relations with Louisiana until the Lower Mississippi Valley underwent an intercolonial repartition in 1762–1763.[38]

IV

Over the mid-eighteenth century the Alibamon, Tallapoosa, and Abehka nations maintained trade ties with Louisiana but managed to

37. MPAFD, V, 59, 129–30. Although his analysis minimizes the economic role of the Choctaws in colonial Louisiana, Richard White also demonstrates the success of what he aptly calls the "Choctaw play-off system" in his formidable Roots of Dependency: Subsistence, Environment, and Social Change among the Choctaws, Pawnees, and Navajos (Lincoln, Nebr., 1983), 34–68. White boldly argues that factionalism preserved Choctaw autonomy by facilitating exchange with both the French and the English without leading the nation into complete dependence on either.

38. MPAFD, V, 115, 183. The Seven Years' War of 1754–1762, known as the "French and Indian War" in some places, had negligible effect on trade and other Indian affairs within the Lower Mississippi Valley. Most of the fighting between Europeans and Indians in the South took place among the Cherokees. See John Richard Alden, John Stuart and the Southern Colonial Frontier: A Study of Indian Relations, War,

remain politically neutral in the French and British tug-of-war for their loyalty. These Indians lived in thirty or so villages along the Coosa and Tallapoosa rivers to the east of the Choctaws. One count from the 1730s listed fifteen Tallapoosa towns with 475 warriors, six Abehka towns with 230 warriors, and six Alibamon towns with 160 warriors. Alliance with these populous and productive villages was keenly desired by colonies on both the Atlantic and Gulf coasts. The Alibamons became the most deeply integrated into the French colonial region, beginning with the construction of Fort Toulouse in 1717. At this nexus of trade, Indians exchanged peltry and food with soldiers and traders and received gifts and hospitality from the post commandants.[39]

But the Alibamons, like the Tallapoosas and Abehkas, kept trade avenues to the English open as well. They intermittently permitted Englishmen to bring their superior and lower-priced goods into the villages while negotiating repeatedly for better terms of trade with the French.[40] They never missed an opportunity to rebuke Louisiana officials for the relative inferiority and scarcity of French merchandise. Reporting in early 1744 that the Tallapoosa villages were asking for several traders, Vaudreuil added, "The Indians see few of our trade goods and as what is sent there in the largest quantities is powder and bullets and guns that are usually rather poor—for a thousand that are sent to this colony, five hundred will always be damaged—that convinces them that the French are entirely poor and do not know how to make goods as the English do."[41]

Partly compensating for Louisiana's uncompetitive situation in Upper Creek country was its provisioning of armaments and, perhaps more reliably, of alcohol to Indian villagers. Explaining why "these Indians do

Trade, and Land Policies in the Southern Wilderness, 1754–1775 (Ann Arbor, Mich., 1944), 38–136. For a study that significantly advances our understanding of Indian-European diplomatic relations across the Southeast, see Michael James Foret, "On the Marchlands of Empire: Trade, Diplomacy, and War on the Southeastern Frontier, 1733–1763" (Ph.D. diss., College of William and Mary, 1990).

39. Relation de la Louisiane. Diplomacy and trade among the Upper Creeks are closely examined in Gregory A. Waselkov *et al., Colonization and Conquest: The 1980 Archaeological Excavations at Fort Toulouse and Fort Jackson, Alabama* (Montgomery, Ala., 1982), 43–101.

40. *MPAFD*, IV, 170, 220–221, 223, 245–246; William L. McDowell, Jr., ed.. *Documents Relating to Indian Affairs, 1754–1765*, Colonial Records of South Carolina, 2d Ser. (Columbia, S.C., 1970), 62–71.

41. *MPAFD*, III, 652–653, IV, 223.

not restrict themselves to commerce with the English . . . and do not abandon the French entirely," Louisiana officials revealed in 1743 the key to their success: "That would doubtless happen if the Indians were not obliged to resort to us for powder and lead, which they obtain with great difficulty from the English, in addition to the liquor, which is brought to them from here in abundance and which, nevertheless, causes a very bad result, since this drink makes them savage and since it is often the cause of fights, not only among themselves, but also with the French who trade it to them and whom they mob when they refuse it to them."[42] Brandy and rum proved to be effective but also destructive substitutes for other, scarcer, trade goods. Addiction to alcohol kept Indians attached, and even indebted, to French traders, who otherwise offered them a skimpier array of merchandise than did the English. The Jesuit chaplain stationed at Fort Toulouse was recalled to New Orleans in 1745 protesting excessive trade in alcohol, and six years later another priest went there and resumed the futile campaign against this abuse. Describing the Alibamons, Tallapoosas, and Abehkas in 1750, Governor Vaudreuil regretted "that some of them are perishing every day because of the illness that is caused them by the trade in liquor," but confessed that it "cannot be suppressed because of the want of merchandise of the qualities [that we have] long asked for without being able to obtain them."[43]

There were some benefits to be gained, however, by the Upper Creeks' neutral position between the French and British empires. They avoided the kind of dependency that dragged the Choctaws into civil war and maximized the opportunity to make themselves indispensable to parties contending for alliance. While a group of Shawnees in 1737 attempted to establish an accord between the Cherokees and the Alibamons, one considered by the French to be detrimental to Louisiana's security, the Alibamon war chief Pacana was negotiating a prisoner exchange with the Chickasaws for the colony. When the Abehkas and Tallapoosas fell into revenge-driven warfare with some Choctaws in 1743–1744 and again in 1751–1752, the French mediated a settlement. In the latter instance

42. MPAFD, IV, 208–209, V, 47.

43. Reuben Gold Thwaites, ed., *The Jesuit Relations and Allied Documents: Travels and Explorations of the Jesuit Missionaries in New France, 1610–1791*, 73 vols. (Cleveland, Ohio, 1900), LXIX, 205; Jean Delanglez, *The French Jesuits in Lower Louisiana (1700–1763)* (Washington, D.C., 1935), 485–487; MPAFD, IV, 146, V, 47.

Governor Vaudreuil persuaded the Choctaws that destroying the Chick-asaws was of greater importance, but confided to Minister of Marine Antoine Louis Rouillé, "As it is the policy of this government that the Choctaws never be perfectly united with the Abehkas and Tallapoosas, nations that are naturally restless and turbulent because of the English, I thought I ought not to extinguish completely the resentment of the for-mer." Upper Creek villagers stayed out of the Choctaw War, but served as middlemen between Choctaws and Englishmen over the ensuing year. In early October 1757, according to three English traders, "some Chactaws arrived at the Alabama Towns in the Upper Creeks to the Number of fifty Men or upwards, brought with them Parcells of Deer Skins, with an Intent to trade with the English Traders in that Nation, but that the French at the Alabama Fort had Influence sufficient over them (the Chactaws) to pre-vent their coming personally to lay out their Deer Skins with the English traders, though very desirous, and persuaded the Chactaws to sell their Deer Skins to the Albama Indians for their old Cloaths with which those Indians procured new ones of the English traders."[44]

In the long run, the most important development on this periphery of the Lower Mississippi Valley was the growth in population and power that began for the Upper Creeks during the mid-eighteenth century. Like other Indian nations in the region, the Alibamons, Tallapoosas, and Abeh-kas gradually acquired a stronger immunity to foreign diseases with each passing epidemic. But through adoption of Natchez, Shawnees, and other refugee Indian groups and avoidance of large-scale war, numbers in these tribes started to rise at an exceptional rate. By 1764, thirty-nine different Upper Creek towns contained 2,625 warriors, which translates into a total population of perhaps 9,000 men, women, and children.[45]

This growing population of Upper Creeks met old and new challenges by collaborating more frequently with Indian neighbors along the Chat-tahoochee River. These Muscogee villages, known to the French as the Caouitas or Kawitas (after the central town of Coweta), dealt principally

44. MPAFD, IV, 146–151, V, 112–113; McDowell, ed., *Documents Relating to Indian Affairs, 1754–1765*, 423.

45. Ress en Sement Des Villages Sauvages de la Poste des Alybamons. Enclosed in Majr Farmar's letter of Jan. 24, 1764, *MPAED*, I, 94–97. For the immigration of the Shawnees into Upper Creek country, see *MPAFD*, IV, 48–49, 222. Also see Jacobs, ed., *Edmund Atkin Report*, 42.

with the English colonies of South Carolina and Georgia. Mounting pressures from westward-migrating settlers and increasing abuses from traders elicited shared responses from peoples who were now becoming known as Upper and Lower divisions of a formative Creek Confederacy. In 1756 the French hosted a conference at Fort Toulouse, attended by both Lower and Upper Creek villagers and even by some Overhill Cherokees who together proclaimed common grievances against the English. On November 3 of that same year, Upper Creek towns assembled as "the Mouth of the Nation," perhaps for the first time, to negotiate with Georgia officials at Savannah. With their economic ties to the Alibamons under greater stress, French traders stepped up their "infamous commerce" in liquor while Louisiana officials struggled to "furnish to the Alibamon nations the trade and assistance which they demand."[46]

v

Indian nations west of the Mississippi strengthened their connections with colonial Louisiana under a combination of circumstances somewhat different from those east of the river. The Atakapas and Opelousas, living in the bayou and prairie country south of Red River, appealed to the colonial government in the early 1730s to send traders into their villages. In exchange for European merchandise, they offered peltries, bear oil, and even horses. The crown encouraged Bienville to investigate the prospects for trade with them; rumors that the Atakapas were cannibals had caused only momentary hesitation. By 1738 French traders were dealing regularly with both groups. In 1754 Joseph Blanpain

46. McDowell, ed., *Documents Relating to Indian Affairs, 1754–1765,* 253–255; Woods, *French-Indian Relations,* 161–165; AC, C13A, XLII, 61–62. The fullest study of the evolution of the Creek Confederacy and its relations with the English during this formative period is James F. Doster, *The Creek Indians and Their Florida Lands, 1740–1823,* 2 vols. (New York, 1974), I, 31–66. Also see John R. Swanton, *Early History of the Creek Indians and Their Neighbors,* Bureau of American Ethnology Bulletin, no. 73 (Washington, D.C., 1922), 97–109. The cultural and political life of the Creek people during the 18th century is reconstructed with fresh insight in Michael D. Green, *The Politics of Indian Removal: Creek Government and Society in Crisis* (Lincoln, Nebr., 1982), 1–36; and Joel W. Martin, *Sacred Revolt: The Muskogees' Struggle for a New World* (Boston, 1991).

even tried to establish a post near the disputed St. Bernard Bay, where he was arrested by Spanish soldiers from the presidio of San Xavier. Upon his release, Blanpain settled for periodic trade excursions to the westernmost Atakapas and to other coastal Texas groups. But Atakapa and Opelousa villages located east of the Sabine River remained firmly within the trade network of Louisiana.[47]

The French traded with a number of different Indian groups along the Red River. Situated closest to its confluence with the Mississippi, the Avoyelles became well known, in the words of Antoine Le Page Du Pratz, "for the services they have done the colony by the horses, oxen, and cows they have brought from New Mexico." Their extensive travels and intimate contact with Europeans and other Indians along the Red River, however, exposed this small tribe to debilitating viruses and liquor, and by the 1750s their village was abandoned. Louisiana traders at Natchitoches gathered peltry and food from several Caddoan-speaking villages in the vicinity and traveled up to the Great Bend of the Red River to trade with the Kadohadachos. Meanwhile, missionaries from Mexico extended their activities into the Hasinai villages between the Sabine and Trinity rivers. These Indians consequently developed no formal ties with Louisiana, although Spanish and French officials cooperated in the maintenance of peaceful relations in this border zone.[48]

---

47. *MPAFD*, I, 204, III, 556; Mathé Allain and Vincent H. Cassidy, "Blanpain, Trader among the Attakapas," *Attakapas Gazette*, III (December 1968), 32–38; AC, C13A, XXXVIII, 136–140v.

48. Antoine Le Page Du Pratz, *Histoire de la Louisiane . . .* , 3 vols. (Paris, 1758), I, 297–298, II, 241–242; *MPAFD*, V, 213, 529–530. For general ethnohistorical information on the Caddoes and Hasinais, see John R. Swanton, *Source Material on the History and Ethnology of the Caddo Indians,* Bureau of American Ethnology Bulletin, no. 132 (Washington, D.C., 1942), 56–73; Helen Hornbeck Tanner, *The Territory of the Caddo Tribe of Oklahoma* (New York, 1974), 19–62; Don G. Wyckoff and Timothy Baugh, "Early Historic Hasinai Elites: A Model for the Material Culture of Governing Elites," *Midcontinental Journal of Archaeology,* V (1980), 225–288; Russell M. Magnaghi, "Changing Material Culture and the Hasinai of East Texas," *Southern Studies,* XX (1981), 412–426; Herbert Eugene Bolton, *The Hasinais: Southern Caddoans as Seen by the Earliest Europeans,* ed. Russell M. Magnaghi (Norman, Okla., 1987). Spanish missionary activities in eastern Texas are summarized in James E. Corbin, "Spanish-Indian Interaction on the Eastern Frontier of Texas," in David Hurst Thomas, ed., *Columbian Consequences,* I, *Archaeological and Historical Perspectives on the Spanish Borderlands West* (Washington, D.C., 1989), 269–276.

As the Red River Indian allies of French Louisiana entered the second half of the eighteenth century, they found themselves being joined by new Indian neighbors and began to reorganize their own communities for better defense. The proliferation of European merchandise around the settlement of Natchitoches attracted other Indians into the exchange network of the Lower Mississippi Valley. Since the early decades of colonization, French explorers and traders had made occasional expeditions to Wichita and Comanche villages in the western interior, but now groups of these southern plains people began to move themselves closer to the Red River. From the 1740s to 1760s, most of the Wichita villages that had occupied the upper Arkansas River valley migrated into the trade zone of Natchitoches. The Tawakonis established their village on the upper Sabine River. The Taovayas, Iscanis, and a few smaller Wichita bands relocated on the Red River about a hundred miles west of the Kadohadachos. All four clusters of Indian migrants numbered approximately one thousand warriors and contributed to a sudden growth in the Indian population on Louisiana's northwestern periphery.[49]

Coinciding with this southward migration of Indians into the exchange sphere of the Lower Mississippi Valley was the northward expansion of Spanish settlement and forts into the Texas interior. Confrontation between Hispanic settlers and Wichita villagers increasingly made the French trade in the area a threat to the security interest of northern Mexico. In response to this newly troubled political border as well as to their own continuing depopulation from disease, the Caddo Indians along the Red River merged into more compact villages and formed a stronger confederacy. As Spanish officials intensified their efforts to restrain French

49. Herbert Eugene Bolton, ed. and trans., *Athanase de Mézières and the Louisiana-Texas Frontier, 1768–1780* [Documents published from original Spanish and French MSS chiefly in the archives of Mexico and Spain], 2 vols. (Cleveland, Ohio, 1914), II, 83. Early French relations with the Wichitas and migration to the Red River area are discussed in John, *Storms Brewed in Other Men's Worlds*, 304–374; Wayne Morris, "The Wichita Exchange: Trade on Oklahoma's Fur Frontier, 1719–1812," *Great Plains Journal*, IX (1970), 79–84; Earl Henry Elam, "The History of the Wichita Indian Confederacy to 1868" (Ph.D. diss., Texas Tech University, 1971), esp. 87–133; Timothy K. Perttula and Bob D. Skiles, "Another Look at an Eighteenth-Century Archaeological Site in Wood County, Texas," *Southwestern Historical Quarterly*, XCII (1988–1989), 417–435.

traders and as the Wichitas aggressively competed for guns, ammunition, and other scarce trade merchandise, the Caddoes reinforced their own political and economic relations with Louisiana.[50]

The Quapaw Indians also strengthened their association with Louisiana during the mid-eighteenth century. If the Upper Creeks and Caddoes, respectively, occupied the eastern and western portals of the French trade network, the several Quapaw villages along the lower Arkansas River guarded the region's northern door at the midsection of the Mississippi Valley. From the opposite side and with less frequency than the Choctaws, they dispatched raiding parties against the Chickasaws and even participated in quelling the Choctaw revolt. More important, the Quapaw nation provided goods, defense, and other services to the French garrison at Arkansas, to hunters in the White and St. Francis river basin, and to convoys traveling to and from the Illinois district. In May 1749, a war party of Chickasaws, rebellious Choctaws, and even some Upper Creeks attacked the Arkansas district, killing six settlers and capturing eight slaves. "Unfortunately for our Frenchmen," reported Governor Vaudreuil, the Quapaws "had been obliged to withdraw . . . five leagues from the fort to find land suitable for planting, their old clearings being flooded by the very high waters. This gave the enemies time to strike their blow before the Arkansas could be warned of it." At the Indians' request and for their own security, the French constructed a new fort farther up the Arkansas River amid the Quapaw villages at Écores Rouges.[51] When the medal chief and seventeen other Quapaw delegates visited New Orleans in the summer of 1753, Governor Kerlérec "amused them, showed them great attention, and entertained them well." He furthermore advised a new commandant for the Arkansas district "to maintain this nation out of concern for covering the space of forty leagues above and below [the

---

50. Bolton, ed. and trans., *Athanase de Mézières,* II, 83, 120; Herbert Eugene Bolton, *Texas in the Middle Eighteenth Century: Studies in Spanish Colonial History and Administration* (Berkeley, Calif., 1915), 42–78, 312, 379. Site locations and changes among the Caddoes are discussed in Clarence H. Webb and Hiram F. Gregory, *The Caddo Indians of Louisiana* (Baton Rouge, La., 1978), 24–32.

51. *MPAFD,* V, 33–35. Quapaw relations with Europeans during this period are discussed in Stanley Faye, "The Arkansas Post of Louisiana: French Domination," *LHQ,* XXVI (1943), 633–721; and W. David Baird, *The Quapaw Indians: A History of the Downstream People* (Norman, Okla., 1980), 21–46.

Arkansas post] on both banks of the [Mississippi] river against the raids and the attacks that some bands of Chickasaws, Cherokees, and Shawnees make from time to time on our boats."[52]

The network of Indian alliance and trade forged during the early decades of French colonization weathered hazardous conditions over the mid-eighteenth century. English traders and their Indian allies, especially Chickasaws and Natchez refugees, repeatedly challenged French hegemony east of the Mississippi. Louisiana officials managed to neutralize English inroads through a policy of military intimidation against the Chickasaws and of gift-giving among other tribes in the region. Trade relations developed steadily west of the Mississippi, even drawing some Plains Indian migrants into the network. The cohesion of the colony's alliance network, however, was chronically weakened by frequent shortages of trade goods resulting from its marginal position in the French empire. Only by imposing inexorable pressure on the Choctaws did colonial officials quell an anti-French rebellion inside the polity of their most important Indian ally. But weak connections with the Atlantic economy and a sparse colonial population, in the long run, actually helped buffer Louisiana's relations with Lower Mississippi Valley Indians by containing commercial agriculture within geographical and economic limits. The production of crops and furs for export expanded together at a slow rate of growth. By the 1760s, when new forces entered the region, the frontier exchange economy had come to dominate the livelihood of most Indians, slaves, and settlers.

52. *MPAFD*, V, 131. Morris S. Arnold, *Unequal Laws unto a Savage Race: European Legal Traditions in Arkansas, 1686–1836* (Fayetteville, Ark., 1985), sheds new light on many dimensions of life in the Arkansas district of colonial Louisiana, including relations with local Indians.

4

CHANGE AND CONTINUITY DURING

THE YEARS OF PARTITION

The treaties that ended the Seven Years' War affected the inhabitants of the Lower Mississippi Valley far more than did the war itself. In 1762 Louis XV offered Louisiana to Charles III in order to persuade the Spanish king to accept France's peace overtures to England. Spain had joined France late in the war, suffered quick losses of territory, and was reluctant to conclude the war. Having already lost Canada to Great Britain, the French court compensated Spanish losses with its remaining, but still marginal, North American colony. In the Treaty of Fontainebleau of November 1762, "the crown of France cedes to that of Spain the country known under the name of Louisiana as well as New Orleans and the island on which this city is situated."[1] Louisiana promised at least to serve Spain as a barrier between its silver mines in Mexico and England's North American possessions. Then with the signing of the Treaty of Paris in 1763, Great Britain officially acquired all territory east of the Mississippi River above Lake Pontchartrain and its adjoining lakes and bayous. The Mississippi thereby became a political boundary between two European powers, and the Lower Mississippi Valley was parti-

---

1. *MPAFD*, V, 281–283. The "island of New Orleans" was a convenient term used to define the territory east of the Mississippi River below the waterways extending from Manchac on the river to Lake Maurepas. This east-west series of bayous, rivers, and lakes situated above New Orleans did not really constitute a single flow of water, but served as a political boundary between the Spanish possessions around New Orleans and the English possessions on the same side of the river.

tioned into the English province of West Florida and the Spanish province of Louisiana.

The political partition lasted only two decades and concluded with Spanish military conquest of English West Florida during the American Revolution. But for its duration, the intercolonial division of West Florida and Louisiana unleashed demographic and economic forces that persisted after 1783, altering life in the Lower Mississippi Valley at an increasingly rapid rate.[2] The size and composition of the colonial population began to change dramatically after 1763, when both Spain and Great Britain implemented vigorous colonization schemes in their respective provinces. Connected to this process was an expansion of plantation agriculture in the Lower Mississippi Valley. Although French Louisiana had been exporting sizable shipments of tobacco and indigo since the 1720s, large-scale production of export crops remained limited to the New Orleans and Pointe Coupée areas. Under Spanish and English dominion, significant increments of capital, labor, and land were added to commercial agriculture. Finally, the deerskin trade, which had become an important network of relations between Indian and colonial inhabitants, entered a phase of rapid commercialization during which the terms of exchange became more rigid. In the Treaty of Paris in 1783 Spain acquired control over the entire Gulf Coast of North America while the United States of America extended its newly won sovereignty over the trans-Appalachian territory. Under this latest geopolitical carving of the Lower Mississippi Valley, processes of change begun earlier accelerated into a profound transformation of the region.

But events that occurred between 1762 and 1783 indicate that these two decades of change were more transitional than transformative. In face of new official efforts to regulate commerce, expand staple agriculture, and enforce political control, inhabitants of the Lower Mississippi Valley—native-born and immigrant alike—clung to intercultural relations

---

2. The history of the Lower Mississippi Valley during this period is very uneven. Largely because its set of records is in English, the colony of West Florida has received much more attention from American historians than has Louisiana. For a review of the literature on early Spanish Louisiana, see Jack D. L. Holmes, "The Historiography of the American Revolution in Louisiana," *LH*, XIX (1978), 309–326. For a historiographical assessment of the entire Spanish period of Louisiana history, see Light Townsend Cummins, "Spanish Louisiana," in Light Townsend Cummins and Glen Jeansonne, eds., *A Guide to the History of Louisiana* (Westport, Conn., 1982), 17–25.

and economic activities within the familiar framework of exchange. The short-lived revolt of New Orleans merchants and planters against Spanish authority is the best-known but not the only form of economic recalcitrance employed during this transitional period. Settlers, slaves, and Indians accommodated to and resisted the newly emerging economic order by pursuing customary production and marketing practices, which now became more like strategies of survival.

Indians responded resourcefully to the political division of the region in various ways. Tribes east of the Mississippi welcomed English trade but tried to maintain relations with Louisiana traders and to secure access to the Spanish government. Frustrated by both English abuse and Spanish negligence, many Choctaws resorted to acts of banditry committed against colonial settlements. The petites nations along the lower Mississippi and other tribes west of the river, meanwhile, transferred their political allegiance and economic relations to the Spanish government in Louisiana, which introduced a stronger licensing system to Indian trade and prohibited any further enslavement of Indian people. Louisiana officials also tried to prevent livestock raiding in the adjacent province of Texas by prohibiting the purchase of horses and mules from western Indians and restricting the opposite flow of munitions. This policy clashed with the raiding-trading practices of the Wichitas, who nonetheless developed stronger ties to Louisiana during the 1770s. Rising intimidation from Indian raiders to the north, especially the Osages, bound all Indian villages on the northwestern periphery of the Lower Mississippi Valley more tightly to the regional exchange network.

Familiar means of livelihood among African-American slaves underwent a parallel process of stressful change and continuity. The economy of the Lower Mississippi Valley still depended upon slaves working in a wide array of roles, as soldiers, hunters, boatmen, herders, peddlers, and interpreters. But the intensification of plantation agriculture during the 1760s and 1770s imposed upon a rapidly growing slave population a spate of ordinances prohibiting evening assemblies, concubinage, and other features of daily life that had facilitated physical and even some social mobility. The marketing activities of slaves received especially anxious attention from slaveowners and officials, partly because they involved trade in stolen goods but more generally because open exchange by slaves with Indians and settlers was increasingly considered subversive. The formation of larger and more aggressive runaway communities signaled a mounting rebelliousness among slaves. Some took advantage of the new political boundary between British West Florida and Spanish Louisiana by running away from one province to another. Growing initiatives among blacks, however, evoked more repressive measures from colonial officials, who even cooperated across the intercolonial line to return runaway slaves to their owners. Once-customary means of subsistence—adapting to inaccessible terrain, possessing firearms, pilfering owners' property, and petty trading—now became forms of slave defiance.

I

Upon their acquisition of Louisiana and West Florida, Spanish and British officials, respectively, administered aggressive policies of immigration. In 1763 the number of colonial inhabitants in the Lower Mississippi Valley totaled only about four thousand whites, five thousand Negro slaves, two hundred mulatto slaves, one hundred Indian slaves, and one hundred free people of color. The vast majority of this populace was born in the colonial region, a status referred to as "creole" in Louisiana. Accustomed to living in a colony neglected by its home country, these people were the creators and benefactors of the frontier exchange economy. In order both to increase the economic value and to secure the political sovereignty of their respective colonies, the new governments at Louisiana and West Florida promoted the immigration of more settlers and slaves into the region.[3]

3. My estimate of the colonial population in 1763 is based on the following sources: General Census taken in New Orleans and in all the districts below the city of New Orleans to Pointe Coupée in the year 1763, in Jacqueline K. Voorhies, comp. and trans., *Some Late Eighteenth-Century Louisianians: Census Records of the Colony, 1758–1796* (Lafayette, La., 1973), 103–105; and Katherine Bridges and Winston DeVille, trans., "Census of Natchitoches Post 1766," *LH,* IV (1963), 156–159.

Derived from the Spanish words *criar* and *colono, creole* was a term used in Caribbean and Latin American colonies in general to describe persons born in America but not ancestrally native to it, distinguishing them from American Indian people and from European or African-born people. Officials in 18th-century Louisiana applied the adjective *creole* to Negro slaves as well as to whites born in the colony. The classification of people as "Creole" emerged during the early 19th century, when Anglo-Americans began to pour into southern Louisiana and colonial descendants sought a social identity distinct from these newcomers. The term went through another process

Initiating this latest wave of migration to the Lower Mississippi Valley, only the second after the Company of the Indies program of the 1720s, were some of the nearly twenty thousand settlers who had been expelled from their homes in Nova Scotia by the British government during the Seven Years' War. Groups of these French-speaking refugees began to trickle down the Mississippi River to Louisiana immediately after the expulsion of 1755, soon forming a new settlement above the German Coast. The large-scale migration of Acadians, however, occurred after 1765, following their temporary stays in American and French ports. Spanish officials desired the immigration of such farming families to Louisiana, and in 1767 the Council of the Indies even allocated twenty-five thousand pesos a year to assist migrants. By 1769 more than 1,000 Acadians had reached the colony and established three new settlements. The Acadian coast, occupying both sides of the Mississippi about seventy miles above New Orleans, included 486 inhabitants. Another 444 Acadians lived at the settlements of Atakapas and Opelousas on Bayou Teche, a long and narrow stream flowing into the Gulf of Mexico about seventy-five miles west of the Mississippi.[4]

The Spanish government followed the land policy of its French predecessor, distributing small holdings along the river banks to settlers. An ordinance issued by Governor Alexander O'Reilly in 1770 fixed the con-

---

of redefinition in the second half of the 19th century under pressure of strict racial classification. White creoles excluded colored creoles from the category, and for colored creoles the category defined a mixed racial ancestry. The changing definitions and uses of the term are explored in Virginia R. Domínguez, *White by Definition: Social Classification in Creole Louisiana* (New Brunswick, N.J., 1986). For evidence of the perpetuation of the "native-born" meaning of *creole* through the antebellum period, see Joseph G. Tregle, Jr., "On That Word 'Creole' Again: A Note," *LH*, XXIII (1982), 193–198. The difference of French Creoles from other French-speaking Louisianians like Cajuns is elucidated in Glenn R. Conrad, "Potpourri Français: The Culture of South Louisiana," *Gateway Heritage*, VI, no. 2 (Fall 1985), 2–9.

4. Carl A. Brasseaux, *The Founding of New Acadia: The Beginnings of Acadian Life in Louisiana, 1765–1803* (Baton Rouge, La., 1987), is the definitive study of Acadian settlement in Louisiana. Documents pertaining to the first wave of Acadian immigration have been compiled in Brasseaux, ed., Brasseaux *et al.*, trans., *Quest for the Promised Land: Official Correspondence Relating to the First Acadian Migration to Louisiana, 1764–1769* (Lafayette, La., 1989). For a demographic analysis of the size and composition of Acadian families, see Andrew S. Walsh and Robert V. Wells, "Population Dynamics in the Eighteenth-Century Mississippi River Valley: Acadians in Louisiana," *Journal of Social History*, XI (1977–1978), 521–545.

dition of land distribution. "Each newly arrived family" received from six to eight arpents of frontage, according to its means of cultivation, and a standard forty arpents in depth. Grantees were required "to make, within the first three years of possession, levees sufficient for the preservation of the land, and the ditches necessary to carry off the water." In addition to being responsible for keeping a road along the levee and for clearing and enclosing the adjacent land, settlers could sell their grants only after three years of possession and with permission from the governor.[5]

A decade after the first major group of Acadians traveled to Louisiana, Spanish-speaking families in the Canary Islands were recruited for colonization. From October 1778 to May 1780, six ships carried two thousand "Isleños" from one of Spain's oldest colonial regions to the Lower Mississippi Valley. Like the Acadians, these families of farmers and fishermen dispersed among several settlements in lower Louisiana. San Bernardo was located downriver from New Orleans, between the east bank of the Mississippi and Lake Borgne. Along Bayou Lafourche, near its confluence with the Mississippi at the Acadian Coast, other Canary Islanders established Valenzuela. The other major settlements included Galveztown, at the junction of the Amite and Iberville rivers, and New Iberia, on Bayou Teche below the Acadian settlement of Atakapas. At least five hundred more Isleños reached Louisiana during the 1780s.[6]

During the summer of 1785, seven ships carried another sixteen hundred Acadians from France to New Orleans. Smallpox and other diseases afflicted these and previous Acadian migrants, especially in the early years of their diaspora, but overall this period of immigration to Louisiana was far less unhealthy than in the 1720s. The lower mortality rate among Acadian and Canary Island settlers resulted from a combination of factors. Spain administered an effective system of hospitalizing infected im-

5. Gustavus Schmidt, trans., "O'Reilly's Ordinance of 1770: Concerning Grants of Land in Louisiana to New Settlers, Fencing of Same, Building of Roads and Levees, and Forfeiture of Strayed Cattle," *LHQ*, XI (1928), 237–239. For a full account of Spain's immigration policy, see Gilbert C. Din, "Early Spanish Colonization Efforts in Louisiana," *Louisiana Studies*, XI (1972), 31–49.

6. Sidney Louis Villeré, comp., *The Canary Islands Migration to Louisiana, 1778–1783: The History and Passenger Lists of the Islenos Volunteer Recruits and Their Families* (New Orleans, 1971). The immigration of Isleños to colonial Louisiana and the life of their descendants into the 20th century are fully examined in Gilbert C. Din, *The Canary Islanders of Louisiana* (Baton Rouge, La., 1988), 15–83.

migrants and supplying all travelers as they ascended the Mississippi River. The support and care provided by migrant families already established in the colony to succeeding immigrants also facilitated healthier diets and speedier recoveries. By the 1780s inoculation against smallpox was under way in Louisiana, especially as both an experimental and a precautionary measure among incoming slaves.[7]

Although their number has not been determined, slaves being shipped from the Caribbean to Louisiana during the 1770s and early 1780s further increased and diversified the African-American population in the colony. In 1776 Spain allowed French merchants to import Negroes from St. Domingue and other West Indies islands in exchange for Louisiana commodities. By the 1780s United States merchants operating in New Orleans also began to invest in the shipment of Jamaican and other English Caribbean slaves to both Louisiana and West Florida.[8]

Colonization of West Florida by Great Britain during this period introduced additional groups of settlers and slaves to the Lower Mississippi Valley. Like their counterparts in Spanish Louisiana, officials in the newly created English province were allowed to grant land freely to immigrating settlers. In 1764 Governor George Johnstone received instructions from the Board of Trade "that one hundred Acres of Land be granted to every Person being Master or Mistress of a Family, for himself or herself, and fifty Acres for every white or black Man, Woman, or Child, of which such Person's Family shall consist."[9] By this means a great deal of land fell into the possession of several influential persons. Daniel Clarke obtained three thousand acres at the old French settlement of Natchez, and twenty

---

7. Brasseaux, *Founding of New Acadia*, 80, 108, 173–174; Gilbert C. Din, "Spain's Immigration Policy and Efforts in Louisiana during the American Revolution," *Louisiana Studies*, XIV (1975), 241–257; Din, "Spanish Immigration to a French Land," *Revue de Louisiane/Louisiana Review*, V (1976), 63–80; John Duffy, ed., *The Rudolph Matas History of Medicine in Louisiana*, 2 vols. (Baton Rouge, La., 1958–1962), I, 198–204.

8. John G. Clark, *New Orleans, 1718–1812: An Economic History* (Baton Rouge, La., 1969), 222–225; Thomas Marc Fiehrer, "The African Presence in Colonial Louisiana: An Essay on the Continuity of Caribbean Culture," in Robert Macdonald *et al.*, eds., *Louisiana's Black Heritage* (New Orleans, 1979), 3–31.

9. Instructions of Board of Trade, quoted in Clinton N. Howard, *The British Development of West Florida, 1763–1769* (Berkeley, Calif., 1947), 8. For a modern analysis of immigration to West Florida, see Robin F. A. Fabel, *The Economy of British West Florida, 1763–1783* (Tuscaloosa, Ala., 1988), 6–21.

thousand acres above Natchez were granted to the earl of Eglinton. But at the same time, hundreds of poorer settlers occupied plots of a few hundred acres and joined the scattered French inhabitants who had decided to remain in the now English province.[10]

By 1774 the migration of Anglo-American settlers and African-American slaves from all parts of the Atlantic seaboard to the Gulf Coast and eastern bank of the Mississippi River increased the colonial population of West Florida to nearly four thousand whites and fifteen hundred blacks.[11] But the greatest influx of English-speaking people came after the outbreak of the American Revolution. By the end of 1775, West Florida became an officially designated asylum for loyalist refugees. Unlike the other groups of migrants entering the Lower Mississippi Valley during these years—the Acadians, Canary Islanders, and even earlier Anglo-Americans—many English loyalists came from a propertied class and brought a large number of Negro slaves with them. These political refugees traveled to West Florida, mostly to the Natchez area, down the Ohio and Tennessee rivers. People of lesser means, especially families from Georgia and Carolina, followed the old Chickasaw route from the Savannah River to the Upper Creek villages, and from there headed either down the Alabama River or westward to the Mississippi. Traveling from Mobile towards the Alibamons in 1777, naturalist William Bartram "met a company of emigrants from Georgia; a man, his wife, a young woman, several young children and three stout young men, with about a dozen horses loaded with their property."[12]

Between 1763 and 1783, the colonial population in all of the Lower

10. Gordon M. Wells, comp., "British Land Grants—William Wilton Map, 1774," *JMH*, XXVIII (1966), 152–160; Howard, *British Development of West Florida*, appendix I, "Analysis of Land Grants," 50–106.

11. Lieutenant Governor Elias Durnford estimated on Jan. 15, 1774, that "there cannot be less than 2,500 Whites and 600 Slaves on the Mississippi, and parts adjacent and about 1,200 Whites from the Lake Pontchartrain to the East of Pensacola, and about 600 Slaves." EPR, VI, 32–34.

12. Robert V. Haynes, *The Natchez District and the American Revolution* (Jackson, Miss., 1976), 11–23; J. Barton Starr, *Tories, Dons, and Rebels: The American Revolution in British West Florida* (Gainesville, Fla., 1976), 48–49; William Bartram, *Travels through North and South Carolina, Georgia, East and West Florida, the Cherokee Country, the Extensive Territories of the Muscogulges or Creek Confederacy, and the Country of the Choctaws* (1791), ed. Francis Harper (New Haven, Conn., 1968), 280–281.

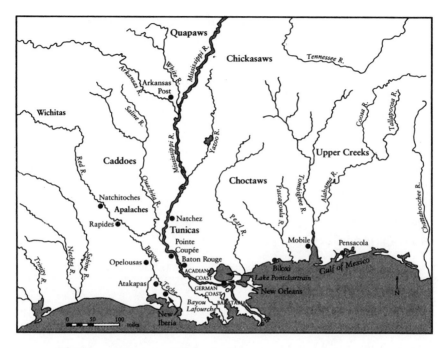

MAP 2. *The Lower Mississippi Valley in the 1770s*

Mississippi Valley increased more than threefold. The province of West Florida reached as many as seven thousand inhabitants before the Spanish conquered all of its major posts during the American Revolution. Following West Florida's transfer to Spain in 1783, about a third of these people abandoned the colony. Most of the Anglo-American immigrants and their Negro slaves who remained in the region had formed three new core areas of settlement: Natchez and the lands adjoining it on the Mississippi and behind it on neighboring streams to the east, the Baton Rouge and Manchac coast downstream on the east bank of the Mississippi, and the lower banks of the Alabama and Tombigbee rivers above Mobile (see Map 2).[13] Meanwhile, old and new settlements in Spanish Louisiana became steadi-

13. Starr, *Tories, Dons, and Rebels,* 230–240, provides a full analysis of available information regarding the number of immigrants to West Florida and the size of its population. Fabel, *Economy of British West Florida,* 18–20, estimates Starr's figure of 7,000–8,000 in 1781 to be somewhat too high and reaches a maximum closer to 6,000.

TABLE 3. *The Colonial Population in the Lower Mississippi Valley,*
1785

Districts	Whites	Free People of Color	Slaves	Total
Red River Valley and Bayou Teche				
Natchitoches	404	8	344	756
Rapides	63	0	25	88
Avoyelles	149	0	138	287
Ouachita	198	0	9	207
Attakapas and Opelousas	1,204	22	1,182	2,408
Banks of the Lower Mississippi River (Descending Order)				
Arkansas (west bank)	148	31	17	196
Natchez (east bank)	1,121	0	438	1,559
Pointe Coupée (west bank)	482	4	1,035	1,521
Baton Rouge and Manchac	68	2	100	170
Galveztown (behind Manchac)	237	0	5	242
Iberville (east bank)	451	0	222	673
Valenzuela (west bank)	306	0	46	352
Fourche (on Bayou Lafourche)	333	0	273	606
Acadian Coast (both banks)	912	18	402	1,332
Second German Coast (both banks)	714	5	581	1,300
First German Coast	561	69	1,273	1,903

ly more populous, and the capital at New Orleans grew into a city of five
thousand residents.[14] By the mid-1780s the entire Lower Mississippi

14. As indicated in Chapter 2, New Orleans had always included a relatively large
percentage of the region's colonial population. The town comprised 24% of all white
and black inhabitants in 1726 and 17% in 1783. Although its population grew at
higher rates after 1783, the overall proportion of urban residents declined over the
ensuing years. For sophisticated demographic and social analyses of the city's population in the 1770s, see Kimberly S. Hanger, "Household and Community Structure
among the Free Population of Spanish New Orleans, 1778," *LH*, XXX (1989), 63–79;
and Hanger, "Avenues to Freedom Open to New Orleans' Black Population, 1769–
1779," *LH*, XXXI (1990), 237–264.

TABLE 3. *Continued*

Districts	Whites	Free People of Color	Slaves	Total
Chapitoulas Coast (both banks)	1,128	263	5,645	7,036
New Orleans (east bank)	2,826	563	1,631	5,028
Bayou St. John (behind New Orleans)	91	14	573	678
Below New Orleans (both banks)	387	67	1,664	2,118
St. Bernardo (east bank)	584	2	0	586
Gulf Coast Area				
Mobile and Tombigbee River	325	51	461	837
Pensacola	384	28	184	596
Total	13,076	1,147	16,248	30,471

Source: Census of Louisiana in the year 1785, app. no. 2 to the Digest of Laws of Louisiana Communicated to Congress, Nov. 29, 1803, in U.S., Congress, *American State Papers: Miscellaneous,* 2 vols. (Washington, D.C., 1832–1834), I, 381.

Valley included a colonial population of sixteen thousand slaves, thirteen thousand whites, and more than one thousand free people of color (see Table 3). A significant demographic watershed was now reached. Although the Indian population began to recover slowly from earlier epidemic shocks, the number of colonial inhabitants roughly equaled that of the Lower Mississippi Valley's Indian inhabitants for the first time since colonization had begun and, henceforth, climbed above it at an accelerated rate.[15]

15. Census of Louisiana in the year 1785, app. no. 2 to the Digest of the Laws of Louisiana Communicated to Congress, Nov. 29, 1803, in U.S., Congress, *American State Papers: Miscellaneous,* 2 vols. (Washington, D.C., 1832–1834), I, 381. For my estimation of some 30,000 American Indians living in the Lower Mississippi Valley during the 1780s, see Daniel H. Usner, Jr., "Decline and Migration: A Population History of Indians in the Eighteenth-Century Lower Mississippi Valley," MS.

11

The surge in migration to the Lower Mississippi Valley occurred in conjunction with plans for economic development administered by the new colonial governments. Spain and Great Britain sought to expand and rechannel commerce, increasing the volume of crops, furs, and timber exported from the region and connecting it more firmly to different European markets. Indians, settlers, and slaves were affected by this process in different ways, but they all struggled to resist and shape it for their own advantages.

The most famous reaction to the new order was an attempted rebellion among Louisiana merchants and planters against Spanish dominion in the 1760s. By the time news of France's cession of the colony to Spain reached New Orleans in October 1764, the wealthy Louisianians who coalesced around the Superior Council had accumulated virtually insoluble debts to French merchants amid a severe shortage of money. The promulgation of Spanish commercial decrees, drawing Louisiana into Spain's colonial sys-- tem, evoked fears of regulation and bankruptcy among the colony's commercial populace. After undue delay in the bureaucratic machinery of Spain, Governor Antonio de Ulloa reached New Orleans with a company of only ninety soldiers on March 5, 1766. Months of protest and plotting by the Superior Council climaxed in late October 1768, when members and their conspirators persuaded about five hundred Acadian and German colonists—who also felt threatened by Spanish trade restrictions— to assemble in the capital and then issued a rebellious memorial. Personally threatened and powerless, Ulloa departed New Orleans for Havana on November 1. In their incendiary decree of October 28, proclaiming indignation against Spain's emissary and swearing loyalty to "Louis the Well-beloved," the petitioners revealed not only their active economic interests but also the commercial ambitions upon which they hoped to climb out of debt.[16]

16. An authoritative study of the Superior Council's plot with special emphasis on Governor Ulloa's position is John Preston Moore, *Revolt in Louisiana: The Spanish Occupation, 1766–1770* (Baton Rouge, La., 1976), 42–164. Carl A. Brasseaux has contributed further to our understanding of this revolt by exploring more deeply than all previous scholars the role of the French colonial government, in *Denis-Nicolas Foucault and the New Orleans Rebellion of 1768* (Ruston, La., 1987), 65–90. The role of German farmers has been recently highlighted in Reinhart Kondert, "The German Involvement in the Rebellion of 1768," *LH*, XXVI (1985), 385–397.

Louisiana merchants and planters worried that restriction of commerce to Spanish ports would reduce the marketability of the colony's particular combination of export commodities. Tobacco from the Lower Mississippi Valley would have to compete directly with the far superior leaves of the St. Domingue product. Guatemala already supplied Spain with "an indigo superior and in larger quantity than its factories need." And the petitioners also pointed out, "Havana and Peru furnish it sugars and lumber far preferable to ours." Of all markets in France or in French colonies to which Louisiana exporters feared losing access, deerskins and other furs seemed to be jeopardized the most, having "so much less value in Spain that they are little used there." Their anxiety was deepened by the fact that open commerce in the Upper Mississippi Valley and along the Missouri River had no sooner been promised to all inhabitants in 1765 than Governor Ulloa began granting monopolies to trade in those regions among several favored individuals.

> To render clearer the first motive of our complaints, it is proper to observe that the trade that is carried on with the Indian nations is one of the principal branches of commerce, of which the interest is so closely united here with that of the cultivator, that one is the spring of the other. This trade is a very advantageous outlet for the products of several manufactures, which will shortly spread by encouragement. It is an abundant mine, of which the opening presents riches, which promises treasures more valuable than those of Potosi, and so much the more considerable as the activity of the trade will dig deeper. From this exhaustless source arises the advantage of the public and of the individual. The merchant finds there a profitable sale for his goods; the laborer, employed in these journeys and in this trade, gets there the means of subsisting and of amassing a competency. The affection of the natives is kept up by frequent intercourse with the French, securing to them the results that necessarily follow from familiar acquaintance. Public security at last, from which this trade with the barbarous nations that surround us has arisen, is preserved by it.[17]

Indeed, not since the designs of La Salle in the 1680s had the prospects of Indian commerce in the Mississippi Valley been so splendidly described.

17. A full translation of the memorial is available in Alcée Fortier, *A History of Louisiana*, 4 vols. (New York, 1904), I, 177–204.

But now in the hyperbole of rebellious times, the general benefits of exporting peltry and other staples were inflated, as were the impending dangers of Spanish rule. Like the more successful rebellion in the Atlantic seaboard colonies of England a decade later, Louisiana's merchant-planter coup reflected a heightening sensitivity of colonial export interests to tighter regulation by their home governments.[18]

Spanish possession of Louisiana was firmly won in July 1769, when Alexander O'Reilly reached the colony with some two thousand troops. The conspirators were quickly arrested, and five were eventually executed in New Orleans. Spain did not really thwart Louisiana's production of exports any more than did France. Its commercial policies actually helped expand commerce in significant directions. For one thing, the granting of a trade monopoly for Indian trade in the Upper Mississippi Valley, which had riled New Orleans merchants excluded from venturing northward, accelerated commerce up the Missouri River and linked the region more closely than ever to the Lower Mississippi Valley. The post of St. Louis was established in 1764 under the partnership of Pierre Laclede Liguest and Gilbert Antoine de St. Maxent. An exclusive trade license granted the previous year to this same company by Governor Kerlérec had irritated other merchants so much that it was revoked in 1767. But St. Maxent received a similar permit from Ulloa in 1768. The Superior Council's enraged reaction to the Spanish governor was quelled. And deerskins, beaver pelts, and buffalo robes from Illinois and Missouri country soon began to flow downriver, commercially overshadowing the intraregional Indian trade within the Lower Mississippi Valley in due time.[19]

Imperial trade policies and the American Revolution caused exports from both Louisiana and West Florida to follow an erratic pattern during the 1760s and 1770s, yet the volume of tobacco, indigo, timber, and peltry exported from the region rose significantly by the end of this period. Spanish governors made frequent exceptions and allowances to the law confining Louisiana commerce to Spanish ships and ports, and in 1776

18. Moore, *Revolt in Louisiana*, 103–123, 185–230. Also see David Ker Texada, *Alejandro O'Reilly and the New Orleans Rebels* (Lafayette, La., 1970).

19. James Julian Coleman, Jr., *Gilbert Antoine de St. Maxent: The Spanish-Frenchman of New Orleans* (New Orleans, 1968), 22–45; Paul Chrisler Phillips, *The Fur Trade* (with concluding chapters by J. W. Smurr), 2 vols. (Norman, Okla., 1961), II, 223–244.

Spain officially opened the colony's trade with France and the French West Indies. Louisiana tobacco, "of excellent quality and very much to the liking of the consumers in all the provinces of the said kingdom," was even awarded a trade monopoly in Mexico.[20] By the 1780s Louisiana was annually exporting an average of 3,000,000 livres worth of indigo, 1,000,000 livres of tobacco, another 1,000,000 livres of timber products, and some 600,000 livres of furs, most of the last going to France and additional European countries other than Spain. From British West Florida during the 1770s, sizable quantities of indigo and timber left the ports of Mobile and Pensacola along with an annual average of fifty tons of raw deerskins and thirty-five tons of Indian-dressed deerskins. Peltries constituted more than 50 percent of that colony's annual value of exports. In 1782 Spain further liberalized commerce with Louisiana and its newly won West Florida, signaling the expanding role of export staples in the economic life of the region.[21]

As during the 1720s, the current push to expand commercial agriculture clashed with means of livelihood and forms of exchange preferred by common settlers in the Lower Mississippi Valley. The latest immigrants seemed eager to take advantage of what creole inhabitants had long discovered—"the facility offered by the country to live on its natural productions," which, according to the French governor in 1764, "has created habits of laziness." Reporting on the arrival of some two hundred Acadians in September 1766, Louisiana's first Spanish governor minimized the returns that one should expect from the money spent to assist their passage: "They are not able to cultivate indigo nor tobacco without having first a competent number of negroes to do the work and they will be reduced to owning a few animals and to cultivating grains and roots for their own consumption, with which they will be rich as far as they are personally concerned but will not enrich the colony nor contribute to the growth of its commerce, because it will never get beyond producing wood,

20. *SMV,* I, 232, 237–238; Brian E. Coutts, "Boom and Bust: The Rise and Fall of the Tobacco Industry in Spanish Louisiana, 1770–1790," *Americas,* XLII (1985– 1986), 289–309.

21. *SMV,* II, 1–5. My estimates of export volumes and values are derived from Clark, *New Orleans,* 181–201; and Robert R. Rea, "British West Florida Trade and Commerce in the Customs Records," *AR,* XXVII (1984), 124–159.

indigo of very poor quality, and tobacco in small quantities and of ordinary quality."[22]

British officials in West Florida similarly worried that most newly arrived settlers would contribute little to the commercial productivity of the province. "From the beginning of November to the latter-end of February," according to Montfort Browne, "a man with his Gun may plentifully supply a Family of Twelve or fourteen with choice Buffaloe Beef, Bears Meat, Venison, Geese, Turkies, Ducks, etc. and in all times of the year Fish may be catched in the greatest abundance." In 1774 a later lieutenant governor, Elias Durnford, reported that a want of provisions forced many emigrants to "take to Hunting." He recommended that food and tools be loaned them "in order to encourage the Men, to apply themselves to the cultivation of their Lands, instead of those practices." As he approached the first English settlement above Lake Pontchartrain several years later, William Bartram noticed how "the inhabitants neglect agriculture; and generally employ themselves in hunting and fishing."[23]

Not only did new immigrants to the Lower Mississippi Valley, like those in earlier times, rely heavily upon subsistence hunting and fishing, but many of them turned to trading as a supplementary, if not primary, means of livelihood. The Indian trade of West Florida produced the province's major staple during its English period, attracted innumerable men from the Atlantic Coast region, and created a serious problem of social and economic control for the colonial government. Without licenses and with only a few kegs of rum, many newcomers—described by one observer as "Deserters, Horse thieves, half breeds and Negroes"—began to wander through Choctaw, Creek, and Chickasaw villages, bartering their alcohol for deerskins and horses and bringing these items to merchants in the Gulf Coast ports.[24]

22. AC, C13A, XLIV, 58; R. E. Chandler, "Ulloa and the Acadians," *LH*, XXI (1980), 90–91.

23. EPR, III, 96, VI, 39–40; Bartram, *Travels*, ed. Harper, 269.

24. "Journal of David Taitt's Travels from Pensacola, West Florida, to and through the Country of the Upper and Lower Creeks, 1772," in Newton D. Mereness, ed. *Travels in the American Colonies* (New York, 1916), 501–512, 525. Also see Peter Chester's address to the General Assembly, Oct. 1, 1778, in Robert R. Rea, comp., *The Minutes, Journals, and Acts of the General Assembly of British West Florida* (University, Ala., 1979), 280.

While the partition of the Lower Mississippi Valley into a British and a Spanish province split the external commerce into two separate flows, the well-established network of exchange linking places on both sides of the river continued to operate. Officials in both West Florida and Louisiana tried to control the movement of traders, especially in order to keep valuable deerskins and other produce within their respective colonies. But Indian villagers and colonial peddlers defied political boundaries and carried merchandise wherever it proved most advantageous or convenient. After 1763, English traders aggressively began to extend their activities across the Mississippi, along the Red and Arkansas rivers, and even up the Missouri.[25] On the other hand, French traders in Louisiana did not abandon their traditional connections with villages that now fell under British colonial administration. Some men with strong ties to the Choctaws, such as Simon Favre and Henry Lafleur, entered the service of the English government as interpreters of Indian languages and thus secured their own commerce by legal means.[26] Others simply continued to travel clandestinely between Spanish Louisiana and the Choctaw nation. One settlement of Frenchmen and Choctaws at Tangipahoa, on the north shore of Lake Pontchartrain and within West Florida's boundaries, was accused of diverting deerskins from the Mobile trade to New Orleans. In March 1770, Daniel Ward asked a member of the West Florida General Assembly "to have a stop put to the trade that's carried on by the inhabitants of New Orleans with the Indians on the English side of the Lake Pontchartrain on the Bay of St. Louis, to the great prejudice of this province and particularly those concerned in the Indian trade." This Mobile-based merchant reported that "at a moderate computation they get at least 20,000 pounds annually."[27]

25. Unzaga to Bucareli, July 8, 1770, Dispatches of the Spanish Governors of Louisiana, Works Progress Administration transcriptions, Louisiana Historical Center, New Orleans.

26. As early as 1755, Simon Favre had served as interpreter at Fort Tombecbé (Payment of Interpreter to the Indians at Tombecbé, New Orleans, Apr. 29, 1755, French Louisiana Documents, 1729–1765, Historic New Orleans Collection, New Orleans). Favre, the Lefleurs, and several other French-speaking traders continued to deal with the Choctaws into the 1780s and later (Juan de La Villebeuvre, List of Choctaw Towns and traders, Nov. 24, 1787, AGI, PC, leg. 200).

27. Rea, comp., *Minutes, Journals, and Acts of the General Assembly of British West Florida*, 146, 230. Also see John Richard Alden, *John Stuart and the Southern Colonial*

The settlement of Manchac, situated a hundred miles above New Orleans on the east bank of the Mississippi, became a pivotal point in the movement of merchandise and produce across the river and between provinces. From the Gulf ports of Pensacola and Mobile, sloops and schooners carried imported goods through the Mississippi Sound, Lakes Borgne, Pontchartrain, and Maurepas, and then through the Amite and Iberville rivers to warehouses behind Manchac—a total distance of about two hundred miles. With the tacit approval or grudging acceptance of governors in New Orleans, settlers up and down the Mississippi River traded with English merchants there. Concern over lost export-import duties and periodic shortages of food supplies in the capital produced, at the most, erratic police action against this contraband trade. Among the West Florida merchants extensively involved in tapping products from settlers and traders along the Mississippi was a Scottish-born resident of Manchac named John Fitzpatrick. In May 1770, for example, Fitzpatrick sent "181 Good Deer Skins in the hair Wt. 386 lb." and "400 Carrots of Choice point Coupee Tobaco" to exporters in Mobile. In return for these and other export commodities, Fitzpatrick provided settlers at places like Pointe Coupée, Natchez, and Natchitoches with cloth, ammunition, rum, and even Negro slaves being shipped into the region by English ships.[28]

III

During the transitional 1760s and 1770s Indians in the Lower Mississippi Valley pursued their own strategies for fitting the new

Frontier: A Study of Indian Relations, War, Trade, and Land Policies in the Southern Wilderness, 1754–1775 (Ann Arbor, Mich., 1944), 235–237; and Rea, "British West Florida Trade and Commerce," AR, XXXVI (1984), 133.

28. Margaret Fisher Dalrymple, ed., The Merchant of Manchac: The Letterbooks of John Fitzpatrick, 1768–1790 (Baton Rouge, La., 1978), 51, 67, 88, 90–91, 108–109, 145, 276. In addition to stationary merchants like Fitzpatrick, there were usually about a dozen English-owned ships operating on the lower Mississippi River. Most of these vessels made only periodic trips into the mouth of the river, some from New England. Spanish governors rarely interfered with this coastal commerce, recognizing its importance to Louisiana settlers. Some locally operated ships always present on the river, called "floating warehouses," also supplied colonists with necessary goods in exchange for their produce. And as explained by Francisco Bouligny, "it is an unavoidable operation despite the effort and vigilance which the governor wanted to employ, since

order into the familiar framework of frontier exchange. The withdrawal of French colonial authority drastically weakened the ability of the large Indian nations in the interior to play off intercolonial rivalry. The Choctaws, Chickasaws, and Upper Creeks suddenly found themselves forced to negotiate with only one European power. As soon as English military personnel moved into Pensacola, Mobile, and Fort Tombecbé during the fall of 1763, signs of potential conflict emerged. The Choctaws and Upper Creeks insisted upon the perpetuation of a protocol that had long been customary in their relations with French officials. English commandants complained immediately about the practices of entertaining and giving gifts to Indian visitors. After hundreds of Choctaws came to visit Mobile in November and December, Major Robert Farmer reported with regrets that only by "giving them Victuals when ever they ask it, and the Government making them Annually considerable Presents" would the English be able to replace successfully the French among these Indians.[29]

The Choctaws and Alibamons naturally turned to their old allies, the French, for assistance in their efforts to keep trade relations bound to the traditional protocol of diplomacy. Before Spain officially occupied Louisiana in 1766, delegations of Indians continued to visit the French governor in New Orleans. On March 5, 1764, Mastabé, chief of the Choctaw town of Oskilakna, told Jean-Jacques Blaise d'Abbadie that "he could not become accustomed to the absence of the French in his village and that everything was melancholy for them." Six months later a group of thirty-three Alibamons arrived to report "their regret at no longer seeing the French," a loss exacerbated by the English decision not to occupy Fort Toulouse. In the presence of John Stuart, the British superintendent of Indian Affairs who happened to be visiting New Orleans, a delegation of Choctaws in December 1764 confirmed their attachment to the French and proceeded to describe new abuses being committed, charging that incoming English traders "beat them with clubs, steal their horses, and debauch their women." The arguments of Abbadie and Stuart that "close bonds of friendship" now existed between the English and the French were warmly received by the Indian delegates. But at least one elder spokesman strongly feared that the English would "poison and destroy

to impede it would require that he place a guard at each house." EPR, VI, 225–283; Dalrymple, ed., *Letterbooks of Fitzpatrick*, 229–230; Gilbert C. Din, ed. and trans., *Louisiana in 1776: A Memoria of Francisco Bouligny* (New Orleans, 1977), 62–63.

29. MPAFD, V, 291–293; MPAED, I, 11–14, 38–39, 113.

the Choctaw nation."[30] Bitter memories of French propaganda and English intrigue, which had cost the Choctaw nation a painful civil war only a generation before, were not easily erased.

By treaties of "peace and friendship" made at Mobile and Pensacola in the spring of 1765, Choctaw, Chickasaw, and Creek leaders formalized relations with the new English province of West Florida. Meeting together at Mobile for the first time in more than forty years, the Choctaws and Chickasaws negotiated treaties with Governor Johnstone and agreed to maintain peace with the English, to return runaway slaves and deserting soldiers, to cede a specified area of land along the Gulf Coast, and to trade according to a schedule of fixed prices. Dignitaries from both the Upper and Lower Creek towns met with Johnstone in Pensacola and agreed to a similar set of conditions, including an identical tariff of exchange rates.[31]

The formal speeches delivered by Choctaw chiefs at the treaty council in Mobile disclose what their people had come to expect from their European trading partners. On April 1 Tomatly Mingo, a great medal chief of the Sixtowns, or southern district, opened with the familiar elaboration of his people's dependence upon "Guns Cloathing and other Necessaries" provided by "white Men." He then told the English, "If I am become their Son, they must Act the Part of a Father in Supplying my Wants by proper Presents and also by furnishing a plentyfull Trade." The Choctaws obviously respected the advantages of European merchandise and undoubtedly were dependent upon much of it, but they never agreed to submit to any European authority. Tomatly Mingo expected the English to show the respect and take the responsibility of "a Father," outlining in detail the specific obligations assumed under that role. Settlement could not extend beyond the boundary set by the cession of coastal land between the Tombigbee and Tickfaw rivers. The garrison at Tombecbé must be maintained, but not with more than thirty soldiers, and it must "be allways well Supplied with Provisions and all sorts of Goods." Finally, the colonial

30. Carl A. Brasseaux, ed. and trans., *A Comparative View of French Louisiana, 1699 and 1762: The Journals of Pierre Le Moyne d'Iberville and Jean-Jacques-Blaise d'Abbadie* (Lafayette, La., 1979), 111, 128, 136.

31. *MPAFD*, I, 211–215, 249–255. The articles in these treaties dealing with cessions of land are explained and mapped in Louis De Vorsey, Jr., *The Indian Boundary in the Southern Colonies, 1763–1775* (Chapel Hill, N.C., 1966), 204–227.

government had to "Caution and restrain" traders who were already mistreating Choctaw men and women.[32]

Alibamon Mingo, now about eighty years old and considered chief of the entire Choctaw nation, spoke highly of French merchandise and hoped that the English would "be equally Bountyfull which must be done if they wish equally to gain the affection of my people." He agreed to replace his French medal with an English one, but not without setting his own conditions concerning future trade and settlement.

> There was one thing I would mention tho' it cannot concern myself, and that is the Behaviour of the traders towards our Women, I was told of old by the Creeks and Cherokees, wherever the English went they cause disturbances for they lived under no Government and paid no respect either to Wisdom or Station. I hoped for better things, that those Old Talks had no truth in them. One thing I must report which has happened within my own knowledge, that often when the Traders sent for a Basket of Bread and the Generous Indian sent his own wife to Supply their wants instead of taking the Bread out of the Basket they put their hand upon the Breast of their Wives which was not to be admitted, for the first maxim in our Language is that Death is preferable to disgrace.
>
> I am not of opinion that in giving Land to the English, we deprive ourselves of the use of it, on the Contrary, I think we shall share it with them, as for Example the House I now Speak in was built by the White people on our Land yet it is divided between the White and the Red people. Therefore we need not be uneasy that the English Settle upon our Lands as by that means they can more easily Supply our wants.[33]

As in most other colonial regions, neither the admonitions of Indian leaders nor the regulations of provincial governments could effectively control the behavior of traders and travelers scattered among native villages. The political realignment and sudden immigration of the 1760s made conditions around Indian trade in the Lower Mississippi Valley more volatile than ever. Unable to check illicit trade with Louisiana and

32. *MPAED*, I, 236–239.
33. *MPAED*, I, 240, 241.

to abate Choctaw recalcitrance, the English abandoned Fort Tombecbé by January 1768 and thereby signified political indifference toward the tribe's problems. The abuses committed in the West Florida hinterland, it should be noted, had more to do with the decline in political power among its Indian nations than with the nationality of traders involved; many Frenchmen continued to operate alongside English newcomers. By 1770 several traders had established their own farms and cowpens near Choctaw, Chickasaw, and Creek villages in violation of the treaties of 1765. Peddlers, packhorsemen, and a growing number of stragglers began to hunt deerskins themselves, cutting into the traditional economic role of Indian hunters in addition to disturbing increasingly fragile hunting grounds.[34] In 1772 Paya Mattaha, head chief of the Chickasaws, not only complained about the presence of white hunters and horse thieves in his country but also reported that traders were cheating his people by using shorter measures and phony scales. West Florida's system of licensing trade proved ineffective because, argued Paya Mattaha, "there are so many white men who are likely to oppose them, and who will probably Influence Red men to join in their opposition."[35]

Increasing quantities of rum carried by traders into their towns indeed constituted a powerful form of influence and caused great hardship among Indians who traded with West Florida. Liquor was an extremely easy and fairly inexpensive means for traders to purchase deerskins. While drunkenness allowed these peddlers to cheat men and women during individual transactions, the addictiveness of alcohol helped deepen Indian dependency upon European commerce and expand their need to produce larger quantities of deerskins. In the spring of 1771, Deputy Superintendent Charles Stuart reported on the disorders being caused in villages by liquor and estimated that a "great part of their Skins are purchased with

34. Minutes of the Congresses held at Pensacola in October and November 1771, with the Chiefs of the Upper Creek Nation, Minutes of the Congress held at Mobile in December 1771 and January 1772 with the Chiefs of the Chickasaw and Choctaw Nations, Mississippi Historical Society, *Publications,* Centenary Ser., V (1925), 108–160 (cited hereafter as *PMHS:CS*); Robert R. Rea, "The Trouble at Tombeckby," *AR,* XXI (1968), 21–39.

35. *PMHS:CS,* V, 142–146. The deleterious effects of English trade upon the Choctaws after 1763 are keenly analyzed in Richard White, *The Roots of Dependency: Subsistence, Environment, and Social Change among the Choctaws, Pawnees, and Navajos* (Lincoln, Nebr., 1983), 69–96.

that Commodity." The next winter in Mobile, Captain Ouma from the Choctaw village of Seneacha pleaded eloquently that "some regulation may be made to prevent the profuse Importation of Rum amongst us." He attributed "all disorder and Quarreling between us and our white men" to the rum that "pours in upon our nation Like a great Sea from Mobille and from all the Plantations and Settlements round about Particularly from the House of Simon Favre [a French trader with the Choctaws for many years] who is Settled upon this River [Mobile]."[36]

The southern Indian nations' discontent over English policy and trade abuses did not erupt into anything like the pan-Indian revolt that swept across the Great Lakes region in the 1760s. Protest and rebellion, instead, stayed at the more prosaic level of social banditry. Indian raiders had pillaged Louisiana settlements and posts before 1763, especially during the Natchez, Chickasaw, and Choctaw wars. A lack of gifts or trade goods, some personal abuse committed by a trader, soldier, slave, or settler, or perhaps an excessive demand upon Indian services or resources periodically provoked bands of Indian men to attack colonial persons and possessions. But after the partition of the Lower Mississippi Valley, Indians in both West Florida and Louisiana resorted more frequently to stealing livestock, pillaging supplies, and other forms of intimidation in order to win demands from colonial governments.[37]

Many Choctaws turned to banditry in their efforts to bypass English West Florida's control and to demand Spanish Louisiana's attentions.

36. *PMHS:CS,* V, 47, 150–151.

37. I am indebted to Eric Hobsbawm's treatment of social banditry, which seems applicable to Indians and slaves in colonial regions. A person becomes a bandit because he does something considered criminal by the state or by local rulers, for example, cattle stealing, revenge killing, and blackmarketing, but for which he is supported or at least sanctioned by the local population. Such acts of protest against oppression or negligence are usually performed by young, single men acting alone or in small bands (E. J. Hobsbawm, *Primitive Rebels: Studies in Archaic Forms of Social Movement in the Nineteenth and Twentieth Centuries* [New York, 1965], 5, 13–29). Informative approaches to banditry in colonial or frontier regions include Silvio R. Duncan Baretta and John Markoff, "Civilization and Barbarism: Cattle Frontiers in Latin America," *Comparative Studies in Society and History,* XX (1978), 587–620; Charles van Onselen, "'The Regiment of the Hills': South Africa's Lumpenproletarian Army, 1890–1920," *Past and Present,* no. 80 (August 1978), 91–121; Richard White, "Outlaw Gangs of the Middle Border: American Social Bandits," *Western Historical Quarterly,* XII (1981), 387–408.

Frederick Haldimand, brigadier general of Great Britain's Southern District of North America, reported in 1768 to General Thomas Gage, "The continual depredations of the Choctaw Indians of the six villages, who hunt in and frequent continually the neighborhood of lakes Pontchartrain and Maurepas where they pillage the inhabitants, kill their animals, and introduce French traders in their country, required that there should be some one of confidence and authority among them who would repress their outbreaks." Meanwhile, Choctaw parties were intimidating Louisiana settlements along the Mississippi River with pleas for food and demands for presents. "These incidents happen," argued the commandant at the newly established Acadian settlement of St. Gabriel, "when they have already been to the English (which they ordinarily do) and get here full of brandy. And as they are drunk on this liquor, they become agitated and ask for everything they can think of with haughtiness and a tone of arrogance, as if we were their tributaries."[38]

In these acts of banditry, excessive consumption of alcohol mingled with general discontent over colonial relations. The abundance of rum sold by English traders was in itself a chronic source of grievance, especially to Indian leaders and women. Furthermore, liquor heated tempers and fueled violent behavior among Indian men already angered by a growing negligence and intolerance displayed by officials. Violations of trade customs and diplomatic protocol often triggered violent retaliation. In 1770 about thirty Choctaws broke into the storehouse at Natchez and took away all of the merchandise and horses from the fort. Informed of the whereabouts of the bandits' camp by two other Choctaws and a Quapaw, a party of whites pursued them in the night, "expecting to find them drunk." The camp was alerted in time and fired thirteen or fourteen shots at the posse. The three friendly Indians led the firing into the camp, drove the bandits away, and retrieved the stolen goods. Two or three Choctaws were killed and two wounded in this skirmish; the Quapaw was wounded along with four white servants. One candid settler attributed

---

38. Clarence Walworth Alvord and Clarence Edward Carter, eds., *Trade and Politics, 1767–1769,* Illinois Historical Society, Collections, XVI (Springfield, Ill., 1921), 413–414; R. E. Chandler, "The St. Gabriel Acadians: The First Five Months," *LH,* XXI (1980), 288–289. For other reports of Choctaw banditry at this time, see the correspondence between Governor Unzaga and the commandant of Pointe Coupée during the spring of 1770: AGI, PC, leg. 188a.

this raid to both the Choctaws' dissatisfaction with the English commandant's unfulfilled promises of presents and the large quantity of rum being
sold to them at Natchez. Among the merchandise retaken from the bandits were fifty to sixty kegs of rum. The return of this large quantity of
alcohol to the storehouse was, in a sense, only more bad news for Indians
and colonists concerned about health and safety. Eventually the same rum
retrieved from a group of bandits would reach other Indians as traders
busily peddled it from village to village.[39]

Indian banditry along the lower Mississippi River also stemmed from
the westward migration of some groups of Choctaws, beginning in the
1760s, into Louisiana. Animosity toward the English, depletion of game
in familiar hunting locations, and continuing relations with Louisiana
traders were major incentives for the movement of many Choctaws down
the Pearl River and their resettlement on the north shore of Lake Pontchartrain. French settlers living in the area and resentful toward British
rule provided useful support to these Indian migrants. Yet Spanish officials
proved to be as unreceptive as their English counterparts to the presence
of apparently "wandering" Indians. Reporting on the Choctaws from
English territory "who would not stop coming" to the post at Iberville,
Governor Alexander O'Reilly observed late in 1769 that "most of the time
they are invited by the people who would have an interest in the pretext of
making them these presents." As hunting and trading increased in this
thickly pine-forested area, other colonial residents at Spanish Galveztown
and English Baton Rouge began exchanging rum, ammunition, and corn
for peltry, game, and bear oil produced by traveling Choctaw families.
Merchants in Pensacola and Mobile with privileged rights over Choctaw
trade were perturbed, and farmers and planters vulnerable to pilferage
also began to protest Indian activities in their neighborhood. Heavy rains
and high floods during the summer of 1782 aggravated tensions. Many
Choctaw were killing cattle as they would deer around Galveztown,
situated on a major road from Choctaw country to New Orleans. After a
Choctaw was fatally beaten in that settlement, vengeful warriors and their
families—numbering more than four hundred people by December—

39. EPR, IV, 101–104; *PMHS:CS*, V, 154–157. For a summary of related cases of
Indian banditry, see Robert R. Rea, "Redcoats and Redskins on the Lower Mississippi,
1763–1776: The Career of Lt. John Thomas," *LH*, XI (1970), 5–36.

marauded the area, forcing inhabitants to give them food and taking poultry and livestock from their yards.[40] The intensity of Indian banditry eventually dissipated, as Choctaw families extended their hunting and trading farther into Louisiana.[41]

IV

While the Choctaws, Chickasaws, and Upper Creeks grappled with new and old problems in West Florida, Indian villagers in other parts of the Lower Mississippi Valley adjusted to changing circumstances under Louisiana's Spanish administration. After Great Britain acquired West Florida, groups of Apalaches, Taensas, Pacanas, Mobilians, Biloxis, Chahtos, Pascagoulas, and Alibamons migrated from the Gulf Coast and Alabama River area to the lower banks of the Mississippi. These Indian migrants soon discovered that Louisiana belonged to Spain, not to the familiar French. Along with the Houmas, Chitimachas, and Tunicas still inhabiting their villages along the Mississippi, these petites nations now found their loyalty being tugged between British West Florida and Spanish Louisiana. Before Spain took possession of Louisiana, Governor Kerlérec had realized the benefits to be derived from the approximately eighty Apalache Indians, "being hunters and farmers," and in September 1763 decided to locate them at the rapids of the Red River. "There," recorded General Commissioner Abbadie, "they will be useful for aiding vessels ascending the river towards Natchitoches. Moreover, through their hunting, they will be able to supply New Orleans."[42]

In establishing authority over the east side of the Mississippi, the En-

40. *SMV*, I, 146–147, II, 20–21, 56, 59, 67–68, 382–384, III, 53–54; James Alexander Robertson, ed., *Louisiana under the Rule of Spain, France, and the United States, 1785–1807*, 2 vols. (Cleveland, Ohio, 1911), II, 103.

41. Lawrence Kinnaird and Lucia B. Kinnaird, "Choctaws West of the Mississippi, 1766–1800," *Southwestern Historical Quarterly*, LXXXIII (1979–1980), 349–370; White, *Roots of Dependency*, 92–96. This movement of some Choctaws to Lake Pontchartrain and of others west of the Mississippi River resulted in the permanent settlement by many in various parts of the present-day state of Louisiana. To follow their history to the present, see Fred B. Kniffen *et al.*, *The Historic Indian Tribes of Louisiana: From 1542 to the Present* (Baton Rouge, La., 1987), 94–98, 299–305.

42. Brasseaux, ed. and trans., *Journals of Iberville*, 101–102, 107, 112.

glish also vied for the services of these Indian migrants. During the spring of 1768, Montford Browne met a group of Chahtos and Mobilians building a new village on the Amite River and was welcomed at the palmetto-covered house of chief Mattaha with a calumet dance. The Indians had already supplied the English at Fort Bute with three boats. As Browne "found them a great deal disgusted against the Spaniards' late behavior," he persuaded them to settle closer to Baton Rouge after the year's harvest. "As these Savages are a good deal civilized, industrious and excellent Hunters," he wrote, "the acquisition will be the greater."[43]

The presence of so many petites nations along the Mississippi in the 1760s testified to their ability to endure nearly a century of severe pressures. Their survival as distinct peoples was largely due to the useful goods and services that they provided colonial society. In order to inaugurate Spanish relations formally with these Mississippi River nations, Governor O'Reilly invited delegations to New Orleans in the fall of 1769. On September 30, chiefs, interpreters, and other persons from the Tunicas, Taensas, Pacanas, Houmas, Bayogoulas, Ofogoulas, Chaouáchas, and Ouachas approached the general's house with song and music. Inside he greeted them under a canopy in the company of prominent residents of New Orleans. Each chief placed his weapon at O'Reilly's feet and waved a feather fan over his head. O'Reilly accepted their fans, smoked their pipes, and clasped their hands. Then the Bayogoula leader spoke for the delegation, offering loyalty to the Spanish and requesting that they "grant us the same favors and benefits as did the French." After exhorting the Indians to treat both the English in West Florida and the Spanish in Louisiana peaceably, O'Reilly placed medals hanging from scarlet ribbon around the chiefs' necks and had presents distributed. This procedure was repeated when the Chahtos, Biloxis, Pascagoulas, and Mobilians arrived on October 22, the Chitimachas on October 29, and the Quapaws on November 16. By January 1770 the approximately twenty villages still situated along the Mississippi River between New Orleans and Arkansas had altogether received 1,270 pesos worth of presents from the new colonial regime, signifying a successful transition from French to Spanish political relations.[44]

The new Louisiana government introduced two important reforms into

43. EPR, III, 94–95.
44. SMV, I, 101–102, 154–155.

the colony's relationship with Indian people. Like his counterpart in British West Florida, Governor Ulloa attempted both to reduce expenses and to regulate commerce with the region's native inhabitants. He attributed the "vicious custom" of gift-giving to the fact that "the merchants who trade with them, in order to secure greater profits, induce the Indians to come to the presidios, telling them that they will receive wonderful presents there." In the summer of 1768, Ulloa ordered "that the territories of the various tribes be distributed among the better class of traders, giving them licenses to enter the tribes to trade for one year and making them responsible for anything which may occur to the detriment of the peace and good relationships." These traders were required to "persuade the Indians not to come to the forts except at the customary times for receiving their presents and to supply them regularly with the things they customarily use so that it may not be necessary for them to come to the forts to ask for these as extra presents because they had not been supplied with them."[45]

In keeping with the Laws of the Indies, by which Spain governed its colonies, O'Reilly issued a proclamation on December 7, 1769, forbidding inhabitants of Louisiana to "acquire, purchase, or take over any Indian slaves." Although the practice of purchasing and enslaving Indians captured by allied tribesmen had diminished since the Chitimacha, Natchez, and Chickasaw wars, some colonists still owned Indian slaves in Louisiana. In 1763 at least one hundred Indians were slaves in the Lower Mississippi Valley, half of them living in New Orleans.[46] From 1770 onward, no more Indians could be enslaved in Louisiana, and those already living under slavery could not be sold by their owners. Avenues to emancipation available under Spanish law undoubtedly contributed to the eventual disappearance of an Indian slave population in Louisiana. But gradual absorption into the rapidly growing non-Indian population, especially African-American slaves, and a tightening racial structure—in which any combination of mixed ancestry was classified as "people of color"—probably did more to eliminate the number of Indian slaves.[47]

45. *SMV*, I, 61–62; Moore, *Revolt in Louisiana*, 92–102.

46. *SMV*, I, 125–126; Voorhies, comp. and trans., *Some Late Eighteenth-Century Louisianians*, 5–103; Katherine Bridges and Winston DeVille, "Natchitoches in 1766," *LH*, IV (1963), 156–159; *SMV*, I, 196.

47. Stephen Webre, "The Problem of Indian Slavery in Spanish Louisiana, 1769–1803," *LH*, XXV (1984), 117–135; Domínguez, *White by Definition*, 23–26. Interra-

Following O'Reilly's arrival at New Orleans in 1769, the Caddoes and their new neighbors on the Red River, the Wichitas, received a great deal of attention from Spanish governments in both Louisiana and Texas. Banditry on the western edge of the Lower Mississippi Valley was increasing as Indian and colonial groups transported livestock eastward from the Texas plains to the woodlands. Not only did the opposite flow of firearms and ammunition from Louisiana traders motivate Wichitas and other Indians to rob livestock from Texas forts and settlements, but the sale of the same items by intermediary native traders to the Apaches actually extended this contraband network even farther west. With Spain now in possession of the entire area and trying to colonize Texas, officials in the adjacent provinces coordinated as much as possible their efforts to prevent Indians from robbing livestock from presidios and rancherias in Texas and selling them to traders in Louisiana.[48]

In 1770 the Louisiana government initiated a series of trade restrictions for the upper Red River valley. O'Reilly prohibited "all persons whatsoever, from purchasing, trading for, or receiving horses or mules . . . which shall be confiscated." Three traders who received licenses to deal with Caddo villagers were not allowed to trade with Comanches or Wichitas. The chiefs of the villages of Grand Caddo and Yatasi agreed "not to furnish any arms or munitions of war to the Naÿtanes, Taouayaches, Tuacanas, Quitseys, etc.," all bands of Wichitas, and also to "have arrested and brought to this post all the *coureurs de bois* [traders and trappers], French, Spanish, or blacks, of whom they have knowledge, wandering in the Indian villages." In 1773 the Spanish disbanded their settlement at Los Adaes in order to reduce contraband trade, but to little

---

cial assimilation of Indian slaves did not alleviate the difficulty surrounding slaves' petitions for freedom, which was eventually inherited by the United States territorial government. As Orleans Territory Governor William Claiborne reported to Secretary of State James Madison in 1803, "In this Territory, there are now several hundred persons held as slaves, who are descended of Indian families" (Dunbar Rowland, ed., *Official Letter Books of W. C. C. Claiborne, 1801–1816*, 6 vols. [Jackson, Miss., 1917], IV, 179–181).

48. Herbert Eugene Bolton, ed. and trans., *Athanase de Mézières and the Louisiana-Texas Frontier, 1768–1780* [documents published from original Spanish and French MSS chiefly in the Archives of Mexico and Spain], 2 vols. (Cleveland, Ohio, 1914), II, 34; Teodoro de Croix to Domingo Cabello, Feb. 1, 1780, Bexar Archives, microfilm in Louisiana Division, New Orleans Public Library.

avail. The old settlers of Los Adaes returned to eastern Texas six years later and formed the town of Nacogdoches. Merchandise and livestock proceeded to flow through this new town as well as through Natchitoches, Opelousas, and Atakapas. Texas Indians continued to raid Spanish herds in order to exchange horses and mules for Louisiana merchandise.[49] As of December 1783, the governor of Texas was still pleading with Louisiana's governor to suppress the flow of arms and ammunition from Louisiana. "The proceeds of this trade," Domingo Cabello reported from San Antonio de Bexar, "serve as a stimulus to encourage them in their hostilities."[50]

The Taovayas and other Wichita villages entered the exchange network of the Lower Mississippi Valley on a more formal basis during the 1770s. Louisiana established official trade relations with them through the diplomatic skill of Athanase de Mézières, lieutenant governor of Natchitoches from 1769 until his death a decade later. At a meeting held in Grand Caddo, seven Wichita chiefs explained to de Mézières that "their discord with the Spaniards" was due to the assistance given by garrisons and missions to their enemies, the Apaches. On October 27, 1771, the Taovayas, the largest group of so-called Nortenos, agreed to "cease their incursions and their attacks upon all of the presidios of his Majesty, his subjects, and property of whatever kind."[51] Peace with these people, as with all other Indians in the Lower Mississippi Valley, required that the Louisiana government provide them with annual gifts and allow them to trade regularly with colonial peddlers. If they had not been able to continue "trading their peltry for guns, munitions, breech-cloths, hunting-knives, beads, and other things which they prize," warned the governor of Texas in 1772, the Wichitas would quite easily steal horses from Spanish settlers and sell them to the familiar French traders of Louisiana and even to the English, "whom they have so close by that only the Misissipi intervenes."[52]

49. Bolton, ed. and trans., *Athanase de Mézières*, I, 135, 148–150, 157–158; Cabello to de Croix, Dec. 20, 1780, Bexar Archives; *SMV*, II, 69–70. The early settlement of Los Adaes and other parts of eastern Texas is examined in Oakah L. Jones, Jr., *Los Paisanos: Spanish Settlers on the Northern Frontier of New Spain* (Norman, Okla., 1979).

50. *SMV*, II, 94.

51. Bolton, ed. and trans., *Athanase de Mézières*, I, 206–212, 256–259.

52. *Ibid.*, 129, 269–270, 300–301. For a closer look at the changing economic involvement of the Wichitas in colonial Louisiana, see Wayne Morris, "The Wichita

Wichita, Caddo, and Quapaw relations with Louisiana were severely tested by a number of challenges that developed during these transitional years. Spanish officials tried to fend off English traders from West Florida and Illinois, who, in the words of Teodorio de Croix in 1778, "lose no opportunity to introduce themselves among the Indians, both for the profit gained from the barter and for the welcome and the gratitude with which the Indians receive and entertain them, since for no Indian of the North is there any jewel more precious than firearms, which they already have in such abundance that they trade them to the citizens of San Antonio de Bejar for any trifle whatever."[53] After English traders began to penetrate the Arkansas district with their own supplies of alcohol, Quapaw villagers repeatedly intimidated the post commandant for a freer trade in liquor. Meanwhile, war parties of Osage Indians were acquiring arms and supplies at Illinois, where French and Spanish merchants aggressively traded from St. Louis and where even English competitors began to visit. The Osages intensified their southward raids against Caddo and Quapaw villages, stealing horses and skins and harming traders and Indians. Amid a devastating smallpox epidemic in 1777–1778, traders found it increasingly difficult to furnish their villages with merchandise at the rates of exchange set by de Mézières.[54]

The Caddoes grew impatient with the Spanish government, especially when they saw the lieutenant governor carrying gifts beyond their towns to the Wichitas. On November 1, 1780, de Mézières' successor at Natchitoches, Antonio Gil Ybamo, reported that the Caddoes "are destroying at every step my flags, staff of command, and medals, saying that they cannot live on the luster of these." By this time even the Taovayas began to feel the shortage. The following week Qui Te Sain, their chief, sent a message to

Exchange: Trade on Oklahoma's Fur Frontier, 1719–1812," *Great Plains Journal,* IX (1970), 79–84.

53. Bolton, ed. and trans., *Athanase de Mézières,* II, 222–223.

54. *Ibid.,* 131, 141–142, 231–232. For conditions along the lower Arkansas River, see Gilbert C. Din, "The Spanish Fort on the Arkansas, 1763–1803," *Arkansas Historical Quarterly,* XLII (1983), 271–293; and Morris S. Arnold, "The Relocation of Arkansas Post to *Ecores Rouges* in 1779," *Ark. Hist. Qtly.,* XLII (1983), 317–331; Arnold, *Unequal Laws unto a Savage Race: European Legal Traditions in Arkansas, 1686–1836* (Fayetteville, Ark., 1985), 66–83. The raiding activities of the Osages are fully documented in Gilbert C. Din and A. P. Nasatir, *The Imperial Osages: Spanish-Indian Diplomacy in the Mississippi Valley* (Norman, Okla., 1983), esp. 31–145.

the governor of Louisiana, which reported that "we are deprived of everything, and have neither hatchets, nor picks, nor powder, nor bullets to defend ourselves from our enemies." For many years to come, Spanish colonial officials grappled with these local problems in what was suddenly becoming one of the most volatile regions of international and intertribal conflict in North America.[55]

V

The period of political partition was also one of transition for African-American slaves in the Lower Mississippi Valley. With the development of plantation agriculture occurring at a faster pace, slaves faced tightening restrictions against social and economic activities that had helped mitigate bondage in Louisiana and had become integral to the frontier exchange economy. What had served as day-to-day means of accommodation became more strictly defined as criminal activities. Familiar forms of resistance, consequently, magnified into deeds of defiance. As in other colonial slave societies, many black Louisianians resorted to *petit marronage,* repetitive and temporary flights into the forests, to cope with the burdens or escape the abuses endemic in slavery. Inseparable from the comings and goings of runaway slaves were their small-scale banditry against plantations and their illicit marketing of goods. Beginning in the 1760s, running away from owners took on a larger significance as many slaves tried to take advantage of changing political conditions and as colonial officials fortified efforts to control a growing slave population.[56]

---

55. *SMV,* I, 390–392.

56. For a sample of petit marronage cases, see *RSCLHQ,* V, 246–247, 593–594, XII, 663, XIX, 768–771. Richard Price, ed., *Maroon Societies: Rebel Slave Communities in the Americas* (Garden City, N.Y., 1973), is an excellent comparative look at marronage in plantation societies across the Western Hemisphere. The long-term significance of African-American initiatives in economic life is explored in Philip D. Morgan, "Work and Culture: The Task System and the World of Lowcountry Blacks, 1700 to 1880," *William and Mary Quarterly,* 3d Ser., XXXIX (1982), 563–599.

Political implications of slave initiatives in the Atlantic seaboard colonies during this same period are explored in Philip D. Morgan, "Black Society in the Lowcountry, 1760–1810," in Ira Berlin and Ronald Hoffman, eds., *Slavery and Freedom in the Age of the American Revolution* (Charlottesville, Va., 1983), 83–141; Peter H. Wood,

Upon the intercolonial division of the Lower Mississippi Valley in 1762–1763, blacks in both British West Florida and Spanish Louisiana correctly perceived potential advantages in the geographical juxtaposition of colonies belonging to competing European nations. By 1766 the prisons in Mobile and New Orleans contained many slaves who tried to benefit from the early tension between provincial authorities by crossing the new boundary. The governor of West Florida, George Johnstone, wrote to Charles-Philippe Aubry refusing to deliver "the Negroes, Deserters from New Orleans, now in Custody at Mobile" until the Louisiana governor rendered "reciprocal Justice." Among the runaways then in the New Orleans prison were a mulatto and a Negro, the only survivors of five slaves who had fled from John McGillivray, a Mobile merchant, "in a Boat in order to go to new Orleans." A storm wrecked their vessel on one of the Chandeleur Islands in the Gulf of Mexico, and three persons died before a French boatman discovered the castaways.[57]

Officials and settlers in both colonies quickly realized the mutual interest in returning runaway slaves to their respective owners. Merchants involved in the sale of black men and women across the colonial boundary, such as John Fitzpatrick of Manchac, played a prominent role in negotiating and carrying out the return of runaways from one colony to another. While in New Orleans during the spring of 1769, Fitzpatrick took into his custody a slave woman and her child belonging to Daniel Ward, who had recently moved from that city to Mobile. "Married to a black Silver Smith and not wanting to quit him at this place," this woman and her child were closely guarded by the merchant until he was able to transport them to their owner in West Florida. Two years later Fitzpatrick reported to another merchant in Mobile that two Negro men had run away from a planter at Pointe Coupée "some time aGo" and were reportedly seen living among the Negroes on a plantation near Mobile.[58]

Such vigilance and cooperation among officials, planters, and merchants made flight from one province to another more difficult, but

---

"'Impatient of Oppression': Black Freedom Struggles on the Eve of White Independence," *Southern Exposure*, XII, no. 6 (November/December 1984), 10–16; Marvin L. Michael Kay and Lorin Lee Cary, "'They Are Indeed the Constant Plague of Their Tyrants': Slave Defence of a Moral Economy in Colonial North Carolina, 1748–1772," *Slavery and Abolition*, VI, no. 3 (December 1985), 37–56.

57. MPAED, I, 316–318.

58. Dalrymple, ed., *Letterbooks of Fitzpatrick*, 45, 110–111.

some slaves were not deterred from seeking freedom. Throughout the 1770s black prisoners were exchanged between the governments. A Negro named York, having fled from his English owner, managed to live on the Spanish side for "some time" until "he was taken up in the acadian Country" and brought to the New Orleans prison in 1778. By this time the costs of capturing, imprisoning, and transporting marrons like York ran very high, causing Governor Peter Chester of West Florida to recommend to his counterpart in Louisiana that "owners, of both nations, have the liberty of seeking their runaway negroes in the territory of each."59 Persistence by runaway slaves made cooperation between the colonies necessary even after war broke out between Spain and Great Britain. Following his siege of Pensacola in 1781, Governor General Bernardo de Gálvez assured the English that "the negroes who from fright have fled from Pensacola during the siege, shall be returned to their owners."60

In order to control enslaved laborers more effectively within both provinces, officials inflicted upon recalcitrant slaves the harshest forms of punishment allowed under their respective codes. "For them," Louisiana Governor Luis de Unzaga insisted, "quick, quite active and severe action, must be taken, and they must be treated with all the sternness of the law." In July 1764, Cesar, owned by a Chapitoulas planter, "was seized and convicted of being a fugitive slave, theft, and of having fired upon the citizens' militia and patrol." For these multiple acts of defiance, this slave had his hand amputated and was then broken on the wheel; his body was publicly exhibited on the road behind New Orleans. In June 1771 the Cabildo of New Orleans (municipal council) sentenced two Negroes, arrested for "whipping their master, Jean Baptiste LeBreton, and setting his hay loft on fire," to be "dragged by the tails of horses, hanged, and quartered."61 Over the ensuing decade the city government instituted a scale of bounties, in order to encourage the return of slaves, ranging from three pesos for the capture of a fugitive Negro within New Orleans to twelve pesos for the capture of one in the vicinity of Natchitoches, Atakapas, and

59. SMV, I, 247; Dalrymple, ed., Letterbooks of Fitzpatrick, 291–292; SPR, I, 189.
60. Gaspar Cusachs, trans., "Diary of the Operations of the Expedition against the Place of Pensacola, Concluded by the Arms of H. Catholic M., under the Orders of the Field Marshall Don Bernardo de Galvez," LHQ, I, no. 1 (January 1917), 82.
61. Unzaga to Bucarelli, June 22, 1771, Dispatches of the Spanish Governors of Louisiana; Brasseaux, ed. and trans., Journals of Iberville, 124.

Opelousas. It also paid free Negroes to pursue runaways and taxed slave-owners living in the city "in order to accumulate sufficient funds to pay for the prosecution and activities which will be made against savage Negroes."[62] Among the English plantations near Baton Rouge, several slaves were arrested in June 1776 for conspiring to assassinate their owners. A speedy trial resulted in the hanging of four men, while "Lesser punishments were inflicted on the less guilty."[63]

Flight to Indian villages in the hinterland, which had long been a risky option for daring slaves, was made less promising by an increase in official efforts to retrieve runaways from interior nations. On March 26, 1765, Governor Johnstone of West Florida informed the Choctaw and Chickasaw chiefs assembled at Mobile, "We farther Expect you will agree to bring in any Negroes who may desert their Masters Service, for which a proper reward will be allowed to the Person who Shall execute this Service." The return of runaway slaves was a customary obligation in these Indian nations' relationship with colonies, reciprocated with bounty payments. Now it was made even more competitive by incentives that West Florida offered to English traders for arresting slaves found in Indian villages.[64] In Spanish Louisiana similar conditions were arranged with old and new Indian allies. Caddo Chiefs visiting Natchitoches, for example, agreed with de Mézières in April 1770 to arrest slaves as well as French or Spanish "persons without occupation" in their villages, for a bounty of one musket and two ells of cloth per returned fugitive. The commandant of Natchitoches had recently issued stern prohibitions against slaves' holding public assemblies, trading with Indians, and possessing firearms and now found his district caught in a scare over slave insurrection.

62. Records and Deliberations of the New Orleans Cabildo, Aug. 27, Oct. 15, 1773, Nov. 17, 1775, Apr. 9, 1779, Sept. 27, 1782, Louisiana Division, New Orleans Public Library. Important contributions to the study of slavery in Spanish Louisiana are James Thomas McGowan, "Creation of a Slave Society: Louisiana Plantations in the Eighteenth Century" (Ph.D. diss., University of Rochester, 1976), 217–424; and Derek Noel Kerr, "Petty Felony, Slave Defiance, and Frontier Villainy: Crime and Criminal Justice in Spanish Louisiana, 1770–1803" (Ph.D. diss., Tulane University, 1983).

63. Eron Dunbar Rowland, comp., *Life, Letters, and Papers of William Dunbar* (Jackson, Miss., 1930), 26–27; Dalrymple, ed., *Letterbooks of Fitzpatrick*, 204. For a good summary of slave codes in the English province, see Fabel, *Economy of British West Florida*, 23–29.

64. *MPAED*, I, 223; Dalrymple, ed., *Letterbooks of Fitzpatrick*, 111.

"Among the vagabonds" whom he managed to retrieve from Indian villages was a slave of mixed Indian and European ancestry belonging to a planter at Pointe Coupée, more than one hundred miles away. Lami, as reported by de Mézières, "for many years has been living with the Cadodachos, being one of these who to flatter the Indians affect to despise our nation."[65]

The formation of larger and more aggressive maroon communities during the 1770s and 1780s signaled mounting rebelliousness among Louisiana slaves and evoked virulent repression from colonial officials. The swamplands bordering New Orleans and plantations along the lower Mississippi River offered slaves a refuge for extended periods of time. Runaways from different owners met in the low-lying forest and formed camps for purposes of plunder and self-defense. These bands mostly wandered from place to place, but some established more sedentary quarters hidden in thickets of oak and cypress trees and tall cane and cattails. Men, women, and children inhabited these makeshift villages and sustained themselves through hunting, fishing, gardening, and trading with Negroes left on the plantations. Adjustment to inhospitable conditions was surely difficult, but the physical hardships were offset by the reward of freedom from a slaveowner's control.

While post commandants became increasingly watchful for fugitives headed toward Indian villages, administrators in New Orleans concentrated on destroying maroon communities. In May 1781 a party of four white men and six armed slaves discovered two runaway villages in the swamps near Pointe Coupée. Six of the approximately fifteen villagers were arrested, and their testimony provided a valuable description of maroon life. Equipped with only an axe, hatchet, knife, file, and bayonet, this group of runaways lived in cane huts and cultivated corn and vegetables. They acquired sugar, salt, wine, lard, meat, and other provisions by pillaging neighboring farms and trading with slaves. They wove baskets, sifters, and other articles made from willow, which slaves on a nearby plantation sold for them in the city. Most alarming to officials and slaveowners, the men of these villages were employed by one settler at cutting and squaring trees at a wage of one and a half reales per squared timber.[66]

65. Ordinance by de Mézières, Jan. 21, 1770, AGI, PC, leg. 188a; Bolton, ed. and trans., *Athanase de Mézières,* I, 157–158, 165. Also see Gerald L. St. Martin, trans., "A Slave Trial in Colonial Natchitoches," *LH,* XXVIII (1987), 57–91.

66. *SJRLHQ,* XVI, 516–520.

In March 1783 an expedition of free Negroes and mulattoes under Lieutenant Guido Dufossat captured 23 inhabitants of a maroon village along Lake Borgne. Through theft and trade the members of this community, aptly called Terre Gaillarde, had accumulated a large quantity of guns and ammunition. The only means of approaching the camp was by wading through reeds and water up to the chest. Under the leadership of a notorious fugitive named San Malo, the marrons raided farms and ambushed travelers. San Malo and some of his comrades were absent when the slave-hunting posse traveled up Bayou L'Anse Vizio and surprised Terre Gaillarde. They ambushed the expedition on its return trip to New Orleans, but failed to rescue their fellow villagers. The destruction of Terre Gaillarde drove San Malo's band to commit further depredations, which intensified anxiety throughout the settler populace. Members of the New Orleans Cabildo became distrustful of the free Negroes and mulattoes employed to capture these bandits. Finally, in June 1783 a large detachment of troops arrested more than 50 runaways, including San Malo, and he and 3 other leaders were executed on June 19 at the town square. Eventually a total of some 120 captives taken during this crackdown on marronage were identified with Terre Gaillarde. The legend of San Malo, however, lasted for a long time among Louisiana slaves.[67]

67. *Ibid.*, XX, 841–865; Records and Deliberations of the New Orleans Cabildo, June 25–26, 1784. Gilbert C. Din, "*Cimarrones* and the San Malo Band in Spanish Louisiana," *LH,* XXI (1980), 237–262, examines this episode in full detail. In "Creole Slave Songs," *Century Magazine,* XXXI (1886), 814–815, George Washington Cable recorded the following dirge still popular among black New Orleanians during the late 19th century:

> Alas! young men, come, make lament
> For poor St. Malo in distress!
> They chased, they hunted him with dogs,
> They fired at him with a gun,
>
> .   .   .   .
>
> They hauled him from the cypress swamp,
> His arms they tied behind his back,
> They tied his hands in front of him;
> They tied him to a horse's tail,
> They dragged him up into the town.
> Before those grand Cabildo men
> They charged that he had made a plot
> To cut the throats of all the whites.
> They asked him who his comrades were;

VI

The partition of the Lower Mississippi Valley between Great Britain and Spain ended with the military conquest of West Florida by Spanish forces during the years 1779–1781. Late in 1776 Spain abandoned its neutrality over the American Revolution and began to provide assistance to the rebellious English colonies. New Orleans became a crucial entrepôt for arms and other supplies delivered to the Continental Congress. Spain openly declared war against Great Britain in 1779, and Governor Bernardo de Gálvez of Louisiana proceeded to organize three major campaigns against British garrisons in West Florida. As in former military expeditions in the region, slaves and Indians were deployed, alongside regular army and militia soldiers, by both provinces.[68]

For the large Indian nations east of the Mississippi River, participation in the Spanish-British war threatened deeper political embroilment than they needed. Choctaws, Chickasaws, and Upper Creeks demonstrated a general reluctance to become involved in this latest European conflict. But military assistance had become an unavoidable accompaniment to trade alliances. Tensions within the interior tribes were renewed, and already unstable relations with West Florida were exacerbated when agents from Spanish Louisiana besought their military services on behalf of the rebellious English colonies. At a conference with British officials in May 1777, a delegation of Choctaw and Chickasaw leaders agreed to patrol

---

Poor St. Malo said not a word!
The judge his sentence read to him,
And they raised the gallows-tree.
They drew the horse—the cart moved off—
And left St. Malo hanging there.
The sun was up an hour high
When on the Levee he was hung;
They left his body swinging there,
For carrion crows to feed upon.

68. For a useful overview of Louisiana's role in the American Revolution, see Light T. Cummins, "Spanish Imperial Policy in Louisiana during the American Revolution," *Revue de Louisiane/Louisiana Review*, VII (1978), 155–165. William S. Coker and Robert R. Rea, eds., *Anglo-Spanish Confrontation on the Gulf Coast during the American Revolution* (Pensacola, Fla., 1982), is a sample of current approaches to the war years in Florida and Louisiana. Details of the three campaigns are fully told in Starr, *Tories, Dons, and Rebels*, 142–215.

the Mississippi River in search of American military convoys. But during the following two years, most Indian villagers preoccupied themselves with their own interests and security. They used every opportunity to remind both the Spanish and English that any military alliance depended upon an adequately supplied and well-regulated trade. Unwilling to furnish them with satisfactory gifts and hospitality, General John Campbell of West Florida failed to secure the number of Choctaw warriors needed to defend Mobile, which quickly fell to Gálvez's army on March 14, 1780. As later warned by agent Farquhar Bethune, "Reason and Rhetoric will fall to the Ground unless supported by Strouds and Duffells."[69]

By the summer of 1780, the intervention of European agents and the scarcity of merchandise began to divide the tribes into wavering factions. In order to recruit warriors for the defense of Pensacola, Campbell hosted a feast in early July. A Spanish officer at Mobile expressed surprise over "the goods which the English are giving to the savages," but did not believe "that they will succeed in attracting all the Choctaws for several have told me that it was only necessity and nothing else that made them go to secure things from the English." As in previous struggles fueled by intercolonial rivalry, the Choctaws disagreed among themselves over which side to support. But now, with the civil war of the 1740s still fresh in their memory, they proceeded with a caution and disinterest shared by the Chickasaws and Upper Creeks. During the closing months of 1780, only a few parties took part in some skirmishes at the military outposts around Mobile and Pensacola. By the time a Spanish army of some four thousand men reached Pensacola Bay, only four hundred Choctaw and one hundred Creek warriors could be mustered to join the one thousand British soldiers, one hundred settlers, and fifty slaves who unsuccessfully defended Pensacola in March and April 1781.[70]

---

69. James H. O'Donnell III, *Southern Indians in the American Revolution* (Knoxville, Tenn., 1973), is the best overview of southeastern Indian diplomacy and warfare during these years. Bethune is quoted by O'Donnell on p. 101. Also see Helen Hornbeck Tanner, "Pipesmoke and Muskets: Florida Indian Intrigues of the Revolutionary Era," in Samuel Proctor, ed., *Eighteenth-Century Florida and Its Borderlands* (Gainesville, Fla., 1975), 13–39.

70. *SMV*, I, 382–383, 419–421; O'Donnell, *Southern Indians in the American Revolution*, 104, 112; Starr, *Tories, Dons, and Rebels*, 182–183. The best modern analyses of Indian strategies include Michael D. Green, "The Creek Confederacy in the American Revolution: Cautious Participants," and Kathryn Holland, "The Anglo-

The Treaty of Paris of 1783 conveyed all of the Floridas below the thirty-first parallel to Spain and recognized claims by the independent United States of America to all other territory east of the Mississippi River. This newest geographical realignment of the Lower Mississippi Valley opened an era of diplomatic contest and economic change that rapidly transformed life in the region for Indians, settlers, and slaves alike. With the hindsight of this subsequent process available to us, the 1760s and 1770s indeed appear to have been ominous. But the people of that time, still producing and trading within the framework of frontier exchange, only dimly perceived that they were engaged in a struggle to maintain a semiautonomous way of life against invasive and overwhelming economic change.

Spanish Contest for the Gulf Coast as Viewed from the Townsquare," in Coker and Rea, eds., *Anglo-Spanish Confrontation*, 54–75, 90–105.

II

THE FRONTIER

EXCHANGE ECONOMY

It is time to explore more closely the frontier exchange economy of the Lower Mississippi Valley. Chapter 5 focuses on the various means of production at Indian villages and camps and at colonial farms and plantations. There, farming, gathering, hunting, fishing, and herding practices freely crossed intercultural lines over the eighteenth century. In such manner Indians, settlers, and slaves balanced their subsistence needs with commercial pressures and confronted the colonial government's efforts to expand the economy's transatlantic exports. They stitched together a patchwork of seasonal activities that harvested plenty of food sources from the rich wetlands and forests. The movement through the frontier exchange network of those foodstuffs is traced in Chapter 6. In this face-to-face exchange of grains, game, and other produce, inhabitants played a diversity of roles that helped shape a unique set of mores and a common culture while sharpening class lines and reshaping their individual cultures. Not least important was the emergence of a distinctive, multicultural cuisine.

The essential but low-status frontier labor of troops and boatmen in this intercultural exchange is studied in Chapter 7. Men from both the colonial and native populations participated widely in Louisiana's military service and water transportation. But the adversities and possibilities faced by army and navy personnel in their daily life would drive many into sundry, and sometimes subversive, relationships with other groups. Chapter 8 describes the widespread exchange and marketing system of peltry, which embraced Indians, settlers, and slaves in a diverse and diffuse network. Although traders increasingly channeled Indian-produced furs directly to coastal ports for export, a significant amount of deerskins moved across the Lower Mississippi Valley through small-scale transactions. At many different points of exchange, a variety of people were able to influence the value of goods, the language spoken, and the means of transportation.

During most of the eighteenth century, change in these economic activities and relations occurred gradually and piecemeal. But those patterns and shifts before the Mississippi Valley was divided between the United States and Spain in 1783 foreshadowed a transformation that eventually swept the region once colonial governments implemented stronger immigration, commercial, and slavery policies. After 1783 this frontier exchange economy began to unravel, as plantation agriculture, racial stratification, and fur trade monopolization undermined the flexibility and fluidity previously enjoyed through older systems of livelihood. Not as easily uprooted as they were controlled, however, the economic customs and intercultural relations fostered over the previous century would endure for many Indians, settlers, and slaves as vital strategies of survival and resistance for a long time to come.

5

FARMING, HUNTING, AND HERDING

Activities surrounding the production of food and other goods among Indians, settlers, and slaves were the foundation of the frontier exchange economy. Various forms of agriculture blended with procurement of wild plants and animals and with the herding of livestock to form a distinct pattern of livelihood. Similar methods of production pervaded Indian and colonial communities, largely because settlers and slaves borrowed practices from Indians. Indian villagers in the Lower Mississippi Valley had a long tradition of mixing the cultivation of crops with hunting, gathering, and fishing. During the eighteenth century they continued producing for their own needs but also participated in the colonial economy by provisioning local markets, hunting white-tailed deer for the overseas market, and even bringing livestock into the region. Many colonists practiced a similar combination of farming, hunting, and trading with varying degrees of commitment to production of export staples. In the course of a year, settlers and slaves planted food crops, tobacco, and perhaps some indigo, raised poultry and livestock, and pursued fish, deer, and smaller animals—for their own subsistence and for periodic exchange with each other.[1]

Some specialized loci of production nonetheless developed, integrating

1. This chapter is by no means an attempt at what is now called the new environmental history. But in its examination of land-use practices among both the native and colonial inhabitants of a region, it does resemble works like William Cronon, *Changes in the Land: Indians, Colonists, and the Ecology of New England* (New York, 1983); and Timothy Silver, *A New Face on the Countryside: Indians, Colonists, and Slaves in South Atlantic Forests, 1500–1800* (Cambridge, 1990).

different areas into the regional network of exchange. Every winter in lowland forests of oak, hickory, and other hardwoods that bordered the meandering waterways, camps of Indian families dispersed to hunt white-tailed deer and black bear for their own subsistence and for the regional economy. In the bountiful maze of lowland forests along the Arkansas, White, and St. Francis rivers, annual hunting expeditions from New Orleans produced increasing quantities of meat for colonial consumption and furs for commercial exportation. Through the intermixture of bayous, lakes, wooded hills, and swampy morasses of lower Louisiana, Indians and colonists transported horses, mules, and cattle eastward from the Texas plains. This major movement of animals provided the original stock for breeding livestock in Indian villages as well as colonial settlements, where people raised small herds on open pasture.

I

The mixture of subsistence activities supporting livelihood across the Lower Mississippi Valley during the eighteenth century originated in the woodland economy developed by Indian villagers over previous centuries. The relative importance of particular means of production like farming or fishing varied from tribe to tribe, depending upon the ecological niche occupied by the group. Life in the floodplain of the Mississippi River revolved more heavily around the seasonal procurement of abundant fishes, mammals, and wild plants available in lowland forests and waters, whereas people living on upland terraces or in the hilly country devoted more of their subsistence cycle to planting corn, beans, and other domestic plants on fertile ground. Regionally, however, Indians had created village economies that efficiently exploited a wide range of resources.[2]

In the alluvial lowlands Indian villages occupied natural levees, where inhabitants cultivated crops on narrow fields during the summer and procured a variety of wild foods into the fall. Deer, opossums, raccoons,

2. Daniel H. Usner, Jr., "A Cycle of Lowland Forest Efficiency: The Late Archaic-Woodland Economy of the Lower Mississippi Valley," *Journal of Anthropological Research*, XXXIX (1983), 433–444.

rabbits, and muskrats were hunted in the swamps, where they could easily be pursued along limited pathways with bow and arrow. October was the best time of year for stalking deer, because the rutting behavior of bucks peaks then. Indians collected a wide variety of fruits and seeds along the levees and waterways, with acorns, pecans, and hickory nuts becoming an important food source by the late autumn.[3] The high density of fish impounded in backwater lakes after spring flooding receded made catching them with a variety of nets and poisonous plants easy during the summer and fall. At an Acolapissa village on the north shore of Lake Pontchartrain, André Pénicaut in 1706 witnessed Indians fishing from boats with trot lines. With some cornmeal dough or meat attached to wooden or bone hooks set a foot apart, they "do not fail to catch fish weighing more than fifteen or twenty pounds." Lines were pulled up about twice a day, which "does not keep them from working in their field, for it can be attended to in less than half an hour."[4]

European observers in the early eighteenth century noted both the diversity of wildlife and the skill with which different species were obtained. The raccoon and opossum especially fascinated foreign visitors, Antoine Le Page Du Pratz reporting that the "wild cat," or raccoon, "may be tamed, and then becomes very frolicksome and full of tricks." Commenting on the accessibility of the "wood rat," as he called the opossum, "it is very rare to see any creature walk so slow; and I have often catched them when walking my ordinary pace." "Every where to be met with," the white-tailed deer was hunted by Indians "sometimes in companies, and sometimes alone." Le Page Du Pratz and Pénicaut both described in detail

3. H. H. Kopman, *Wildlife Resources of Louisiana: Their Nature, Value, and Protection,* Louisiana Department of Conservation, Bulletin, no. 10 (New Orleans, 1921); G. H. Lowery, *The Mammals of Louisiana and Its Adjacent Waters* (Baton Rouge, La., 1974), 492; Bruce D. Smith, *Middle Mississippi Exploitation of Animal Populations,* University of Michigan Museum of Anthropology, Papers, no. 57 (Ann Arbor, Mich., 1975), 37–38.

4. Richebourg Gaillard McWilliams, ed. and trans., *Fleur de Lys and Calumet: Being the Pénicaut Narrative of French Adventure in Louisiana* (Baton Rouge, La., 1953), 109 (hereafter cited as *Pénicaut Narrative*); Antoine Le Page Du Pratz, *The History of Louisiana,* ed. Joseph G. Tregle, Jr. (London, 1774; facs. rpt., Baton Rouge, La., 1975), 287; Victor W. Lambou, "Fish Populations of Backwater Lakes in Louisiana," American Fisheries Society, *Transactions,* LXXXVIII (1959), 7–15.

how Indians stalked deer by approaching a buck with the dried head of a deer over themselves and making sounds to attract it close enough for the kill. In the fall Indians also burned dry grass, both to improve its feeding potential and to ease the movement of small animals. As explained by Le Page Du Pratz, "The game spread themselves all over the meadows, and delight to feed on the new grass; which is the reason why travelers more easily find provisions at this time than at any other." Small herds of buffalo scattered across the Gulf Plain, and Indian uses of bison meat and robes were observed by Europeans in the late seventeenth and early eighteenth centuries. But the migration of these large mammals into the southeastern woodlands seems to have been a fairly recent phenomenon. Their arrival had perhaps been facilitated by the Indian practice of burning, but was suddenly reversed by intensive hunting during the early colonial period.[5]

From late summer through autumn, an abundance of fresh fruits, berries, and nuts was also prominent in the Indian diet. Father Jacques Gravier, who visited the Tunicas in November 1700, remarked that "there are such quantities of piakimina [persimmon] that whole families go together to the woods to gather it." Indian women across the Lower Mississippi Valley mixed nuts and fruits into a variety of dishes and even made breads from wild plants. In making persimmon bread, according to Le Page Du Pratz, they "squeeze the fruit over fine sieves to separate the pulp from the skin and the kernels." From the resulting paste, "they make cakes about a foot and a half long, a foot broad, and a finger's breadth in thickness." Wild plants harvested in autumn were also dried and stored for use during other parts of the year.[6]

Over the winter months Indians dispersed into camps along lakes and bayous in order to exploit food sources that were less mobile and diverse than those of other seasons. With the shedding of antlers by bucks and the scarcity of vegetation during this time, deer confined themselves to the most heavily wooded swamps. Consuming much less food, bucks and

---

5. Le Page Du Pratz, *History*, ed. Tregle, 134, 256, 264–265; *Pénicaut Narrative*, 112; Erhard Rostlund, "The Geographic Range of the Historic Bison in the Southeast," Association of American Geographers, *Annals*, L (1960), 395–407.

6. Reuben Gold Thwaites, ed., *The Jesuit Relations and Allied Documents: Travels and Explorations of the Jesuit Missionaries in New France, 1610–1791*, 73 vols. (Cleveland, Ohio, 1896–1901), LXV, 133–135; Le Page Du Pratz, *History*, ed. Tregle, 233.

does lost a lot of weight in winter.[7] So Indian hunters turned more attention to the black bear, an important source of meat and oil. Bears in the hardwood bottomlands would gain weight between October and December and hibernate, usually inside the hollow trunk of a fallen tree, for weeks at a time from November to March. When Indians discovered a "fat and lazy" bear, as observed by Le Page Du Pratz, they "gather a heap of dried canes, which they bruise with their feet, that they may burn the easier, and one of them mounting upon a tree adjoining to that in which the bear is, sets fire to the reeds, and darts them one after another into the breach; the other hunters having planted themselves in ambuscade upon other trees. The bear is quickly burned out of his habitation, and he no sooner appears on the outside, than they let fly their arrows at him, and often kill him before he gets to the bottom of the tree."[8]

Winter hunting bands also procured fish and fowl from watered areas across the floodplain. Although some villagers used nets to catch fish annually trapped by flooding in the small backwater lakes, Indians generally used a hook and line to catch catfish and trout, among an array of different fishes found in plentiful rivers, lakes, and estuaries. In the deltas they gathered clams, oysters, and crabs while also taking advantage of the density of migratory waterfowl. "When winter came," Pénicaut and his Indian hosts "went out to the channel and into the woods to kill bustards, ducks, and wild geese that are much bigger than the geese in France. During that season unbelievable numbers of them are attracted to Lake Pontchartrain, and there they stay along the lake shore."[9]

With spring marked by rising water levels on the rivers, Indians returned to their villages situated on protected natural levees or bluffs. Here

7. Kopman, *Wildlife Resources of Louisiana*, 34–36; Louisiana Wildlife and Fisheries Commission, *Seasonal Variation in Food Consumption and Weight Gain in Male and Female White Tailed Deer*, 12th Biennial Report (New Orleans, 1968), 129.

8. Le Page Du Pratz, *History*, ed. Tregle, 261–262; Lowery, *Mammals of Louisiana*, 409.

9. *Pénicaut Narrative*, 101–102, 112, 138; Ruth Lapham Butler, trans., *Journal of Paul Du Ru (February 1 to May 8, 1700), Missionary Priest to Louisiana* (Chicago, 1934), 30–37; James Warren Springer, "The Prehistory and Cultural Geography of Coastal Louisiana" (Ph.D. diss., Yale University, 1973); J. Richard Shenkel, *Oak Island Archaeology: Prehistoric Estuarine Adaptations in the Mississippi River Delta*, Report for the Jean Lafitte National Historical Park, National Park Service (New Orleans, 1980).

they concentrated on mammals driven upland by flooding. Deer would scatter into sparse herds and feed on a generally less than desirable browse in the piney forests. Sometimes especially high water forced Indians to hunt farther than usual and even to abandon their own towns. When Pénicaut visited the Quapaws in the spring of 1700, he observed that "they could give us only a little food, because the Missicipy River had overflowed its banks and beasts had withdrawn to more than sixty leagues from the river bank."[10] Spring-ripening fruits like mayhaws and blackberries were also gathered then. And once the rivers began to recede from their banks, Indians turned to agriculture.

In order to start new fields in forested lowlands, Indians had to clear thick patches of cane and sometimes remove oak and cypress trees before planting their crops. Cutting and burning proved to be effective methods of removal. Le Page Du Pratz observed Indian farmers cutting the canes in early March and peeling a ring of several feet of bark off the base of the trees, "as then the sap is in motion in that country." Two weeks later when the dry canes were set afire, "the sap of the trees are thereby made to descend, and the branches are burnt, which kills the trees." Fields prepared in this way acquired high fertility without much labor and without animal fertilizers. The seeds of corn were sown directly into the nutritive ashes of burnt wood and cane. "Such as begin a plantation in woods, thick set with cane," noted Le Page Du Pratz, "have an advantage in the maiz, that makes amends for the labor of clearing the ground." This system of agriculture, however, required that bottomland fields be left fallow after several harvest seasons for new vegetation to grow. What were impenetrable canebrakes one decade became productive fields the next, and vice versa. The actual longevity of Indian fields remains uncertain, but the periodic relocation of fields in lowland forests probably contributed to some of the change in village locations during the eighteenth century.[11]

10. P. D. Goodman and V. H. Reid, "Deer Browsing in the Longleaf Pine Belt," Society of American Forestry, *Proceedings, 1958* (1959), 139–143; Henry A. Pearson and Herbert S. Sternitzke, "Deer Browse Inventories in the Louisiana Coastal Plain," *Journal of Wildlife Management,* XL (1976), 326–329; *Pénicaut Narrative,* 34–35.

11. Le Page Du Pratz, *History,* ed. Tregle, 184. For a general discussion of slash-and-burn agriculture, see Ester Boserup, *The Conditions of Agricultural Growth: The Economics of Agrarian Change under Population Pressure* (Chicago, 1965), 15–30; and Marshall D. Sahlins, *Tribesmen* (Englewood Cliffs, N.J., 1968), 30–31. The effects

11

The forms of production practiced by settlers and slaves in colonial Louisiana resembled those long used by Lower Mississippi Valley Indians, mainly because such a mixture of farming, hunting, fishing, and gathering protected them from the environmental and economic uncertainties of living in a strange land. Cultivation of food plants that worked for Indians, on small plots of bottomland, secured a livelihood for most colonial inhabitants. Few farmers could afford to devote all of their agricultural production to export crops like tobacco or indigo. At best they sought a balance between commercial and subsistence farming. Even on the largest plantations, slaves spent much of their time producing their own food sources. Settlers and slaves also pursued wild plants and animals in neighboring forests and waters in order to round out their diet. Sometimes a flood, drought, or hurricane wiped out colonial and Indian fields, making alternative sources of food essential.

Most settlers in the Lower Mississippi Valley cultivated a mixture of food crops, especially corn and rice, on farms of fewer than 200 acres. During the 1720s small farms called *habitations* gradually spread along the banks of the Mississippi between the New Orleans area and the settlement of Pointe Coupée. In order to keep colonists there and to encourage agriculture, the Company of the Indies offered settlers moderately sized tracts of free land, usually with 5 arpents of river frontage and 40 arpents deep from the bank (200 arpents, or 170 acres). "A man with his wife or his partner," wrote Father Paul Du Poisson in 1727, "clears a little ground, builds himself a house on four piles, covers it with sheets of bark, and plants corn and rice for his provisions; the next year he raises a little more for food, and has also a field of tobacco; if at last he succeed in having three or four Negroes, then he is out of his difficulties." Resembling a village of sorts, neighboring farms composed a single settlement or district.[12] Ordinances prohibiting speculation and providing free conces-

---

of Indian agriculture on the vegetation of the Southeast are discussed in Erhard Rostlund, "The Myth of a Natural Prairie Belt in Alabama: An Interpretation of Historical Records," Association of American Geographers, *Annals*, LXVII (1957), 392–411.

12. Thwaites, ed., *Jesuit Relations*, LXVII, 283. The significance of corn and rice in the Louisiana diet will be discussed in Chapter 6.

sions during the French period did not completely prevent land monopolization, but they did ease the process of settlement for many propertyless immigrants. This pattern of long, thin grants of land stretching back from frontage on the river and averaging fewer than 200 acres was adopted by Spain and Great Britain in their later efforts to colonize the region with families of farmers. Each farmer received a grant of land on the Mississippi or some other waterway and was obliged to cultivate the soil within a year and to maintain a levee to control flooding.[13]

Some continuity between Indian and colonial farming can be attributed to use of Indian fields and of Indian laborers in early Louisiana. Abandoned native villages became prime sites for the location of concessions granted by the Company of the Indies. Previously cleared areas appropriated by Europeans in colonial North America were known to the English as "Indian old fields" and to the French as "vieux villages." In Louisiana they included both scattered fields left fallow by Indian cultivators and entire townsites deserted because of epidemics, wars, or migrations. The concession granted to Paris Duvernay was located about seventy miles above New Orleans at the old village of the Bayogoulas. Situated seven or eight arpents west of the riverbank of the Mississippi and relatively safe from flooding, this site contained, according to a company official, "two hundred and fifty arpents of land in which the plough may pass everywhere." Ten miles downriver most of the German families who had endured their migration to Louisiana formed a settlement "on very good land where there were formerly Indian fields easy to cultivate."[14] In some cases individual settlers and soldiers purchased parcels of farm land directly from Indian villagers in order to begin planting their own crops more easily. Rarely were Indian lands coerced from them, but Indian labor

13. Lewis Cecil Gray, *History of Agriculture in the Southern United States to 1860*, 2 vols. (Washington, D.C., 1933), I, 337–340; John G. Clark, *New Orleans, 1718–1812: An Economic History* (Baton Rouge, La., 1969), 52, 183–186. To compare land distribution in Louisiana with that in Canada, see Richard Colebrook Harris, *The Seigneurial System in Early Canada: A Geographical Study* (Madison, Wis., 1966), 20–40, 117–138.

14. Heloise H. Cruzat, trans., "Louisiana in 1724: Banet's Report to the Company of the Indies, Dated Paris, December 20, 1724," *LHQ*, XII (1929), 121–133; Cruzat, trans., "Sidelights on Louisiana History," *LHQ*, I, no. 3 (January 1918), 99–100. Also see Marcel Giraud, *Histoire de la Louisiane française*, IV, *La Louisiane après le système de law (1721–1723)* (Paris, 1974), 196–215.

was expropriated through warfare. Between 1708 and 1722 the number of Indian slaves working on Louisiana farms increased from 80 to 169. These men and women undoubtedly showed Europeans and Africans working beside them some useful techniques for raising food.[15]

Gradually an increasing number of petits habitants committed their farms to the production of export crops, especially if they managed to purchase a few slaves. They and a small number of wealthier planters introduced new forms of production to the Lower Mississippi Valley—operations geared toward producing larger quantities of tobacco, indigo, and other commodities for the Atlantic market. In addition to the financial shortcomings suffered as producers in a marginal colony, Louisiana planters specializing in commercial crops faced the environmental hazards of heavy rains and floods, hurricanes, and even periodic droughts. Excessive rain during the summer of 1728 ruined most of Louisiana's tobacco crop, including twenty thousand pounds owned by Governor Périer, who joked bitterly, "I did not at first feel my loss because I thought that the deluge of water that we have experienced for fifty days would carry me away after my tobacco." Just two years later a severely dry season prevented the governor and others from even planting tobacco, and then in 1732 three-fourths of the tobacco seed from a very successful harvest was destroyed by a hurricane that struck on August 29. With planting delayed in the spring of 1734 by three months of flooding, Louisiana officials prematurely lamented: "This country is subject to such great vicissitude that one can almost not count on the crops at all. Now there is too much drought, now too much rain." Levees and canals were constructed in time and allowed tobacco and indigo producers to withstand seasonal risks, but exportation of commercial crops from the Lower Mississippi Valley remained erratic until the end of the eighteenth century.[16]

15. Le Page Du Pratz, *History,* ed. Tregle, 20–22, 27–28; Jean François Benjamin Dumont de Montigny, "Historical Memoirs of M. Dumont" (1753), in B. F. French, ed., *Historical Collections of Louisiana,* 5 vols. (New York, 1846–1853), V, 31; Charles R. Maduell, Jr., comp. and trans., *The Census Tables for the French Colony of Louisiana from 1699 through 1732* (Baltimore, 1972), 16–27; Glenn R. Conrad, ed. and trans., *Immigration and War: Louisiana, 1718–1721: From the Memoir of Charles Le Gac* (Lafayette, La., 1970), 61–62.

16. MPAFD, I, 168–170, II, 586–587, III, 637–638, IV, 43; Clark, *New Orleans,* 61–87; Jacob M. Price, *France and the Chesapeake: A History of the French Tobacco*

After the destruction of the early plantations at Natchez by the Indians in 1729, until resettlement of that area during the 1770s, settlers at the more defensible settlement of Pointe Coupée cultivated most of the tobacco shipped from Louisiana. By 1745 the population of Pointe Coupée consisted of 260 whites, 426 blacks, 23 Indians, and 15 mulattoes. Slaves belonged to 75 percent of the district's sixty-one households, which included a garrison and church. Monsieur Trenaunay, the settlement's largest propertyholder, owned thirty-eight Negro slaves and one Indian slave who cultivated a combination of tobacco, corn, and beans on 120 arpents of cleared land. Half of all slaves at Pointe Coupée inhabited only eight farms, with twenty or more slaves, but the average number of slaves per farm was nine. Among the aspiring, smaller tobacco planters there was a free Indian woman named Marie, who with seven slaves and a white husband cultivated twenty arpents of cleared land.[17]

Production of tobacco demanded many months of meticulous labor and dragged farmers through moments of grueling uncertainty. Seeds had to be sown on the open field by February in order for the growing plants to be removed to a carefully cleared and fenced tobacco garden during the rainy season. After replanting them at three feet apart in straight rows, workers daily had to remove the worms, weeds, and buds from the delicate plants. As explained by one Louisiana tobacco planter, "You must look over every plant, and every leaf, in order to sucker it, or pull off the buds, which grow at the joints of the leaves; and at the same time you must destroy the large green worms that are found on the tobacco, which are often as large as a man's finger, and would eat up the whole plant in a night's time." Farmers also had to worry about the possibility of heavy rain destroying these pampered plants. As soon as the leaves became brittle, usually by August, workers had to cut the tobacco and hang it inside a tobacco shed. Many a time, the planter must have looked up and wondered whether his leaves were of marketable quality. Once they became completely dry, the leaves were stripped from their stalks and prepared for shipment to New Orleans.[18] Then one had to worry about the

---

Monopoly, 1674–1791, and of Its Relationship to the British and American Tobacco Trades, 2 vols. (Ann Arbor, Mich., 1973), I, 302–360.

17. Bill Barron, ed., Census of Pointe Coupée, Louisiana, 1745 (New Orleans, 1978).

18. Jean François Benjamin Dumont de Montigny, Mémoires historiques sur la Louisiane, 2 vols. (Paris, 1753), I, 34–43. Vol. II of Dumont's Mémoires is translated in

price of tobacco dropping again (as it tended to do after 1730) or about one's crop rotting en route or on the levee before a merchant ship reached the colony. When Joseph Herbert brought nineteen cases of tobacco from Pointe Coupée to New Orleans in September 1741, his creditor, J. B. Piemont, found "most of the lot wet and rotten and the rest very poor and marred by infectious influence of rotten portion, unfit for export." If prices dropped too low or if merchants refused to buy his crop, the planter went into deeper debt to purchase the clothing, tools, wine, brandy, and other imported goods needed to start the cycle of production all over again.[19]

Involving more capital investment, larger labor forces, and even greater financial entanglement than tobacco farming, the production of indigo was limited to a small group of planters who lived around New Orleans. Increasing from about fifteen in the 1730s to fifty by the 1760s, indigo plantations produced Louisiana's most valuable export commodity per pound in the form of a blue dye highly demanded by European clothing manufacturers.[20] The cultivation of indigo was far less complicated than that of tobacco, but as described by one Louisiana observer the conversion of these plants into the lucrative export commodity still was labor-intensive:

When the plant is ripe, it is cut down and brought to a twenty-foot-high shed that has a roof held up by poles instead of walls. In this shed there are three vats placed in such a way that water from one can run into the next. The indigo leaves and a certain amount of water, in which they are permitted to rot, are placed in the highest vat. When the man in charge of the operation decides, after frequent inspection, that the time is right, he opens a spout, and the water runs into the next vat. . . .

When all the water is in the second vat, it is beaten until the overseer, through his long experience, decides that the process is to stop. The water is then permitted to settle, and the indigo forms a sediment at the bottom of the vat. As the liquid becomes clear, it is

vol. V of the already cited *Historical Collections of Louisiana.* I have also used the original manuscript of the *Mémoires* in the Edward E. Ayer Collection, Newberry Library, Chicago.

19. *RSCLHQ*, V, 466–477, XI, 136–137; *SJRLHQ*, VII, 185.
20. *MPAFD*, V, 39, 114–115; AC, C13A, XXIII, 134, XXXVIII, 261.

run off in gradual stages through a series of spouts placed one beneath the other.

The indigo is then removed from the vat and is . . . permitted to seep. It is then dried on boards and cut into little squares, which are packed into barrels for shipment to Europe.[21]

The production of naval stores—another important set of export commodities—occupied many settlers and slaves, especially during months of slow agricultural activity. By the 1730s several pitch-and-tar manufacturers operated along the north shore of Lake Pontchartrain, in one of the region's thickest pine forests. As split pieces of pine trees were burned over pits, the resin dripped into them and drained through interconnected canals dug into the ground. In order to make pitch, red-hot cannon balls were thrown into some of the tar pits. The tar then ignited, the remaining moisture dissipated, and the substance turned into a hardened pitch. The owners of naval store operations in Louisiana usually hired slaves from planters for short periods of time. On April 29, 1735, for example, Jean François Pasquier leased fifteen Negroes to tar manufacturer Antoine Aufrere for a term of six months and a fee of 1,125 livres.[22] During the autumn and winter months many planters themselves sent their slaves into swamps behind the plantations to cut valuable cypress trees and float the timber along canals draining into the Mississippi. Cargoes of pitch and tar went to shipyards in France, and most of the lumber and staves produced in Louisiana went to the West Indies.[23]

Even on farms inextricably tied to the Atlantic market, settlers and slaves combined subsistence and commercial activities into their seasonal cycle of production. Farmers supplemented their diet with game, fish, and other wild foods taken from local forests and waters. Slaves hunted,

21. Seymour Feiler, ed. and trans., *Jean-Bernard Bossu's Travels in the Interior of North America, 1751–1762* (Norman, Okla., 1962), 205. Also see Dumont, *Mémoires historiques*, I, 44–48.

22. *MPAFD*, III, 638, 645; Le Page Du Pratz, *History*, 217–218; *RSCLHQ*, V, 264, VI, 288.

23. Philip Pittman, *The Present State of the European Settlements on the Mississippi* (1770), ed. Robert R. Rea (facs. rpt., Gainesville, Fla., 1973), 23–24; *SJRLHQ*, X, 588–589; Eron Dunbar Rowland, comp., *Life, Letters, and Papers of William Dunbar* (Jackson, Miss., 1930), 48. The importance of lumber to Louisiana as an export commodity is demonstrated in John Hebron Moore, "The Cypress Lumber Industry of the Lower Mississippi Valley during the Colonial Period," *LH*, XXIV (1983), 25–47.

fished, and collected edible plants for their own use, for their owners' kitchens, and for the regional food market.[24] Philippe Haynault's farm at Pointe Coupée was a typical unit of agricultural production for the mid-eighteenth century, in which daily economic life revolved around the production of food and tobacco. At his death in 1743, Haynault owned 280 arpents of land, six cattle, seven hogs, and ten chickens, along with two horses owned jointly with another farmer. His labor force consisted of two African men, an Indian woman and her daughter—all slaves—and a white overseer. Haynault lived in a cypress-shingled house, thirty by fourteen feet, built on posts, while his slaves inhabited separate huts. Food provisions stored on the farm included twenty-four barrels of corn, two barrels of beans, and a barrel of Illinois flour. Among Haynault's personal possessions were one Indian trade blanket, nine worn Indian trade shirts, six Indian pots, and three Indian sifters. The Indian woman probably took care of the corn and bean crops, with some assistance from the other slaves at planting and harvesting time, and she undoubtedly prepared meals for the farm's residents with some of her traditional cookware. When not busy with planting, replanting, weeding, and drying tobacco, the men spent much of their time tending the livestock and hunting for wild game (see Plate 5 for a sketch of a tobacco farm).[25]

Slaves who lived on large plantations probably exerted greater control over production of food. Those on smaller farms, like that of Haynault, lived under tighter supervision by owners who often worked alongside them in the fields. But on the indigo plantations around New Orleans, slaves were allowed to cultivate their own gardens and raise their own poultry and even, as will be seen presently, to market their produce. In 1738 the concession of Chaouachas, located about fifteen miles below New Orleans on the west bank of the Mississippi, housed 153 slaves, who

24. For references to plantation slaves serving as hunters, see *RSCLHQ*, V, 385, VII, 334–336, XIX, 211–228. An informative glimpse at how plantation laborers divided their time between producing food and export crops is the diary of William Dunbar, who owned a plantation near Baton Rouge during the 1770s; see Rowland, comp., *Life, Letters, and Papers of William Dunbar*, 23–34.

25. *RSCLHQ*, V, 466–477. Farms like this were common at the settlements of First and Second German Coasts, Pointe Coupée, and Natchitoches, where the average number of slaves in 1766 ranged from 2.5 to 6 per farm. See Jacqueline K. Voorhies, comp. and trans., *Some Late Eighteenth-Century Louisianians: Census Records of the Colony, 1758–1796* (Lafayette, La., 1973), 163–214.

PLATE 5. *Drawing of His Farm on the Mississippi River.* By Jean François Benjamin Dumont de Montigny. Circa 1730. *Courtesy of Edward E. Ayer Collection, Newberry Library, Chicago*

Explication des
chiffres

1 maison principale
2 grange
3 jardin
4 poulailler
5 colombier
6 maison des negres
7 terres nouvellement
Defrichées
8 debarquement

fossé

L. ouis

sur le fleuve

produced large quantities of rice, tobacco, and indigo and raised a herd of seventy cattle for the owner-investors in Paris. Comprising forty different nuclear families, these people lived in twenty separate cabins upriver from the manager's house and the plantation fields of rice, tobacco, and indigo. Behind their quarters, "surrounded by stakes, roofed by Palmetto" like a distinct village, were fields on which the slave families cultivated their own food. The short distance from New Orleans made it easy for slaves from Chaouachas to market their goods in town on weekends. "In several barns belonging to different negroes," an inventory taken on January 24, 1738, found "eighty-six barrels of rice, twenty-five barrels of beans and four barrels of potatoes" in addition to grains that "have not been threshed" (see Plate 6).[26]

The pervasive importance of hunting in colonial Louisiana meant that many slaves handled firearms regularly and that laws regulating possession of guns were difficult to enforce. Armed slaves in a frontier society, whether serving as soldiers or hunters, made the institution of slavery always vulnerable to the possibility of revolt. The Code Noir had prohibited slaves from carrying firearms, but many owners allowed slaves who hunted for them to keep guns handy in their cabins. Other slaves took advantage of this flexibility by possessing firearms even without their owners' permission. In an ordinance issued in 1744 to prevent the dangerous firing of guns by hunters too close to populated areas, slaves were "forbidden to carry rifles or any other firearms without written permission from their masters," under penalty of "whipping and confiscation of arms by the arresting party."[27]

26. *RSCLHQ*, VIII, 602–620. A diagram of the Chaouachas concession was drawn by Jean François Benjamin Dumont de Montigny and is in his manuscript *Mémoires*, 355, Edward E. Ayer Collection, Newberry Library, Chicago. It is reproduced here as Plate 6. Sidney W. Mintz argues that unsupervised production of food crops provided the basis of an open market system and abetted the emergence of a protopeasantry in Jamaica (*Caribbean Transformations* [Chicago, 1974], 194–195). Michael Craton, however, has suggested that cultivation by slaves for their food did not necessarily allow greater mobility (*Searching for the Invisible Man: Slaves and Plantation Life in Jamaica* [Cambridge, Mass., 1978], 161–162).

27. AC, C13A, XXXV, 283; Tamara D. McGinnis, trans., "Ordinance Regulating the Bearing of Arms, 1744," *LH*, XXIX (1988), 228. Black hunters in colonial South Carolina, where frontier conditions closely resembled those of Louisiana, were not restricted until the threat of rebellion in 1712; see Peter H. Wood, *Black Majority:*

Slaves who hunted occupationally for the plantation received special privileges from their owners and enjoyed higher prestige within the slave community. To threaten the status or limit the mobility gained by such a person sometimes proved dangerous, as events at a Chapitoulas plantation on the night of May 31, 1771, reveal. Seeing a fire consume one of the outbuildings, planter Jean Baptiste Cezaire Lebreton ran out onto his gallery in the dark to alert his slaves of the fire. Within seconds a musket ball and some birdshot pierced his chest, killing him instantly. An extensive investigation, which included the torture of two men on the rack, uncovered an assassination plot led by a slave hunter called Temba. Temba, whose Christian name was Pedro Nicolas, had been scolded and threatened by his owner earlier that evening for sleeping away from the plantation too often. Infuriated by Lebreton's demands, Temba persuaded the blacksmith to set fire to the shed in order to expose the planter to the deadly fire of his hunting rifle. Immediately following the shooting, the overseer gathered as many as six guns from the slave cabins on Lebreton's plantation, all of them usually used for hunting. As frontier conditions gradually gave way to more rigid norms of plantation slavery, firearms once tolerated for food production would be increasingly confiscated to prevent rebellion.[28]

III

Farming and hunting practices among American Indians in the Lower Mississippi Valley changed according to how particular groups participated in the frontier exchange economy. People living in the petites nations interspersed with colonial settlements responded with versatility to the demand for food products. They harvested surplus crops and wild plants, caught extra fish, and hunted enough game to trade with settlers and slaves. Small-scale exchange of surpluses between communities was probably a long-standing form of trade among the region's Indian population. Despite massive depopulation and frequent dislocation, the small

Negroes in Colonial South Carolina from 1670 through the Stono Rebellion (New York, 1974), 127.
    28. SJRLHQ, VIII, 6–22.

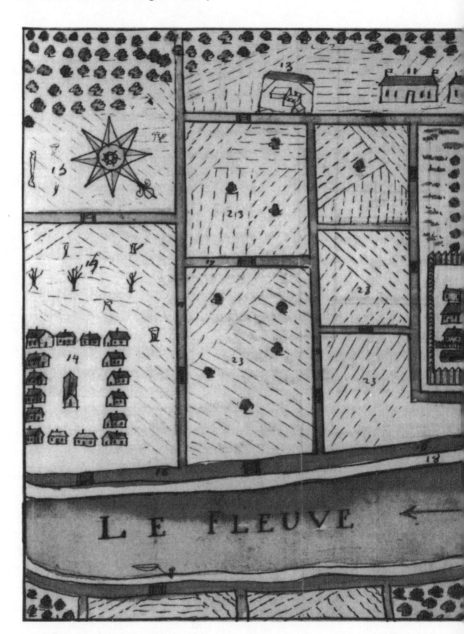

PLATE 6. *Drawing of the Chaouachas Concession.* By Jean François Benjamin Dumont de Montigny. Circa 1730. *Courtesy of Edward E. Ayer Collection, Newberry Library, Chicago*

Concession des chaoüacha
appartenante cy devant a Mgr
le duc de belleisle et associés
Explication des chiffres

1 maison du regisseur
2 cuisinne
3 forge
4 magazin
5 m. du chirurgiens
6 menuiscrie
7 parc aux bestiaux
8 colombiers
9 poulailler
10 jardins
11·12 granges
13 indigoterie
14 hab. des negres
15 leurs terrains
16 fossé
17 écoulemeur des
eaux

18 levées
19 débarquent
20 cloche pour
appeller les
Negres au
travailler
21 Croix des
missions
22 ponts
23 terres
defrichées

SAINT LOÜIS

nations maintained themselves as productive villages functioning much like colonial settlements in the regional economy. "The Houma, Chitimacha, and other Indian communities that were dispersed among the plantations," cartographer and naturalist Bernard Romans noted, "served as hunters, and for some other laborious uses, something similar to subdued tribes of New England." Another Englishman reported in 1769 that the Houmas, Taensas, and Alibamons "are to the full as civilized as our poorer sort of People; they are very industrious, and have been very usefull to the French."[29]

Indians hunting for colonial settlers formed personal bonds that sometimes created moments of frustration or even fear. A planter whose meals benefited from game sold to him by Indian hunters occasionally wondered how they spent their time around his slave quarters. An investigation into a slave conspiracy at Natchitoches in 1770 disclosed the nature of such exchanges. Noël Verret, overseer on the de Mézières plantation, saw a group of Indians land their pirogue at the hut of a slave named Christopher, where they joined some Negroes in shucking corn. One Indian named Miguel informed Verret that "there was a great deal of game at the lake and that he would bring me some in exchange for some ammunition." When Miguel returned with one turkey, the overseer "complained about how little that was." The hunter apologized and asked for another advance of lead and gunpowder. So Verret "only furnished him with lead this time in order to try to extract payment." Meanwhile, according to separate testimony, a slave named Otis was selling a gun, which he had acquired from a mulatto, to an Indian "for deerskin and oil."[30]

In 1773 there were still some ten Indian villages along the Mississippi below its confluence with the Red River. The main town of the Houmas, consisting of about forty gunmen, stood on the east bank sixty miles above New Orleans. Another Houma village was situated opposite the river. A league below Manchac the Taensas, Pacanas, and Mobilians lived

29. MPAFD, III, 535–536; Bernard Romans, A Concise Natural History of East and West Florida . . . (1775; rpt., New Orleans, 1961), 69–71; EPR, III, 94–95, IV, 20–21. For other descriptions of these Indian villages, see Pittman, Present State of the European Settlements on the Mississippi, ed. Rea, 22–35; and Edward Mease, "Narrative of a Journey through . . . West Florida in the Years 1770 and 1771," Mississippi Historical Society, Publications, Centenary Ser., V (1925), 63–67.

30. Gerald L. St. Martin, trans., "A Slave Trial in Colonial Natchitoches," LH, XXXVIII (1987), 65–66, 86.

on the west bank in a single town of about thirty gunmen. The Alibamons counted thirty-seven gunmen and lived just above Manchac on the east side. While some Chitimachas were moving down Bayou Plaquemine, about fifteen gunmen and their families remained along the Mississippi. Down the bayou other Chitimachas and some Atakapas and Opelousas totaled another fifty gunmen. The Tunicas still occupied their town, numbering about thirty-five gunmen, on the east bluff above the Pointe Coupée plantations. Above Tunica stood a village of ten to twelve Chahto gunmen and another of fifteen Pascagoula gunmen on the west bank. The Biloxis, numbering nearly one hundred gunmen, had just moved from the west to the east bank a short distance below the Red River. Methods of farming, hunting, fishing, and gathering employed by these Indian villagers changed a little since precolonial times. Firearms were now used to hunt game, and metal replaced bone and wood for hooks. The proportion of farming or hunting in a single town's livelihood changed somewhat, according to local needs in the colonial economy, and livestock entered the landscape. But overall, there was continuity in planting and harvesting techniques as well as in the availability of wild plants and animals.[31]

Men in these and other Indian villages along major routes in Louisiana regularly hired themselves to military and commercial expeditions as subsistence hunters. Traveling on the Mississippi during the fall of 1770, Jean-Bernard Bossu employed two Tunicas who "obtained for us an abundance of food while we were going up the river." When one of these hunters happened to shoot a poisonous snake swimming near the boat, Bossu awarded him a bottle of tafia (an inferior rum). But the Tunica's reward did not end there. Upon reaching the Arkansas post, he was honored by the Quapaws "with the title of Captain among red men and at the same time Chevalier of the Rattlesnake." As Bossu explained the ceremony, "They designed and tattooed around his body the figure of a serpent with its head falling on a place which ladies will permit me to let them guess."[32]

31. List of the Several Tribes of Indians inhabiting the banks of the Mississippi, Between New Orleans and Red River, with their number of gun men and places of residence, Jan. 1, 1773, William Haldimand Papers, British Museum, microfilm in the Louisiana Division, New Orleans Public Library; Pittman, *Present State of the European Settlements on the Mississippi*, ed. Rea, 24, 35–36.

32. Samuel Dorris Dickinson, ed. and trans., *New Travels in North America by Jean-Bernard Bossu, 1770–1771* (Natchitoches, La., 1982), 36–37.

Production activities among Indian villagers in the larger, interior tribes of the Lower Mississippi Valley changed slowly and subtly as a result of their participation in the regional economy. Farming and hunting methods were only slightly altered, as Indians adopted livestock and some new crops into their village agriculture and produced larger quantities of deerskins for the commercial market. By the 1770s livelihood inside the Choctaw nation showed many signs of continuity. Although reduced to half of their precolonial size, the Choctaws numbered approximately 13,000 people living in some fifty villages. Towns averaged about 250 inhabitants each and altogether occupied some four thousand square miles of what is now eastern Mississippi and western Alabama. Most Choctaw villages stood on hilly prairies surrounded by winding bayous and swampy ground. The cabins in each village were divided into hamlets separated from each other by streams and lowlands. Between hamlets and along the springs that separated them stood rich fields of corn, beans, and other crops.[33]

Groups of entire families planted and harvested the Choctaw villages' large fields, and women grew beans, small corn, tobacco, and vegetables gradually adopted from Europeans and Africans in smaller household gardens. After the gardens were sown and as soon as bayou waters receded, usually by the beginning of May, the Choctaws planted their staple corn, pumpkins, and melons on the village bottomlands. From then until the harvest in August, the women generally weeded and tended to all of the crops, misleading some passing observers to believe that Indian men

33. *MPAFD*, I, 95–96, 155, V, 226 n. 43; H. S. Halbert, "Bernard Romans' Map of 1772," Miss. Hist. Soc., *Publs.*, VI (1902), 420–421. For useful descriptions of terrain in the Choctaw country, see *MPAFD*, I, 81–117, 136–154; and Mease, "Narrative of a Journey," Miss. Hist. Soc., *Publs.*, Cent. Ser., V (1925), 82–90. Also see John R. Swanton, *Source Material for the Social and Ceremonial Life of the Choctaw Indians*, Bureau of American Ethnology, Bulletin, no. 103 (Washington, D.C., 1931); Jerome A. Voss and John H. Blitz, "Archaeological Investigations in the Choctaw Homeland," *American Antiquity*, LIII (1988), 125–145. In a provocative interpretation of Choctaw livelihood, Richard White argues that these Indians had recently migrated from the Big Black, Tombigbee, Pearl, and Yazoo River valleys—over the late 17th and early 18th centuries—to the upland forest in order to escape epidemics and slaving expeditions. While applying old farming practices along the smaller streams in their new location, Choctaws relied upon the vacated lowlands of the major rivers for hunting deer. See White, *The Roots of Dependency: Subsistence, Environment, and Social Change among the Choctaws, Pawnees, and Navajos* (Lincoln, Nebr., 1983), 1–33.

did not till the soil. Generalizations regarding the sexual division of labor and the absence of private landholdings among American Indian societies reveal more about the attitudes of eighteenth-century observers than about the livelihood of Indians in the Lower Mississippi Valley.[34] Men and women in some tribes worked the fields together at planting and harvesttime much as European peasants, the essential difference being that the fields in Choctaw, Chickasaw, and other Indian villages belonged to female lineages. When Regis Du Roullet requested military assistance from the Choctaw village of Boucfouca in May 1732, the men "begged me please to ask for people from the neighboring villages, since they could not furnish me all I needed on account of their planting." At every spring planting, as reported by Bernard Romans in 1775, the men "help their wives in the labour of the fields."[35]

Aside from disturbances caused by epidemics and wars, the Choctaws managed to control the impact of colonial relations upon village life. Houses remained circular structures made from wood and clay. Around the inner walls of each cabin, the Choctaws built a two-foot-high platform that served as beds and shelves. The fireplace stood in the middle of the dirt floor, and a small hole in the ceiling and a small doorway provided the only openings. These compact, smoke-filled apartments protected their occupants from summer heat, winter cold, and ubiquitous insects. In

34. Francis Jennings, *The Invasion of America: Indians, Colonialism, and the Cant of Conquest* (Chapel Hill, N.C., 1975), 60–84; Cronon, *Changes in the Land,* 43–44, 51–52; James Axtell, *The Invasion Within: The Contest of Cultures in Colonial America* (New York, 1985), 148–167. Travelers through rural France, especially persons of bourgeois or urban origins, often commented on the amount of work performed by peasant women in the fields. As a new ideal of womanhood evolved among middle-class Europeans, their descriptions of the treatment and behavior of women in the countryside resembled those used by observers of Indian village life in America, emphasizing the "savage" customs of "lazy" peasant men. See the discussion of this phenomenon in Jean-Louis Flandrin, *Families in Former Times: Kinship, House-hold, and Sexuality in Early Modern France,* trans. Richard Southern (Cambridge, 1979), 112–118. Mary Beth Norton, *Liberty's Daughters: The Revolutionary Experience of American Women, 1750–1800* (Boston, 1980), 18–20, 94–95, explicitly relates observations about Indian women to sexual roles being promoted in late 18th-century American society.

35. MPAFD, I, 146; Romans, *Concise Natural History of East and West Florida,* 58. For a summary of sexual roles and property rights among southeastern Indians, see Charles Hudson, *The Southeastern Indians* (Knoxville, Tenn., 1976), 264–269, 312–313.

separate structures raised eight feet above ground, the Choctaws stored their grain. Men continued to carve out of hickory trees the mortars and pestles needed to pound corn. Women carried on the production of cane baskets for sifting and storing food and even found a ready market for these products in colonial settlements. Hooked sticks still served as primary farming implements, although an increasing number of households acquired metal pickaxes and hoes for turning soil and pulling weeds. Outside the cabin stood the technology for processing deerskins—a beam over which to spread the soaked skins while removing the hair, a large mortar and pestle with which to soften them in cornmeal and water, and two upright posts for stretching and drying the skins.[36]

The most perceptible changes in village livelihood occurred in the seasonal routine of activities. People devoted more of their time to producing corn, bear oil, tallow, and deerskins for the regional market, and the European merchandise received in exchange—particularly blankets, kettles, and axes—replaced some traditional manufactures. Women nevertheless continued to make their family's clothing, only increasingly with cloth, needles, and thread acquired through trade. Men's sphere of village life was most drastically affected by the introduction of firearms and alcohol. Chickens, hogs, and newly introduced vegetables, much of it raised for the colonial food market, further changed the landscape of Indian villages by the third quarter of the eighteenth century. Hickory rails were built around household gardens, and boys added the management of livestock to their traditional role as small-game hunters.[37]

36. Mease, "Narrative of a Journey," Miss. Hist. Soc., *Publs.*, Cent. Ser., V (1925), 83–84. Supporting ethnographic evidence for technological continuity includes David I. Bushnell, Jr., *The Choctaw of Bayou Lacomb, St. Tammany Parish, Louisiana,* Bureau of American Ethnology, Bulletin, no. 18 (Washington, D.C., 1909); T. N. Campbell, "Choctaw Subsistence: Ethnographic Notes from the Lincecum Manuscript," *Florida Anthropologist,* XII (1959), 9–24; Muriel H. Wright, "American Indian Corn Dishes, *Chronicles of Oklahoma,* XXXVI (1958), 155–166; Margaret Zehmer Searcy, "Choctaw Subsistence, 1540–1830: Hunting, Fishing, Farming, and Gathering," in Carolyn Keller Reeves, ed., *The Choctaw before Removal* (Jackson, Miss., 1985), 32–54.

37. *MPAFD,* I, 28–29; Relation de la Louisiane [ca 1735], 140 (anonymous MS), Edward E. Ayer Collection, Newberry Library, Chicago; Romans, *Concise Natural History of East and West Florida,* 42–46, 55–67; James Adair, *The History of the American Indians, Particularly Those Nations Adjoining to the Mississippi, East and West Florida, Georgia, South and North Carolina, and Virginia* . . . (London, 1775), 436.

Indian production of deerskins for colonial trade occurred mostly in the camps that the Indians formed during the winter, in keeping with the familiar pattern of eastern woodlands livelihood. The significant change over the colonial period was that winter hunting became, in addition to a form of food procurement, a means of producing commodities for the Atlantic market.[38] Hunting parties of ten or so Choctaw families dispersed along rivers and bayous were such a regular feature of life in the Lower Mississippi Valley that they rarely seemed noteworthy except to visitors like Bernard Romans. In January 1772 he spotted along the Tombigbee River "a hunting camp of Choctaws . . . who invited us on shore, treated us very kindly, and spared us some venison, bear's meat and oil." Only at these hunting camps, Romans observed, did they "entertain a stranger at free cost." He also noticed that whenever members of the camp killed a deer or bear, they divided the liver up and sent a piece to each fire in the camp, whereupon the men of the family burned it. Excluded from this ceremony but certainly active in these camps, the women stayed near the palmetto huts in order to prepare the meat, skins, and oil. On returning to his camp from the day's chase, each hunter, according to an early nineteenth-century observer, "relates with minuteness every incident that occurred, and talks with much humor of the casual accidents that happened."[39]

The distances traveled to winter hunting grounds from the home villages seemed to vary widely, but the deerskin trade imposed mounting pressures to pursue game as far away as possible. Hunters from the Choctaw town of Shumotakali spent their winters into the 1730s only two miles away, whereas the Alibamons reputedly traveled nearly three hundred miles during a hunting season in the 1750s. Toward the end of the eighteenth century, the depletion of deer in some areas forced many camps

38. For general discussions of how commercial trade affected Indian hunting practices, see Gregory A. Waselkov, "Evolution of Deer Hunting in the Eastern Woodlands," *Midcontinental Journal of Archaeology,* III (1978), 15–34; Charles M. Hudson, Jr., "Why the Southeastern Indians Slaughtered Deer," in Shepard Krech III, ed., *Indians, Animals, and the Fur Trade: A Critique of "Keepers of the Game"* (Athens, Ga., 1981), 155–176; White, *Roots of Dependency,* 69–96; Silver, *A New Face on the Countryside,* 68–72, 88–97.

39. Romans, *Concise Natural History of East and West Florida,* 56, 215; Choctaw Indians, John A. Watkins Manuscript, Special Collections Division, Howard-Tilton Memorial Library, Tulane University, New Orleans.

to travel farther than before. Upper Creek and Chickasaw hunters had to frequent the Tennessee Valley more often, bringing them into increasing conflict with the Cherokees. Hunting sojourns on the western side of the Mississippi River by more and more Choctaw camps caused tensions with settlers and other Indians in Louisiana.[40]

IV

Most of the surplus food items, deerskins, and other goods traded in the frontier exchange economy were produced on farms and plantations or in villages and camps scattered across the Lower Mississippi Valley. At all of these points of production, people blended various activities into a livelihood based on self-sufficiency and yet periodically involved in commerce. Two sets of production activities developing in colonial Louisiana, however, involved geographical specialization and long-distance transportation. The lowland forests in the St. Francis Basin, an area drained by the St. Francis, White, and Arkansas rivers at the upper edge of the Lower Mississippi Valley, became a bountiful source of wildlife for the regional economy. Convoys of professional hunters annually traveled on the Mississippi River between this rich animal habitat and the town of New Orleans. The other important network of production in the region was the eastward movement of livestock from the Texas plains into Louisiana settlements and villages. Both sets of activities employed a diverse number of people and encompassed widespread intercultural interaction.

By the 1720s Louisianians began to treat the St. Francis Basin as a regional center of large-scale hunting for meat, oil, and fur. For the 1725–1726 winter expedition from New Orleans to this rich lowland, Guillaume Allain hired himself to an experienced Canadian hunter named Sieur Lefevre. His wages consisted of 200 francs cash, forty pounds of tallow, fifty pounds of meat, four pots of bear grease, and half of the

40. AC, C13A, XI, 174–176; Relation de la Louisiane, 198; Seymour Feiler, ed. and trans., *Jean-Bernard Bossu's Travels in the Interior of North America, 1751–1762* (Norman, Okla., 1962), 146; Halbert, "Bernard Romans' Map of 1772," Miss. Hist. Soc., *Publs.*, VI (1902), 419–420; John Sibley, *A Report from Natchitoches in 1807*, ed. Annie Heloise Abel (New York, 1922).

pecans that he could gather. When he fell sick on the journey and replaced himself with François Le Moyne, however, Allain's employer refused to pay the terms of their agreement. Disputes over the lucrative proceeds of St. Francis Basin expeditions continued into the Spanish period. On March 24, 1770, the deputy sheriff of New Orleans seized Jean Baptiste Boyer's two boats, after the hunter's employee, Lavigne, refused to pay the debts claimed by merchants Conard and Clermont. Boyer's crew had recently returned to the city with forty animals' worth of salted meat, fourteen hundred pounds of tallow, four pots of bear oil, and about two hundred skins of beaver, deer, bear, and otter. Boyer, who was still at Arkansas, had a number of creditors, including some laborers who had accompanied him on his last expedition. Joseph Jobert, for example, had received only four pots of oil and was still entitled to one hundred pounds of meat and 375 livres in cash. Boyer's entire shipment sold for 2,724 livres, all of which went to his creditors. Among those reimbursed, François Bouguignon received 700 livres for his fifteen months of service to Boyer.[41]

Many hunters like Boyer were advanced merchandise needed for their expeditions by New Orleans merchants; they agreed to pay their debts with specified quantities of skins, meat, and oil. In 1746 Pierre and Michel Clermont promised to pay 2,250 pounds of tallow to Nicolas Judice for goods provided to them. Some farmers even ventured upriver to participate in a winter hunt. Jean François Besson and his wife, Marianne Bourselice, temporarily transferred their one hundred arpents of land and eleven cattle to a son-in-law in August 1762, before they left on a hunting trip to the White River. In 1776 Manchac merchant John Fitzpatrick, who regularly credited merchandise to upriver hunters and traders, sent 200 pounds of gunpowder and 244 pounds of balls to Arkansas hunters named Hoopock and Stampley.[42]

A growing number of hunters who lived in the St. Francis Basin devel-

41. *RSCLHQ*, III, 149–150; Clermont vs. Boyer, Mar. 19–Apr. 28, 1770, Spanish Judicial Records, Louisiana Historical Center, New Orleans. Morris S. Arnold, *Unequal Laws unto a Savage Race: European Legal Traditions in Arkansas, 1686–1836* (Fayetteville, Ark., 1985), 54–59, discusses several other cases involving hunters' wages and debts.

42. *RSCLHQ*, XV, 516, XXIV, 246–247; Margaret Fisher Dalrymple, ed., *The Merchant of Manchac: The Letterbooks of John Fitzpatrick, 1768–1798* (Baton Rouge, La., 1978), 201.

oped a bad reputation because of what colonial officials considered unlawful and immoral customs. In 1770 Athanase de Mézières, lieutenant governor of Natchitoches, called them "the most wicked persons, without doubt, in all the Indies." "They live so forgetful of the laws," he reported to Governor Unzaga, "that it is easy to find persons who have not returned to Christian lands for ten, twenty, or thirty years, and who pass their scandalous lives in public concubinage with the captive Indian women whom for this purpose they purchase among the heathen, loaning those of whom they tire to others of less power, that they may labor in their service, giving them no other wage than the promise of quieting their lascivious passions; in short they have no other rule than their own caprice, and the respect which they pay the boldest and most daring, who control them." Perhaps of greater concern than their sexual affairs, many of these hunters allegedly furnished munitions to the Osages, whose raids against colonial settlements and other Indian groups were on the rise. But as long as hunters in the Arkansas district continued to produce valuable commodities like furs, meat, and oil, government efforts to regulate their disorderly behavior remained ineffective.[43]

The colony of Louisiana suffered a chronic shortage of domestic beef and horsepower during its early years, only partly mitigated by the abundance of game, fish, and fowl in the Lower Mississippi Valley. By 1718, settlers had managed to accumulate four hundred head of cattle and two hundred horses from small numbers shipped to the colony, but this livestock diminished rapidly in the subsequent years of famine and immigration. Efforts to import livestock from St. Domingue and Florida during the 1720s failed to materialize. Stocks of chickens, pigs, and sheep slowly increased in colonial settlements, but an increase in horses and cattle became dependent upon moving livestock across land from Texas eastward into Louisiana.[44]

The evolution of an intercultural network that transported livestock into the Lower Mississippi Valley actually began before the eighteenth century. Louisiana settlers then entered this formative network and accel-

43. Herbert Eugene Bolton, ed. and trans., *Athanase de Mézières and the Louisiana-Texas Frontier, 1768–1780*, 2 vols. (Cleveland, Ohio, 1914), I, 166–169; Arnold, *Unequal Laws unto a Savage Race*, 78–86.

44. *MPAFD*, II, 594, III, 268; Conrad, ed. and trans., *Memoir of Charles Le Gac*, 2, 53; Myldred Masson Costa, trans., *The Letters of Marie Madeleine Hachard, 1727–28* (New Orleans, 1974), 57.

erated the movement of animals needed within the new colony. Caddo Indian villages along the rivers of eastern Texas had for a long time hosted summer fairs, at which Indians from afar traded their goods for salt, corn, and orange bowwood produced by the Caddoes. Jumano Indians brought to the Caddoes turquoises and cotton blankets from Rio Grande Pueblos along with produce from their own buffalo hunting. By the mid-seventeenth century they began to bring horses and metal goods acquired from the Spanish in New Mexico. Indian herds of horses sprang up across the vast territory of Texas, being stocked with animals rustled from Spanish settlers or purchased at Pueblo trade fairs. When La Salle's men were wandering through eastern Texas in 1686–1687, they managed to acquire horses from Caddo villagers.[45]

From these beginnings, Indian villagers and French traders worked inconspicuously to move livestock farther eastward, down the Red River, to Louisiana settlements. As commandant of Natchitoches from 1721 to 1744, Louis Juchereau de Saint-Denis maintained a friendly trade relationship with Spanish settlers around Los Adaes and shipped small numbers of livestock downriver. Spanish and French settlers in the Eastern Timbers area of Texas, where the Great Plains meets the Eastern Woodlands, employed Indians to herd livestock on their ranches. In violation of Spanish law, they exchanged horses and cattle with Natchitoches traders for French merchandise. During the 1730s Saint-Denis sent from sixty to eighty head of cattle each spring toward New Orleans, where two butchers were selling beef at six sous per pound.[46]

45. Jean Delanglez, ed. and trans., *The Journal of Jean Cavelier: The Account of a Survivor of La Salle's Texas Expedition, 1684–1688* (Chicago, 1938), 73; John Gilmary Shea, ed., *Discovery and Exploration of the Mississippi Valley: With the Original Narratives of Marquette, Allouez, Membré, Hennepin, and Anastase Douay* (New York, 1852), 211. For a full discussion of the Caddoes and their trade with the Jumanos during the 17th century, see Elizabeth A. H. John, *Storms Brewed in Other Men's Worlds: The Confrontation of Indians, Spanish, and French in the Southwest, 1540–1795* (College Station, Tex., 1975), 165–195.

46. *MPAFD*, III, 314–315, 486; Hiram Ford Gregory, "Eighteenth-Century Caddoan Archaeology: A Study in Models and Interpretation" (Ph.D. diss., Southern Methodist University, 1973), 46–57; AC, C13A, XXII, 148–151; Agreement between Jacques Larche and Jean Thomas Machinet, Nov. 4, 1737, Records of the Superior Council, Louisiana Historical Center, New Orleans. For the 1739 expedition against the Chickasaws, cattle and horses were driven from the Illinois country. But a downriver shipment of beef from the upper valley did not become significant until the 19th

Indians participated in this livestock trade network, from its source at the western edge of the colonial region to final delivery points at New Orleans and other lower Louisiana settlements, in a variety of ways. Whether as rustlers, herders, or breeders, Indian involvement reflected a group's own interest in the process. The most experienced horse dealers in the region, Caddoes herded animals that were undoubtedly stray and some that probably belonged to settlers. They then exchanged these horses and cattle with French traders and with other Indian groups, including the Quapaws and Illinois from the central Mississippi Valley. The Wichitas contributed their rustling and trading skills to this network as they migrated to the upper Red River at midcentury. From their pivotal villages near the junction of the Red and Mississippi rivers, Tunica and Avoyelle Indians also transported horses, oxen, and cows to colonial settlements.[47] Choctaw and Chickasaw Indians east of the Mississippi, meanwhile, tapped into the eastward flow of horses and became skillful breeders and outfitters in their own right. As described by trader James Adair, they made fine saddles with buffalo hide sewn onto white oak boards and mounted their horses from the right-hand side. From Choctaw and Chickasaw villages, horses reached the Creeks and Cherokees and even some English settlers.[48]

By 1748 there were an estimated ten thousand head of cattle in Louisiana colonial settlements, but livestock production suffered a severe blow when an epizootic broke out and lasted three years. Both the extensive

---

century. Margaret Kimball Brown, "Allons, Cowboys!" *Journal of the Illinois State Historical Society*, LXXVI (1983), 273–282.

47. *Pénicaut Narrative*, 138; John, *Storms Brewed in Other Men's Worlds*, 338–344; Pierre François Xavier de Charlevoix, *Journal of a Voyage to North-America*, 2 vols. (London, 1761), II, 279–280; Le Page Du Pratz, *History*, ed. Tregle, 166–167.

48. Relation de la Louisiane, 163; Mease, "Narrative of a Journey," Miss. Hist. Soc., *Publs.*, Cent. Ser., V (1925), 73; Romans, *Concise and Natural History of East and West Florida*, 42; Adair, *History of the American Indians*, 340, 457–459; H. B. Cushman, *History of Choctaw, Chickasaw, and Natchez Indians* (Greenville, Tex., 1899), 235–236, 390–391. According to a manuscript of Nathaniel Folsom used by Cushman, the first cattle were brought into the Choctaw Nation by traders during the 1770s. At one point in his discussion, Cushman quotes "the first neat cattle" from the manuscript, which does not preclude the possibility that some of the more wild bovines from the west had not reached Choctaw villages earlier. Cushman furthermore quotes Folsom as stating: "There was abundance of horses. There were many hogs in the Nation when I first came."

spread of this disease and the rapid recovery by the colony attest to the continual influx of livestock being handled by Indian and white traders. In 1750 General Commissioner Michel issued permits to several individuals "to go trade for cattle at the Natchitoches and to bring them to the Bayogoulas, there to multiply the species, which has considerably decreased in the colony because of the diseases of the preceding years, which still continue this year."[49] An acceleration of livestock traffic over the ensuing thirty years actually enlarged both the number and size of herds within the region. Natchitoches and Pointe Coupée became major herding centers, from which merchants and planters purchased horses, mules, cows, bulls, and oxen.[50] By 1766 the inhabitants of Louisiana and West Florida possessed nearly thirty thousand head of cattle and almost four thousand horses and mules, and the avenues of importation from the west continued to expand.[51]

The settlement of Bayou Teche by Acadian farmers during the 1760s opened an additional route for livestock transportation into the Lower Mississippi Valley. The new districts of Atakapas and Opelousas became

49. *MPAFD*, V, 53; N. M. Miller Surrey, *The Commerce of Louisiana during the French Régime, 1699–1763* (New York, 1916), 258–259.

50. Dalrymple, ed., *Letterbooks of Fitzpatrick*, 42; Rowland, comp., *Life, Letters, and Papers of William Dunbar*, 69. Terry G. Jordan, *Trails to Texas: Southern Roots of Western Cattle Ranching* (Lincoln, Nebr., 1981), 25–82, traces an Anglo-Saxon influence upon Texas cattle ranching to the Carolinas and follows its diffusion through the Gulf Coastal Plain. He challenges previous assertions about the primacy of Spanish influence on ranching in Texas. But Jordan misses the intercultural dimension of livestock trade because the 18th-century trails *from* Texas are ignored. For a study of Texas ranching that does examine the eastward movement of cattle and horses into Louisiana, see Sandra L. Myres, *The Ranch in Spanish Texas, 1691–1800* (El Paso, Tex., 1969), 43–50.

51. This estimate is derived from the 1766 census of Spanish Louisiana and from more impressionistic descriptions of British West Florida. Farms along the lower Mississippi River contained 6,356 cattle and 1,064 horses. Those along Red River and Bayou Teche had 3,360 cattle and 1,235 horses, and the ranches at Atakapas claimed as many as 15,000 more cattle and 300 more horses and mules. See Table 4. Farms located between Pensacola and the east bank of the Mississippi above Manchac, most of them owned by French families, possessed about another 5,000 cattle and 1,000 horses. See James Crawford to Lieutenant Governor Browne, Oct. 9, 1769, EPR, IV, 26–28; and Bernard Romans, "An Attempt towards a Short Description of West Florida," in P. Lee Phillips, ed., *Notes on the Life and Works of Bernard Romans* (Deland, Fla., 1924), 120.

instant markets for horses and cattle being smuggled eastward from Texas ranches. Athanase de Mézières reported in 1777 that during the autumn season, "when the rivers are fordable and the pasturage good," a trader with a few servants could easily "conduct droves of cattle, sheep, horses, and mules" from San Antonio de Bexar to Opelousas, a distance of some four hundred miles, within a month's time. A complex interethnic network of exchange evolved in which Atakapas and Opelousas as well as white dealers traveled to the mouth of the Trinity River and purchased livestock stolen and delivered by Indians from the interior. The traders, many of whom were Acadian ranchers, then transported these contraband animals to Bayou Teche.[52]

Settlers at Atakapas and Opelousas quickly accumulated their own herds of livestock. In addition to participation in the eastward movement of livestock, this process was facilitated by an arrangement made between some Acadian immigrants and Antoine Bernard d'Auterive, a retired infantry captain who owned *vacheries,* or ranches, at Bayogoulas, Barataria, and Atakapas. D'Auterive owned at least six thousand head of cattle, the product of many years' commerce with the Atakapas Indians and other livestock traders. On April 4, 1765, he agreed to furnish "five cows with calves and one bull to each of the Acadian families during each of six consecutive years." The Acadians could sell a few cows or bulls, provided they kept a record of all transactions. "At the end of six years, they will each return the same number of cows and calves, of the same age and kind, that they received initially; the remaining cattle and their increase . . . will be divided equally between said Acadians and Mr. Dauterive."[53]

With their livestock increasing from two thousand cattle and seven hundred horses in 1766 to more than ten thousand cattle and two thousand horses by the mid-1770s, the districts of Opelousas and Atakapas became a major source of supply for buyers in other parts of Louisiana. Livestock moved from Bayou Teche pastures eastward to Mississippi River settlements over both land and water. When New Orleans merchant

52. Bolton, ed. and trans., *Athanase de Mézières,* I, 179, II, 105–106, 242; Cabello to Lucas Fontenau, Oct. 28, 1786, Bexar Archives, microfilm in the Louisiana Division, New Orleans Public Library.

53. Grover Rees, trans., "The Dauterive Compact: The Foundation of the Acadian Cattle Industry," *Attakapas Gazette,* XI (Summer 1976), 91.

Jean Baptiste Macarty purchased 180 head of oxen from Atakapas, he employed a crew of one Indian, a Negro slave, and four or five whites to drive the animals around some bayous and to ferry them across others.[54] Pirogues were as important as horses in these cowboys' efforts to round up and drive cattle in the Atchafalaya Basin. Such present-day sites as Berwick and Breaux Bridge, Louisiana, served as entrance points into this network of bayous, lakes, and marshes. From there livestock and other trade items were barged toward the Mississippi along Bayou Plaquemine, if destined for the New Orleans area, or along the Atchafalaya River, if going to the Natchez area. Herds of a hundred or more cattle purchased by merchants were usually gathered in the spring and transported during the summer and autumn months.[55]

V

The growing number of livestock in colonial settlements began to alter landscape and livelihood in the Lower Mississippi Valley perhaps more than any other by-product of the colonial economy. By 1766 the average number of cattle per farm along the Mississippi River approached fourteen and that of horses nearly two. Livestock holdings were even higher in the indigo- and tobacco-producing areas: for example, twenty-six cattle per farm at Chapitoulas and twenty per farm at Pointe Coupée.[56] While the cattle and horse populations appear to have increased almost as much by driving animals into the region as by breed-

54. Voorhies, comp. and trans., *Some Late Eighteenth-Century Louisianians*, 280–318; *SJRLHQ*, XXI, 1257–1260.

55. Petition of Hilario Bouttet, July 23, 1784, Records and Deliberations of the Cabildo; Realty sale, Dec. 29, 1785, at Fort Bute de Manchac, Archives of the Spanish Government of West Florida, I, 12, Louisiana Historical Center, New Orleans; Charles César [Claude C.?] Robin, *Voyage to Louisiana, 1803–1805*, trans. Stuart O. Landry, Jr. (New Orleans, 1966), 183–185; Thomas Ashe, *Travels in America, Performed in 1806* . . . (London, 1808), 325–326.

56. See Table 4. For comparable average holdings of livestock in English colonial regions of North America, see James T. Lemon, *The Best Poor Man's Country: A Geographical Study of Early Southeastern Pennsylvania* (Baltimore, 1972), 162; Carville V. Earle, *The Evolution of a Tidewater Settlement System: All Hallow's Parish, Maryland, 1650–1783* (Chicago, 1975), 124; Robert D. Mitchell, *Commercialism and Frontier Perspectives on the Early Shenandoah Valley* (Charlottesville, Va., 1977), 185.

TABLE 4. *The Agricultural Structure of Louisiana in 1766*

A. Farm Population

Districts (North to South)	No. of Farms	Rural Population	No. of Settlers	Slaves No./Avg. per Farm
Pointe Coupée	117	1,199	509	690/5.8
Upper Acadian Coast	87	269	253	16/.2
Lower Acadian Coast	60	163	142	21/.4
Second German Coast	118	816	574	242/2.1
First German Coast	77	648	340	308/4.0
Chapitoulas	50	1,151	185	966/19.3
First below New Orleans	60	1,449	193	1,256/20.9
English Turn	66	646	288	358/5.4
Ten Indian villages between settlements	331	1,159		
Overall on Mississippi[a]	966	7,500	2,484	3,857/6.0
Natchitoches	99	632	382	250/2.5
Opelousas	75	281	196	85/1.1
Atakapas	50	161	137	24/.5
Old ranches in Atakapas		50		
Overall inland[b]	224	1,124	715	409/1.6
Overall[c]	1,190	8,624	3,199	4,266/5.0

[a]Average excludes Ten Indian villages.   [b]Average excludes Old ranches.   [c]Average excludes Ten Indian villages and Old ranches.

TABLE 4. *Continued*

B. Farm Holdings

Districts (North to South)	No. of Farms	Cattle No./Avg. per Farm	Horses, Mules No./Avg. per Farm	Arpents No./Avg. per Farm
Pointe Coupée	117	1,122/9.6	235/2.0	30,400/260
Upper Acadian Coast	87	13/.2	0/	26,200/259
Lower Acadian Coast	60	118/2.0	4/.1	17,280/288
Second German Coast	118	1,410/12.0	199/1.7	29,880/253
First German Coast	77	942/12.2	144/1.9	18,680/243
Chapitoulas	50	1,306/26.1	174/3.5	28,400/568
First below New Orleans	60	1,321/22.0	245/4.1	23,640/394
English Turn	66	1,246/18.9	63/1.0	56,120/850
Ten Indian villages between settlements	331			
Overall on Mississippi[a]	966	7,478/10.8	1,064/1.7	230,600/284
Natchitoches	99	1,006/10.2	558/5.6	32,600/329
Opelousas	75	1,350/18.0	423/5.6	29,080/388
Atakapas	50	1,004/20.1	254/5.1	17,500/350
Old ranches in Atakapas		15,000/	300/	
Overall inland[b]	224	18,360/14.5	1,535/5.5	79,180/353
Overall[c]	1,190	25,838/12.6	2,599/2.7	309,780/381

[a]Averages exclude Ten Indian villages.   [b]Averages exclude Old ranches.   [c]Averages exclude Ten Indian villages and Old ranches.

Sources: Jacqueline K. Voorhies, comp. and trans., *Some Late Eighteenth-Century Louisianians: Census Records of the Colony, 1758–1796* (Lafayette, La., 1973), 163–214; List of the Several Tribes of Indians inhabiting the banks of the Mississippi, Between New Orleans and New River, with their number of gun men and places of residence, Jan. 1, 1773, William Haldimand Papers, British Museum (microfilm in the Louisiana Division, New Orleans Public Library).

ing them around settlements, the quantity of hogs and sheep rose largely through the steady reproduction of animals descended from early colonial imports. The overall number of hogs and sheep on colonial farms cannot be accurately determined, because these animals were rarely counted, as they browsed freely through open forests and prairies. But by 1770 the 130 farms located below New Orleans each had an average of three and a half hogs and twelve sheep, and the 152 farms on the Acadian Coast each had an average of twelve hogs and less than one sheep per household. Most of the swine in the Lower Mississippi Valley ran freely in the woods and canebrakes around colonial settlements and Indian villages alike. Not countable by any means were the hogs and poultry raised by slaves on plantations and in towns.[57]

Endeavors by habitants to produce meat and dairy products for the local food market resulted in the establishment of several livestock enterprises around New Orleans. In 1738 Paul Cezant and his wife, Barbe Mary, settled on a plantation owned by Pierre Dupart at Barataria, agreeing to "care for the cattle and poultry and to make butter and cheese which they will bring or send to New Orleans." Their remuneration for the three years of service that they agreed to provide included half of the progeny of the cattle, hogs, and poultry and a salary of 150 livres per year. To assist this white couple in raising the animals and processing the food, Dupart sent a Negro man and a Negro woman, both slaves, to Barataria.[58]

---

57. Le Page Du Pratz, *History*, ed. Tregle, 19; Voorhies, comp. and trans., *Some Late Eighteenth-Century Louisianians*, 217–253, 441–486. For descriptions of hogs at Indian villages, see "Thomas Campbell to Lord Deane Gordon: An Account of the Creek Indian Nation, 1764," *Florida Historical Quarterly*, VIII (1930), 160; Romans, *Concise Natural History of East and West Florida*, 57, 64; Adair, *History of the American Indians*, 436. Frank Owsley, who clearly demonstrated the importance of livestock grazing to the majority of farmers in the antebellum South, argued quite correctly that the livestock found in the interior by early 19th-century settlers belonged to Indians: "These droves of livestock, both wild and domesticated, in the Indian nations were doubtless important sources from which the white frontiersmen obtained many of his cattle and long-legged, razorback hogs. They explain in part the remarkable development of the grazing industry during the first part of the nineteenth century, especially after the War of 1812." *Plain Folk of the Old South* (Baton Rouge, 1949), 28–30.

58. Agreement between Sieur Dupart and Paul Cezant and wife, Dec. 2, 1738, Records of the Superior Council.

African-American herders played a prominent role in the spread of livestock production across Louisiana, as they did in South Carolina and other plantation colonies. When Joseph Le Kintrek and Daniel Bopfé formed a livestock-raising partnership on the German Coast in 1741, seven of Le Kintrek's slaves—three men, two women, and two children—helped drive his cattle to the new *vacherie,* where they would stay to take care of sheep, hogs, and poultry as well as cows.[59] In gathering cattle from the fields and forests, Negro *vacheres,* or cowherds, enjoyed a mobility and responsibility similar to slave hunters'; in some cases, the same individuals performed both roles. In 1739 Jean Gonzalez accused Joseph Chaperon of harboring his mulatto slave, Pierre, in order to keep him as a cowherd. When Navy Lieutenant Jean Charles Pradel and Superior Council Judge Nicolas Denis Foucault established a livestock and poultry farm in 1763, "one Negro caretaker" was assigned to oversee its cows, sheep, hogs, turkeys, and chickens. Jean Baptiste Prevost's *vachere* at English Turn, a twenty-five-year-old slave named Caesar, had thirty-two head of cattle, nine horses, and four hogs to look after in 1769.[60]

Around points of livestock production in the frontier exchange economy, the interests of different ethnic and economic groups frequently clashed in ways that prefigured divisions that would fester in the region long after the eighteenth century. The scarcity of high ground in the alluvial Mississippi Valley, before large levees were built, made herding and driving livestock a difficult and, sometimes, belligerent task. African-American slaves familiar with similar environmental conditions in the Senegal River valley were prepared to handle the challenge of keeping their owners' stray cattle from mixing with others on the narrow natural levees. This proved especially hard to do during flood season. On one occasion a slave cowherd from the de Blanc plantation was shot in his left

59. Agreement between Le Kintrek and Bopfé, Sept. 12, 1741, in Winston DeVille and Elizabeth Becker Gianelloni, comps., *Calendar of Louisiana Colonial Documents,* III, *St. Charles Parish* (Baton Rouge, La., 1965), 2. For a discussion of black cowherds, or "cowboys," in South Carolina, see Wood, *Black Majority,* 31, 105–106, 212–213.

60. *RSCLHQ,* VI, 661, IX, 454, XXVI, 205–206. See Milo B. Howard, Jr., and Robert R. Rea, trans., *The Mémoire Justificatif of the Chevalier Montault de Monberaut: Indian Diplomacy in British West Florida, 1763–1765* (University, Ala., 1965), 89, for a Mobile area planter's boast, "My herdsmen, while watching my herds, occupy themselves in hunting and ordinarily bring me enough game of all sorts to maintain a table that would pass for sumptuous in town."

eye while trying to separate his cattle from those being guarded, perhaps too vigilantly, by a free Negro employee of Sieur Bellair of the neighboring plantation.[61]

A desire for beef occasionally motivated people who lacked their own animals to lead a cow or two away from plantation herds. In 1721 a fine of three hundred livres was imposed on habitants who killed livestock belonging to others.[62] Theft by settlers did not stop, but by the second quarter of the century Indians and slaves were mostly accused of raiding cattle. Indians often killed livestock to test their power over these new animals, to defend their fields against strays, or to intimidate encroaching owners. During the spring of 1723, disgruntled Natchez villagers stole and killed precious livestock on the neighboring French concessions, and downriver, around Chapitoulas, two runaway Indian slaves had been killing and butchering cattle for some time in order to eat the meat. As time went on, Indians throughout the colonial region developed a taste for domestic beef, which became partly responsible for attacks on settlement herds.[63]

Runaway black slaves, whose West African background made them more familiar than Indians with cattle, appear to have been the most numerous and most skillful rustlers in the Lower Mississippi Valley. In 1727 a group of recently arrived Africans fled from their labor on the public levee, and by the end of November Governor Périer "had five of them arrested by the Indians two weeks ago who killed two of Sieur Filard's cows which we had to replace with those of the [company] plantation." Throughout the eighteenth century, small bands of extremely mobile marrons traveled from plantation to plantation and fed off cattle,

61. RSCLHQ, V, 249. Along the Senegal and Gambia rivers of West Africa, there was a sharp occupational division between pastoralists, who raised livestock on the *jeeri,* or higher ground, and cultivators, who farmed on the *waalo,* or floodplain. Philip D. Curtin, *Economic Change in Precolonial Africa: Senegambia in the Era of the Slave Trade* (Madison, Wis., 1975), 17–18.

62. AC, C13A, XXIII, 29. For examples of settlers' stealing cattle, see RSCLHQ, XXII, 239–250; and SJRLHQ, XXI, 1257–1260.

63. RSCLHQ, I, 109; AC, C13A, VII, 302. By the second half of the century Choctaw delegates expected to be furnished beef at Mobile and Pensacola and even on their journey to and from the towns. See Howard and Rea, trans., *Mémoire Justificatif of the Chevalier Montault de Monberant,* 111; and Elias Durnford, Memorial for payment of Cattle supplied to the Choctaw Indians who passed by Belle fountain on their way to and from Pensacola in August 1779, EPR, VIII, 621–622.

hogs, and poultry, sometimes with assistance from the local slaves. In this manner blacks in colonial Louisiana maintained their own underground market in domestic meats, supplementing on their own initiative the meager diets provided by many owners.[64] Some slaves also managed to take horses. According to the Superior Council in 1751, they "break down all the horses of the colony by pursuing them immoderately, and by stealing them, not only out of the woods, but also out of their stables." Police regulations issued on February 18 of that year permitted "said negroes to be shot at when they are thus met on horseback, and when they refuse to stop on their being hailed."[65] A heightening consciousness by officials of slavery's vulnerability to frontier conditions provoked sterner punitive measures against black Louisianians.

In general the dispersed pattern of livestock production blurred distinctions between strayed and stolen animals and between private and common grazing grounds. By the 1780s most settlers in the cattle-rich districts of Atakapas and Opelousas still owned, on the average, fewer than fifty head of cattle and fewer than four hundred arpents of land. Indians still living around Bayou Teche also raised small herds of cattle. Since enclosing cattle in pens required excessive amounts of labor to cut the forests for pasturage and fences, Acadian and other herders chose to pasture their livestock on natural levees and other scattered ground above the bottomland. Even those individuals who managed to build enclosures allowed their animals to graze in open woods and prairies, particularly during the winter months. European observers like Charles Robin were astonished at such a practice, especially when thirsty for a cup of milk: "During the dry seasons the herds had already scattered and most of the inhabitants let them all go out without bothering to keep near them a cow or two for their daily needs."[66]

64. *MPAFD*, II, 563; *RSCLHQ*, XIII, 135.
65. AC, C13A, XXXV, 39–52.
66. Robin, *Voyage to Louisiana*, trans. Landry, 195–196; Lauren Post, "The Old Cattle Industry of Southwest Louisiana," *McNeese Review*, IX (1957), 43–55; Post, "Some Notes on the Attakapas Indians of Southwest Louisiana," *LH*, III (1962), 221–242. Of the 316 households constituting Opelousas in 1788, 72% owned fewer than 50 head of cattle and fewer than 20 arpents of land facing Bayou Teche (Voorhies, comp. and trans., *Some Late Eighteenth-Century Louisianians*, 280–318). For a description of herding along Bayou Lafourche in the 20th century that seems applicable to earlier times, see Works Projects Administration, *Louisiana: A Guide to the State* (New York, 1941), 415:

With free use of rangeland becoming an irritant to rising interests in plantation agriculture and more commercialized animal husbandry, regulations mounted against open grazing. According to an ordinance issued by Governor O'Reilly in 1770, cattle would be "permitted to go at large, from the eleventh of November of one year, to the fifteenth of March of the year following; and at all other times the proprietor shall be responsible for the damage that his cattle may have done to his neighbors." Although branding had been practiced all along by well-established farmers and ranchers, less-propertied and more recent settlers as well as Indians and slaves "hunted" cattle belonging to others and therefore resisted the use of brands, which made the identity of appropriated animals too clear. O'Reilly ordered that "all cattle shall be branded by the proprietors." Settlers who did not brand their cattle at the age of eighteen months would surrender any claim to them. "Nothing being more injurious to the inhabitants than strayed cattle, without the destruction of which tame cattle cannot increase," the ordinance of February 18, 1770, authorized proprietors to "collect and kill, for their use, the said strayed cattle" until July 1, 1771, "after which time they shall be considered wild and may be killed by any person whomsoever."[67]

In this nascent struggle between small farmers and their wealthier neighbors, practices that had commonly been used in the frontier economy began to run up against measures to control or outlaw them. Burning forests to hunt wildlife and to clear fields, a method borrowed from Indian inhabitants, blended into the issue of open grazing. In response to damages suffered by planters from spreading fires, the General Assembly of West Florida passed an act in 1770 prohibiting hunters from setting fire to "grass, herbage, trees, or shrubs upon any land or lands in the said Province not being his, her, or their property, except between the first day of February and the fifteenth day of April, and being ten miles distant from

---

Because of the limited farm land, cattle are pastured on the ridges and mounds that rise a few feet above the swamps bordering the bayou. Pirogues, instead of horses, are employed by the herdsmen in rounding up their hardy livestock, and trained cow hounds are used to find cattle that have bogged in muck. Dairy animals, pastured on *coteaux* (little hills) nearer the levee, go back and forth to their grazing islets through fended-in lanes called *manches*.

67. Gustavus Schmidt, trans., "O'Reilly's Ordinance of 1770: Concerning Grants of Land in Louisiana to New Settlers, Fencing of Same, Building of Roads and Levees, and Forfeiture of Strayed Cattle," *LHQ*, XI (1928), 239–240.

any town or settlement."[68] In 1773 Ana Judith Chenal, widow of Jean Baptiste Grevembert, complained that "the residents of Opelousas have been killing much of my live-stock at my dairy-farm giving as a reason that they are straying." Responding to this petition, Governor Luis de Unzaga urged the commandant of Opelousas that "the residents must cease, at once, this odious practice of driving home the animals of their neighborhood which legitimately belong to known owners." In 1787, owners of large cattle herds at Opelousas, like Martin Duralde with one thousand head of cattle and Joseph Cormier with nearly seven hundred, renewed demands that stray cattle "in the woods and prairies of Plaquemines Brulées" be destroyed by firearms, because a few cattle from their own pens tended to join the strays during each winter pasturage. Previous attempts to capture them had failed, according to the petitioners, because of "the indolence of the employees" and "the self-interest of scoundrels."[69]

The frontier exchange economy was shaped by and, in turn, reshaped many different production activities among the Indians, Europeans, and Africans brought together in the Lower Mississippi Valley. Most of the early changes in production, however, occurred through a gradual mixing of their subsistence practices. Indians contributed useful farming and hunting techniques to the colonial economy, and economic life around their villages was altered by commercial hunting and livestock raising.

68. Robert R. Rea, comp., *The Minutes, Journals, and Acts of the General Assembly of British West Florida* (University, Ala., 1979), 376–377; Romans, *Concise Natural History of East and West Florida*, 11; Robin, *Voyage to Louisiana*, trans. Landry, 194. The persistence of fire techniques adopted from Indians in the hunting, herding, and farming practices of the South is examined in Stephen J. Pyne, *Fire in America: A Cultural History of Wildland and Rural Fire* (Princeton, N.J., 1982), 71–83, 143–160; and Albert E. Cowdrey, *This Land, This South: An Environmental History* (Lexington, Ky., 1983), 15–16, 54–55, 94.

69. *SJRLHQ*, XI, 233–235; Carl A. Brasseaux, trans., "Petition of the Habitants for the Destruction of Stray Cattle," *Attakapas Gazette*, XI (Summer 1976), 78–79. The cultural and economic significance of open-range grazing in the 19th-century South is receiving renewed attention from various perspectives. Major contributions include Forrest McDonald and Grady McWhiney, "The South from Self-Sufficiency to Peonage: An Interpretation," *American Historical Review*, LXXXV (1980), 1095–1118; J. Crawford King, Jr., "The Closing of the Southern Range: An Exploratory Study," *Journal of Southern History*, XLVIII (1982), 53–70; Steven Hahn, *The Roots of Southern Populism: Yeoman Farmers and the Transformation of the Georgia Upcountry, 1850–1890* (New York, 1983), 58–63.

Africans found much of their labor coerced into the production of tobacco, indigo, and naval stores for exportation, but managed to supplement their own livelihood through various subsistence practices—practices that they both carried to Louisiana themselves and borrowed from
other groups. Many settlers also minimized their dependency on the
production of export crops. A combination of subsistence practices on
and around their farms helped safeguard them against natural hazards
and market uncertainties.

In their various but interconnected cycles of production, inhabitants of
the Lower Mississippi Valley tried to balance subsistence with commercial
activities. This effort became more difficult, however, toward the end of
the eighteenth century. The interests of planters and merchants committed
to expanding export production grew stronger after 1763, with help from
immigration and commercial policies implemented by colonial governments. Ordinances regulating possession of firearms and livestock and the
use of forests and fields began to erode some of the autonomy and
flexibility that petty producers had managed to maintain at their villages,
farms, camps, and plantations. But this clash with export-oriented interests never fully drove long-standing subsistence practices from the landscape. Instead, subsistence-oriented Indians, settlers, and slaves channeled
their customary pattern of production and exchange into strategies of
survival and resistance within the tightening grip of a plantation economy.

6

FOOD MARKETING AND THE

EVOLUTION OF REGIONAL FOODWAYS

Marketing systems reveal a good deal about the relationships among the various groups that compose a society; and, furthermore, they serve as a useful comparative measurement of the similarities and differences between societies.[1] This maxim, familiar to anthropologists, has much to offer historians of North American colonial and frontier regions. But the economic activities of Indian and colonial societies have long been separated by prevalent conceptualizations of frontiers either as boundaries between primitive and commercial economies or as transitional zones through which stages of economic development rapidly progress.

Modern scholarship on fur trade networks has exposed the multiplicity of roles and relationships that American Indians formed as participants within dynamic frontier economies. It reflects a new anthropological understanding of economic life among historians, one that takes day-to-day, informal episodes of exchange as well as the more formal institutions of commerce into account.[2] But when it comes to goods other than or in

---

1. Sidney W. Mintz, in his many works—from "Peasant Markets," *Scientific American*, CCIII, no. 2 (August 1960), 112–122, to "Reflections on Caribbean Peasantries," *Nieuwe West-Indische Gids/New West Indian Guide*, LVII (1983), 1–17—has illuminated dimensions of food marketing that should interest North Americanists.

2. Landmark studies of Indian trade that were influenced by economic anthropology include Arthur J. Ray, *Indians in the Fur Trade: Their Role as Trappers, Hunters, and Middlemen in the Lands Southwest of the Hudson Bay, 1660–1870* (Toronto, 1974);

addition to furs, particularly food, the older impressions of the frontier as backward or self-sufficient still seem to obscure the many forms of exchange that occurred between the different groups of people who inhabited American colonial regions.

Examination of how food marketing evolved in the Lower Mississippi Valley brings the groups who participated and the goods that they exchanged into focus. But food is never simply an object of exchange; it is also a means of exchange. By trading in particular food items, Indians, Africans, and Europeans interacted closely and influenced each other culturally. Colonies were "dietary frontiers," as Fernand Braudel has observed, where "eating other people's bread" involved both profound change and stubborn conflict. Production and peddling of foodstuffs in small quantities constituted a sphere of social interaction that generated a unique creole diet in North America while also serving as a source of economic autonomy for Indians, settlers, and slaves in the eighteenth-century Lower Mississippi Valley. The respective meanings of food exchange to the different peoples who traded provide evidence of how participants presented themselves to each other as members of distinct social groups.[3]

I

Food marketing between Indians and colonists arose immediately in Louisiana, as in other nascent North American colonies, be-

Calvin Martin, *Keepers of the Game: Indian-Animal Relationships and the Fur Trade* (Berkeley, Calif., 1978); Neal Salisbury, *Manitou and Providence: Indians, Europeans, and the Making of New England, 1500–1643* (New York, 1982); Richard White, *The Roots of Dependency: Subsistence, Environment, and Social Change among the Choctaws, Pawnees, and Navajos* (Lincoln, Nebr., 1983).

3. Fernand Braudel, *The Structure of Everyday Life: The Limits of the Possible*, trans. Siân Reynolds, Civilization and Capitalism, Fifteenth–Eighteenth Century, I (New York, 1980), 163–172; Bernard S. Cohn, "History and Anthropology: The State of Play," *Comparative Studies in Society and History*, XXII (1980), 198–221. For other articulations of the anthropological search for meaning in social and economic relations, see Natalie Zemon Davis, *Society and Culture in Early Modern France* (Stanford, Calif., 1975), xvi–xvii; William H. Sewell, Jr., *Work and Revolution in France: The Language of Labor from the Old Regime to 1848* (Cambridge, 1980), 5–13;.Rhys Isaac, *The Transformation of Virginia, 1740–1790* (Chapel Hill, N.C., 1982), 323–357.

cause of a combination of factors: tenuous supply lines with the mother country, the ability of local Indians to trade food surpluses, and a reluctance among colonists to plant their own food crops. Sent by France late in 1698 to establish a military post near the mouth of the Mississippi River and to forestall Spanish and English advances in the region, naval captain Pierre Le Moyne d'Iberville encountered dismal prospects for sustaining what he hoped would become a colony. Already overextended across other colonies and facing shortages of food at home, the French crown was not prepared to deliver supplies with any regularity to the Gulf Coast. Under these circumstances Iberville's isolated outpost was desperately dependent upon food provided by Indian villages.[4]

While sailors and soldiers from France and some Canadian traders and trappers who had joined them on the coast were constructing Louisiana's first colonial fort at Biloxi Bay, the Pascagoulas, Mobilians, and other Gulf Coastal Indians eagerly traded their surpluses of corn, beans, and meat for axes, beads, and other curious items of European manufacture. During the first decade of the eighteenth century, colonial officials regularly sent boats up the Mobile and Mississippi rivers to purchase supplies of maize from Indians. In order to facilitate their trade with the French, some villages even began to relocate closer to the coast and to plant larger quantities of grain. When the Houmas abandoned their old town several miles east of the Mississippi, for example, they settled downriver along the west bank near Bayou Lafourche—a convenient way station for French explorers and travelers. By 1708, when the colony of Louisiana numbered fewer than 300 people (122 military men, 80 Indian slaves, and 77 settlers), Indians in the vicinity of Mobile regularly exchanged meat and grain for firearms and gunpowder. For ten deer carried to Fort St. Louis in 1710, an Indian hunter could acquire his first musket.[5]

Indian willingness to trade food, however, did not automatically solve Louisiana's early subsistence problems. The French initially hoped to

4. Early food problems in Louisiana are described fully in Marcel Giraud, *A History of French Louisiana*, I, *The Reign of Louis XIV, 1698–1715* (1953), trans. Joseph C. Lambert (Baton Rouge, La., 1974), 91–194.

5. Richebourg Gaillard McWilliams, ed. and trans., *Iberville's Gulf Journals* (University, Ala., 1981), 78, 170 (hereafter cited as *Iberville's Gulf Journals*); McWilliams, ed. and trans., *Fleur de Lys and Calumet: Being the Pénicaut Narrative of French Adventure in Louisiana* (Baton Rouge, La., 1953), 98–103 (hereafter cited as *Pénicaut Narrative*); MPAFD, II, 32–34, 52–53.

maintain their own eating habits, but they failed in attempts to grow wheat at Biloxi and Mobile on the coast and at Bayou St. John near the Mississippi. Reluctance to eat other people's bread, furthermore, threatened the colony repeatedly with open conflict. Reporting on the increasing palatability of Indian corn to settlers in 1706, Jean-Baptiste Le Moyne de Bienville stated that "the men who are in Louisiana are accustoming themselves to eat it, but the women who are for the most part from Paris eat it reluctantly." Despite the women's threats to abandon the colony, Bienville continued to purchase corn "at a low price from the Indians." Wheat shipped by brigantine from Veracruz was "extraordinarily dear."[6]

Whenever food shortages struck the garrisons at Mobile and Biloxi, the governor avoided famine and mutiny by allowing groups of soldiers, sailors, and workers to stay in Indian villages for extended periods of time. These seasonal visitors expressed no fear, at least in written form, of being poisoned or polluted by their hosts—a good sign that some common ground existed between cuisines and that everyday relations across cultural lines were genial. Features of Indian fare most noteworthy to early Louisiana colonists from Europe were the diversity of both wild and cultivated food sources, the innumerable ways people cooked maize, and their casual eating manners (although the last did not necessarily fascinate all Europeans, among whom use of tables and forks was only slowly spreading during the eighteenth century).[7] French carpenter André Pénicaut recalled his visit in 1699 to a Pascagoula village, where he and others received smoked meats of buffalo, bear, and deer, several kinds of melons and wild fruits, and sagamité, "which is a kind of pap made from maize

6. *MPAFD*, II, 59, 75, 208–209, III, 32, 112, 151–152. Setting the tone for a century of retelling, Louisiana historian Charles Gayarré poked fun at the "comical" insurrection threatened by the 20 or so "French girls" transported to Louisiana in 1704, who were "indignant at being fed on corn" (*History of Louisiana*, 4 vols. [New York, 1854–1866], I, 86–87). But women played a crucial role in the struggle to preserve traditional subsistence and marketing practices in 18th-century France. Their resistance to imposed change in customary habits should not be dismissed. See Olwen Hufton, "Women and the Family Economy in Eighteenth-Century France," *French Historical Studies*, IX (1975), 1–22.

7. Antoine Le Page Du Pratz, *Histoire de la Lousiane . . .*, 3 vols. (Paris, 1758), III, 12–13; *Pénicaut Narrative*, 105–109. For relevant eating customs in early 18th-century French households, see Braudel, *Structures of Everyday Life*, 203–243; and Jean-Louis Flandrin, *Families in Former Times: Kinship, Household, and Sexuality in Early Modern France*, trans. Richard Southern (Cambridge, 1979), 102–105.

and green beans that are like those in France." He admired the wooden dishes and clay pots made by the Pascagoulas and remarked that the women cooked large quantities of sagamité in "great earthen pots" for a few families to share. Pénicaut furthermore observed that, "however abundant their provisions may be, they do not overindulge themselves, but eat only what they need, yet very untidily, most of them eating only with their fingers, though they possess spoons, which they make from buffalo horns." Indians, on the other hand, evinced reluctance to eat items significant in the French diet, particularly salads, soups, wine, and poultry. By 1700 the Houma Indians had raised plenty of chickens from some hens and cocks left by seventeenth-century explorers, but they did not eat them and may even have considered the strange birds to be sacred. As Father Jacques Gravier reported: "When one wishes to obtain chickens from them, He must not say that he intends to kill or eat them. They would give them with reluctance; but they willingly sell these fowls when they are not killed in their presence, or when they are told that they will be taken away to be reared as with them."[8]

The availability of Indian produce tempted some officials to profiteer from the sale of food. Louisiana's first political conflict, in fact, centered upon accusations—not entirely false—that the Le Moyne brothers engrossed "the meat and other produce that the Indians have brought to Mobile," trading with the king's merchandise and marking up the price of food for their own profit. Far away from France, where local governments and traditional constraints still protected buyers of food from profiteering middlemen, colonial merchants and administrators were in a convenient position to intercept corn and game from Indian suppliers and resell the food to consumers at exorbitant prices.[9] The Superior Council assumed responsibility for fixing the price of basic food items, ordering on Septem-

8. *Pénicaut Narrative,* 18–19; *Iberville's Gulf Journals,* 78; Reuben Gold Thwaites, ed., *The Jesuit Relations and Allied Documents: Travels and Explorations of the Jesuit Missionaries in New France, 1610–1791,* 73 vols. (Cleveland, Ohio, 1896–1901), LXV, 151.

9. *MPAFD,* III, 64. The conflict between the pro–Le Moyne and anti–Le Moyne factions, much of which centered on the distribution of food supplies, is fully explored in Charles Edwards O'Neill, *Church and State in French Colonial Louisiana: Policy and Politics to 1732* (New Haven, Conn., 1966), 47–77. For the regulation of food marketing in the ancien régime, see Steven L. Kaplan, *Bread, Politics, and Political Economy in the Reign of Louis XV,* 2 vols. (The Hague, 1976), I, 65–68.

ber 27, 1721, "that no venison shall be sold in the future at a price above sixteen livres for an entire deer, eight livres for a half and four livres for a quarter." According to a fuller tariff issued the following year, buffalo beef was set at eight sous per pound, cattle beef at ten sous per pound, chickens at three livres apiece, and eggs at fifty sous per dozen. These and subsequent regulations, however, never stopped commandants of military posts from attempting to monopolize food supplies and other goods delivered by neighboring Indian villagers.[10]

Many early Louisiana settlers became irreversibly accustomed to direct exchange with Indians for their subsistence. Looking back on France's feeble commitment to the colony during its first two decades, Jean Beranger noted that the habitants had consequently "done nothing else than try to get a little trading merchandise to obtain from the savages their sustenance, consisting of Indian corn, beans, pumpkins, or small round pumpkins, game and bear grease." What began as a necessity in an unfamiliar land became a preference over other sources of food. Colonial officials like Marc-Antoine Hubert, *commissaire ordonnateur* in 1716, lamented the settlers' reluctance to till the soil themselves. The "idle and lazy life" seen by observers eager for Louisiana to become an export-producing colony was testimony to the vitality of cross-cultural exchange among inhabitants. "Trade with the Indians," Hubert complained, gave colonists "what they need day by day."[11]

But when the Company of the Indies sent a flood of immigrants to Louisiana between 1717 and 1721, dependence on Indian supplies of food actually expanded. Seven thousand settlers and two thousand slaves disembarking on the Gulf Coast, deprived of adequate provisions and infected by diseases, created a severe food crisis. Soldiers and workers, now employed by the company, continued to be sent into nearby Indian villages. Bulk shipments of corn were, meanwhile, sought from interior tribes. Even as this food crisis subsided, the survivors frustrated company officials by staying reliant on Indian trade for their subsistence.[12]

10. *MPAFD*, II, 263, III, 326. For selected examples of profiteering by post commandants, see AC, C13A, XI, 174–176, XXIX, 142, XLIV, 21–22.

11. William M. Carroll, trans., Frank Wagner, ed., *Béranger's Discovery of Aransas Pass: A Translation of Jean Béranger's French Manuscript* (Corpus Christi, Tex., 1983), 33; *MPAFD*, II, 232.

12. Jean François Benjamin Dumont de Montigny, *Mémoirs historiques sur la Louisiane*, 2 vols. (Paris, 1753), II, 41–42; Glenn R. Conrad, ed. and trans., *Immigra-*

Many of the several thousand African slaves who were shipped to Louisiana during the 1720s to develop the colony's commercial agriculture also turned to food marketing as a means of sustenance and self-determination. Their own desire to cultivate familiar foods, combined with the economic interests of their owners, made slaves active producers in the emerging food market. Managing the Company of the Indies plantation across the river from New Orleans from 1726 to 1734, Antoine Le Page Du Pratz recognized the inclination among slaves to satisfy personally their own subsistence needs and eating tastes. He recommended that owners give "a small piece of waste ground" to their slaves, "engage them to cultivate it for their own profit," and purchase their produce "upon fair and just terms."[13] Planters thereby acquired goods to resell to other colonists, although the slaves themselves preferred direct participation in the marketplace. Small-scale cultivating and marketing of foodstuffs by slaves had several advantages in Louisiana, as in other plantation colonies. It helped owners to maintain slaves at a level of subsistence minimizing hardship, death, and rebellion, it provided consumers with a larger quantity and wider array of foods than would otherwise have been available, and it gained for slaves some measure of autonomy from their masters. Colonial officials intermittently enforced regulations upon slave peddlers, requiring them by 1751 to carry written permits from their owners, but the open marketing of goods by slaves benefited too many people for the prohibition against it to be enforced before the last quarter of the century.[14]

II

Foodstuffs produced in both Indian villages and colonial settlements circulated through a diffuse network of cross-cultural ex-

---

tion and War: Louisiana, 1718–1721: From the Memoir of Charles Le Gac (Lafayette, La., 1970), 108, 130–135; Jean Baptiste Bernard de La Harpe, The Historical Journal of the Establishment of the French in Louisiana, ed. Glenn R. Conrad, trans. Joan Cain and Virginia Koenig (Lafayette, La., 1971), 113, 154, 167–173; O'Neill, Church and State in French Colonial Louisiana, 121–122.

13. Antoine Le Page Du Pratz, The History of Louisiana, ed. Joseph G. Tregle, Jr. (London, 1774; facs. rpt., Baton Rouge, La., 1975), 387.

14. Jean François Benjamin Dumont de Montigny, "Historical Memoirs of M. Dumont" (1753), in B. F. French, ed., Historical Collections of Louisiana . . . , 5 vols. (New

change. Food surpluses were periodically traded in bulk to areas in short supply, but more importantly for the long-term evolution of the region, Indians, settlers, and slaves frequently exchanged food items in small-scale, face-to-face transactions. France treated Louisiana as an importer of flour, alcohol, and a few more luxurious foodstuffs, but supply lines were too tenuous and shipments always too small or spoiled for colonists to rely upon external sources for grain and meat. Settlers accused merchants who exported flour from France of shipping inedible and short-measured supplies. The Illinois country eventually became one reliable source of wheat for the colonists downriver.[15] Food marketing within the Lower Mississippi Valley, meanwhile, was stimulated by the presence of numerous military personnel in the region and the fact that about 25 percent of Louisiana's colonial population lived in New Orleans by mid-century. Corn, game, and other provisions consumed at interior posts like Natchitoches, Arkansas, and Tombecbé came from neighboring Indian villagers who bartered for metalware, brandy, cloth, and other trade goods directly with the soldiers. Sometimes Indians sold food to military officers on a more formal basis. The colonial government also purchased large quantities of grain for its troops from settlers along the Mississippi River.[16]

Residents of New Orleans and Mobile benefited from food crops and meats, even from prepared items like persimmon bread, cornmeal, and

York, 1846–1853), V, 120; AC, C13A, XXXV, 39–52; Records and Deliberations of the New Orleans Cabildo, Jan. 10, 1772, Louisiana Division, New Orleans Public Library. The advantages gained by slaves from food production and marketing are underscored in Sidney W. Mintz, *Caribbean Transformations* (Chicago, 1974), 192.

15. *MPAFD*, II, 347; N. M. Miller Surrey, *The Commerce of Louisiana during the French Régime, 1699–1763* (New York, 1916), 265–266, 291–299; John G. Clark, *New Orleans, 1718–1812: An Economic History* (Baton Rouge, La., 1969), 30, 59–60; Clark, *La Rochelle and the Atlantic Economy during the Eighteenth Century* (Baltimore, 1981), 170–173.

16. *MPAFD*, III, 423, 535–536; Heloise H. Cruzat, trans., "Louisiana in 1724: Banet's Report to the Company of the Indies, Dated Paris, December 20, 1724," *LHQ*, XII (1919), 126. Examples of military contracts with colonists for food supplies include *RSCLHQ*, V, 377–378, VI, 287, XIII, 157, 309. The influence of heavy urbanization upon Louisiana's marketing system is suggested in J. Zitomersky, "Urbanization in French Colonial Louisiana (1706–1766)," *Annales de démographie historique 1974: Études, comptes rendus, documents, bibliographie* (Paris, 1974), 263–278.

PLATE 7. *Drawing of the Savages of Several Nations, New Orleans, 1735*. By Alexandre de Batz. *Courtesy of Peabody Museum of Archaeology and Ethnology, Harvard University, Cambridge, Mass.*

bear oil, that were sold by Indian people. Indians from the large, interior nations occasionally supplied these towns with corn, poultry, and vegetables, but the petites nations participated more regularly in urban markets (see Plate 7).[17] During the 1720s those Acolapissas, Chitimachas, and Houmas who had resettled closer to New Orleans were producing corn, fish, and game for city dwellers and travelers. On the Pearl River, between New Orleans and Biloxi, the Pensacolas, Biloxis, Pascagoulas, and Capinas furnished "an abundance of meat to all the French who are near enough to trade for it." Of a group of Chaouachas who migrated from Florida to the Mobile River outside the town of Mobile, Bienville declared that "their sole occupation is to produce corn by means of which they obtain from the French what they need." The migration of Alibamons, Biloxis, Pascagoulas, and Chahtos from British West Florida to the lower

17. Bernard Romans, *A Concise Natural History of East and West Florida* . . . (New York, 1775; rpt., New Orleans, 1961), 57; Romans, "An Attempt towards a Short Description of West Florida," in P. Lee Phillips, ed., *Notes on the Life and Works of Bernard Romans* (Deland, Fla., 1924), 120.

Mississippi during the 1760s meant that New Orleans gained access to a larger number of Indian peddlers at the expense of Mobile.[18]

In time, colonial farmers from the surrounding countryside brought grains, vegetables, fruits, and poultry to the multiethnic market at New Orleans. German immigrants who settled above the city during the 1720s became notable food provisioners. "They bring every day to the market," observed one contemporary, "all kinds of produce to the city." When raids by Choctaw rebels caused them to flee from the German Coast to the city in 1748, New Orleans became, as Governor Vaudreuil reported, "deprived of the comforts that those settlers provided for it by their industry and their thrift."[19] Thomas Jefferys later called the Germans "the purveyors of the capital, whither they bring, weekly, cabbages, salads, fruits, greens, and pulse of all sorts, as well as vast quantities of wildfowl, salt pork, and many excellent sorts of fish," and described their pattern of marketing by the 1760s:

> They load their vessels on the Friday evening, towards sunset, and then placing themselves two together in a pirogue, to be carried down by the current of the river, without ever using their oars, arrive early on Saturday morning at New Orleans, where they hold their market, whilst the morning lasts, along the bank of the river, selling their commodities for ready money. After this is done, and when they have provided themselves with what necessaries they want, they embark again on their return, rowing their pirogues up the river against the stream and reach their plantations in the evening with provisions, or the money arising from the produce of their labours.[20]

The German farmers were joined by other groups of independent producers who marketed their foodstuffs in the city. French and free Negro families also provisioned New Orleans from their gardens and fields.

18. *MPAFD,* III, 535–536; Le Page Du Pratz, *History,* ed. Tregle, 202, 233, 262–263; EPR, III, 94–95, IV, 20–21; Philip Pittman, *The Present State of the European Settlements on the Mississippi* (1770), ed. Robert R. Rea (facs. rpt., Gainesville, Fla., 1973), 22–35.

19. AC, C13A, XIV, 138; Relation de la Louisiane [ca. 1735], 19 (anonymous MS), Edward E. Ayer Collection, Newberry Library, Chicago; *MPAFD,* V, 30.

20. T. Jefferys, *The Natural and Civil History of the French Dominions in North and South America* . . . (London, 1761), 147; Helmut Blume, *Die Entwicklung der Kulturlandschaft des Mississippideltas in kolonialer Zeit* . . . (Kiel, 1956), 50–56.

During the 1760s newly arriving Acadian and Canary Island settlers began to plant corn, rice, and other food crops and became important producers in the local food market. Individual transactions performed by these colonists were usually small, but collectively they amounted to a substantial volume of provisions. The temptation for many farmers in Spanish Louisiana to sell their produce across the river to English West Floridians caused officials to complain during the 1760s and 1770s that the city of New Orleans suffered occasional food shortages.[21] Colonial towns were also provisioned by resident hunters and fishermen who sold their goods on the streets and levees. In 1770 an English traveler observed that along Lake Pontchartrain behind New Orleans, at the mouth of Bayou St. John, there were "Fishermen and fowlers and when unemployed in that business they gather wood and burn it into charcoal."[22]

African-Americans were the most ubiquitous peddlers of food in Lower Mississippi Valley towns. Many planters sent slaves into Mobile, New Orleans, Natchez, and Natchitoches to sell poultry, meats, vegetables, and milk on their owners' behalf. Slaves took this opportunity to sell independently their own foodstuffs and other items. Slaves residing in the towns also took advantage of urban markets to sustain trade practices independent of the economic interests of their owners. Along the riverfront and in the streets black New Orleanians purchased foodstuffs for themselves as well as their masters from slaves and farmers who carried produce in from the countryside. In these transactions a slave could barter with combinations of his owners' cash and his own belongings and thereby skim some indeterminable amount from the deal for personal use. Some urban blacks hunted, fished, or gardened in order to peddle their own provisions.[23]

21. Carl A. Brasseaux, ed. and trans., "Official Correspondence of Spanish Louisiana, 1770–1803," *Revue de Louisiane/Louisiana Review*, VII (1978), 172–173; Charles César [Claude C.?] Robin, *Voyage to Louisiana, 1803–1805*, trans. Stuart O. Landry, Jr. (New Orleans, 1966), 114–115; Thomas Ashe, *Travels in America, Performed in 1806* . . . (London, 1808), 316–317.

22. Edward Mease, "Narrative of a Journey . . . through West Florida in the Years 1770 and 1771," Mississippi Historical Society, *Publications*, Centenary Ser., V (1925), 63. The June 1778 census of New Orleans lists 12 hunters living in the city. For this and other evidence of town hunters, see Albert J. Robichaux, Jr., ed. and trans., *Louisiana Census and Militia Lists, 1770–1789: German Coast, New Orleans, below New Orleans, and Lafourche* (Harvey, La., 1973), 23–68.

23. Records and Deliberations of the New Orleans Cabildo, Jan. 10, 1772; *SMV*, I, 239–241.

Women in general played a prominent role in town markets, but African-American women became perhaps the most influential buyers and sellers of food in New Orleans. Women from Indian villages and colonial households actively participated in all forms of petty exchange, placing themselves in an intermediary role between cultures.[24] Slave women were assigned to the cooking and grocery chores of white households, but other factors were also involved in their marketing activities. In West African societies women traditionally dominated the distribution of foodstuffs in local markets, not simply for economic reasons but as a means of periodically reinforcing kinship ties beyond the households of their husbands. Black women used familiar street marketing skills in the slave colony of Louisiana to establish a sphere of life apart from their owners' control. In some cases they even purchased their freedom.[25]

Many slaves perceived food marketing as something more than a means of subsistence. Acts of pilferage often interwove with exchanges of food.

24. Important insights into the marketing activities of women in colonial or interethnic situations can be found in Robert Steven Grumet, "Sunksquaws, Shamans, and Tradeswomen: Middle Atlantic Coastal Algonkian Women during the Seventeenth and Eighteenth Centuries," in Mona Etienne and Eleanor Laycock, eds., *Women and Colonization: Anthropological Perspectives* (New York, 1980), 43–62; Ulrich Köhler, "Patterns of Interethnic Economic Exchange in Southeastern Mexico," *Journal of Anthropological Research*, XXXVI (1980), 316–337; Mary Beth Norton, "The Evolution of White Women's Experience in Early America," *American Historical Review*, LXXXIX (1984), 593–619.

25. B. W. Hodder and U. I. Ukwu, *Markets in West Africa: Studies of Markets and Trade among the Yoruba and Ibo* (Ibadan, Nigeria, 1969), 50–52, 71–93; Solange Faladé, "Women of Dakar and the Surrounding Urban Area," in Denise Paulme, ed., *Women of Tropical Africa*, trans. H. M. Wright (Berkeley, Calif., 1971), 217–229. Among the 248 free people of color in New Orleans in 1778, women composed a significant majority. Whereas the number of adult white males 13 years and older was greater than that of adult white females (358 to 398), the number of free Negro men was much smaller than that of free Negro women (19 to 69), as was the number of free men of mixed color to that of free women of mixed color (40 to 92) (*SMV*, I, 290). The dominance in New Orleans street marketing of African-American women, many of whom probably bought their freedom, is vividly illustrated in Lyle Saxon *et al.*, comps., *Gumbo Ya-Ya: A Collection of Louisiana Folk Tales* (New Orleans, 1945), 27–49. For the role of women in other African-American urban markets, see Mintz, "Peasant Markets," *Sci. Am.*, CCIII, no. 2 (August 1960), 114–118; Mintz, *Caribbean Transformations*, 210–211; Michael M. Horowitz, *Morne-Paysan: Peasant Village in Martinique* (New York, 1967), 33–38.

Taking small quantities of food sources here and there served slaves in a variety of capacities—protesting deprivation under their owners' control, supplementing nutrition within the slave community, and sometimes facilitating flight from bondage. In 1729 a group of young runaway slaves from plantations between New Orleans and Chapitoulas stole a heifer, bacon, corn, and some hens. Changereau, a Bambara from the Senegal region of West Africa, admitted to eating some of the meat but denied stealing it. Another captured member of this group, François, said he did not kill any cattle but confessed that he "stole some bacon and sold it to another negro for tobacco." Although claiming not to have joined these marrons, Sabany told the prosecutor that they had given him fresh meat in one of the Bienville plantation cabins. Throughout the eighteenth century, small fugitive camps fed themselves from plantation herds and storehouses, traded leftovers with other slaves, and even channeled goods into the open market. The fifteen or more inhabitants of one camp, discovered behind the Bienvenue estate in 1781, survived by killing stray cattle, by growing patches of corn and vegetables, and by making "baskets, sifters, and other articles made of willow," which slaves on a nearby plantation sold for them in New Orleans.[26]

Most day-to-day pilferage on plantations and in towns occurred without much official notice, but cases in which theft led to arrest and prosecution reveal the variety of ways that slaves illicitly exchanged food with other Louisianians. After Alexandre Boré discovered one hundred chickens and five quarters of rice missing from his plantation at Cannes Brus-lées in 1753, one of his many slaves was flogged into admitting that he had traded them away for tafia. The settler who bartered with him, one Faussier of Chapitoulas, was sentenced to pay fifty livres indemnity to Boré as well as a fine of one hundred livres. Meanwhile, the pilferer managed to break his chains, steal a gun, and flee into the forest. On June 3, 1782, a twenty-six-year-old slave named Juan was arrested in New Orleans; his interrogation disclosed how pilfered food financed an ambitious escape. He crossed Lake Pontchartrain to the city after taking from his owner a pirogue, a gun and ammunition, a shirt, and some sweet potatoes. On the way he stole turkeys and hens from the La Chaise plantation and, after selling them in New Orleans, stole five more hens from a courtyard in town. Juan sold the hens to a Frenchman named La Rochelle for cash, with which he had intended to buy gunpowder.[27]

III

The multiple roles played by Indians, settlers, and slaves in producing, marketing, and processing food items in the Lower Mississippi Valley created ripe conditions for the evolution of a colonial diet fluorescent in cross-cultural influences. As it linked different ethnic groups together in an environment rich in fish, fowl, game, and seasonings, the regional food market undoubtedly shaped culinary tastes and cooking techniques. Although no exact lines or precise moments of influence can be detected, the origins of Louisiana's legendary creole cuisine lie in the syncretic process of cultural change that accompanied economic relations during the eighteenth century. The long-term outcome proved to be unique to the Gulf Coastal area around New Orleans, but the process by which immigrant and indigenous groups influenced each other's foodways was common in all colonial regions.[28]

The most extensive influence upon diet in the Lower Mississippi Valley, one shared by the entire southeastern section of North America, was American Indian uses of corn. Settlers and slaves not only adopted maize

27. RSCLHQ, 229–230, 250; SJRLHQ, XVIII, 1004–1011. For illicit marketing among slaves in other colonies, see Peter H. Wood, Black Majority: Negroes in Colonial South Carolina from 1670 through the Stono Rebellion (New York, 1974), 211–217; and Thomas J. Davis, A Rumor of Revolt: The "Great Negro Plot" in Colonial New York (New York, 1985), 2–11.

28. For modern work on foodways in other North American colonial and frontier regions, see Maryellen Spencer, "Food in Seventeenth-Century Tidewater Virginia: A Method for Studying Historical Cuisines" (Ph.D. diss., Virginia Polytechnic Institute and State University, 1982); Elizabeth J. Reitz and Stephen L. Cumbaa, "Diet and Foodways of Eighteenth-Century Spanish St. Augustine," in Kathleen Deagan, ed., Spanish St. Augustine: The Archaeology of a Colonial Creole Community (New York, 1983), 151–185; Linda Keller Brown and Kay Mussell, eds., Ethnic and Regional Foodways in the United States: The Performance of Group Identity (Knoxville, Tenn., 1984); Sarah F. McMahon, "A Comfortable Subsistence: The Changing Composition of Diet in Rural New England, 1620–1840," William and Mary Quarterly, 3d Ser., XLII (1985), 26–65.

as a food crop but learned from Indians various ways of preparing it for consumption. Jean François Benjamin Dumont estimated that Indians in colonial Louisiana cooked corn in "42 styles, each with its special name." To make their basic bread, or *paluska holbi,* Choctaw women stirred boiling water into cornmeal, pounded it into a stiff dough, and shaped the dough into small rolls. After wrapping these rolls inside clean corn shucks and tying them with strips of shuck, they then cooked the bread under hot ashes. Sometimes they added chestnut or hickory oil to the cornmeal for a richer taste. The Choctaw also ate *bunaha,* a bread prepared by mixing dried beans, wild potatoes, or hickory meat with cornmeal, making rolls wrapped in shucks, and boiling them in water.[29]

An important item in the Choctaw diet was *tanfula,* called by the French *sagamité à la lessive* and by the English lye hominy, which Indians always offered hungry travelers and occasionally carried into colonial settlements. Choctaw women made, and still make, *tanfula* by covering finely pounded and well-sifted corn with boiling water, mixing in some wood-ash lye, and maintaining a boil for a few hours. Eighteenth-century observers usually explained the use of lye in terms of adding flavor, color, or bulk to sagamité. One visitor to Choctaw country before the middle of the century, for example, noted, "by way of seasoning they have a pot hung in the air in which are ashes of corn silk, bean-pods, or finally oak ashes, on which having thrown water they take the lye which has fallen into a vessel provided underneath, and with it season their stew which is called sagamité."[30] We now know, however, that high-alkaline lye derived from ashes actually enhances the nutritional quality of corn protein and protects people who eat a corn-based diet against pellagra. To produce an alkaline solution, Choctaw women poured cold water over clean wood ashes placed in a hopper. As the water seeps into the ashes, a yellow lye

29. Dumont, *Mémoires historiques,* I, 32–34; Le Page Du Pratz, *History,* ed. Tregle, 227–233; Relation de la Louisiane, 128; James Adair, *The History of the American Indians; Particularly Those Nations Adjoining to the Mississippi, East and West Florida, Georgia, South and North Carolina, and Virginia . . .* (London, 1775), 437–439; H. B. Cushman, *History of Choctaw, Chickasaw, and Natchez Indians* (Greenville, Tex., 1899), 31–32. Two essential essays on the Choctaw diet are Herbert B. Battle, "The Domestic Use of Oil among the Southern Aborigines," *American Anthropologist,* N.S., XXIV (1922), 171–182; and Muriel H. Wright, "American Indian Corn Dishes," *Chronicles of Oklahoma,* XXXVI (1958), 155–166.

30. Relation de la Louisiane, 128.

drips down the trough and into a small container. The mixture of this lye with cornmeal maximized the concentration of essential amino acids. Describing the various ways in which the people of Louisiana prepared corn, an early nineteenth-century traveler suggested that they recognized the nutritional value of cooking sagamité: "It is believed that this last method is the healthiest, and it is especially refreshing."[31]

Among other Indian foodways that infiltrated the colonial diet was the mixture of wild fruits and nuts into a variety of dishes and the use of animal oils in cooking. Bear oil produced by hunters was a commonly traded item in the frontier exchange economy. Indians processed the oil by boiling bear flesh and fat together and stored it in deer heads—plugged with a paste made from fat and ashes—or in dried bladders. During the 1720s they usually received a gun or a yard of cloth for each "Deer of Oil" sold to the French. Colonial and native inhabitants used bear oil for both cooking and curing. They boiled the fat in a kettle, sprinkling in some laurel and salt, and after a week of settling, the clear oil that rose to the surface was ready either for frying food or for applying to rheumatic parts of the body.[32]

African-Americans influenced the colonial diet in Louisiana with their own methods of preparing food. A previous knowledge of cultivating and cooking maize helped African slaves adapt to American Indian horticulture and facilitated, in the long run, the persistence of some distinct features of the Indian diet in southern foodways. People in the Upper Guinea region of West Africa, where a vast majority of Louisiana's slaves originated in the eighteenth century, were generally more familiar with maize than were their European contemporaries. Introduced to West Africa by Portuguese traders in the sixteenth century, American corn

31. Robin, *Voyage to Louisiana*, ed. and trans. Landry, 199; Wright, "American Indian Corn Dishes," *Chron. Okla.*, XXXVI (1958), 158–160; Daphne A. Roe, *A Plague of Corn: The Social History of Pellagra* (Ithaca, N.Y., 1973); Solomon H. Katz *et al.*, "The Anthropological and Nutritional Significance of Traditional Maize Processing Techniques in the New World," in Elizabeth S. Watts *et al.*, eds., *Biosocial Interrelations in Population Adaptation* (The Hague, 1975), 195–231.

32. Le Page Du Pratz, *History*, ed. Tregle, 202, 262–263; Robin, *Voyage to Louisiana*, 138, 151; Battle, "Domestic Use of Oil among the Southern Aborigines," *Am. Anthr.*, N.S., XXIV (1922), 171–182; Surrey, *Commerce of Louisiana during the French Régime*, 262–263.

served as a major food source for the slave trade and quickly entered the cuisine of some societies in present-day Nigeria and Dahomey.[33]

West African knowledge of another grain crop further diversified the diet of colonial Louisianians during the 1720s, as it had already done for Carolinians on the Atlantic seaboard. In 1718 the Compagnie d'Occident instructed the captains of two slave ships bound for Louisiana to buy at least a few Africans "who know how to cultivate rice" as well as some "hogsheads of rice suitable for planting." Whereas Indian or colonial farmers often had to wait for the waters to retreat from their fields before planting corn, rice could be sown before the rivers overflowed every spring and promised, therefore, to protect the colony from delayed or deficient grain supplies. Slaves in Louisiana, most of them from the Senegal River region, soon were planting rice along the seasonally flooded banks of the Mississippi. By 1724, slave owners in Louisiana had begun to pay their debts to the company with rice, realizing the hope of colonial planners for a new export commodity. More important for the development of the local economy, rice was already becoming a major domestic food for settlers and slaves alike. "I admit that this is not a great return for France," reported Bienville in 1726, "but it is a great comfort for the colony and it will be the riches of the little settlers. . . . There are no bad years for rice after what we have seen these last three years."[34]

African-Americans soaked and pounded rice into a batter, using a method similar to the way American Indians made cornmeal. Slaves were able to use rice and corn interchangeably to make, among other dishes, what Le Page Du Pratz heard some call "couscou." They may even have encouraged the combination of the two grains in the colonial diet. "Rice cooked in milk is very common," wrote an Ursuline nun who reached the colony in 1727, "and we eat it often along with sagamité, which is made from Indian corn that has been ground in a mortar and then boiled in

33. Margaret Jones Bolsterli, "The Very Food We Eat: A Speculation on the Nature of Southern Culture," *Southern Humanities Review*, XVI (1982), 119–127. For the use of maize in the slave trade and the forms of maize consumption in West Africa, see Marvin P. Miracle, *Maize in Tropical Africa* (Madison, Wis., 1966), 87–106.

34. Elizabeth Donnan, ed., *Documents Illustrative of the History of the Slave Trade to America,* 4 vols. (Washington, D.C., 1930–1935), IV, 635–638; MPAFD, II, 310, 351, III, 519–520. The role of Africans in building the more successful rice export economy of South Carolina is examined in Wood, *Black Majority,* 35–91.

TABLE 5. *Price List of the Louisiana Food Market, 1777*

Item	Livres	Sous	Deniers
Fresh beef, the pound		6	3
Fresh pork, ditto		6	3
Rendered lard		12	6
Quarter mutton	3	2	6
Quarter lamb	1	5	
Hen	1	5	
Capon	1	17	6
Big hens and pullets		12	6
Pair of grain fed pullets		18	9
Dozen eggs		12	6
Turkey hen, 18 mo. old	3	15	
Year old turkey hen and old turkey hen	2	10	
Young turkey	1	17	6
Jar of milk to November 1st		12	6
After Nov. 1st, to end of March		18	9
A pound of fresh butter	1	5	
Jar of lard	2	10	
Jar of bear grease	2	10	
A pound of veal		8	
A quarter of young venison	1	17	6
A quarter of old venison	2	10	
1 quarter of unhulled rice	6	5	
1 quarter of hulled rice	22	10	
Red and white apalachian beans	6	5	
Barrel of white corn	6	5	

water with butter or bacon fat. Everyone in Louisiana considers this an excellent dish."[35]

The diversity of food sources shaping the diet of eighteenth-century Louisianians can be gleaned from a list of items, with prices fixed by the New Orleans Cabildo, that was issued in July 1777 (see Table 5). Euro-

35. Le Page Du Pratz, *History*, ed. Tregle, 185–186, 386; Myldred Masson Costa, trans., *The Letters of Marie Madeleine Hachard, 1727–28* (New Orleans, 1974), 18.

TABLE 5. *Continued*

Item	Livres	Sous	Deniers
Barrel of ground corn	2	10	
Barrel of dry kidney-beans	15		
Jar of lentils	1	5	
Barrel of English peas and beans	10		
Pair of pigeons		18	9
French domestic duck	1	5	
Mallard duck	1	11	3
Wild game meat, the pound		5	
Wild beef tongue	1	17	6
Pound of ordinary fish like meuil, casseburgos, etc.		5	
Pound of choice fish like bass, red fish, etc.		6	3
Barrel of sweet-potatoes	3	2	6
Cord of wood, taken from the levee	18	15	
Cord of drift wood, ash, oak, etc.	7	10	
Cord of drift wood, all kinds of wood	6	5	
French wild duck	1	5	
Other wild ducks		18	9
Teal duck		6	3
Two water hens for one teal duck			
Cartage charges in the city		18	9

Source: Proclamation by Bernardo Gálvez Fixing Prices, July 15, 1777, *SMV,* I, 239–241.

pean domestic fowls and meats, American corn and beans, and local game, fish, and waterfowl were all sold side by side by a multiethnic group of peddlers.[36] Less visible than the basic ingredients sold in the marketplace were the combinations of food prepared inside colonial households. Uncertain etymologies befuddle efforts to trace definite origins, but some characteristic dishes of Louisiana creole culture represent the cross-cultural influences that originated during the colonial period. The thick

36. *SMV,* I, 239–241.

base, or roux, from which all forms of gumbo are made is produced by cooking either sliced okra or powdered sassafras in a slowly heated oil. The name of the finished stock of seafood, poultry, meat, or any combination of these ingredients has been attributed to the Angolan word for okra, *guingombo,* a vegetable brought to the region by African slaves, or to the Choctaw word for sassafras powder, *kombo ashish,* which local Indians continued to market into the twentieth century. The elusive origins of another spicy, rice-based dish, jambalaya, have led one folklorist to suggest that a creolization of the French *jambon,* "ham," and the Choctaw *falaya,* "long," went into naming this meat-stretching meal.[37]

IV

The marketing of food in the Lower Mississippi Valley, more than any other sphere of exchange in the frontier economy, brought Indians, settlers, and slaves together under flexible circumstances. Multiple roles in production spilled over into fluid participation in distribution of foodstuffs. Economic exchange across cultural lines, however, faced a complex of forces in colonial society that minimized the leveling potential of food marketing and shared foodways. The institution of slavery, European class divisions, racism, colonial policy, and violent conflict all contributed to the buildup of racial barriers in eighteenth-century Louisiana, especially after the population scale tipped unfavorably for Indians. The transformation of the Lower Mississippi Valley into an agricultural export economy, which began to surface by the 1760s, further intensified the hierarchical stratification of both race and class. Particular features of food marketing, therefore, reinforced interethnic distinctions and foreshadowed the full-blown racial system that was to come.

Sheer demographic force explains the gradual marginalization of American Indians in the regional food economy. As settlers increased in number and grew their own crops, the volume and variety of foodstuffs provided by Indian communities declined. Scattered bands of Louisiana Indians

37. Ernest Gueymard, "Louisiana's Creole-Acadian Cuisine," *Revue de Louisiane/ Louisiana Review,* II, no. 1 (Summer 1973), 8–19; John Miller, "A Brief Look at Creole," *Mississippi Folklore Register,* XIII (1979), 33–37. For a summary of the etymology of *gumbo,* see William A. Read, *Louisiana-French* (Baton Rouge, La., 1931), 122.

began to concentrate on bartering venison and bear oil with travelers and settlers mostly during winter months. The declining political and economic importance of Indians also manifested itself in the formal sphere of relations, where gifts of food had customarily bound parties into a reciprocal partnership.

Through most of the eighteenth century, tribes maintained a sharp division between two kinds of food exchange in their relations with colonists. In casual day-to-day trade with outsiders, Indians in the Lower Mississippi Valley clearly allowed food to have a market value. But food played a deeply ritual function within their own societies, so in more formal relations with Europeans food was treated as a gift that held participants together in a kinshiplike relationship. Describing a welcome given by the Natchez, Le Page Du Pratz observed that upon shaking hands and being seated, "a silence of a few minutes then ensues till the stranger begins to speak, when he is offered some victuals, and desired to eat. You must taste of what they offer you, otherwise they will imagine that you despise them." The "unfeigned hospitality" of Choctaws among whom Horatio Cushman lived a century later still involved a period of "the most profound silence" before the visitor stated his purpose and then an offering of food with the words, "Chishno upah," or "You eat." "It became your duty to partake a little of every thing the hospitable wife had placed before you," Cushman instructed, "otherwise you would, though unwittingly, cause your host and hostess to regard your neglect of duty as a plain demonstration of contempt for their hospitality—purposely intended and offered." In 1738, chiefs of the Tunica village, who regularly engaged in marketing cattle and other food sources, greeted the officers of a military convoy on the Mississippi with fowls and vegetables, which, according to the chaplain, "we cannot refuse, and after rewarding their generosity with other presents, we take our leave."[38]

The French were by no means indifferent to this special meaning of food and understood that its exchange involved important political obligations. Expensive banquets occasionally held by villages in France for their seigneurs or other visiting nobles not only were rituals of respect and deference but demonstrated their dependence upon the guardianship of

38. Le Page Du Pratz, *History*, ed. Tregle, 367; Cushman, *Choctaw, Chickasaw, and Natchez Indians*, 173–174; Jean Delanglez, ed. and trans., "The Journal of Pierre Vitry, S.J., 1738–1740," *Louisiana Studies*, III (1964), 260.

their superiors.[39] In Louisiana the French generally abided by the etiquette of food gifts. As French officer and interpreter Chevalier Montault de Monberaut told English officials in West Florida, "The Indians have been accustomed by the French to very affectionate treatment; their chiefs, every time they would come to a settlement, were first entertained, as were their warriors." Whenever on a diplomatic journey to a colonial post or town, the Choctaws carried just enough food to reach their destination, expecting official hosts to provision them hospitably during the stay and for the return trip. Shortly after Father Du Poisson arrived at his mission in 1726, the men from the Arkansas village of Sauthouis came to perform "sans dessein la danse de la découverte" for him, "without design," meaning "that they are making a present without any anticipation of return." But when they finished dancing at noon, the French Jesuit "saw well that I must not send them away without giving them a great kettle [*chaudiere haute*]." To make this "great kettle," or feast, Du Poisson "gave them corn without stint," and the Indians prepared it with ceremony.[40]

If food shared would help maintain cordial relations, food denied could start hostilities. A breakdown in the food-giving protocol occasionally resulted in Indian acts of banditry against the livestock and crops of settlers. Toward the end of the eighteenth century, as Louisiana underwent the drastic changes in population, economy, and politics that culminated in annexation by the United States, the disruption of exchange rituals reached chronic proportions. A reduction in the level of intercolonial rivalry over Indian allegiance tended to diminish the enthusiasm of Louisiana officials for furnishing gifts of food to visiting Indians and, therefore, reduced food to a strictly market commodity. Boundaries went up exactly where bonds had once formed. On the way to the Mississippi River in September 1782, three Choctaw men forced a settler near Galveztown to feed them and then stole some of his chickens. "A Negro who serves as interpreter" told the commandant that "these same Indians said we are

39. See, for example, Thomas F. Sheppard, *Lourmarin in the Eighteenth Century: A Study of a French Village*, Johns Hopkins University Studies in Historical and Political Science, 88th Ser., no. 2 (Baltimore, 1971), 141–142.

40. Milo B. Howard, Jr., and Robert R. Rea, trans., *The Memoire Justificatif of the Chevalier Montault de Monberaut: Indian Diplomacy in British West Florida, 1763–1765* (University, Ala., 1965), 88; Relation de la Louisiane, 121–123; Thwaites, ed., *Jesuit Relations*, LXVII, 251–253.

trembling with fear, and that Spain was not good, because it killed them with hunger and did not give them anything to eat thus making it necessary for them to steal in order to live."[41] Diplomatic visits to Mobile, New Orleans, and Natchez also became more and more disappointing to Indian delegates. Spain's agent to the Choctaws reported from the village of Boucfouca in 1793 that "all the Choctaws are complaining" over mistreatment by the interpreter in New Orleans, Monsieur Forneret. Among their grievances were this man's not allowing them "to spit in his house nor smoke there" and "the small amount of food they are given when they return home."[42]

Stingier provision of food offered by government officials and more frequent raids against the fields and herds of white farmers by Indian bandits signaled, in one way, the decline in political power and economic status of Indians in the Lower Mississippi Valley. But even though their role in the regional market began to diminish rapidly after the 1760s, Indians continued throughout the nineteenth century to peddle foodstuffs and other goods along the Mississippi River and in the towns of Mobile, Natchez, and New Orleans. Petty trading actually became more like a strategy for surviving complete encirclement by the dominant society. Association with the sale of particular goods, such as herbs and spices, handcrafts and game, secured for small Indian groups a distinct identity, albeit diminutive in the eyes of many whites.[43] At the end of the eighteenth century, hundreds of Louisiana Indians—Choctaws, Houmas, Chitimachas, Tunicas, and others—camped on the outskirts of New Orleans, usually during the late winter, and peddled in the city an array of foods and food-related items: venison, waterfowl, and other game; baskets, sieves, and can blowguns; and kindling wood, wild fruits, medicinal

41. *SMV*, II, 59. See Lewis Hyde, *The Gift: Imagination and the Erotic Life of Property* (New York, 1983), 3–108, for an insightful discussion of the differences between gift and market exchanges and of what happens when the market displaces the gift.

42. Villebeuvre to Carondelet, Boukfouka, Mar. 30, 1793, East Tennessee Historical Society, *Publications*, no. 30 (1958), 101–102.

43. Daniel H. Usner, Jr., " 'Fragments of This Erratic Race': The Presence of American Indians in Nineteenth-Century New Orleans," MS; James H. Merrell, *The Indians' New World: Catawbas and Their Neighbors from European Contact through the Era of Removal* (Chapel Hill, N.C., 1989), 267–271.

herbs, and such culinary spices as filé, the powder ground from sassafras leaves and used by Louisianians to make "filé gumbo."[44] Indian families also seasonally traveled Louisiana's waterways during the nineteenth century, trading the same kinds of goods with both planters and slaves.[45]

V

Complementary marketing roles held by distinct groups, as anthropologists have shown, can actually maintain and reinforce boundaries between them.[46] Although roles were not rigid, racial fragmentation did exist in the food economy of eighteenth-century Louisiana. Distribution of property rights to food dramatized daily the great difference in status between slaves and free people. Whether Louisiana blacks engaged in illicit trade or not, they understood that their gardening, hunting, and peddling of foodstuffs occurred with the permission of owners and under the vigilance of colonial officials. On the other hand, whenever resident or runaway slaves stole something from plantations either to eat or to trade, they asserted their claim to the labor being coerced from them. The economic activities of slaves fell under increasing scrutiny as government tried to prevent pilferage and rebellion. Ordinances that prohibited people from trading with slaves who lacked permits appeared more frequently after the middle of the century. In a proclamation issued upon his military occupation of Louisiana for Spain, Alexander O'Reilly declared in August

44. Paul Alliot, "Historical and Political Reflections on Louisiana: Lorient, July 1, 1803; New York, April 13, 1804," in James Alexander Robertson, ed. and trans., *Louisiana under the Rule of Spain, France, and the United States, 1785–1807*, 2 vols. (Cleveland, Ohio, 1911), II, 81–83; Berquin-Duvallon, *Travels in Louisiana and the Floridas, in the Year 1802, Giving a Correct Picture of Those Countries*, trans. John Davis (New York, 1806), 96–99; Christian Schultz, Jr., *Travels on an Inland Voyage . . .*, 2 vols. (New York, 1810), II, 198; Fortescue Cuming, *Sketches of a Tour to the Western Country* (1810), vol. IV of Reuben G. Thwaites, ed., *Early Western Travels* (Cleveland, Ohio, 1904), 365–366.

45. John Francis McDermott, ed., Albert J. Salvan, trans., *Tixier's Travels on the Osage Prairies* (Norman, Okla., 1940), 55–59, 81–82; Meloncy C. Soniat, "The Tchoupitoulas Plantation," *LHQ*, VII (1924), 309–310.

46. Fredrik Barth, ed., *Ethnic Groups and Boundaries: The Social Organization of Culture Difference* (Boston, 1969).

1769: "Several inhabitants have pointed out to us that individuals in the city and the country were using no restraint about selling goods to slaves of both sexes and without distinction as to age, and were making no inquiries as to the source of the money with which they were paid; and that they are likewise continuing to buy from the said negro slaves everything which they bring either to market or elsewhere, without express permission from their masters, despite the various prohibitions made." Marketing joined possession of firearms and livestock as customary practices in the frontier exchange economy that became increasingly intolerable during its transformation into an agricultural export economy.[47]

The role of slaves in food exchange was directly threatened by general changes in the region's economy. By the 1780s a large number of people in New Orleans had become professional peddlers, or *marchands,* who bought foodstuffs from producers and resold them to consumers. Increasing commercialization and the growing volume of trade made traditional price tariffs issued by the government less effective. "The peddlers are moving around in different parts of the City," reported the Cabildo, "and their wares cannot be inspected by the officials and for this reason they sell the good as well as the spoiled commodities at an arbitrary price so they will not lose anything in their business." Accordingly, in September 1784 the government established a marketplace and required food *marchands,* both free and slave, to rent stalls. Slaves sent daily to sell "vegetables, milk, wild fowl, quartered venison and mutton" for their owners continued "to enjoy the liberty to sell their commodities in the City as they did before." Farmers bringing their own produce to town were allowed to sell directly to the public for three hours, after which their goods had to be sold at wholesale to the licensed traders. The formation of an institutionalized marketplace in New Orleans, with fees to be paid and goods closely watched, contributed to the gradual relegation of black producers and peddlers to a subordinate status in the food market. Without either an owner's permit or an official license, slaves found it more difficult to trade openly. One visitor to New Orleans in 1797 observed that blacks vended "to raise a scanty pettance" from small stalls located between the levee

47. AC, C13A, XXXV, 39–53; *SMV,* I, 89–90; Marc de Villiers Du Terrage, *The Last Years of French Louisiana* (1904), ed. Carl A. Brasseaux and Glenn R. Conrad, trans. Hosea Phillips (Lafayette, La., 1982), 184.

and the first row of houses. But he found that more "were obliged to account to the master for the profits of the day."[48]

As their marketing opportunities deteriorated in an increasingly commercial economy, black Louisianians had to become more surreptitious and deal with middlemen. A growing number of peddlers traded for foodstuffs and other products across the Louisiana countryside, operating on credit annually provided by New Orleans merchants. One early nineteenth-century traveler noted that Catalans were particularly active and successful *marchands,* but "they seem to be held to be on a level with Negroes." This status was at least partially due to their willingness to buy goods from slaves, like another group of peddlers who traded from pirogues. "Principal victuallers" of New Orleans, these *caboteurs*—French, Spanish, and English in origin—"take in payment, chickens, eggs, tallow, lard, hides, honey, bear-oil, corn, rice, beans, in fact anything they can sell in town." In explaining the lucrative illicit trade that *caboteurs* maintained with slaves, Charles Robin captured the plight of the marketer who was also treated as marketable property: "True, the Negroes do have chickens and pigs of their own, but they can sell nothing without the permission of their masters. It is better for both the buyer and seller to do without the permission. The inhabitants complain continually of the thefts committed by their Negroes encouraged by the *caboteurs,* and they curse and revile the latter."[49]

Although American Indians and African-Americans were being driven into the margins of a changing economy, they did not relinquish means of subsistence and trade that had worked in the frontier exchange economy. State laws and militia patrols never completely prevented pilfering and peddling by slaves. Even after the large tribes of the Gulf South were removed, Indians obstinately continued to produce and provision goods from their homeland. When he landed at the New Orleans levee on a foggy January morning in 1819, architect Benjamin Henry Latrobe witnessed, although "everything had an *odd* look" to his biased eyes, what was still a vital legacy of food marketing and foodways from colonial Louisiana:

48. *SMV,* I, 239–241; Records and Deliberations of the New Orleans Cabildo, Sept. 10, 1784; Francis Baily, *Journal of a Tour in Unsettled Parts of North America in 1796 and 1797,* ed. Jack D. L. Holmes (Carbondale, Ill., 1969), 165.

49. Robin, *Voyage to Louisiana,* trans. Landry, 36–37, 118–119.

Along the levee, as far as the eye could reach to the West and to the market house to the East were ranged two rows of market people, some having stalls or tables with a tilt or awning of canvass, but the majority having their wares lying on the ground, perhaps on a piece of canvass, or a parcel of Palmetto leaves. The articles to be sold were not more various than the sellers. White men and women, and of all hues of brown, and of all classes of faces, from round Yankees, to grisly and lean Spaniards, black negroes and negresses, filthy Indians half naked, mulattoes, curly and straight-haired, quarteroons of all shades, long haired and frizzled, the women dressed in the most flaring yellow and scarlet gowns, the men capped and hatted. Their wares consisted of as many kinds as their faces. Innumerable wild ducks, oysters, poultry of all kinds, fish, bananas, piles of oranges, sugar cane, sweet and Irish potatoes, corn in the Ear and husked, apples, carrots and all sorts of other roots, eggs, trinkets, tin ware, day goods, in fact of more and odder things to be sold in that manner and place, than I can enumerate. The market was full of wretched beef and other butchers meat, and some excellent and large fish. I cannot suppose that my eye took in less than 500 sellers and buyers, all of whom appeared to strain their voices, to exceed each other in loudness.[50]

Behind the color and din witnessed by Latrobe at his foggy New Orleans landing was a century of cross-cultural exchange that had connected diverse inhabitants of the Lower Mississippi Valley. Early Louisiana colonists could not afford to close any avenue to food supplies, Indians acquired desirable European merchandise with produce from their fields and forests, and Africans gained some autonomy through their gardening and gathering foods. Alimentary trade was a sphere of exchange less susceptible than other economic relationships to racial and class barriers. Economic usefulness, however, did not ameliorate the subordinate status ascribed to Indians and blacks in colonial society. Relations in the food market were not entirely open and benign. Indians had to struggle to maintain the protocol of gift exchange that signified their political sovereignty. Denied full rights to their own labor and property, slaves relied upon pilferage and illicit trade to supplement food production.

50. Benjamin Henry Boneval Latrobe, *Impressions respecting New Orleans: Diary and Sketches, 1818–1820*, ed. Samuel Wilson, Jr. (New York, 1951), 21–22.

Growth of the colonial population and expansion of commercial agriculture reduced dependence upon Indian food supplies and undermined advantages attained by slaves in marketing. Indian producers and peddlers eventually became marginal participants in the region's food economy, as waning intercolonial rivalry decreased the political leverage of Indian nations. The economic activities of slaves were confined more rigidly to the production of agricultural staples, as the rising plantation economy devalued the self-sufficiency of African-Americans. Nevertheless, these changes neither eradicated the presence of Indians and blacks from the food market nor reversed their influence on Louisiana foodways. Peddling food items continued to provide an important means of livelihood, evidenced throughout the nineteenth century by itinerant camps of Indians selling game and herbs across the countryside and by African-Americans who vended on the streets of Natchez, Mobile, and New Orleans. But the most persistent remnant of eighteenth-century food marketing rests in the food itself, from the ubiquitous ingredients of corn and rice to the delicate uses of sassafras and okra.

7

SOLDIERS, SAILORS, AND ROWERS

The international contest among Spain, France, and England over North America created frequent wars involving Europeans, Indians, and Africans. Since Francis Parkman's multivolume study of this struggle in the Northeast, historians have been very attentive to the military theatre of colonial and Indian relations, often at the expense of other forms of intercultural contact. Modern scholarship has fortunately turned to military service and warfare in colonial America with an eye on how they reflect society and politics in general. This new kind of military history is helping us reconstruct social relations within colonies while bringing combat down to earth and placing war more realistically within the larger context of political and economic change.[1]

Before the American Revolution, none of the European wars fought in North America directly reached the Lower Mississippi Valley. Most of the region's warfare originated in conflicts between Louisiana and neighboring Indians, although sentiments among the latter were partly influenced

1. My thinking about this new approach to military service has been strongly influenced by John Shy, *Toward Lexington: The Role of the British Army in the Coming of the American Revolution* (Princeton, N.J., 1965); W. J. Eccles, "The Social, Economic, and Political Significance of the Military Establishment in New France," *Canadian Historical Review*, LII (1971), 1–22; Larry E. Ivers, *British Drums on the Southern Frontier: The Military Colonization of Georgia, 1733–1749* (Chapel Hill, N.C., 1974); Gary B. Nash, *The Urban Crucible: Social Change, Political Consciousness, and the Origins of the American Revolution* (Cambridge, Mass., 1979); John E. Ferling, *A Wilderness of Miseries: War and Warriors in Early America* (Westport, Conn., 1980); and Fred Anderson, *A People's Army: Massachusetts Soldiers and Society in the Seven Years' War* (Chapel Hill, N.C., 1984).

by English traders. European soldiers, Negro slaves, and Indian warriors were mobilized into major colonial campaigns during the Natchez War and the subsequent Chickasaw wars. The Seven Years' War brought a large number of French troops to Louisiana, but no action was seen in the region.[2] Colonial Louisiana, therefore, invites a case study into the daily lives and social relations of colonial soldiers whose routine was not frequently interrupted by marching and fighting. Soldiering in the Lower Mississippi Valley actually constituted an array of laborious and tedious tasks expected from troops in most colonies. But a particular combination of geographical and economic conditions in Louisiana also brought soldiers and associated occupational groups—sailors and other boatmen—into close contact with peoples of different cultures.

Both military service and water transportation in the Lower Mississippi Valley involved daily activities and relationships that greatly influenced the evolution of a frontier exchange economy. Soldiering was performed by a wide cross-section of the region's inhabitants and brought individuals from different ethnic groups together under particularly trying circumstances. The tedium of garrison life in Louisiana was broken only a few times during the eighteenth century for large-scale military action against Indian and European enemies. During the periodic campaigns and battles outlined in Part I, European soldiers traveled and fought alongside Indian warriors and African-American volunteers and conscripts. Underpaid, low in status, and unmarried, European soldiers experienced personal contact with blacks and Indians daily, as they faced a diversity of hardships, tasks, and limited opportunities. Because transportation on rivers and lakes was crucial to colonial administration and communication, men who rowed, paddled, and sailed boats also played an integral role in connecting different peoples of the Lower Mississippi Valley.

I

The earliest months at Fort Maurepas in 1699 epitomized conditions that many eighteenth-century soldiers later encountered in colonial Louisiana. Construction of buildings from huge pine trees along

2. Guy Frégault, *Canada: The War of the Conquest,* trans. Margaret M. Cameron (Toronto, 1969).

Biloxi Bay was frequently interrupted during the spring, at some satisfaction to the weary soldiers, by delegations of neighboring Indians who
visited the commandant. On one such visit by the Bayogoulas in May,
chief Antobiscania urged Sauvolle de La Villantry to "put the soldiers on
the alert" before the women crossed the bay to see the fort. He feared that
disrespect would be shown by these strange men, "hollaring that his wife
was there, and that they must give her the same homage as they give him."
Reconnaissance and hunting journeys over land and water occasionally
took the soldiers away from the fort. By June the corn burned beneath the
sweltering sun, fresh water became scarce, and alligators were seen "at
every moment." Dysentery and heavy rainfall made the summer miser-
able, and worm-eaten bastions and boats demanded continual repair.
Southwesterly breezes and rations of alcohol offered some relief. But when
a ship from Saint Domingue arrived with spoiled flour and inferior brandy
in late August, the soldiers' spirits sank even lower.[3]

Living and working conditions hardly improved for Louisiana soldiers
once the colony staggered toward permanence. Military service under a
government, and for a while under a company, attempting to cut corners
and reduce costs made the soldier's life as difficult as a slave's. In addition
to guard duty, an order to row or unload a boat was always imminent.
When the Company of the Indies ordered that the wages of soldiers be
reduced below nine livres a month in 1721, General Commissioner La
Chaise graphically pleaded their case:

How do you expect, Gentlemen, this soldier who is not given lodging
since there are no barracks, from whom are retained three livres for
bread and forty-five sous for clothing, to be able to live here for three
livres and fifteen sous in copper money and pay twelve livres a month
for his rent? It is not possible. A handful of peas costs fifty to sixty
sous, a watermelon three livres. An egg costs at present sixteen and
eighteen sous. The inhabitants sell salt at the rate of three livres a
pound. Bear oil is at ten and twelve livres a *pot*. In short, everything is
of extraordinary dearness. If they could work by the day and earn
something that would be good, but they have too many duties and the

3. Jay Higginbotham, ed. and trans., *The Journal of Sauvole: Historical Journal of the
Establishment of the French in Louisiana by M. de Sauvole (May 3, 1699–August 4,
1701)* (Mobile, Ala., 1969), 23–32.

detached service that they are obliged to perform weakens the companies.[4]

Given the living conditions and demands for labor imposed upon them, it comes as no surprise that of the nine hundred noncommissioned officers and privates sent to Louisiana between 1717 and 1725 only four hundred survived or remained by the end of 1726.[5] The first permanent brick barracks for troops stationed in New Orleans were finally built in 1738 and not without some penny-pinching and delay by the royal government. Meanwhile, soldiers had to sleep in temporary houses "made of piles driven into the ground covered with wretched bark of trees on the verge of falling off, without floors, without chimneys and consequently in a continual humidity." The ordinary *fusilier,* or private, was, therefore, always "subject to infirmities that make him a burden on the hospital when they do not render him incapable of serving." Reporting in 1741 that mattresses, bolsters, and blankets were needed at Fort Condé in Mobile, Major Beauchamp quipped to the minister of marine, "I am quite convinced that your intention is not that the soldiers should be made to sleep like dogs." At the interior posts of Toulouse, Tombecbé, Natchez, Arkansas, and Natchitoches, where repairs and rations were always needed, soldiers lived under even more precarious conditions.[6]

High rates of death and desertion throughout the eighteenth century made transportation of replacements to Louisiana a continual necessity. Mostly young and unmarried, the stream of new recruits brought physical mobility and occupational diversity to the colony. Between March 31, 1752, and April 25, 1758, eighteen ships carried 662 soldiers from France to Louisiana. The recruits who reached the colony during this period included 95 *laboureurs* (farm laborers), 62 *maçons* (masons), 48 *cordonniers* (shoemakers), 32 *tisserands* (weavers), 25 *tailleurs* (tailors), and 13 *vignerons* (winegrowers). The rest came from various other occupations, all of which apparently did not provide them with enough employment or could not fulfill their particular needs in France. But employment in the colonial army was far from being a safe or promising alternative. Within

4. *MPAFD,* II, 317–318, III, 348.

5. Glenn R. Conrad, comp. and trans., *The First Families of Louisiana,* 2 vols. (Baton Rouge, La., 1970), I, 1–193, 227.

6. *MPAFD,* III, 237–238, 348–349, 590, 593–594, IV, 175–176, 190.

the same six years of these recruits' arrival, 217 soldiers died in the colony, and 82 soldiers deserted from their companies.[7]

A quick look at the individual fates of several soldiers who embarked for the colony between 1752 and 1758 vivifies the various conditions of military life only suggested by this rough statistical sketch. Claude Lassaigne, born in Grenoble and a mason by trade, left France on March 31, 1752. Two years later, on April 10, 1754, he died in the military hospital at New Orleans. A fellow passenger on *Le Rhinoceros,* clothmaker Pierre Perriers of Montauban drowned at Natchez seven months after Lassaigne's death. Pierre Artaud, a shoemaker born in Eydein, embarked for Louisiana on October 17, 1752. In September 1757 he deserted, and in July of the following year was condemned, in absentia, to be executed by a firing squad. Not long after his arrival in 1756, a Rouen linenmaker named Joseph François Bazille was executed (as we will see) for assassinating an officer. A farm laborer born in Jeanviel, Antoine Excrousailles embarked for Louisiana in the spring of 1752, served for four years, and returned to France in 1756, probably feeling very fortunate just to have survived life in the colonial army. François Vinet, a winegrower from the town of Provins, reached Louisiana in 1756 and served until 1764. After his discharge Vinet married Marie La France and began farming below New Orleans. By 1770 this forty-year-old veteran and his twenty-four-year-old wife had three children between the ages of one and five. Their farm consisted of eight hundred arpents of land, forty cattle, and three hogs.[8]

Officials in Louisiana complained often that not enough soldiers followed the path taken by François Vinet. In 1751 Governor Vaudreuil and Commissioner Michel signed a letter to the minister of marine complaining that "very few have an inclination to marry, but a much smaller number have enough ambition and strength to undertake to clear a tract of land, since they have lived all their lives in great debauchery and

---

7. Winston DeVille, ed., *Louisiana Recruits, 1752–1758: Ship Lists of Troops from the Independent Companies of the Navy Destined for Service in the French Colony of Louisiana* (Cottonport, La., 1973); DeVille, *Louisiana Troops, 1720–1770* (Baltimore, 1965).

8. DeVille, ed., *Louisiana Recruits;* DeVille, *Louisiana Troops;* Jacqueline K. Voorhies, comp. and trans., *Some Late Eighteenth-Century Louisianians: Census Records of the Colony, 1758–1796* (Lafayette, La., 1973), 234.

without restraint." The royal government intended to issue two discharges per company every year to soldiers desiring to settle down in Louisiana, offering them three years of rations and an allowance "as if they had remained in the troops." Requests for discharges by the infirm and other qualified men were abundant, but Vaudreuil and Michel charged that too many libertines "prefer to continue in the service rather than to begin at a suitable age to put the rope about their necks to plow." Not putting any hope in the "bandits and vagabonds" being recruited through the military for Louisiana, they warned, "If you do not send, my lord, good peasants from the lands where the earth is well worked, likewise good laborers who work to better advantage than the few who remain here, together with a supply of negroes who will be sold on credit for two or three years to these settlers and especially to the new ones, the colony will languish forever."[9]

I I

Although prone to exaggerate disrepute and debauchery in the ranks, officials could not deny that disease, poor shelter, and inadequate food supplies caused pervasive ill health and recalcitrance among Louisiana soldiers. Smallpox epidemics accompanied most military campaigns, especially during the 1730s and 1770s, afflicting white and black soldiers as well as Indian warriors. In addition to sickness and death caused by periodic mobilizations of troops into and through the region, soldiers stationed in the Lower Mississippi Valley suffered from more endemic diseases like malaria, scurvy, dysentery, pneumonia, and syphilis. Late summer and fall were the cruelest seasons for new recruits unacclimated to the swampy Gulf Coast and suddenly exposed to the heat, humidity, and mosquitoes. Of the 583 deaths among soldiers recorded between 1730 and 1770, 50 percent occurred in the months of August, September, October, and November. Some years were worse than others. Nearly one-fourth of the deaths during this same period came in 1751. From August through November of that year eighty-nine men died from sickness, two by drowning, and three by execution. All year round, the

9. *MPAFD*, V, 81–83. For a look at this issue in Canada, see Peter N. Moogk, "Reluctant Exiles: Emigrants from France in Canada before 1760," *William and Mary Quarterly*, 3d Ser., XLVI (1989), 500–503.

military hospital in New Orleans usually housed between thirty and fifty soldiers.[10]

At midcentury, colonial troops stationed widely in the Lower Mississippi Valley numbered between six hundred and nine hundred soldiers and constituted about 30 percent of the region's white male population. According to a summary made in 1754, there were 21 soldiers at the mouth of the Mississippi River, 141 at Mobile, and 473 at New Orleans. Among the settlements on the Mississippi there lived 69 soldiers at English Turn, 23 at the German Coast, 10 at Pointe Coupée, and another 10 at the Indian town of Tunica. Occupying the interior posts were 45 troops at Natchitoches, 50 at Arkansas, 50 at Natchez, 36 at Tombecbé, and 33 at Toulouse or Alibamons. Among those stationed at New Orleans and Mobile were five companies of Swiss mercenary soldiers numbering approximately 150 men. This regiment of Germans, Swedes, Danes, and Poles was recruited for Louisiana in 1731 and held a position semi-autonomous of the regular French troops, especially in the enforcement of discipline.[11]

In the hierarchy of free workers in colonial Louisiana, private soldiers stood at rock bottom. Military wages lagged far behind the rise in the cost of living and frequently reached the colony a year or two behind schedule. To a segment of the populace more dependent upon currency than most colonial people for sustenance, all of this brought serious troubles. Many soldiers resorted to either buying goods on credit from merchants and tavernkeepers or stealing merchandise that belonged to others. Men stationed at the interior posts occasionally distributed among themselves the trade goods reserved for Indian villagers, but more frequently relied

10. Conrad, comp. and trans., *First Families*, II, 82–123. Of the 420 deaths recorded in New Orleans from Jan. 1, 1724, to Dec. 31, 1728, 280, or 59%, occurred between Aug. 1 and Nov. 30. For examples of widespread sickness among colonial troops being reported, see *MPAFD*, II, 41, 239; AC, C13A, XIII, 104, XXXVI, 129–130; *MPAED*, I, 289.

11. *MPAFD*, IV, 116–117, V, 67–70, 141–142. René Chartrand, "The Troops of French Louisiana, 1699–1769," *Military Collector and Historian*, XXV (1973), 58–65, is a descriptive summary of the number and conditions of soldiers, with four color plates illustrating various uniforms. The Swiss regiment is examined in David Hardcastle, "Swiss Mercenary Soldiers in the Service of France in Louisiana," in Alf Andrew Heggoy and James J. Cooke, eds., *Proceedings of the Fourth Meeting of the French Colonial Historical Society* (Washington, D.C., 1979), 82–91.

upon their own personal exchange of merchandise with Indian men and women.[12]

Soldiers' wages remained low throughout the French period, and when the first Spanish governor refused to pay more than the seven livres per month that they had been receiving, some three hundred soldiers returned to France. In order to attract the remaining French soldiers into Spanish service, the ministry authorized an increase to thirty-five livres per month, the standard scale for Spanish colonial troops. An annual salary of 96 pesos by 1766, however, compared poorly with the salaries paid to other government employees: 192 pesos to first sergeants, the highest-paid noncommissioned soldiers in the colony; 500 pesos to the Indian interpreter at New Orleans; 600 pesos to the midwife at the hospital; and 2,400 pesos each to the colonel of the First Battalion and to the procurator general of the Judicial Council.[13]

The discipline and punishment inflicted on soldiers were not unlike those suffered by slaves in colonial Louisiana. Men stationed at remote garrisons were especially vulnerable to severe, and sometimes cruel, treatment by their officers. The contempt toward recruits expressed by some governors perhaps gave license to abusive post commandants. The worst case of excessive action was committed against a small detachment of Swiss and French soldiers on Cat Island, several miles off the Mississippi coast. Their commanding officer, an ensign named Duroux, was apparently a tyrant. He forced his twelve or so men to work for him without compensation and to eat spoiled bread while he sold away the garrison's allocated flour. When a soldier refused to tend his garden or make lime from sea shells, according to Jean-Bernard Bossu, he was tied naked to a tree and exposed to mosquitoes. The breaking point came when Duroux demanded that his men return all goods cast ashore from a wrecked

---

12. *MPAFD*, II, 293, IV, 251–252; AC, C13A, XII, 166, XXVIII, 153–156; Antoine Le Page Du Pratz, *The History of Louisiana*, ed. Joseph G. Tregle, Jr. (London, 1774; facs. rpt., Baton Rouge, La., 1975), 36. For close-up examinations of subsistence and trade at two interior garrisons, see Ian William Brown, "Early Eighteenth Century French-Indian Culture Contact in the Yazoo Bluffs Region of the Lower Mississippi Valley" (Ph.D. diss., Brown University, 1979); and Gregory A. Waselkov *et al., Colonization and Conquest: The 1980 Archaeological Excavations at Fort Toulouse and Fort Jackson, Alabama* (Montgomery, Ala., 1982).

13. *MPAFD*, III, 352; *SMV*, I, 6–10; A. P. Nasatir, ed., "Government Employees and Salaries in Spanish Louisiana," *LHQ*, XXIX (1946), 888–907.

Spanish ship, which they had gathered for themselves. The ensign was summarily killed on April 22, 1757. The mutineers then released Jean Baptiste Baudreau, a settler from the mainland with intimate friends in the Choctaw nation, whom Duroux had put in chains for refusing to return items salvaged from the Spanish shipwreck. Seven soldiers fled the island in two boats, accompanied by Baudreau, who officials now believed had conspired with the assassins and would guide them into English territory.[14]

The arrest and court-martial of these deserters occurred under the governorship of Louis Billouart de Kerlérec, who did not conceal his animosity toward the latest recruits sent to reinforce Louisiana. "Made up only of professional deserters and of more vicious characters," these reinforcement companies were accused by the governor of being "more dangerous to the colony than the enemy himself." With the help of Alibamon and Tallapoosa Indians, officers from Mobile and Fort Toulouse captured the Cat Island deserters. Following a trial at New Orleans in June 1757, Baudreau and a soldier named Joseph François Vidou "were condemned to be broken, alive, to death upon the wheel, and their bodies quartered and thrown onto the rubbish dump, which was carried out three hours after the sentence was pronounced, in front of the troops." The Swiss soldier accused of murdering Duroux was turned over to the commander of his corps, who condemned him "to be axed, his head and his hand cut off, both to be displayed on a gallows for a week." What Governor Kerlérec called "exemplary justice" was a well-tested means of discouraging recalcitrance among soldiers as well as slaves.[15]

III

Closely related to soldiers in their demanding and often dangerous performance of frontier labor were the numerous rowers, sailors, and pilots who moved products and people by water through the Lower Mississippi Valley. Like military service, water transportation

14. MPAFD, V, 185–186; Seymour Feiler, ed. and trans., *Jean-Bernard Bossu's Travels in the Interior of North America, 1755–1762* (Norman, Okla., 1962), 178–181.

15. MPAFD, V, 186–188.

brought Indians, Europeans, and Africans into close contact under phys-ically trying but socially flexible circumstances. Boatmen constituted an especially mobile and volatile group of residents. Along with sailors they participated widely in the frontier exchange economy.

During the first twenty years of colonization, the number of men avail-able to row and steer boats along the Gulf Coast and up the rivers remained inadequate, requiring soldiers occasionally to man the vessels. By 1706 most of the sailors employed by the royal navy for this purpose had already deserted to the Spanish at Pensacola "because they are not paid until the end of the year." At least eight men were needed during these early years in order to sail a "bark of about forty-five to fifty tons" along the banks of the Mississippi and trade with Indian villagers for corn, and another ten had to be always ready to row between Dauphine Island and Mobile with official correspondence and other kinds of information. With the arrival of slaves from West Africa, economy-minded officials began to advocate the employment of "negroes to serve as sailors" instead of "your convicts and your white men who must have French provisions." Already in 1723, two Africans from Suratte had proved to be good sailors, encour-aging the Company of the Indies to "make sailors" of more.[16]

Many blacks arrived at Louisiana already possessing skills needed to handle boats on the region's peculiar waters. In the Senegal region of West Africa, which has often been compared geographically with the Lower Mississippi Valley, the Company of the Indies relied upon the naval services of many of its inhabitants to transport merchandise and slaves up and down the rivers. The name for any African who worked for the French as sailors, soldiers, translators, or laborers was actually *lap-tot,* a Gallicized form of the Wolof word for sailor. Familiar with sea-sonal flooding, shifting sandbars, and crocodiles, Senegalese men became equally useful sailors in Louisiana; only in the colony they generally worked as enslaved, instead of free, employees of the same French com-pany. One freed Negro who died in Louisiana on September 29, 1724, a man named Scipion, had perhaps bought or been rewarded his freedom as a sailor on the company's ship *Le Dromadaire.*[17] By 1727, fifty-five

16. *Ibid.,* II, 22, 107–109, 346, 565. For a discussion of France's problems with manning its navy, see James Pritchard, *Louis XV's Navy, 1748–1762: A Study of Organization and Administration* (Kingston, 1987), 71–88.

17. Conrad, comp. and trans., *First Families,* II, 83. For discussions of black boatmen in the Senegal Valley, see André Delcourt, *La France et les établissements française au*

company-owned Negroes lived at the mouth of the Mississippi River. Their jobs included rowing to meet incoming ships, guiding them upriver, and removing the floating timber that seasonally amassed and endangered passage. Upon preparing boats to transport tobacco from upriver farms, officials in New Orleans reported to company directors, "We shall diminish the naval expenses every day by making only blacks, and few white men, sailors." At Mobile in 1733, twelve government slaves manned the boat that regularly plied the waters between that port and Fort Tombecbé, Fort Toulouse, and New Orleans.[18]

Partly because of the availability of skillful slave sailors, free boatmen commanded a wage rate only slightly higher than that of soldiers who themselves were employed occasionally to power vessels cheaply. The pay scale during the 1720s ranged from fifteen livres per month for sailors to sixty livres for captains. Of the fifteen sailors residing in New Orleans on July 1, 1727, ten were *engagés*, public workers indebted to the company for passage to the colony, and only five were married. By midcentury, sailors usually earned two hundred livres each year for about eight months of service, or a monthly wage of twenty-five livres. They sometimes had to sue for their wages when an employer failed to pay them on time or in the obligated amount.[19] Rations and working conditions, furthermore, were not always adequate, and sailors generally lived a poor life. On July 29, 1744, Joseph St. Maurice complained that his employer, one Duplanty, mistreated him and provided only "big hominy and a little rice" for his nourishment en route to Arkansas. When sailor Martin Ripars died at New Orleans on July 6, 1763, the value of his personal belongings—some pieces of worn clothing and a small mattress—fell far below the amount owed to his landlord for board and burial.[20]

Considering the harsh living and working conditions experienced by

Sénégal entre 1713 et 1763 (Dakar, 1952), 128–131; and Philip D. Curtin, *Economic Change in Precolonial Africa: Senegambia in the Era of the Slave Trade* (Madison, Wis., 1975), 112–115, 178–179.

18. *MPAFD*, II, 565, III, 388–392, 439–443; AC, C13A, XXIV, 158–160.

19. *MPAFD*, III, 399, 449; AC, C13A, VIII, 455; Conrad, comp. and trans., *First Families*, II, 35–47; *RSCLHQ*, X, 269, XII, 315–317.

20. *RSCLHQ*, XIII, 143, XXV, 558–559. By the end of the 18th century, Louisiana sailors in the employ of Spain received from 11 to 15 pesos per month plus rations. Abraham P. Nasatir, *Spanish War Vessels on the Mississippi, 1792–1796* (New Haven, Conn., 1968), 44.

soldiers and sailors alike, the founding of Charity Hospital in New Orleans at the bequest of a former sailor seems more than appropriate. Jean
Louis came to Louisiana in the employ of the French navy. After working
for the Company of the Indies as a sailor, Louis entered the business of
boat building some time before 1727. After running a small but successful
operation in New Orleans, he wrote a will on November 16, 1735,
committing two hundred livres of his property "to the poor of this city
who are ashamed to beg," one hundred livres "to procure clothes for the
most needy orphans," and the remainder "to the founding of a hospital
for the sick of the city of New Orleans." The sailor-turned-boatbuilder
died the following year and left an estate valued at ten thousand livres.
The Kolly House was purchased and served as a hospital for poor and
transient patients until it was destroyed by a hurricane in 1779.[21]

Negroes participated in water transportation either as free men employed directly by boat owners or as slaves hired out by their owners. A
free black of New Orleans named Scipion hired himself in August 1736 as
a rower on Madame Labuissonniere's boat going to the Illinois country.
For 200 livres he agreed to serve on board until the vessel returned and to
work during the rest of the year for François Trudeau. Three years later
Scipion agreed to take charge of René Petit's barge from New Orleans to
Illinois for 250 livres, 50 of which he received in advance. Agreements
made between slaveowners and boat owners indicate that blacks were
often hired out as rowers on convoys up and down the Mississippi in
exchange for certain quantities of flour. On July 6, 1739, for example,
Pierre Baron of Pointe Coupée hired a Negro rower named Jacob to
Messieurs Bienvenue and Mathurn for two thousand pounds of flour. On
the Chickasaw campaigns and other military expeditions, slaves served as
both rowers and longshoremen, loading and unloading the necessary
supplies and equipment. At midcentury each boat in the Illinois convoy
was manned by a Negro owned by the royal government "to help in
relieving the masters on these journeys, which are fatiguing."[22]

Indians in the Lower Mississippi Valley naturally formed the largest and

21. Henry P. Dart, ed., "Cabildo Archives: French Period," *LHQ*, III (1920), 554–
559; Charles Maduell, comp. and trans., *The Census Tables for the French Colony of
Louisiana from 1699 through 1732* (Baltimore, 1972), 14, 92, 137.

22. *RSCLHQ*, VI, 663, VIII, 489, 490; Agreement between Scipion and René Petit,
Mar. 10, 1739, Records of the Superior Council; *MPAFD*, V, 79.

most skilled group of boatmen for most of the eighteenth century, and they made fundamental contributions to colonial water transportation. The Choctaw word *bayuk* was quickly adopted by French travelers and became the standard reference in the regional dialect to the small rivers or creeks that abound in lower Louisiana.[23] The French furthermore learned how to produce and use native-style boats hollowed from cypress trunks. To make their boats, as Pénicaut observed the procedure in 1699, Indian men

> kept a fire burning at the foot of a tree called *cypress* until the fire burned through the trunk and the tree fell; next, they put fire on top of the fallen tree at the length they wished to make their boat. When the tree had burned down to the thickness they wanted for the depth of the boat, they put out the fire with thick mud; then they scraped the tree with big cockle shells as thick as a man's finger; afterward, they washed it with water. Thus they cleared it out as smooth as we could have made it with our tools. These boats may be twenty-five feet long. The savages make them of various lengths, some much smaller than others. With these they go hunting and fishing with their families and go to war or wherever they want to go.[24]

Within months the French were making several dugout canoes about thirty feet long, called pirogues, for reconnaissance and trade. Instead of burning the log hollow as the Indians did, colonial workers dug them out with axes and adzes. Manned by as many as twenty rowers and sometimes equipped with sails, pirogues were the most widely used type of boat through most of the eighteenth century.[25] Although many vessels were

23. William A. Read, *Louisiana Place-Names of Indian Origin* (Baton Rouge, La., 1927), xii; Robert C. West, "The Term 'Bayou' in the United States: A Study in the Geography of Place Names," Association of American Geographers, *Annals,* XLIV (1954), 63–74.

24. Richebourg Gaillard McWilliams, ed. and trans., *Fleur de Lys and Calumet: Being the Pénicaut Narrative of French Adventure in Louisiana* (Baton Rouge, La., 1953), 8–9 (hereafter cited as *Pénicaut Narrative*).

25. Antoine Le Page Du Pratz, *Histoire de la Louisiane,* 3 vols. (Paris, 1758), II, 188–189; *RSCLHQ,* VIII, 271. For useful discussions of the various kinds of boats used in the colony, see N. M. Miller Surrey, *The Commerce of Louisiana during the French Régime, 1699–1763* (New York, 1916), 55–81; and William B. Knipmeyer, "Folk Boats of Eastern French Louisiana," ed. Henry Glassie, in Don Yoder, ed., *American Folklife* (Austin, Tex., 1976), 105–149.

built by slaves and soldiers directly employed by the colony, Louisiana officials often depended upon renting from settlers those pirogues needed to transport supplies and trade goods between posts. Indians frequently sold pirogues to the colonial populace and government. On his way from the Choctaw village of Yowani to that of Boucfouca in May 1732, for example, Regis Du Roullet had a resident of Chickasawhay build a pirogue for him to cross the Yowanis Creek. In 1767 Jean Baptiste Brazillier at Bayou St. John purchased a boat from some Indians with Jean Tuon's trade merchandise. Instead of delivering it to his neighbor, as promised, Brazillier kept the pirogue, and thereby evidence of his exchange with Indian boatbuilders entered the Superior Council Records.[26]

Indian villagers living near the Gulf Coast and the Mississippi River often rowed boats for colonial passengers or transported them in their own pirogues. During the 1720s Indians navigated pirogues that were carrying supplies and crops between New Orleans and Natchez and even guided ships through the mouth of the Mississippi at Balize. Governor Vaudreuil complained in 1749 about the Choctaws employed to escort boats between Mobile and Fort Tombecbé: "They ask exorbitant prices, and the fact that we need them makes us put up with everything that they wish and this spoils them completely."[27] Indian men not only provided their labor, usually in exchange for trade merchandise, but also provided their white and black companions with information needed to manipulate vessels through the tricky waterways and to survive a journey's hazards. Mobilians, Tohomes, Biloxis, and other Mobile Bay villagers, assisting some soldiers in the transportation of goods to the Tombecbé and Toulouse posts in 1759, showed them how to read the currents and tides of the rivers, how to catch and cook catfish, and, equally important, how to keep unbearable mosquitoes off their bodies at night. "To protect ourselves from them," reported the commanding officer, "we stuck big reeds into the ground and bent them to form arches. We covered these with a cloth and put a bearskin, which served as a mattress, under them."[28]

26. *MPAFD*, I, 143, IV, 268, 329; Records of the Superior Council, July 1, 1767.

27. *RSCLHQ*, III, 427; Jerome J. Salomone, "Mississippi River Bar-Pilotage: The Development of an Occupation," *Louisiana Studies*, VI (1967), 41–42; *MPAFD*, V, 22.

28. *MPAFD*, V, 224–225; Feiler, ed. and trans., *Jean-Bernard Bossu's Travels*, 129–130, 156–160.

Convoys between New Orleans and Illinois, which became more regular by midcentury, employed the single largest group of boatmen on their annual journeys. Each *bateau,* a sharp-bowed vessel made of flattened timber capable of carrying up to forty tons of cargo, was manned by a captain, a slave owned by the king, about twenty rowers (often soldiers), and a few armed soldiers. Increasing from only a few during the 1720s to more than ten by the 1770s, the *bateaux* usually left New Orleans in August or September in order to beat the winter ice. The thousand-mile trip upriver proceeded at a laborious rate of approximately one mile per hour, moving against an autumn current of two miles per hour, and usually took from three to four months to complete. A day's rowing began at dawn and continued until noon, with a brief pause every two hours. The crew went ashore for lunch, which consisted of salt pork or beef, some boiled rice or ground corn, and a biscuit. If they had been fortunate enough to trade with Indians on a passing pirogue, their meal might be enhanced by some fresh game or fish. Travel resumed at two o'clock and ended at sundown. Bedding consisted of a bearskin and a couple of blankets. Breakfast and dinner had to be eaten on the move, but three or four times in the course of a day rowers received a *filet,* or ration, of tafia to keep them going. The return voyage, which usually left Illinois in February or March, was much easier. Driven by a spring current of five to six miles per hour, the *bateaux* reached New Orleans in less than a month's time.[29]

Owners of private boats employed a growing number of sailors and rowers to move trade goods between New Orleans and other settlements. The coastal route from the Gulf Coast towns of Pensacola and Mobile, through Lakes Borgne and Pontchartrain, and to New Orleans or Manchac became increasingly important to import-export merchants trying to tap the interior market. Captains of the vessels that plied this course by the 1760s were often accused of charging excessive freight fees and of carrying contraband merchandise, like deerskins and gunpowder, across the

---

29. MPAFD, III, 706, V, 79; Philip Pittman, *The Present State of the European Settlements on the Mississippi* (1770), ed. Robert R. Rea (facs. rpt., Gainesville, Fla., 1973), 6–7; Charles César [Claude C.?] Robin, *Voyage to Louisiana, 1803–1805,* trans. Stuart O. Landry, Jr. (New Orleans, 1966), 102–104; Surrey, *Commerce of Louisiana,* 46–74.

colonial border between Louisiana and West Florida.[30] Losing crewmen to sickness or desertion at Cat Island in 1770, Alexander McIntosh's boat from Mobile picked up eight Indian men on the north shore of Lake Pontchartrain to row his goods to the Manchac landing for one blanket and shirt each. En route from Mobile to Manchac in the summer of 1777, naturalist William Bartram traveled in "a handsome large boat with three Negroes to navigate her" into Lake Pontchartrain and along its marshy shore frequented by alligators. This routine voyage over two hundred miles of water took only about a week to complete, whereas passage to the same destination by way of the Mississippi River would have required more than a month's time.[31]

IV

Intimacy with women of color, participation in petty trade, and heavy consumption of alcohol were important avenues of release for military and transportation personnel that often got them in trouble with colonial officials. Soldiers were the most visible of European men who engaged frequently in both sexual abuse against and cohabitation with Indian and Negro women. During the earliest years of the colony, they joined traders and trappers from Canada to live in Indian villages when food supplies fell short in the garrisons. Mutually agreeable partnerships were made between these men and their Indian hostesses, but there were also incidents of rape and other brutal treatment that periodically exacerbated tensions between Louisiana and its neighboring Indian nations.[32]

The enslavement of Indian captives during the first two decades of the eighteenth century brought many native women into intimate contact

30. Records of the Superior Council, Aug. 3, 1765; "Journal of Captain Harry Gordon, 1766," in Newton D. Mereness, ed., *Travels in the American Colonies* (New York, 1916), 484–485.

31. Margaret Fisher Dalrymple, ed., *The Merchant of Manchac: The Letterbooks of John Fitzpatrick, 1768–1790* (Baton Rouge, La., 1978), 94; Mark Van Doren, ed., *Travels of William Bartram* (1928; New York, 1955), 334–338; Captain Thomas Hutchins to Lord George Germain, Jan. 24, 1779, EPR, VIII, 288.

32. *Pénicaut Narrative*, 80–81, 106; *MPAFD*, II, 68–69; Jay Higginbotham, *Old Mobile: Fort Louis de la Louisiane, 1702–1711* (Mobile, Ala., 1977), 401; Carl A. Brasseaux, "The Moral Climate of French Colonial Louisiana, 1699–1763," *LH*, XXVII (1986), 27–41.

with soldiers as well as settlers. "The Canadians and the soldiers who are not married," Governor Antoine de La Mothe Cadillac reported in 1713, "have female Indian slaves and insist that they cannot dispense with having them to do their washing and to do their cooking." As commandant at Detroit before moving to Louisiana, Cadillac had adhered to the policy that allowed marriage between Frenchmen and Christianized Indian women for the sake of Frenchifying Indians. But it seemed that too many Louisiana soldiers preferred concubinage with their servants over legitimate marriage; sometimes they even sold their own children born to these relationships. Also few Indian women, according to General Commissioner Jean-Baptiste Duclos, desired a permanent marriage with Frenchmen. The Ministry of Marine in Paris responded to requests that French-Indian matrimony be permitted by noting, "The children that come from these marriages are extremely dark-skinned and by this means the colony would be populated with half-breeds who are by nature idle, loose and even more rogues such as are those of the Spanish colonies."[33]

The immigration of more European women to Louisiana after 1717 created a more balanced sex ratio within the colonial population, making intermarriage with Indian women less necessary to individuals and less threatening to the colony's order. The Code Noir implemented in 1724 prohibited sexual intercourse between slaves and colonists, but interracial cohabitation certainly did not end. Although "the number of those who maintain young Indian women or negresses to satisfy their intemperance is considerably diminished," Father Raphaël reported from New Orleans in 1726, "there still remain enough to scandalize the church and to require an effective remedy." One "remedy" taken by some soldiers was to enter into legitimate marriage with free Indian and African-American women. In 1736 a French soldier named Jean Baptiste Brevel married a Nasoni Caddo woman named Anne, two months after the birth of their first child. Another soldier at Natchitoches, Joseph Le Duc, married Marie Anne Gueydon—the daughter of Jacques Gueydon and a Caddo woman named Marie Anne Therese.[34]

33. *MPAFD*, II, 169, 211–212, 218–219; Charles Edwards O'Neill, *Church and State in French Colonial Louisiana: Policy and Politics to 1732* (New Haven, Conn., 1966), 80–92, 248–252.

34. AC, C13A, X, 46; Elizabeth Shown Mills, comp., *Natchitoches, 1729–1803: Abstracts of the Catholic Church Registers of the French and Spanish Post of St. Jean Baptiste des Natchitoches in Louisiana* (New Orleans, 1977), 4, 7, 16; Winston

Soldiers stationed at Louisiana garrisons engaged in petty trade as well as in sexual intercourse with Negroes and Indians, and both forms of contact occasionally incited personal conflict. One incident over trade between military personnel and Indians at Natchez actually exploded into more general combat in 1722. A Natchez of the White Apple village owed a soldier some corn for merchandise earlier advanced. In an argument over this debt, the two came to blows, and the Indian and some of his companions were fatally shot by the fort's guards. Indian retaliatory raids lasted for a year until Governor Bienville led colonial troops against the Natchez. Meanwhile, the Louisiana Superior Council issued two decrees in June 1723 forbidding soldiers and settlers "to go to trade at the village of the Natchez under any pretext whatsoever without the permission of the commandant of the place" and "to sell, trade or exchange to the Indians any muskets with bayonets."[35] Soldiers nevertheless continued to barter with Indians as well as with slaves and settlers for highly desired or much-needed items.

Alcohol proved to be the most troublesome object of exchange among both soldiers and boatmen, frustrating the colonial administration's efforts to preserve order and bringing together a mixture of people under frequently volatile circumstances. In that first summer of French occupation in 1699, commandant Sauvolle de La Villantry expressed anger over the effects of "l'eau de vie" (brandy) upon his garrison, calling it "the most pernicious drink for the health as well as for the arguments and the quarrels that result from it." Military service and other tedious forms of frontier labor tended to invite immoderate consumption of alcohol, a condition from which many colonists tried to reap benefits. "Inasmuch as . . . there are many persons here who have no other trade than that of selling brandy and other drinks at exorbitant prices, and even grant credit to all the soldiers, workmen and sailors who in their drunkenness take no thought of the fact that they are ruining themselves," the Superior Council issued an ordinance in October 1725 that "forbids all bar-keepers, sellers

DeVille, *Marriage Contracts of Natchitoches, 1739–1803* (Nashville, Tenn., 1961), 4–5. Kathleen Deagan, *Spanish St. Augustine: The Archaeology of a Colonial Creole Community* (New York, 1983), 103, discloses that a significant proportion of marriages among Indian and mestizo women in St. Augustine were with soldiers.

35. *MPAFD*, II, 293.

of brandy, or other liquors to grant any credit to any soldier, workman or sailor under penalty of losing the amount due."[36]

This and other measures did not inhibit the flow of alcohol to and from Louisiana's soldiers. Upon urging that additional troops be stationed at Pointe Coupée in 1741, General Commissioner Edmé Gatien Salmon derisively explained that movement of some "would be so much the easier because there are three companies and half of a Swiss company at New Orleans, which are necessary there only to make the canteens prosperous by getting drunk every day." In a new set of police regulations issued ten years later, the government licensed only six taverns in New Orleans, forbidding them to sell drink to Indians, Negroes, and soldiers, and consigned a liquor shop each to the two officers commanding the French troops and the Swiss regiment "so that the military shall drink at the places only designated for them." Within a few months, however, the general commissioner reported that the soldiers were taking wine and spirits from these stores and reselling them to Indians and Negroes. Governor Kerlérec feared during the Seven Years' War that his garrison was "more dangerous to the colony than the enemy himself."[37]

Instructions issued by Governor Ulloa in March 1767 for the expedition of two boats to the Illinois country represented one Spanish official's desire to "reform abuses" inherited from the French regime. "Soldiers or sailors shall not be permitted to take provisions at their discretion as is the custom among the French," but instead would be issued each evening their rations of food "by weight and measure." Furthermore, brandy was excluded from the ration because the customary *filé* (or measure) caused "intoxication and disorder." "The sailor or soldier who is in the habit of drinking may take it on his own account," the instruction read, "but even so, he shall not be allowed to use it to excess."[38]

Drunkenness was responsible for innumerable acts of violence among soldiers and sailors, and many reported incidents involved altercations

36. Higginbotham, ed. and trans., *Journal of Sauvole,* 32; *RSCLHQ,* III, 74.

37. *MPAFD,* IV, 192, V, 185; Brasseaux, "Moral Climate," *LH,* XXVII (1986), 39. Also see Henry P. Dart, "Cabarets of New Orleans in the French Colonial Period," *LHQ,* XIX (1936), 71–99.

38. Louis Houck, ed., *The Spanish Regime in Missouri: A Collection of Papers and Documents Relating to Upper Louisiana,* 2 vols. (Chicago, 1909), I, 3.

with Negroes and Indians. Details of fights with Indians at the interior posts are hard to come by, but general references indicate that drinking bouts and drunken brawls often brought soldiers and Indians to blows. Liquor reaching Upper Creeks through Fort Toulouse, as reported by Governor Vaudreuil and Commissioner Salmon in 1743, "makes them savage and since it is often the cause of fights, not only among themselves, but also with the French who trade it to them and whom they mob when they refuse it to them." "It has happened several times that the soldier, the officer, and even the missionary have been obliged in their houses to repel force with force, the drunken Indians being capable of pillaging, striking, even killing those whom they happen to meet."[39]

Blacks occasionally found themselves at odds with military personnel under various circumstances, although the influence of liquor was evident in most documented cases. In January 1742 a twenty-five-year-old slave named Pierre, "of the Sango nation," was arrested and confined at Natchez. Having been previously owned by Monsieur Brunot at Balize and being a baptized, fluent speaker of French, Pierre was probably very familiar with French soldiers. His new owner, Madame L'Epiné of Arkansas, now accused him of running away. Under the influence of liquor, Pierre struck a soldier named Jean Laurent Bergerot in the face with a piece of iron, later asserting that he had been mistreated by soldiers inside the fort. For this assault upon Bergerot, Pierre was sentenced "to be flogged every day and on Sundays at the crossings of the City by the public Executioner of High Justice, his right ear to be cut off, and to carry a chain on his foot of the weight of six pounds for the remainder of his days."[40] In May 1747 at New Orleans, Étienne La Rue, a twenty-two-year-old mulatto from Senegal and a pilot of the ship *L'Unique* undergoing repairs, fell in with three soldiers outside the royal hospital. Jacques Ferrand, Mathieu Monet, and Jean Gaillard—all in their twenties and convalescing in the hospital—insulted La Rue as he walked from the farm of a free Negro named Simon. "Bonsoir Seigneur Négrette" (Good night, Lord Little Negro), Gaillard called, and La Rue responded with "Bonsoir Seigneur Jean foutre" (Good night, Lord Jack Fool). When fighting broke out, La Rue was grabbed and struck by Sieur Tixerant. La Rue's pistol then fired as a corporal pulled his arm to arrest him, lead hitting both La Rue and the

39. *MPAFD*, IV, 209.
40. *RSCLHQ*, XI, 288–292.

corporal. Witnesses testified at the proceedings that La Rue was drunk, and he asserted that soldiers had beat him severely before and after the arrest. The Superior Council sentenced La Rue to a fine of one hundred livres of alms for the poor and ten livres for the king.[41]

In June 1752 an apparently drunken soldier, twenty-five-year-old Pierre Antoine Dochenet from Picardy, stabbed two Negro women who were washing clothes on the bank in front of the Ursuline convent at New Orleans. It seems that he made a sexual advance to one of them, Babet, and struck her in the stomach with his bayonet. When Louison, the other, approached to rescue Babet, the soldier began jabbing at her. "Dochenet ordered her to her knees to beg his pardon," Louison testified at the trial, "but he continued his attack upon her with his bayonet and was stopped only by the arrival of Baptiste, her husband, and the police, who overpowered and arrested him." Dochenet claimed that "he was so drunk that it is impossible for him to remember anything that happened prior to his arrest." Nevertheless, the soldier was sentenced to be hanged in the New Orleans public square.[42]

V

Relations of military personnel with colonists, slaves, and Indians occurred under severe stresses imposed by colonial government. Soldiers often found assistance from colonial and native inhabitants to be useful and even essential in efforts to evade or mitigate harsh conditions. Very conscious of the dangers posed by Indian and Negro cooperation with rebellious soldiers, colonial officials employed various means of heightening racial divisions. Indian nations were obligated by treaties to capture and return military deserters, making safe passage to or through their country more improbable. Soldiers, of course, were the European individuals who personally fought against Indians and blacks on military campaigns and slave patrols. But the colonial government did not hesitate

41. Heloise H. Cruzat, trans., "The Documents Covering the Criminal Trial of Etienne La Rue, for Attempt to Murder and Illicit Carrying of Arms," *LHQ*, XIII (1930), 377–390.

42. AC, C13A, XXXVI, 267; Criminal proceedings against Dochenet, June 8–28, 1752, Records of the Superior Council.

to employ black Louisianians as well as Indians to inflict punishment upon or even to execute soldiers convicted of crimes.

Following several years of no pay and short rations, many soldiers deserted Louisiana between 1713 and 1716, some fleeing to Florida and Carolina, others taking refuge in Indian villages. Their replacements turned out to be no more tolerant of the colony's adverse conditions. Complaints, rebelliousness, and desertion persisted and occasionally climaxed in acts of violence. The government relied upon vigorous pursuit and severe punishment, much of which was carried out by non-Europeans. When seventeen French deserters were retrieved during the brief hostilities against Spanish Pensacola in 1719, they were sent "under the guard of fifteen Indians" to Mobile, where their heads were broken at Bienville's orders. At a court-martial in February 1720, a soldier named Jean Baptiste Porcher was condemned in New Orleans, for robbery, "to be flogged during three days by a negro and to serve the Company, during three years, as a convict." In 1721 the officers at Fort Toulouse turned to the Alibamons for assistance after most of the garrison along with eight deserters from Mobile mutinied and fled toward Carolina. The Indians responded "with such briskness that in less than two hours there were two hundred and fifty men who pursued them" and at about thirty miles distance "attacked them, killed eighteen of them on the spot and took the rest alive whom the officers of that garrison tried before a court martial [and] condemned the sergeant who remained to be tomahawked immediately and all the others to be convicts for life."[43]

Indians, Negroes, and even disgruntled European workers were accomplices in the efforts of many soldiers to desert. When New Orleans soldiers harassed Sieur Brulé with continual visits to his house demanding their pay, he hesitated to order their arrest, fearing that "there might be some plot made among the soldiers and the workmen of the concessions and of the Company who have finished their time and others who have been discharged who are refused passage [to France] contrary to the terms of their agreements." One soldier and two sailors were arrested that summer at the Balize, trying to escape in the bilander (a small, two-masted vessel) of a Spanish trader. Three French soldiers who deserted from the Arkan-

43. *MPAFD*, II, 214–216, III, 183, 247, 279–280, 316–317; *RSCLHQ*, III, 282–283.

sas post in 1748 relied heavily upon Indian assistance and guidance in order to reach Taos in Spanish New Mexico.[44] Above all other groups in the colonial region, servants and slaves had good reason to assist and accompany soldiers who attempted desertion. A plot to desert to the English at Carolina, uncovered in May 1728, involved a cross-section of military personnel and bound laborers: a young Indian slave named Bontemps, a black runaway named Guillory, a female engagé named Jeanne Coroy, and three soldiers (Jacques Mermillian, Claude Babaz, and Jacques François Jacquet) were among the accused. Two runaway slaves who stowed away on a royal ship headed for Cuba in 1746 disclosed, upon their arrest and return to Louisiana, that the town of Havana contained a small community of slaves and soldiers who had fled the colony together back in 1739.[45]

Rebellion and desertion among colonial troops pervaded the Lower Mississippi Valley during the 1740s and 1750s, when the number of soldiers stationed in Louisiana rose and shortages of provisions became chronic. General Commissioner Lenormant's enforcement of price increases for merchandise needed by soldiers and Indians alike created a storm of sedition in 1745. Soldiers grew "disgusted with eating nothing but very bad cornbread," Lieutenant Henri de Louboey reported from Mobile, where seventeen French and eighteen Swiss soldiers "had plotted to carry off a shallop loaded with rice and corn which was coming from New Orleans, to pillage what they might find in the warehouses, and to flee to Carolina." While soldiers in Mobile and New Orleans were refusing to eat "munition bread," others stationed at the interior posts deserted because of a lack of food and clothing and the high cost of trade merchandise.[46]

Amid this spiraling series of desertions and punishments, Indian leaders became increasingly perturbed by the endless brutality and killing inflicted upon captured soldiers. In 1737 the Alibamons had agreed to pursue five deserters from Fort Toulouse "only on condition that the lives of those

---

44. *MPAFD*, II, 318–319, III, 350–352; Herbert Eugene Bolton, "French Intrusions into New Mexico, 1749–1752," in Bolton, *Bolton and the Spanish Borderlands,* ed. John Francis Bannon (Norman, Okla., 1964), 155–159.

45. *RSCLHQ*, VII, 686–688, XIX, 479.

46. *MPAFD*, IV, 257, V, 94–105; *RSCLHQ*, XIV, 263–267.

that they might bring back would be spared." They also exhorted the commandant that an agreement should be made with the English for the mutual return of deserters. When a large Choctaw delegation returned seven deserters to Fort Tombecbé in June 1751, Alibamon Mingo and other spokesmen forcefully requested that they be pardoned because of "the infinite pain that it would give the Choctaws to see shed the blood of people who every day bring them the things they need, and that with great difficulty." They retrieved "your Frenchmen who had lost their senses," as explained by Imataha Mingo of the village of Ebitoupougoula, "firmly expecting that no harm will befall them." Five deerskins were presented as a "white sign . . . which shows that the blood of these Frenchmen must not be shed inasmuch as it would be the Choctaw nation that would be the cause of their death." The Choctaws assumed a personal responsibility for the fate of soldiers whom they captured, but indicated that they had no objection to future deserters' being executed: "We pardon children when they err the first time, but if they repeat the offense, we chastise them in anger."[47]

Upon learning two years later that these seven soldiers were being kept in the prison at Fort St. Louis in Mobile, Alibamon Mingo and his entourage protested in person to Governor Kerlérec what they considered an infraction of their treaty. "Since a promise to them on a subject to which they were known to be so attached was broken, they declared themselves freed from their agreement [and] promised consequently no longer to oppose the passage of any soldiers who might conceive a desire to desert, but that on the contrary they would furnish them with guides to facilitate their desertion." Kerlérec took this threat seriously and, in the presence of the Choctaw delegation and the Mobile garrison, he and his council of officers granted pardons to the convicted deserters. The Choctaws renewed their pledge to deliver all soldiers who in the future might desert through their country. Kerlérec took some comfort, amid his concession to Choctaw demands, in the Indians' promise to regard deserters "as their enemies and ours and to treat accordingly those who try to defend themselves and do not surrender at their demand," since this was stated "in the presence of several soldiers [who were] spectators."[48]

On June 20, 1756, a Quapaw delegation under Guedelonguay, medal

47. MPAFD, III, 697, V, 89–93.
48. MPAFD, V, 125–126.

chief of the nation, met with Kerlérec at the government house in New Orleans to seek pardons for four French soldiers who deserted from the Arkansas fort and took refuge in the Indians' temple. Guedelonguay explained that anyone finding sanctuary in the sacred cabin of his people "is regarded as washed clean of his crime." He then warned with bowed head that if the soldiers "were put to death, he would not answer for the dangerous attacks and the rebellions that the chief of the sacred cabin could bring about." The Quapaw chief also reminded the governor "that his nation having lately been at war against the Chickasaws as a mark of affection for the French, his son was killed there and his daughter wounded, and it is because of this that he asks that the loss of the one and the spilled blood of the other be repaid by the pardon that he asks for the four soldiers." Kerlérec grudgingly granted Guedelonguay's request in exchange for a promise "to hand over to him in the future all deserting soldiers or malefactors or other culprits, with no restriction or condition whatever."[49]

Military service and water transportation, which employed a significant proportion of the region's colonial and native populations for a long time, conveniently illuminate the multifarious forms of cross-cultural interaction that occurred among ordinary people in the eighteenth-century Lower Mississippi Valley. Given their precarious living conditions, low social status, and geographically dispersed economic tasks, colonial soldiers, sailors, and boatmen engaged commonly in face-to-face exchange with slaves and Indians. Government efforts to separate and widen the interests of these groups proved partly successful, but many people defied restrictions and dangers in order to trade, cohabit, or conspire. Services essential for holding Louisiana together were performed by a subculture of disdained laborers. When pushed to the margins of subsistence or to the extremes of discipline, soldiers and sailors became a subversive presence in the colony, sometimes allying themselves with the very groups they were supposed to control.

49. *MPAFD*, V, 173–178.

8

THE DEERSKIN TRADE AS A

MARKET SYSTEM

In mid-March of 1699, three men and a woman from the Indian village of Bayogoula were piroguing on the Mississippi River when hailed by a reconnaissance party of Frenchmen. Pierre Le Moyne d'Iberville had just passed the mouth of Bayou Lafourche and needed fresh provisions for his crew. A hunting party of Bayogoulas had already discovered the infant colony at Biloxi a month before, and these four villagers were quite willing to sell some corn to Iberville. At the Bayogoula town during the next few days, Iberville distributed axes, knives, blankets, shirts, mirrors, and needles. In return he received twelve large but worm-eaten deerskins—"their most precious possessions"—from which his ragged men made shoes. To the Bayogoulas and other Indian villagers in the Lower Mississippi Valley, deerskins meant much more than a source of clothing. Inside their temple the Bayogoulas placed bundles of deer, bear, and buffalo skins on a platform, offering thanks and prayers for bountiful hunting. Tanned deerskins and other precious items also served an important function in rituals of exchange both within and between Indian groups. To colonial Louisianians deerskins promised also to become something more than readily available clothes: a promising commodity for shipment to the mother country. Shortly after Iberville's small exchange with the Bayogoulas, Indians and settlers together began to develop an extensive export trade in deerskins.[1]

1. Richebourg Gaillard McWilliams, ed. and trans., *Iberville's Gulf Journals* (University, Ala., 1981), 58–62. For the material and ceremonial uses of deerskins by Indians

244

For historians, the informal, unsystematic trade in deerskins that actually evolved in Louisiana has long been overshadowed by a sequence of French efforts to create a commercial empire in the Mississippi River valley. Beginning in the 1680s, René Robert Cavelier, Sieur de La Salle, attempted, but failed, to expand commerce in bison robes and beaver pelts. Then at the threshold of the eighteenth century, while his men were barely surviving the rigors of building an outpost on the Gulf Coast, Iberville promoted a grand scheme to entrench French power in North America. A system of trading posts and tanneries was to serve as points of concentration for well-armed Indian allies in the Mississippi Valley. Antoine Crozat's plans for Louisiana commerce in 1712 included hopes of profitably controlling the fur trade throughout the region. Paling beside these mercantile designs, the Indian trade in the Lower Mississippi Valley was shaped by a complex of more pedestrian circumstances. A small number of colonial troops with minimal support from the crown had to be dispersed among a few select posts. Intertribal conflicts and English trade with Indians in the region determined when and where French stations were constructed and, furthermore, continued to destabilize Louisiana's trade. The irrepressible eastward flow of beaver skins from the Upper Mississippi Valley to Canada also affected the trade network in Louisiana, making the lower valley a separate, predominantly deerskin-producing region.[2]

Once the network of trade took shape by the 1720s, Indian commerce in the Lower Mississippi Valley did not expand significantly in either area or volume over the next half-century. The deerskin trade was constrained by the same problems that Louisiana's peripheral position in the French colonial system inflicted on the agricultural export sector of the regional economy. Shortages of trade merchandise and the inferior quality of goods chronically thwarted mercantile efforts to manage and expand trade with Indians. Harassed by more aggressive English traders on the eastern edge of the region, the French improvised with selective and localized strategies. As already illustrated, Louisiana officials maintained

---

in the region, see Charles Hudson, *The Southeastern Indians* (Knoxville, Tenn., 1976), 261–264.

2. For a survey of the deerskin trade in Louisiana, which furthermore exemplifies the emphasis on plans and policies, see Paul Chrisler Phillips, *The Fur Trade* (with concluding chapters by J. W. Smurr), 2 vols. (Norman, Okla., 1961), I, 220–245, 361–376, 448–483, 536–540, 569–573.

a modicum of control over Indian trade by fueling Choctaw-Chickasaw rivalry, supplying the Upper Creeks with disproportionate quantities of brandy and firearms, and distributing gifts to tribal leaders annually.[3] Within this geopolitically disadvantageous framework, the deerskin trade in colonial Louisiana was characterized by weak regulation, dispersed points of exchange, and diverse participation—features that deserve as much scrutiny as more commercialized and centralized economic networks.

I

Despite its low level of commercialization before the 1760s, trade with Indians produced French Louisiana's most consistent export commodity. Although data regarding annual exports are incomplete, the number of skins exported from Louisiana between 1720 and 1780 averaged fifty thousand per year. Following a typical hunting season, Bienville reported on February 4, 1743, that "the trade in deerskins amounts at present to more than one hundred thousand pounds." Deerskins averaged two pounds each and were worth two livres apiece in France at that time.[4] In some years, especially those marked by warfare, peltry exports fell below the average volume, but during very good years they climbed to as many as one hundred thousand deerskins. In the long-term significance of deerskins as an export commodity amid agricultural development, Louisiana closely resembled South Carolina. During the 1730s and 1740s, after rice had become its principal export, South Carolina shipped an average of about one hundred thousand skins, or two hundred thousand pounds of peltry, per year. In the year from November 1, 1747, to November 1, 1748—when rice constituted more than half of South Carolina's export value—deerskins still accounted for 22 percent.[5]

3. See Chapters 1–4 for the political context of the deerskin trade in the Lower Mississippi Valley. Noteworthy for their penetrating treatment of politics and diplomacy surrounding trade with the Choctaws are Patricia Galloway, "Choctaw Factionalism and Civil War, 1746–1750," JMH, XLIV (1982), 289–327; and Richard White, The Roots of Dependency: Subsistence, Environment, and Social Change among the Choctaws, Pawnees, and Navajos (Lincoln, Nebr., 1983), 34–146.

4. MPAFD, III, 538, 776–777, IV, 209; N. M. Miller Surrey, The Commerce of Louisiana during the French Régime, 1699–1763 (New York, 1916), 161–165.

5. Verner W. Crane, The Southern Frontier, 1670–1732 (Durham, N.C., 1928), 112,

The relative value of deerskins among Louisiana's total exports fluctuated under various circumstances. Production of tobacco, indigo, and timber products expanded steadily after the Natchez War, but at midcentury, peltry still accounted for approximately one-third of the total value of commodities being exported from Louisiana. Just beginning to recover from a decade of heavy rains, droughts, and hurricanes, tobacco and indigo harvests produced 40 percent, and timber, pitch, and tar constituted most of the remaining export value. Between 1756 and 1760, when the region experienced a steady improvement in agricultural production, the relative value of deerskins dropped to about 10 percent. A total volume of 620,000 pounds of skins, however, left Louisiana during those five years, indicating that the Indian trade was still vigorous and even expanding at the end of the French period.[6]

The exportation of deerskins from Louisiana was generally handled by the same merchants who shipped tobacco, indigo, and other staples to Europe and to other colonial regions. The most active exporters by midcentury included Gerard Pery, Mayeaux de Lormaison, and Pierre Rasteau. On May 30, 1739, Rasteau loaded twenty bundles of deerskins along with some indigo on the *Comte de Maurepas,* one of the ships belonging to his father's firm in La Rochelle. In May 1747 Rasteau shipped 154 packages of deerskins to St. Augustine in Spanish Florida as payment for a shipment of flour received from a merchant there.[7] The

330–331; Peter A. Coclanis, *The Shadow of a Dream: Economic Life and Death in the South Carolina Low Country, 1670–1920* (New York, 1989), 81.

6. Surrey, *Commerce of Louisiana,* 204–211; Jacob M. Price, *France and the Chesapeake: A History of the French Tobacco Monopoly, 1674–1791, and of Its Relationship to the British and American Tobacco Trades,* 2 vols. (Ann Arbor, Mich., 1973), I, 346–347; Marc de Villiers Du Terrage, *The Last Years of French Louisiana* (1904), ed. Carl A. Brasseaux and Glenn R. Conrad, trans. Hosea Phillips (Lafayette, La., 1982), 168–169. Exports from Louisiana dramatically increased during the Seven Years' War (1756–1763), a period of temporary decline in France's overall colonial commerce. The colony's peripheral position in the world economy probably worked to its advantage during the war, attracting vessels unable to reach other, blockaded colonies. For a general discussion of France's overseas commerce at midcentury, see Pierre H. Boulle, "Patterns of French Colonial Trade and the Seven Years' War," *Histoire Social/Social History,* VII (1974), 48–86.

7. *RSCLHQ,* VI, 659, XXVIII, 430–431. For a discussion of these and other French merchants in New Orleans, see John G. Clark, *New Orleans, 1718–1812: An Economic History* (Baton Rouge, La., 1970), 88–106. For extant records of other deerskin shipments, see *RSCLHQ,* V, 255, 425, X, 421, XIV, 595, XIX, 232–233, XXI, 305.

vulnerability of deerskins to heat, worms, and moths posed a peculiar problem for exporters. Ideally the skins should have left the Gulf Coast ports by the end of the spring, as the skins arrived from the villages and before the severely hot season began. But the arrival and departure of ships did not always coincide with this schedule, and many damaged cargoes of deerskins reached the French ports. In his discussion of Louisiana's exportable "pelleteries," Antoine Le Page Du Pratz observed that "some persons have discouraged the traders from taking them from the Indians under the pretext that the moths would set upon them when being carried to New Orleans because of the heat; but I know some people of the trade who are acquainted with the means to preserve them."[8]

Most of the deerskins exported from Louisiana during the French period and even after Spanish acquisition apparently went to the port city of La Rochelle. From there merchants either sent them to the nearby town of Niort or reexported them to Switzerland and other parts of Europe. As explained by Le Page Du Pratz, deerskins "at first did not please the manufacturers at Niort, where they are dressed, because the Indians altered the quality by their way of dressing them; but since these skins have been called for without any preparation but taking off the hair, they make more of them, and sell them cheaper than before."[9] Tanneries in Niort and other European cities used deerskins imported from America to manufacture two different kinds of products. The better-quality skins were processed into such soft leather goods as hand gloves. Others were simply unhaired, wetted and limed, and then stretched at ordinary temperatures until they became sheets of parchment, from which many eighteenth-century bookbindings were made.[10] Although not as aggres-

8. *RSCLHQ*, V, 255, XXI, 304–305; Antoine Le Page Du Pratz, *Histoire de la Louisiane*, 3 vols. (Paris, 1758), III, 377–378.

9. Émile Garnault, *La commerce rochelais au XVIIIe siècle d'après les documents composant les anciennes archives de la Chambre de Commerce de La Rochelle . . .* , 5 vols. (La Rochelle, 1888–1900), III, 70, V, 364–372; Le Page Du Pratz, *Histoire de la Louisiane*, III, 218. The commercial connection between Louisiana and La Rochelle is examined in John G. Clark's excellent business history of that French port, *La Rochelle and the Atlantic Economy during the Eighteenth Century* (Baltimore, 1981), 30, 167–168, 188. From 1730 to 1769 Rochelais merchants outfitted 158 vessels destined for Louisiana. During those decades, skins and furs composed a significant portion of the total value of imports to the city, reaching 37% in 1754.

10. Jerome Le Français de La Lande, *Art de faire le parchemin* (Paris, 1762), 5, 30–36; R. Reed, *Ancient Skins, Parchments, and Leathers* (London, 1972), 119, 132.

sively pursued by European mercantilists as were tobacco and other agricultural staples, deerskins produced throughout the eastern wood-lands of North America found a ready market in the growing leather industry of Europe.

II

Given the importance of the deerskin trade to Louisiana's export commerce as well as to its Indian policy, colonial officials needed to exert regulation over this regional market. But efforts to organize and control peltry marketing were repeatedly frustrated by the various inter-ests of its many different participants: Indians and their leaders, post commandants and traders, and even settlers and slaves. As in other North American colonies, the Louisiana government administered rates of ex-change in the Indian trade. In 1721 for example, the Choctaws and the French agreed to trade at the following prices: a quarter of an ell (ell = about one meter) of woolen cloth or one axe for four dressed deerskins, one blanket or tomahawk for two dressed deerskins, and two-thirds of a pound of gunpowder or twenty gun flints for one dressed deerskin.[11] As the cost of European manufactures rose and additional goods entered the regional economy, new tariffs were negotiated from time to time by colonial and tribal leaders. But once a new set of fixed prices was estab-lished, officials still had to contend with the latest complaints from traders and Indians alike about inadequate supplies or inappropriate prices.

The widespread dependence of Louisiana settlers upon Indian trade made regulation especially difficult during the first third of the eighteenth century. Deerskins acquired directly or indirectly from Indian hunters were a principal means with which many colonists purchased imported goods. Operating between a fixed ceiling of rates set between tribal and colonial governments and a rising floor of costs charged by import mer-chants, traders tended to have, as noted at a Superior Council meeting in December 1728, "a greater share in the complaints that have been made about the high price of the goods than the Indians themselves." In order to mitigate some of the risk and uncertainty at the coastal end of the Indian trade network, the Company of the Indies decided in 1729 to make its

11. MPAFD, III, 303.

warehouse in Louisiana the exclusive exporter of deerskins. After 1732, royal officials tried to fill the company's role "by entrusting in small lots the merchandise that he sends, to settlers who will trade it to the Indians and who will settle their accounts with his Majesty with the skins that they have taken in trade." But the difficulty in finding among the traders "people of sufficiently well known integrity" made it "almost impossible to avoid bad debts," so the deerskin trade soon fell into the hands of "solvent inhabitants who have given security for the merchandise."[12] Consequently, the many anonymous individuals who traded in the Indian villages became middlemen between the Indians who hunted and processed the skins and the colonial merchants who were able to acquire and forward imported trade goods. "On their return from the Indians," as one observer described these traders, "they disperse in the city their peltries or produce, which they bring in payment to those from whom they have borrowed in order to carry on their trade."[13]

Some colonial officials helped undermine regulation by their own attempts to take personal advantage of key positions in the Indian trade network. As commandant of Mobile from 1728 to 1738, Bernard Diron d'Artaguette grabbed a large share of the Choctaw trade. Acquiring an exclusive trade grant in 1726, he advanced merchandise to village chiefs and sent hired traders into the villages to gather peltry, bear oil, tallow, corn, and beans. He complained repeatedly about financial losses incurred in this commerce, most vociferously when Governor Périer reduced prices of trade goods in 1729. Although it was rumored that thefts by his employees actually caused his trouble, Diron d'Artaguette decided to raise the prices of his merchandise. When Mingo Tchito, a chief of the Choctaws, carried his skins to Mobile shortly before the Natchez War broke out in November 1729, the commandant handed him only one blanket for the twenty deerskins dropped at his feet. Mingo Tchito refused to make the exchange and returned angrily to his village. With the retrocession of Louisiana to the king in 1731, the trade with the Choctaws along with other branches of the deerskin market was opened to all reputable settlers who would receive goods from the royal warehouse and agree to sell at the

12. *MPAFD*, II, 613–614, 647–648, III, 565, 596, 651–652.

13. Relation de la Louisiane [ca. 1735], 158–159 (anonymous MS), Edward E. Ayer Collection, Newberry Library, Chicago.

tariff prices. But Diron d'Artaguette's command over the Mobile district gave him a continuing advantage in the Indian trade.[14]

Later attempts by influential Louisianians to monopolize the Choctaws' deerskin trade included a partnership formed in December 1745 between the commandant of Tombecbé, Lieutenant François Hazeur, the royal storekeeper at Mobile, Charles de Lalande, and New Orleans merchant Paul Rasteau. Governor Vaudreuil was suspected of having some interest in this operation, to which he advanced 41,700 livres worth of trade goods from the royal warehouse. The Choctaw revolt that broke out the following summer, however, quickly aborted this promising scheme and cost its investors about 42,000 livres in lost merchandise. Vaudreuil was reprimanded and Hazeur replaced, but commerce at Fort Tombecbé continued to benefit, in the words of a subsequent governor, "some favored traders who should have been subjected to regulations."[15]

Although Indian chiefs expected colonial officials to enforce price controls and other protective measures, their efforts to exploit European competition for peltry also contributed to the unmanageable character of Louisiana's deerskin trade. They repeatedly compared the expense and quality of French merchandise with English. By threatening to deal instead with English traders, Indians bargained hard for more advantageous exchange rates. Colonial merchants and officials bent on tilting the trade relationship in their own favor through commercial privileges, therefore, were inhibited by the determination of tribal leaders to keep the deerskin market firmly attached to the diplomatic contest.[16]

The Choctaws proved to be particularly adept at wresting new concessions from the Louisiana government, to the great frustration of traders who sought higher profits from that nation's potentially lucrative deerskin

14. AC, C13A, XI, 174–176; *MPAFD*, I, 22, 51–52, II, 614–615, III, 565–566, IV, 21, 25–26, 36, 54.

15. Partnership between Hazeur, Lalande, and Rasteau to engage in Choctaw trade, Dec. 4, 1745, Records of the Superior Council, Louisiana Historical Center, New Orleans; *MPAFD*, IV, 265–269; AC, C13A, XXXII, 37–39, XLIV, 21–22.

16. *MPAFD*, I, 261–263, III, 497, IV, 39, 208–209. The weak hold that merchants had over the terms of trade with Indian producers of furs, especially among large interior tribes like the Choctaws and Upper Creeks, is amplified in Eric R. Wolf, *Europe and the People without History* (Berkeley, Calif., 1982), 193–194; and Philip D. Curtin, *Cross-Cultural Trade in World History* (Cambridge, 1984), 225–229.

trade. In the mid-1730s Governor Bienville was forced to build a garrisoned post on the Tombigbee River and to raise the exchange value of deerskins in order to prevent larger amounts of Choctaw-produced peltry from flowing to English traders in Upper Creek and Chickasaw towns. The Choctaws continued to complain, however, about the inferiority of French cloth and the failure of French traders to provide sufficient quantities. In the spring of 1738, Father Michael Beaudouin reported from Fort Tombecbé that within a single month "more than three hundred Choctaws loaded with skins have come to trade and that he has been obliged to send them back dissatisfied for lack of merchandise." The revolt of 1746–1750 violently climaxed the attempt by many Choctaws to expand their commerce with the English. By the 1750s the schedule of prices fixed to meet Choctaw demands, together with the chronic shortage of merchandise, discouraged Governor Vaudreuil from farming out, as done in Canada, this largest branch of Louisiana's Indian trade. When General Commissioner Michel delivered only thirty thousand livres worth of merchandise for the Choctaw trade in 1751, Vaudreuil blamed him for producing "in this nation, although reunited, many malcontents who have gone to trade their skins to the English, who have thereby made fresh attempts to enter into commercial relations with it."[17]

III

Lacking the centralization and commercialization desired by colonial authorities, the deerskin trade nevertheless attracted a wide array of participants. As in the other spheres of economic life, inhabitants of the Lower Mississippi Valley sought opportunities for exchange that did not depend upon the success of merchants or officials to administer policy. Many settlers and even slaves exchanged something for deerskins once in a while, and innumerable colonists passed in and out of the deerskin trade as a temporary means of livelihood. At times peltry changed hands in major transactions inside colonial society. In July 1732, for example, the Superior Council itself purchased five thousand livres worth of hospital supplies with deerskins. At twenty-five sous per pound, this particular exchange involved four thousand pounds of peltry, or approx-

17. AC, C13A, XXI, 117–119; MPAFD, I, 342, III, 699, 716, V, 75–76, 111–112.

imately two thousand deerskins. Individuals more commonly bartered for small quantities of skins in order to meet personal needs. Father Mathurin Le Petit, the Jesuit priest who began a mission at the Choctaw town of Chickasawhay in 1727, traded beads, knives, and other items with the villagers for corn and deerskins. According to the vicar general of Louisiana, the six-hundred-livre salary granted to missionaries was inadequate and forced priests like Le Petit to carry on "commerce of this sort which is not at all proper for our profession." Father Beaudouin, Le Petit's successor at Chickasawhay who lived among the Choctaws for eighteen years, also marketed deerskins and was accused more than once of taking "a hand in everything except his mission."[18]

Many colonists made a lifetime occupation from seasonally trading imported merchandise for peltry and other native products. The identities of some professional traders among the Choctaws offer informative glimpses into the diversity of men and women involved in the deerskin market. Marc Antoine Huché grew up among the Choctaws, was hired in 1721 as interpreter for the Company of the Indies at "five hundred livres per year with two rations for himself and his wife," and traded for Mobile commandant Diron d'Artaguette. As reported by General Commissioner Edmé Gatien Salmon in 1732, the great chief of the Choctaw nation considered Huché to be "brave, firm and faithful." Another employee of Diron d'Artaguette and later an independent trader, Joseph Poupart *dit* Lafleur, sent 581 skins to the Mobile commandant in July 1729, along with a letter describing the activities of English traders among the Chickasaws. A decade later his widow, Marie Roy, ran a warehouse among the Alibamons, which had to be withdrawn in 1740 because of trouble with English traders in the area.[19] In 1739 Jean Daniel, Jacques Huber, and Antoine Chauvin formed a partnership to trade among the Choctaws. Twelve years later General Commissioner Honoré Michel de La Rouvilliere described Chauvin as "a famous trader who is set forth as an oracle" by the Choctaw Indians.[20]

18. *MPAFD*, II, 518, 594, III, 645, 684; Surrey, *Commerce of Louisiana*, 161–165; Jean Delanglez, *The French Jesuits in Lower Louisiana (1700–1763)* (Washington, D.C., 1935), 453–456.

19. *MPAFD*, I, 21, 86, 95, 103, III, 303–304, IV, 13–16, 17–19, 170–171.

20. Contract between Daniel, Huber and Chauvin des Islets, Partners for the Choctaw trade, July 28, 1739, Records of the Superior Council; *MPAFD*, IV, 196, 198, 285, V, 89–93, 97–104.

Various persons of European and African descent also traded for deer-skins among Indian nations west of the lower Mississippi River. In 1738 Joseph Le Kintrek and Joseph Blanpain became partners in the trade of southwestern Louisiana. Two Negro slaves of Le Kintrek, Michel and Janvier, and an unnamed slave of Blanpain were employed by the part-nership. Also contracted to accompany Blanpain into villages of the Ata-kapas and Opelousas Indians was Alexandre Portier. On January 30, 1740, Iherosme and Marie Elizabeth Dupont, husband and wife, signed an agreement to trade for Le Kintrek and Blanpain for two hundred livres a year.[21] Another deerskin merchant who traded with the Atakapas was André Fabry de La Bruyère, secretary of the Marine. In October 1744 Fabry hired the services of five Negro adults and one Negro boy, slaves of Madame Marthe Frémont, for seventeen hundred livres. By July 1746 he delivered more than three thousand pounds of deerskins to the agent of a La Rochelle merchant in payment for merchandise received the year before. Jacques Courtableau, son of a cooper who had migrated to Loui-siana in 1719, succeeded in the Indian trade around the settlement of Opelousas. He married Marguerite Le Kintrek, daughter of the earlier trader, in 1765 and accumulated much land and property, including nine slaves, before his death in 1772.[22]

A diversity of traders and merchants also delivered merchandise to Caddo, Quapaw, and other villages in the northwestern interior of the Lower Mississippi Valley. In December 1743 Louis Duval of Natchitoches obligated himself to send as many deerskins as he could gather in six months, at forty sous each, to Renée Courmy, widow of Louis Blard.[23] In 1770 Alexis Grappé, Pedro Dupain, and Fazende Moriere were advanced merchandise by Natchitoches merchant Juan Piseros to trade at Grand Caddo, Petit Caddo, and Yatasis, respectively. They agreed to deliver to

21. *RSCLHQ*, VI, 283, X, 258; *MPAFD*, I, 204, III, 556; Mathé Allain and Vin-cent H. Cassidy, "Blanpain, Trader among the Attakapas," *Attakapas Gazette*, III (December 1968), 32–38.

22. *RSCLHQ*, XIII, 309, XVI, 334–335; Winston DeVille, *Opelousas: The History of a French and Spanish Military Post in America, 1716–1803* (Cottonport, La., 1974), 27–31, 69–71.

23. Contract for deerskins between Duval and Gourmy, Dec. 18, 1743, Records of the Superior Council. For other agreements between Natchitoches traders and New Orleans merchants, see *RSCLHQ*, XIX, 1096, XXI, 313.

Piseros, by the spring of 1771, deerskins at thirty-five sous apiece, bear oil at twenty-five sous per pot, and buffalo hides at ten livres each. From the new post of Rapides, Valentine Layssard—appointed commandant at the age of twenty-three in 1770—traded very successfully with Indians who hunted in the rich Ouachita River basin, including the Apalache community that had recently migrated into the area from Mobile Bay. Operating out of Natchitoches, a free mulatto named Jeanot was a trader among the Caddoes. In 1779 the chief of the Grand Caddo village requested that Lieutenant Governor Athanase de Mézières permit Jeanot to serve as his guide and interpreter on visits to Natchitoches.[24]

After 1762 the number of traders operating in Indian villages increased with the growth of the colonial population, adding to the difficulty faced by Louisiana and West Florida governments trying to regulate the deerskin market. By the mid-1780s Spanish officials estimated that five hundred traders, employees, and transients were living in and around Choctaw and Chickasaw towns, and nearly three hundred more operated in Creek towns. Considered "vagabonds and villains" by colonial administrators interested in orderly commerce, many of these men married Indian women and became affiliated with specific villages. A "List of Choctaw Towns and Traders" compiled by Juan de La Villebeuvre in 1787 reveals the names of an array of persons involved in the deerskin trade. Frenchmen identified as Favre, Louis, Chastany, and Petit Baptiste lived, respectively, in the eastern district towns of Yanabe, Ouatonloula, Yazoo, Loukfata, and Bitabogoula. In three other villages of the same district "there are many whites, both Traders and Vagabonds." Among the people trading with particular towns in the western district of the Choctaw nation were Englishmen Alexander Fraizer and three employees at West Yazoo; Louis Mulatto, evidently employed at Cushtusha by Simon Favre; Frenchman Louis Leflore at Caffetalaya; the Pitchlynn brothers, English traders at Tchanké; and an American, Moise Forstar, at Mongoulacha. A similar mixture of traders and employees occupied villages in the Sixteen district. The children born to this generation of traders and their Indian

24. Herbert Eugene Bolton, ed. and trans., *Athanase de Mézières and the Louisiana-Texas Frontier, 1768–1780*, 2 vols. (Cleveland, Ohio, 1914), I, 75–92, 135–136, 143–146, II, 253; Sue Eakin, *Rapides Parish History: A Sourcebook* (Alexandria, La., 1976), 7–8; Katherine Bridges and Winston DeVille, "Natchitoches in 1766," *LH*, IV (1963), 156–159.

wives belonged to the clans of their mothers, and some became important tribal leaders by the beginning of the nineteenth century.[25]

Englishmen and their offspring became an increasingly higher proportion of traders in the Lower Mississippi Valley during these transitional years. The deerskin market offered many Anglo-American migrants to the region a springboard for successful settlement around, as well as inside, Indian country. Adam Tate first reached West Florida in 1767 and traded between Mobile and the Choctaw nation until 1773, when the death of his father sent him back to North Carolina. After returning to West Florida amid the impending rebellion in his home colony, Tate married the daughter of another Anglo-American immigrant, and within a few years they increased their household to include two children and three slaves. In 1776 he sought and received a grant of 350 acres on the west bank of the Tombigbee River, situated about sixty miles above Mobile.[26]

IV

The patterns of exchange that constituted the deerskin market in the Lower Mississippi Valley largely remained the same through most of the eighteenth century. The quantity of goods usually carried by traders was naturally limited by the distance and means of transportation involved. Along the land routes that had connected Indian villages long before European contact, colonial peddlers transported their merchandise on packhorses. By midcentury these small horses were actually being bred by Indians and referred to as Atakapa, Chickasaw, or Choctaw ponies— depending on tribal areas—or more generally as "creole horses." The Choctaws bred these *isuba* for their own hunting and trading expeditions as well as to sell them to white traders and to other Indians. They even designed a special packsaddle that held three bundles firmly in place, one on each side and a third on top. With each bundle weighing about 50

25. *SMV*, II, 137, 143–147; Juan de La Villebeuvre, List of the Choctaw Towns and Traders, Nov. 24, 1787, AGI, PC, leg. 200; H. B. Cushman, *History of Choctaw, Chickasaw, and Natchez Indians* (Greenville, Tex., 1899), 386ff; Alexander Spoehr, *Changing Kinship Systems: A Study in the Acculturation of the Creeks, Cherokee, and Choctaw* (Chicago, 1947).

26. Albert Tate, Jr., "The First Tates of the Evangeline–St. Landry Parish Area," *Attakapas Gazette*, XIII (Fall 1978), 109–120.

pounds, these rugged little horses carried up to 150 pounds of deerskins plus some rum kegs and poultry cages that were strapped to their backs. Traders moved their packhorses in single file and usually traveled together in caravans, which dispersed as each party reached its destination. Trading caravans traveled at an average rate of twenty-five miles a day, indicating that a trip from Mobile to the northernmost Choctaw village of Bouktchito (near present-day Philadelphia, Mississippi) probably took about seven days.[27]

The rate at which someone could move a pirogue on a river or stream was determined by various conditions, including the season of the year, the direction of travel, and the manpower employed. A single peddler going upriver in the spring, or high-water season, could travel only a few miles a day, even if he knew how to use the countercurrents close to the banks. Going downriver during the same time of the year, he would advance at least six miles an hour! The size of a small trader's exchange zone was greatly constrained by the seasonal currents of the Gulf Coast rivers, two miles per hour throughout most of the year and six during spring floods recorded on the Mississippi.[28]

The annual rhythm of the deerskin trade varied widely according to different geographical conditions or changing economic and political circumstances. A pattern of travel and exchange among the Choctaw Indians was observed by the 1730s. Traders left Mobile for their villages usually after Choctaw delegations had completed their ceremonial visits to the colonial town to receive gifts—either before the planting season or after harvesttime. Indians from the Mobile area or Choctaws who stayed be-

27. Francis Harper, ed., *The Travels of William Bartram: Naturalist's Edition* (New Haven, Conn., 1958), 136–137; Cushman, *Choctaw, Chickasaw, and Natchez Indians,* 235–236; Lauren C. Post, "Some Notes on the Attakapas Indians of Southwest Louisiana," *LH,* III (1962), 221. Albert James Pickett, who actually interviewed many of the old Indian traders of the late 18th century, estimated the average rate of travel at 25 miles a day in his *History of Alabama . . . ,* 2 vols. (Charleston, S.C., 1851), II, 131–133. Traveling in a trade caravan in 1777 when he entered the Gulf Coastal Plain, William Bartram journeyed from the Lower Creek town of Apalachucla to the Upper Creek town of Talasse, a distance of 60–70 miles, in three days (*Travels of William Bartram,* 251).

28. Charles César [Claude C.?] Robin, *Voyage to Louisiana, 1803–1805,* trans. Stuart O. Landry, Jr. (New Orleans, 1966), 100; Thomas Hutchins, *An Historical Narrative and Topographical Description of Louisiana and West-Florida* (1784), ed. Joseph G. Tregle, Jr. (facs. rpt., Gainesville, Fla., 1968), 24–25, 28.

hind for this purpose accompanied the traders as porters, packhorsemen, and hunters. On reaching his destination, a trader was escorted into the house of the village chief. He entered without speaking and smoked the pipe thrown to him. Finally, the chief would open the conversation by saying, "You have arrived then," and the trader proceeded to describe his merchandise. On the next day the chief announced to the villagers what the trader had to sell. Each person then dealt directly with the trader. "These journeys," according to an anonymous witness, "usually take two or three months, and two hundred percent is earned, but it is necessary to know their language well."[29]

Deerskin traders learned to speak the language of the tribe with whom they dealt, depended on interpreters, or relied on a trade patois understood across tribal boundaries. A lingua franca called Mobilian was spoken by many Louisiana colonists instead of or in addition to distinct tribal languages. "When one knows it," noted Lieutenant Jean François Dumont, "one can travel through all this province without needing an interpreter." Antecedents of Mobilian may have existed in the Lower Mississippi Valley before European contact, but economic relations with the colonial populace of Louisiana undoubtedly accelerated and expanded its use—resembling the evolution of Delaware, Occaneechee, and Catawba into trade languages along the Atlantic coast. Based upon the western Muskhogean grammar of the Choctaw, Chickasaw, and Alibamon languages—all mutually intelligible—Mobilian served as a second language, mixing, with wide variation, lexicon and phonology derived from both Indian and European speech. André Pénicaut spent many of his early days in Louisiana at Indian villages around Biloxi and St. Louis bays and thereby "learned their languages tolerably well . . . especially Mobilien, the principal one, which is understood in all the nations."[30] Well before the mid-eighteenth century, Mobilian became familiar to colonists and Indians west of the Mississippi River. All Caddo villages, as reported by Antoine Le Page Du Pratz, contained someone who could speak this "Langue vulgaire." Mobilian was a convenient second language for many settlers and slaves as well as traders to use among Indians, and

29. Relation de la Louisiane, 121–125.

30. Jean François Benjamin Dumont de Montigny, *Mémoires historiques sur la Louisiane*, 2 vols. (Paris, 1753), I, 181–182; Richebourg Gaillard McWilliams, ed. and trans., *Fleur de Lys and Calumet: Being the Pénicaut Narrative of French Adventure in Louisiana* (Baton Rouge, La., 1953), 81.

through the nineteenth century it continued to be spoken by Indians, Negroes, and whites in southern Louisiana and eastern Texas.[31]

V

   Deerskin traders distributed a wide variety of merchandise among Indian villages throughout the Lower Mississippi Valley. Commodities exchanged most often for skins included clothing, munitions, and metalware. These items along with the gifts annually received by Indians represented a significant proportion of the total merchandise imported into Louisiana and introduced significant new technologies into native society. By 1750 the Choctaw trade alone required five thousand ells of limbourg cloth and four thousand pounds of gunpowder. Indian demand for trade and gift merchandise, although often unmet because of shortages, exerted an influential pull on European imports into Louisiana. A list of goods needed for the Choctaw trade in 1750 (Table 6) indicates the kinds and quantities of items being purchased by the region's largest Indian nation at midcentury.[32]

31. Le Page Du Pratz, *Histoire de la Louisiane*, II, 242. For major contributions to our understanding of Mobilian, see James M. Crawford, *The Mobilian Trade Language* (Knoxville, Tenn., 1978); Emanuel Johannes Drechsel, "Mobilian Jargon: Linguistic, Sociocultural, and Historical Aspects of an American Indian Lingua Franca" (Ph.D. diss., University of Wisconsin, Madison, 1979); and Drechsel, "Towards an Ethnohistory of Speaking: The Case of Mobilian Jargon, an American Indian Pidgin of the Lower Mississippi Valley," *Ethnohistory*, XXX (1983), 165–176.

32. *MPAFD*, III, 652–653; Vincent Guillame Le Senechal d'Auberville to nephew of M. Blondel, Dec. 15, 1755, Dauberville-Bouligny Papers, Historic New Orleans Collection, New Orleans. For trade to carry on with the Choctaw Indians (1750), AC, C13A, XXXIII, 230v. In an excellent business history of a French firm involved in colonial commerce, Dale Miquelon points out the role of Indians as consumers of European imported merchandise in Canada (*Dugard of Rouen: French Trade to Canada and the West Indies, 1729–1770* [Montreal, 1978], 64–65):
   A large portion of the hardware and dry goods was destined for the Indian trade and, so far as the white population was concerned, filled an economic role similar to that of most of the barrelled beef exported to Martinique, which sustained the sugar export economy by feeding slaves. The Indian fitted into the mercantile economy better than did the slave because he not only provided an export staple, but was a good consumer of manufactures, perhaps a better customer than a French peasant. Indian or white, the Canadian population showed the same dependence upon French manufactures that characterized the Creole populations.

TABLE 6. *Annual Trade with the Choctaw Indians, circa 1750*

5,000 *ells* [1 ell = 1.2 meters] of Limbourg, half blue and half red
1,000 white blankets with two points
200 white blankets with three points
500 blankets with stripes
2,500 regular trade shirts, for men, as long in front as in back
150 ordinary trade muskets
4,000 pounds of gun powder
300 pieces of scarlet colored, woolen ribbon
250 pounds of rough vermilion in small one-pound sacks and in barrels
   of 100 and 50 pounds
150 pounds of red lead (a vermilion or red pigment made specifically
   from mercuric sulfide)
200 pounds of blue and white drinking glasses of assorted sizes
30 gross of woodcutter knives
18,000 musket flints
4 gross of trade scissors
3 gross of flint-locks
3 gross of awls
400 mirrors in cases

Source: For trade to carry on with the Choctaw Indians (1750), AC, C13A,
XXXIII, 230v.

A contract between Natchitoches merchant Juan Piseros and three traders in 1770 offers useful information on the volume and variety of European merchandise brought to three particular Indian villages at the end of
the French period. The agreement made by Piseros with Alexis Grappé,
trader at Grand Caddo, Pedro Dupain at Petit Caddo, and Fazende Moriere at Yatasis includes a "list of goods necessary for the annual Supply" for
each village (see Table 7). The high proportion of guns and ammunition
(about 51 percent of total merchandise value) earmarked for these three
villages underscores both the commercial importance of hunting for the
peltry trade and the military dependence of the colony upon Indian allies. More munitions promised more deerkills, which yielded more skins
needed to buy more munitions. Behind this vicious cycle lay the rising

demand for European merchandise among Indians and the steadily profitable market for peltry in Europe. Limbourg cloth, blankets, and shirts composed as much as 26 percent of the total value of goods being exchanged for deerskins and other furs. European-manufactured textiles, and not just the glass beads and trinkets popularly associated with Indian trade, were a significant means of commercial expansion into native communities of North America.[33]

Although the exchange of deerskins and other items for trade goods occurred largely in the form of immediate barter—a few skins directly handed over for perhaps one gingham shirt—credit gradually infiltrated the relationship between Indian and trader. Receiving merchandise on credit from colonial merchants, many deerskin traders found it practical to advance these goods to Indian hunters before they sought their prey. This obligated Indian trade partners to a particular trader, but the latter had to wait and hope for payment at a later date. While nervously awaiting the arrival of more Indians at Natchitoches in the autumn of 1749, Louis Jobard reminded his New Orleans creditor that "without giving credit to the Indians nothing can be done with them." In 1752 widow Françoise Le Kintrek and her new husband, Pierre Couturier, agreed to pay the nearly five thousand livres owed to Jean Baptiste Destrehan "as soon as possible and at latest when the pelts expected by them arrive from Atakapas."[34]

As credit arrangements became more essential to the deerskin market, all parties became increasingly vulnerable to mischance or misdoing. Merchants sometimes charged exorbitant interest on merchandise advanced to traders and were not afraid to drag their debtors into court. In September 1746 Joseph Blanpain, who by then owned a plantation at Houmas on the German Coast, was ordered to pay 1,175 deerskins or the

33. Bolton, ed. and trans., *Athanase de Mézières*, I, 143–146. To compare the relative-value figures in Table 7 with those of Indians in another North American Indian trade region, see Arthur J. Ray, *Indians in the Fur Trade: Their Role as Trappers, Hunters, and Middlemen in the Land Southwest of Hudson Bay, 1660–1870* (Toronto, 1974), 149–153.

34. *RSCLHQ*, XVIII, 705, 708; *Juan de la Villebeuvre and Pedro Chabert v. Simon Favre* [later interpreter for the Indians], Oct. 20, 1783, Spanish Judicial Records, Louisiana Historical Center, New Orleans; Louis Jobard to Pierre Ancelin, Sept. 24, 1749, Records of the Superior Council; *RSCLHQ*, XIII, 309, XVI, 334–335, XXI, 1249.

TABLE 7. *Goods Traded at Three Caddo Villages, 1770–1771*

Grand Caddo (155 Families)				
Item	Quantity	Value in Pesos	% of Total Known Value	Quantity per Family
Staple fusils	40	140	16	.26
Limbourg, ells	60	120	14	.39
Woolen blankets	30	30	3	.19
French gunpowder, lbs.	400	180	21	2.6
Balls, lbs.	900	135	15	5.8
Pickaxes	30	15	2	.19
Hatchets	30	40	4	.19
Tomahawks	30	40	4	.19
Shirts	50	62.5	7	.32
Hunters' knives	144	14.4	2	.93
Pocket knives	144	14.4	2	.93
Awls	72	7.2	1	.46
Vermilion, lbs.	6	12	1	.04
Combs	72	7.2	1	.46
Scissors	72	7.2	1	.46
Mirrors	72	7.2	1	.46
Glass beads, lbs.	60	45	5	.39
Flints	1,000	—		6.4
Steels	72	—		.46
Copper wire, lbs.	12	—		.08
Total		877.1	100	

Value of goods per family (pesos): 5.52

Number of deerskins (@ .35 pesos apiece) needed to buy goods per family: 15.8

TABLE 7. *Continued*

Yatsis (70 Families)				
Item	Quantity	Value in Pesos	% of Total Known Value	Quantity per Family
Staple fusils	15	52.5	12	.21
Limbourg, ells	30	60	14	.43
Woolen blankets	20	20	5	.29
French gunpowder, lbs.	200	90	21	2.9
Balls, lbs.	450	67.5	16	6.4
Pickaxes	10	5	1	.14
Hatchets	10	13.3	3	.14
Tomahawks	10	13.3	3	.14
Shirts	30	37.5	9	.43
Hunters' knives	72	7.2	2	1
Pocket knives	72	7.2	2	1
Awls	72	7.2	2	1
Vermilion, lbs.	4	8	2	.06
Combs	72	7.2	2	1
Scissors	0			
Mirrors	36	3.6	1	.5
Glass beads, lbs.	30	22.5	5	.43
Flints	500	—		7.1
Steels	72	—		1
Copper wire, lbs.	6	—		.08
Total		422.0	100	

Value of goods per family (pesos): 5.87
Number of deerskins (@ .35 pesos apiece) needed to buy goods per family: 16.8

TABLE 7. *Continued*

	Petit Caddo (63 Families)			
Item	Quantity	Value in Pesos	% of Total Known Value	Quantity per Family
Staple fusils	30	105	20	.48
Limbourg, ells	40	80	15	.63
Woolen blankets	40	40	7.5	.63
French gunpowder, lbs.	200	90	17	3.2
Balls, lbs.	450	67.5	13	7.1
Pickaxes	20	10	2	.32
Hatchets	20	26.6	5	.32
Tomahawks	20	26.6	5	.32
Shirts	24	30	6	.38
Hunters' knives	72	7.2	1	1.1
Pocket knives	72	7.2	1	1.1
Awls	0			
Vermilion, lbs.	4	8	1	.06
Combs	72	7.2	1	1
Scissors	0			
Mirrors	24	2.4	.5	.38
Glass beads, lbs.	30	22.5	5	.48
Flints	500	—		7.9
Steels	48	—		.76
Copper wire, lbs.	6	—		.09
Total		530.2	100	

Value of goods per family (pesos): 8.41

Number of deerskins (@ .35 pesos apiece) needed to buy goods per family: 24

TABLE 7. *Continued*

| | Aggregate (288 Families) | | | |
Item	Quantity	Value in Pesos	% of Total Known Value	Quantity per Family
Staple fusils	89	297.5	16	.29
Limbourg, ells	130	260	14	.45
Woolen blankets	90	90	5	.31
French gunpowder, lbs.	800	360	20	2.78
Balls, lbs.	1,800	270	15	6.25
Pickaxes	60	30	2	.21
Hatchets	60	79.9	4	.21
Tomahawks	60	79.9	4	.21
Shirts	104	130	7	.36
Hunters' knives	288	28.8	2	1
Pocket knives	288	28.8	2	1
Awls	144	14.4	1	.50
Vermilion, lbs.	14	28	1	.05
Combs	216	21.6	1	.75
Scissors	72	7.2		.25
Mirrors	132	13.2	1	.46
Glass beads, lbs.	120	90	5	.42
Flints	2,000	—		6.94
Steels	192	—		.67
Copper wire, lbs.	24	—		.08
Total		1,829.3	100	

Value of goods per family (pesos): 6.35
Number of deerskins (@ .35 pesos apiece) needed to buy goods per family: 18.1

Sources: Athanase de Mézières to Gálvez, Mar. 21, 1779; also in Herbert Eugene Bolton, ed. and trans., *Athanase de Mézières and the Louisiana-Texas Frontier, 1768–1780*, 2 vols. (Cleveland, Ohio, 1914), II, 244.

sum of 2,349 livres to J. B. Piemont for trade goods furnished by the New Orleans merchant. In another instance, Joseph Montard proposed to pay thirteen packs of skins to Juan Macarty, but the merchant refused them because the delivery came a year and a half late and during the summer, when the market value of pelts was at its annual nadir.[35] Under such circumstances, it is not surprising that traders often inflated the price of merchandise offered Indians in order to minimize their risks. Indians influenced the chain of credit in their own ways. Unfavorable hunting conditions or warfare often delayed payment of their debts to traders. Indian hunters sometimes evaded their creditors in order to deliver deerskins to other traders and thereby stretch their access to European goods. For the most part, Indians refused to pay interest on merchandise advanced to them—no matter how much time elapsed before meeting an obligation.[36]

Traders whose livelihood depended upon the deerskin market operated on a fluid borderline between the frontier exchange economy and the commercial export economy. Many settlers and slaves traded merchandise for peltry once in a while, in what was just another momentary episode in their various frontier exchange activities. But professional Indian traders, like many tobacco farmers along the Mississippi River, found themselves straddling both the informal world of face-to-face exchange and the more formal world of transatlantic commerce. Their deepening dependency upon import-export merchants in a network of dispersed and unpredictable transactions marked a slow but steady commercialization of economic life in the Lower Mississippi Valley.[37]

35. *RSCLHQ*, X, 271–272, XIII, 137–138, XVII, 185; *SJRLHQ*, XIV, 608–610.

36. Amos Stoddard, *Sketches, Historical and Descriptive, of Louisiana* (Philadelphia, 1812), 445.

37. The symbiotic relationship between such traditional forms of exchange as itinerant peddling and more modern channels of commerce during a transitional period is illuminated in Clifford Geertz, *Peddlers and Princes: Social Change and Economic Modernization in Two Indonesian Towns* (Chicago, 1963), 28–42; and Brian S. Osborne, "Trading on a Frontier: The Function of Peddlers, Markets, and Fairs in Nineteenth-Century Ontario," in Donald H. Akenson, ed., *Canadian Papers in Rural History*, II (Gananoque, Ont., 1980), 59–81. The adaptability and resilience of peddling are asserted in Fernand Braudel, *The Wheels of Commerce*, trans. Siân Reynolds, Civilization and Capitalism, Fifteenth–Eighteenth Century, II (New York, 1982), 75–80.

The intermediary position between the people who produced the deer-skins and those who shipped them abroad was a precarious, and sometimes painful, experience for traders. In 1774 a free mulatto woman named Nelly Price was trading with Indians and colonists at the new settlement of Grand Gulf, situated about fifty miles above Natchez. She owed a considerable debt for cloth, rum, and other goods furnished her by merchants. That year John Fitzpatrick of Manchac traveled to Grand Gulf and insisted on inspecting Price's record book, realizing that she could not pay her debt to him until she collected on the goods advanced to the Indians. The time of the year being February, she was expecting some Indians to bring their deerskins to her any day. Fitzpatrick grew impatient and on seeing her books, which did not show to his satisfaction how she had distributed the merchandise, he abruptly asked what she had done with his goods. According to the merchant, Nelly Price answered with the forwardness that she was known for: "Damn your Blood I have fucked them away[!]" Fitzpatrick responded by striking the woman and running her out of her own house. Price retaliated by charging that Fitzpatrick stole a piece of cloth and twenty gallons of rum from her room.[38]

By the 1780s Louis Pochet had for years traded in the Natchez area and interpreted for the Choctaws. St. Germain, as Pochet was called, owed large sums of money to his creditors and was owed a great deal by his own debtors. He owed a thousand dollars to John Blommart and similar amounts to James Willing and Carlos de Grand Pré. In addition to the many small debts owed by various hunters and settlers, St. Germain was seeking payment of some 8,000 deerskins due from Indians at Rapides, a post on the Red River. In the spring of 1783, he managed to forward 1,365 skins, 125 pounds of tallow, and six barrels of bear oil to Grand Pré in New Orleans, but the barrels were not full, and most of the skins were reportedly damaged. St. Germain received another thousand dollars worth of merchandise from Grand Pré the following June, promising to pay in December. When he died after falling from a tree in a cypress swamp, St. Germain's land, cattle, slaves, and other property were appraised at nearly seven thousand dollars in 1786. Like many other traders,

38. Margaret Fisher Dalrymple, ed., *The Merchant of Manchac: The Letterbooks of John Fitzpatrick, 1768–1798* (Baton Rouge, La., 1978), 347–350; Mrs. Nicholas (Elizabeth House) Trist Diary, 1783–1784, June 30, 1784, Southern Historical Collection, University of North Carolina, Chapel Hill.

St. Germain had lived with an Indian woman, by whom he had three children. Not married under colonial law, this woman still inhabited their house at St. Germain's death and was trying desperately to claim the property. His urgent creditors, however, seized and sold the plantation, fearful that the woman and her kin would "plunder the effects which they consider their own."[39]

VI

During the partition of the Lower Mississippi Valley into British West Florida and Spanish Louisiana, the deerskin trade expanded in volume, and the process of commercialization began to accelerate. A new surge of pressures (as already seen in Chapter 4) fell upon Indians, who now produced more pelts for more predictable supplies of trade merchandise. Tribes east of the Mississippi confronted larger quantities of alcohol, physical abuse, and land encroachment from a rising number of English traders just as their diplomatic leverage began to topple. But the Choctaws and their neighbors welcomed the opportunity to trade with Englishmen. Alibamon Mingo urged them in 1763 to be as "Bountyfull" as the French had been, "which must be done if they wish equally to gain the affection of my people." Recalling how long his men had been using "Guns of France," the aging Choctaw wished that he was young enough "to try the Guns and English Powder both of which I hope will flourish and rejoice the Heart of the Hunters thro' the land and Cover the Nakedness of the Women."[40]

West Florida merchants exported a growing volume of deerskins as peltry produced by Choctaws, Chickasaws, and Upper Creeks was shipped from the ports of Pensacola and Mobile to London. English officials intensified efforts to regulate prices in the deerskin market (see Table 8) and tried to cut off Indian trade with the now Spanish province of Louisiana.[41] But many interior Indians attempted to perpetuate exchange

39. May Wilson McBee, comp., *The Natchez Court Records, 1767–1805: Abstracts of Early Records* (Greenwood, Miss., 1953), 3–6, 19, 33–34, 40–41, 299, 303–306, 311.

40. *MPAED*, I, 240.

41. Dalrymple, ed., *Letterbooks of Fitzpatrick;* Robert R. Rea, "British West Florida Trade and Commerce in the Customs Records," *AR*, XXXVII (1984), 124–159; Robin

relations with New Orleans–based traders in order to mitigate dependency upon the British; some resorted to acts of banditry to defy and protest adverse changes. Even the ascending Creek Confederacy found it difficult to fend off new trade abuses, notably the farming and hunting being undertaken in their country by the English traders themselves. "Formerly our Old Women and motherless Children used by exchanging a Little Corn for goods, to be able to Cover their nakedness," lamented Emistisiguo in 1771, "but they are now deprived of this resource and often obliged on the Contrary to purchase Corn from the Traders. I remember it was formerly agreed That we should meet in the Woods, but notwithstanding that agreement, there are many white men in our nation, who follow no other business but that of Hunting."[42]

Meanwhile, in Spanish Louisiana, Indians west of the Mississippi traded with familiar exchange partners under less disruptive conditions (see Table 9 for a selected tariff). Traders and Indians alike, however, did face the likelihood of losing access to desirable merchandise from France. In a report on the products exported from the colony, Governor Bernardo de Gálvez emphasized in 1778 the importance of providing French trade goods to Louisiana Indians:

> Let it be added that the principal branch [of commerce] which that province supports is peltry. This is obtained from the Indians not in exchange for money but for French goods, which are the only ones that they esteem because they are the only ones to which they are accustomed. Among these people usage is stronger than reason. A gun from Madrid or a piece of scarlet cloth is to them valueless in comparison with a scrap of Limbourg cloth and a French musket that costs from two and a half to three pesos among them. Even if the Indians did not give French goods the preference, the traders would take no other kind, because with these alone can they make a profit. The Indian is already accustomed to give so many skins for a musket, a knife, a pot, etc. These articles cost the trader very little and the sale of the skins to the merchant leaves him a moderate profit which hardly compensates him for the hardships and dangers to which he is

---

F. A. Fabel, *The Economy of British West Florida, 1763–1783* (Tuscaloosa, Ala., 1988), 54–60, 199–200.

42. Emistisiguo at Congress of Upper Creeks in Pensacola, Oct. 31, 1771, Mississippi Historical Society, *Publications,* Centenary Series, V (Jackson, Miss., 1925), 125.

TABLE 8. *Tariff for Indian Trade in West Florida, 1770*

Item	Pounds of Deerskins (Dressed)
Two yards of strouds	8
One blanket striped duffit	8
One, ditto, shaggend	5–6
One white shirt plain	3–4
One check, ditto	3–4
Fringed housings	8–10
Laced, ditto	6
Gartering, one piece of scarlet strip	4
Common figured	3
Dutch pretties, one piece	1–2
Silk ferret, from two to three, ditto	1
Indian calicoes, one, ditto	3–4
Romal handkerchiefs, one	2
Saddles according to quality	16–40
Snaffle bridles, one	3–4
Five strands barleycorn beads	1
Twenty to thirty strands common, ditto	1
Trading scissors, one pair	1
Knives, common trading and cutteaux, according to size	1–3
Trading razors, one	1
Vermillion, one ounce	1
Brass wire, three spans	1
Brass kettles, according to size	—
Tin, ditto, ditto	—
Trading guns	16

TABLE 8. *Continued*

Item	Pounds of Deerskins (Dressed)
Gunflints, according to quality, from ten to twenty	1
Hawk's-bills, ten	1
Gunpowder, half to three-quarters of a pint	1
Bullets, forty to fifty	1
Earbobs, one pair	2
Silk Bengals, large	4
Ditto, small	3
Fifteen pea buttons	1
Cadice	2–3
Common check, one yard	1
Fine, ditto	2
Gun locks	6
Broad hoes	3–4
Hatchets according to size	1–4
Coarse garlix	1
Fine, ditto	2
White plains, one and a half yards	3
Oznaburg shirts	4
One yard Oznaburgs	1
Gilt belts	2

Source: An Act for the Better Regulation of the Indian Trade in the Province of West Florida, May 10, 1770, in Robert R. Rea, comp., *The Minutes, Journals, and Acts of the General Assembly of British West Florida* (University, Ala., 1979), 381–382.

TABLE 9. *Trade Prices at Rapides in Louisiana, 1775*

Item	No. of Deerskins
One *L'aune* [= 1.2 meters] of limbourg	6
A 3 point blanket	8
A 2½ point blanket	7
A gingham shirt	3
White common shirt	3
Trimmed shirt	5–6
One pound of gunpowder	2
50 musket balls	1
One *L'aune* of printed Provence calico	1
One *L'aune* of Holland calico	3
30 gun flints	1
4 flint locks	1
2 large woodcutter knives	1
3 small knives	1
2 pounds of raw sugar	1
1 pound of soap	1
3 skeins of Renne thread	1
5 skeins of white thread	1
1 Chollet handkerchief	1
3 blue and red handkerchiefs	4–5
1 *L'aune* of thread	2
1 pound of vermilion	10

Source: Valentine Layssard to Governor Unzaga, Apr. 20, 1775, AGI, PC Legajo 189-2.

exposed while traveling about among these barbarous tribes. Substitute Spanish articles and they will be dearer, the trader will not buy them, the Indians would not have them, and consequently the internal commerce of the province will be done for, exposing us to the loss of the Indians' friendship and the colonists' tranquility.[43]

During the 1770s both French and English merchandise reached Indian villages, most through indirect means, and most of Louisiana's deerskin exports ended up in France and Great Britain. Direct access to merchants in France was resumed in 1782, when Spain opened Louisiana commerce to selected French ports.[44]

The most significant change in Spanish Louisiana's deerskin market, one marking an incipient transformation of the regional exchange network, was the expansion of trade in the Upper Mississippi Valley. The fur trade in the Illinois country began to contribute sizable quantities of various peltry for exportation from New Orleans, as French and Spanish merchants established at St. Louis after 1764 diverted their growing commerce from Canada, now an English province. Deerskins as well as beaver pelts and buffalo robes from the Missouri River Valley became increasingly important to commerce on the lower Mississippi and eventually overshadowed the intraregional Indian trade of the Lower Mississippi Valley. English merchants, meanwhile, aggressively diverted some of this peltry through Manchac to West Florida ports.[45]

Changes in the deerskin trade implemented by Spain after 1783 signaled a transformed system. The frontier exchange network stitched together by inhabitants over two-thirds of the eighteenth century had begun to unravel. Transitional patterns of the 1760s and 1770s culminated in an altered process. Indians of the large interior nations, who had close ties to many traders, entered this period with high expectations of further commerce. Following the withdrawal of Great Britain from West Florida, the Choctaws, Chickasaws, and Upper Creeks negotiated new trade tariffs with the Spanish government in June 1784. The deerskin trade, however,

43. Arthur P. Whitaker, ed. and trans., *Documents Relating to the Commercial Policy of Spain in the Floridas, with Incidental Reference to Louisiana* (Deland, Fla., 1931), 13–15.

44. Clark, *New Orleans*, 172–180, 193–201; Clark, *La Rochelle*, 167.

45. Phillips, *Fur Trade*, II, 169–183; James Julien Coleman, Jr., *Gilbert Antoine de St. Maxent: The Spanish Frenchman of New Orleans* (New Orleans, 1968).

rapidly slipped under the control of a few merchant houses. The English firm of Panton, Leslie and Company received exclusive privileges from Spanish authorities to trade with the Indian nations east of the Mississippi.[46] On the other side of the river, traders likewise gave way to better-financed and more organized merchants. Accelerated commercialization of the deerskin market inexorably upset its traditional customs and patterns. Traders carried ever larger quantities of liquor into Indian villages, and the distribution of gifts occurred less often. Indian hunters fell into chronic debt to dominant merchant houses, amid declining prices for peltry and depleted game in some areas, and thereby became vulnerable to pressures against their land by the beginning of the nineteenth century.[47]

Trade in deerskins before the 1780s created a regional network linking Indian villages across the Lower Mississippi Valley to colonial port towns on the Gulf Coast. Commercial expansion of this market, however, was thwarted under the French regime by chronic shortages of trade merchandise and by stiff competition from English traders. Within this feebly regulated trade system, many different people participated in the marketing of deerskins—as in the case of foodstuffs—at widely dispersed points of exchange. A weak presence of the French empire in the region, which limited profit making in the fur export business, provided latitude for many less commercial participants to engage in the trade. Conflicting interests between monopolists, traders, and Indians helped keep the deerskin trade in a state of flux and thereby made it conducive for petty exchange. Traders nevertheless became prominent figures in the market. They constituted an ethnically diverse occupation that interacted closely

46. Tariff for Trade with the Chickasaw, Choctaw, and Alibamon Nations established at a congress in Mobile, June 22–23, 1784, Papers of Panton, Leslie and Company, University of West Florida Library, Pensacola; White, *Roots of Dependency,* 97–146; William S. Coker and Thomas D. Watson, *Indians Traders of the Southeastern Spanish Borderlands: Panton, Leslie and Company and John Forbes and Company, 1783–1847* (Pensacola, Fla., 1986).

47. J. Villasana Haggard, "The House of Barr and Davenport," *Southwestern Historical Quarterly,* XLIX (1945–1946), 66–88; Dan L. Flores, "The Red River Branch of the Alabama-Coushatta Indians: An Ethnohistory," *Southern Studies,* XVI (1977), 55–72; Daniel H. Usner, Jr., "American Indians on the Cotton Frontier: Changing Economic Relations with Citizens and Slaves in the Mississippi Territory," *Journal of American History,* LXXII (1985–1986), 297–317.

with free and enslaved employees as well as with Indian villagers. In face of rising regulation and monopolization by the end of the eighteenth century, many Indians and non-Indians struggled to perpetuate a familiar form of frontier exchange. Eventually, but grudgingly, they had to accept that a cotton and sugar plantation economy would supersede the century-old trade in deerskins.

CONCLUSION

Long before what Martin Luther King aptly called the "cotton curtain" fell on the Deep South, slavery had evolved under circumstances that remain obscure to this day. The cotton economy of the nineteenth and early twentieth centuries concealed racial oppression from outsiders but also concealed an older pattern of race relations from future generations. As in other colonial regions, the world created by European settlers, African slaves, and American Indians in Louisiana was not simply a faint or quaint background to antebellum southern society. The lives of many people living in the eighteenth century were touched by confrontations and transactions of various kinds. Their initiatives and frustrations, alliances and hostilities, must be understood in terms of that era's own demographic and economic conditions. Only then can we begin to grasp how significant was the transformation of livelihood and culture that began toward the end of the century.

Over the first half of the eighteenth century, colonial trade and settlement expanded slowly and side by side across the Lower Mississippi Valley. Daily subsistence, military protection, and commercial development remained interdependent in early Louisiana for a long time. A weak mercantilist regime and muted rivalry between European powers facilitated the rise of an indigenous exchange network allowing fluid intercultural relations among the region's various inhabitants. The deerskin trade with Indians provided a spatial framework for various kinds of exchange. Efforts by mercantile interests to build an export-oriented, plantation economy were stalled by the preferences of a fluid and diverse colonial society, which included among other groupings European ser-

vants, African craftsmen, and Indian slaves. Relations with Indian societies also were flexible and variant, ranging from formal alliances with
populous interior tribes to informal exchanges with Indian peddlers and
wage earners from neighboring villages.

But the alacrity that these inhabitants of the Lower Mississippi Valley exhibited in their economic practices and intercultural relations was
matched by the determination of merchants and planters to build a more
rigid colonial order. Turbulence at Natchez and New Orleans in 1729–
1730 violently exposed internal divisions within the expanding colonial
society and its external tensions with Indian nations. The Chickasaw wars
and the Choctaw revolt in the 1730s and 1740s resulted from pressures
imposed on Indian nations by the intercolonial contest between France
and Great Britain. Unable to match English competition with enough
trade supplies on a steady basis, Louisiana officials relied on an Indian
alliance policy of intervention and intimidation that proved especially
dangerous to the Choctaws.

Before the 1760s Louisiana's marginal position in the French overseas
empire left settlers, slaves, and Indians still much to their own designs in
the frontier exchange economy. Commercialization of economic relations
and growth of the colonial populace were inhibited, to the frustration of
officials charged with governing one of the most neglected colonies of
Louis XV. A governor could still complain in 1764 that "the facility
offered by the country to live on its natural production has created habits
of laziness."[1] Closer scrutiny of habits that were scorned by unsympathe-
tic officials, however, reveals that livelihood in and around the colony
involved a much more active process. Inhabitants of the Lower Mississippi Valley pieced subsistence and commercial endeavors together into
a patchwork of farming, herding, hunting, gathering, trade, and transportation activities.

Despite significant differences between cultures and official efforts to
manipulate those differences, Indians, slaves, and settlers forged a network of cross-cultural interaction that routinely brought individuals into
small-scale, face-to-face episodes of exchange. Slaves performed a wide
variety of economic roles outside their principal function of agricultural
production, working as boatmen, soldiers, hunters, peddlers, and inter-

1. AC, C13A, XLIV, 58.

preters. Indians also participated flexibly in the regional economy. In addition to producing abundant deerskins for the export market, they provided transportation and military services and traded food and livestock with colonial residents. European settlers based their livelihood likewise on diverse subsistence activities and engaged in myriad exchanges with both Indians and slaves. Everyday interaction in this frontier exchange economy encouraged cultural osmosis among the participants. Social relations between different ethnic groups, therefore, strayed from the norms that were only partly effected by the colonial elite. Throughout most of the eighteenth century, the character of slavery and of race relations in general was determined more by the demographic and economic conditions within the Lower Mississippi Valley than by the cultural and political designs originating in France, England, or Spain.[2]

Two decades of political partition between 1763 and 1783 spawned new demographic and economic turbulence that continued thereafter to alter life in the Lower Mississippi Valley at a faster and faster rate. Each involved more direct and more successful government intervention than the region had previously witnessed; altogether they represented competitive colonial efforts to expand commerce and to secure territory. The size and composition of the colonial population began to change dramatically in 1763, as both Spain and Great Britain implemented vigorous colonization schemes in Louisiana and West Florida. The movement of new groups of European-Americans and African-Americans into the region continued even after Spain assumed sovereignty over the entire Gulf Coast in 1783, setting a pattern of in-migration that simply expanded when the United States purchased Louisiana in 1803. Connected to this first process was an expansion of plantation agriculture in the Lower Mississippi Valley. Although French Louisiana had been exporting sizable shipments of tobacco and indigo since the 1720s, large-scale production of export crops remained limited to the New Orleans and Pointe Coupée areas. Under Spanish and English dominion, significant increments of capital, labor, and land were added to agriculture. Cotton and sugar also began their ascendancy over other commercial crops. Meanwhile, the deerskin trade, which had been such an important network of exchange between Indian and colonial inhabitants, underwent a process of rapid commercialization.

2. David C. Rankin, "The Tannenbaum Thesis Reconsidered: Slavery and Race Relations in Antebellum Louisiana," *Southern Studies*, XVIII (1979), 5–31.

The demographic profile of the Lower Mississippi Valley had a lot to do with the persistence of a frontier exchange economy into the 1760s, until new rulers in Louisiana and West Florida initiated measures to increase the number of colonial inhabitants. In 1763 the colonial population contained approximately 4,000 whites, 5,000 black slaves, 200 mulatto slaves, 100 Indian slaves, and 100 free people of color. This relatively small population consisted mostly of the descendants of Europeans and Africans who had reached Louisiana during the 1720s, the only period of large-scale immigration under French dominion. Eighty percent lived along the Mississippi from just below New Orleans to Pointe Coupée (as many as 1,300 people residing within the town limits of New Orleans). The Indian population in the Lower Mississippi Valley, although it suffered a catastrophic decline from epidemics, was still larger than the colonial population. More than 3,000 Indian villagers lived along the Mississippi River below the Arkansas post, another 4,000 inhabited the banks of the Red River, and 25,000 composed the large interior nations of Choctaws, Chickasaws, and Upper Creeks. In fact, this population of 32,000 or so Indians living in the region during the 1760s stood at the beginning of a new era of demographic growth, following a century of steady decline from a population of more than 100,000.[3]

In order to improve economic productivity as well as to secure political control in Louisiana and West Florida, respectively, Spanish and British governments promoted immigration of more white settlers and black slaves into the Lower Mississippi Valley. Both provinces offered generous grants of land to encourage colonization and received recruits from scattered sources. Spain attracted thousands of Acadians and Canary Islanders to the Mississippi Delta, and Great Britain colonized Natchez and other parts of West Florida with loyalists from the rebellious North American colonies.[4] The African-American population also became larger and more

3. The significance of these and other kinds of population change in the colonial South is explored in Peter H. Wood, "The Changing Population of the Colonial South: An Overview by Race and Region, 1685–1790," in Wood et al., eds., *Powhatan's Mantle: Indians in the Colonial Southeast* (Lincoln, Nebr., 1989), 35–103.

4. Gilbert C. Din, "The Canary Islander Settlements of Spanish Louisiana: An Overview," *LH*, XXVII (1986), 353–373; Carl A. Brasseaux, *The Founding of New Acadia: The Beginnings of Acadian Life in Louisiana, 1765–1803* (Baton Rouge, La., 1987), 73–115; J. Barton Starr, *Tories, Dons, and Rebels: The American Revolution in British West Florida* (Gainesville, Fla., 1976), 230–240; Bernard Bailyn, *Voyagers to the West: A Passage in the Peopling of America on the Eve of the Revolution* (New York,

diverse during this new wave of immigration. English-speaking slaves were brought into the region by their West Florida owners, and beginning in 1776 Spain allowed French merchants to import blacks from St. Domingue and other West Indies islands into Louisiana. In the 1780s United States merchants operating in New Orleans began to invest in shipments of Jamaican and other English Caribbean slaves to the Lower Mississippi Valley.[5]

By the mid-1780s the colonial population reached 30,000 (16,000 slaves, 13,000 whites, and 1,000 free people of color), and new demographic patterns were set in motion. With Spain still committed to populating Louisiana and West Florida for defensive and commercial reasons, Governor Esteban Rodriguez Miró y Sabater (1785–1791) openly encouraged disgruntled backcountrymen from the United States to migrate into the Lower Mississippi Valley. Anglo-American migrants, some bringing slaves with them, contributed increasingly to population growth in the region. A direction was set for the great wave that followed United States acquisition at the opening of the nineteenth century.[6] The series of immigrations that began in the 1760s, furthermore, quickened the rate at which the number of Indian inhabitants was surpassed by the number of non-Indian inhabitants. Although the Indian population in the Lower Mississippi Valley was steadily growing to about 40,000 people by 1803, the total number of settlers and slaves already exceeded 50,000.[7]

1986), 475–494; Robin F. A. Fabel, *The Economy of British West Florida, 1763–1783* (Tuscaloosa, Ala., 1988), 6–21.

5. John G. Clark, *New Orleans, 1718–1812: An Economic History* (Baton Rouge, La., 1969), 222–225; Fabel, *Economy of British West Florida*, 29–38; Thomas Marc Fiehrer, "The African Presence in Colonial Louisiana: An Essay on the Continuity of Caribbean Culture," in Robert R. MacDonald *et al.*, eds., *Louisiana's Black Heritage* (New Orleans, 1979), 3–31; Paul F. LaChance, "The Politics of Fear: French Louisianians and the Slave Trade, 1786–1809," *Plantation Society in the Americas*, I, no. 2 (June 1979), 162–197.

6. Gilbert C. Din, "Spain's Immigration Policy in Louisiana and the American Penetration, 1792–1803," *Southwestern Historical Quarterly*, LXXVI (1972–1973), 255–276; Allan Kulikoff, "Uprooted Peoples: Black Migrants in the Age of the American Revolution, 1790–1820," in Ira Berlin and Ronald Hoffman, eds., *Slavery and Freedom in the Age of the American Revolution* (Charlottesville, Va., 1983), 143–171.

7. "Schedule of the Whole Number of Persons in the Mississippi Territory, 1801," MS, Mississippi Territorial Census Returns, Territorial Governor RG 2, Mississippi Department of Archives and History, Jackson; Clarence Edward Carter, ed., *The*

As significant as this growth in numbers was the increase in ethnic heterogeneity that resulted from migrations during the Spanish period. Too long overshadowed in historiography by the legendary conflict between "Creoles" and "Americans," the composition of Louisiana's colonial population had rapidly diversified over the years preceding United States possession: creole blacks of principally Senegalese descent were joined by slaves from French and English Caribbean islands and English North America, creole whites of French and German descent by Acadians, Canary Islanders, and Anglo-Americans. In its impact upon society and economy, this process probably resembled pre-Revolutionary migrations to British colonies along the Atlantic seaboard—especially the arrival of Germans, Scotch-Irish, and West Africans over the mid-eighteenth century.[8]

Theoretically, a growth in population was supposed to enhance prosperity in the export sector of the Louisiana and West Florida colonies. Desiring more productive settlers than French Louisiana had been known for, policymakers encouraged newcomers to plant commercial crops and offered large landholdings to immigrants who brought agrarian laborers. Spain's restrictive mercantile laws at first inhibited commercial expansion by confining Louisiana products to Spanish ships and ports. But governors frequently made allowances and exceptions. Spain officially opened the colony's trade to French merchants during the American Revolution and further liberalized commerce in the Lower Mississippi Valley after winning the Floridas back from Great Britain. By the 1780s Louisiana was annually exporting an average of three million livres worth of indigo, one million livres of tobacco, and another million livres of timber products.[9]

Plantations producing the bulk of these export commodities went through a transition during the 1790s. Governmental encouragement had induced producers to invest heavily in growing tobacco and indigo. But mounting indebtedness among many farmers suddenly coincided with

---

Territory of Orleans, 1803–1812 (Washington, D.C., 1940), 32, vol. IX of *The Territorial Papers of the United States.*

8. See D. W. Meinig, *The Shaping of America: A Geographical Perspective on Five Hundred Years of History,* I, *Atlantic America, 1492–1800* (New Haven, Conn., 1986), 213–231, for an attempt at comparing and categorizing patterns of ethnic heterogeneity.

9. *SMV,* II, 1–5; Clark, *New Orleans,* 181–201.

deteriorating market conditions. Experimentation with cotton and sugar was rewarded by successful harvests and rising prices in these products. Cotton production took off before the beginning of the nineteenth century, especially in the Natchez area, where more than a million pounds were being annually harvested by 1800. In the delta zone of the Mississippi Valley, sugar cane replaced indigo as the most profitable crop. "Nature," in the words of New Orleans merchant James Pitot, "gave to cotton, as it did throughout the tropics, the one commodity that could supplement its exportation."[10]

But nature did not work alone in determining the expansion of this new economy. The accelerated influx of settlers and slaves, the expansion of plantation agriculture, and the commercialization of Indian trade altogether contained important man-made origins of a new socioeconomic structure in the Lower Mississippi Valley—commonly called the Cotton Kingdom. An export-directed economy was supplanting a frontier exchange economy, with profound effect upon economic relations between different cultural groups. In order to reinforce this transformation, colonial officials intensified measures to control interaction among settlers, slaves, and Indians. The flexible and variational roles that they previously enjoyed were circumscribed by more numerous codes, stronger enforcement, and sterner punishment from the 1760s onward. As might be expected by students of other colonial regions, the years of Louisiana's burgeoning integration into the world market witnessed a heightening of social conflict—particularly in the forms of slave defiance and Indian banditry.

Within areas of rapid plantation development, small farmers began to suffer disadvantages in the market and even displacement from their land. With cotton and sugar planters seeking larger landholdings along the Mississippi River and adjacent waterways, many small producers found it increasingly difficult to hold on to their valuable riverfront property. Those who could not afford to maintain the levees and roads required by

10. James Pitot, *Observations on the Colony of Louisiana from 1796 to 1802*, trans. Henry C. Pitot (Baton Rouge, La., 1979), 72–77. Lewis Cecil Gray, *History of Agriculture in the Southern United States to 1860*, 2 vols. (Washington, D.C., 1933), I, 76–84, II, 687–688, 739–740, is a good overview of this transition. For the best close-up analysis of developments in the Natchez area, see Jack D. L. Holmes, *Gayoso: The Life of a Spanish Governor in the Mississippi Valley, 1789–1799* (Baton Rouge, La., 1965), 86–101.

law succumbed to the temptation of selling their land to wealthier new-comers or neighbors and moving deeper into the backcountry. Others lost their property to creditors because they borrowed too heavily in efforts to expand their own commercial production. This economic stress exacer-bated ethnic tensions as a growing number of Anglo-American planters and their African-American slaves moved into Louisiana. Acadian, Ca-nary Island, and Creole farmers resented the aggression exerted by newly arriving slaveowners and feared the insurrection that seemed imminent from their slaves.[11]

The growing number of slaves, meanwhile, faced stronger efforts to confine their labor to plantation agriculture. The marketing, hunting, and even gardening activities of slaves came under closer scrutiny. In the 1780s slaves were prohibited from devoting Sundays to their own work and were required to carry passes indicating their owners' approval to sell designated goods. By 1795 they could not "sell any thing without the permission of their master, not even the production of their own Fields, under penalty of Twenty-five Lashes." In this same ordinance issued after an abortive slave rebellion at Pointe Coupée, Governor Francisco de Carondelet permitted no settler to keep more than two hunters, who "shall oblige themselves to deliver up their arms and amunition upon their return from hunting." Any slave found in possession of munitions would be "punished three days with thirty Lashes each day." As the government increased patrols during the 1780s and 1790s, runaway slaves found it increasingly difficult to form maroon camps in the backcountry thickets and wetlands of Louisiana. Indians and free people of color were encour-aged to participate in these slave-catching expeditions, fueling animosity between cultural groups while getting the immediate job done.[12]

11. James H. Dormon, *The People Called Cajuns: An Introduction to an Ethnohis-tory* (Lafayette, La., 1983), 25–30; Brasseaux, *Founding of New Acadia*, 172–176, 192–197; Gilbert C. Din, *The Canary Islanders of Louisiana* (Baton Rouge, La., 1988), 80–90.

12. James A. Padgett, ed., "A Decree for Louisiana Issued by the Baron of Carondelet, June 1, 1795," *LHQ*, XX (1937), 596, 602–603. Important contributions to the study of slavery during these decades include James Thomas McGowan, "Creation of a Slave Society: Louisiana Plantations in the Eighteenth Century" (Ph.D. diss., University of Rochester, 1976), 217–424; Derek Noel Kerr, "Petty Felony, Slave Defiance, and Frontier Villainy: Crime and Criminal Justice in Spanish Louisiana, 1770–1803" (Ph.D. diss., Tulane University, 1983); and Gilbert C. Din, "*Cimarrones* and the San Malo Band in Spanish Louisiana," *LH*, XXI (1980), 237–262.

The rapid growth in the number of settlers and slaves around them would probably have done enough on its own to undermine the advantages formerly held by American Indians in the Lower Mississippi Valley. But the quickening entrenchment of plantation agriculture combined with their deepening dependency upon the deerskin trade to cause a severe socioeconomic crisis among Indian communities after 1763. Indians found themselves having to hunt more and more deer in order to keep up with their purchases from colonial merchants, just as their physical mobility and economic flexibility were becoming less and less tolerable to agricultural interests. To make matters worse, the partition of the region between England and Spain reduced the political leverage available to interior tribes. Now inside British jurisdiction east of the Mississippi, the Choctaws, Chickasaws, and Creeks no longer enjoyed a borderland position between competing European empires. Among the Caddoes and other groups west of the river, smuggling and raiding between Texas and Louisiana became prohibited, since both provinces now belonged to Spain. Indian producers of deerskins became increasingly vulnerable to the use of alcohol and credit by traders, and colonial officials slackened the customary protocol of distributing gifts to Indian delegations and discouraged Indians from traveling and trading freely among the settlements.

The supplanting of the frontier exchange economy by the agricultural export economy affected Indian groups in different ways and, therefore, elicited different strategies of accommodation and resistance to the changing economic order. Because of their proximity to the settlements, Indian villages along the Lower Mississippi River were better able to buffer their livelihood against declining deerskin prices and mounting trade debts. Employment as boatmen, guides, hunters, and farm laborers gave the Houmas, Chitimachas, Tunicas, Biloxis, and Alibamons a range of alternatives to the deerskin trade. These small groups of Indians interspersed among the plantations also continued to produce foodstuffs for the local market, sharing this role in the economy with Acadian and Canary Island farmers.[13]

More dependent than the settlement tribes upon the deerskin trade, the

---

13. Daniel H. Usner, Jr., "American Indians in Colonial New Orleans," in Wood *et al.*, eds., *Powhatan's Mantle*, 104–127. For a similar process in another colonial region, see James H. Merrell, *The Indians' New World: Catawbas and Their Neighbors from European Contact through the Era of Removal* (Chapel Hill, N.C., 1989), 226–233, 266–271.

Choctaws, Chickasaws, and Creeks faced diminishing options from the 1760s through the 1790s. At first they tried to mitigate English control in West Florida by asserting rights to Spanish Louisiana's attention. Tribal leaders asked the new regime west of the Mississippi River to support familiar traders from Louisiana and keep old trade routes to their villages open, but with little success. Rebuffed by officials in both colonies, especially through their withholding of gifts, Indian parties resorted to stealing livestock and crops, pillaging storehouses, and other forms of banditry against the colonial populace. When Panton, Leslie and Company began to dominate the deerskin trade, Indians tried to deal with as many different traders as possible in order to evade paying their debts to the monopolizing firm. This economic strategy was accompanied by an increasing frequency of Choctaw, Chickasaw, and Creek hunting expeditions west of the Mississippi River, where a greater abundance of game made it easier to produce the volume of deerskins necessary for continued commerce. The movement of these hunting camps through the Louisiana countryside, of course, increased conflict with settlements and with other Indian groups.[14]

As governments scrutinized and restricted economic activity more intensively, native-born and immigrant inhabitants clung tenaciously to production and marketing activities within the familiar framework of exchange. Customary means of subsistence became subversive strategies of survival through which subordinate groups sought some measure of autonomy within the new social order. The plantation economy overshadowed, but never totally replaced, the frontier exchange economy. Practiced in the informal spheres of the cotton economy, frontier exchange activities persisted in the shadow of formal commerce well into the nineteenth century.[15] Yeoman farmers raised livestock and hunted game in the

14. Lawrence Kinnaird and Lucia B. Kinnaird, "Choctaws West of the Mississippi, 1766–1800," *Southwest. Hist. Qtly.*, LXIII (1979–1980), 349–370; Richard White, *The Roots of Dependency: Subsistence, Environment, and Social Change among the Choctaws, Pawnees, and Navajos* (Lincoln, Nebr., 1983), 97–146.

15. Gavin Wright, *The Political Economy of the Cotton South: Households, Markets, and Wealth in the Nineteenth Century* (New York, 1978), 69–74, argues that the relationship between subsistence farms and staple-growing plantations was more of a continuum than a bipolarity. For a theoretical discussion of how formal and informal spheres of economic activities are implicated with, rather than separate from, each other, see Philip Harding and Richard Jenkins, *The Myth of the Hidden Economy:*

forests, intermittently grew cotton alongside their food crops, and sometimes exchanged goods with plantation slaves.[16] Many slaves cultivated
their own gardens and hunted for extra food, or pilfered and traded petty
goods, in order to ease the subjugation of their labor to commercial
agriculture.[17] American Indians continued to exchange peltry and food
with both whites and blacks. Even after the removal era, small itinerant
groups of Indians provided goods and services on the margins of an
increasingly bifurcated racial system.[18] Without some of the resilience and
diversity in economic relations carried forward from an earlier time, the
caste system of the cotton South would have been even more oppressive to
Indians, slaves, and settlers marginalized in a transformed society.

Towards a New Understanding of Informal Economic Activity (Philadelphia, 1989),
172–181.

16. Frank Lawrence Owsley, *Plain Folk in the Old South* (Baton Rouge, La., 1949),
1–90; Forrest McDonald and Grady McWhiney, "The South from Self-Sufficiency to
Peonage: An Interpretation," *American Historical Review*, LXXXV (1980), 1104–
1111; John Solomon Otto, "Southern 'Plain Folk' Agriculture: A Reconsideration,"
Plantation Society in the Americas, II, no. 1 (April 1983), 29–36; Steven Hahn, *The
Roots of Southern Populism: Yeoman Farmers and the Transformation of the Georgia
Upcountry, 1850–1890* (New York, 1983), 50–85, 239–289.

17. Eugene D. Genovese, *Roll, Jordan, Roll: The World the Slaves Made* (New York,
1974), 535–540; Ira Berlin, "Time, Space, and the Evolution of Afro-American Society
on British Mainland North America," *AHR*, LXXXV (1980), 61–66; Philip D. Morgan, "The Ownership of Property by Slaves in the Mid-Nineteenth Century Low
Country," *Journal of Southern History*, XLIX (1983), 399–420.

18. Daniel H. Usner, Jr., "American Indians on the Cotton Frontier: Changing
Economic Relations with Citizens and Slaves in the Mississippi Territory," *Journal of
American History*, XXVII (1985–1986), 297–317; Fred B. Kniffen *et al., The Historic
Indian Tribes of Louisiana: From 1542 to the Present* (Baton Rouge, La., 1987), 95–
98.

INDEX